INVESTOR CAPITALISM

INVESTOR CAPITALISM

How Money Managers Are Changing the Face of Corporate America

MICHAEL USEEM

BasicBooks
A Division of HarperCollinsPublishers

FIRST EDITION

Designed by Elliott Beard

Library of Congress Cataloging-in-Publication Data
Useem, Michael.
    Investor capitalism : how money managers are changing the face of corporate
America / Michael Useem. — 1st ed.
        p.   cm.
    Includes bibliographical references and index.
    ISBN 0-465-05031-X
    1. Institutional investments—United States.   2. Investment advisors.   I. Title.
HG4910.U83   1996
658.15—dc20   96-7847
                                                                               CIP

96 97 98 99 00 ❖/HC 10 9 8 7 6 5 4 3 2 1

Contents

INVESTOR CAPITALISM

⟋S⟍

Introduction

DURING SEVERAL FATEFUL MONTHS in 1992–93, General Motors and IBM dismissed their chief executives and dropped thousands of employees. American Express forced out its top executives and reconstituted its board. Westinghouse pressed its chairman into early retirement and restructured top management. Sears cut employment, closed its catalog, and auctioned divisions. American Airlines, Bell Atlantic, Digital Equipment, and GTE and other blue-chip companies set about reengineering their operations.

The companies' announcements of these changes cited a host of disparate causes: Japanese competition, declining sales, bloated payrolls, defaulted real estate, even management failures. So too had the announcements accompanying an array of restructurings during the 1980s. To regain competitiveness, Xerox and AT&T had slashed employment and improved quality. RJR Nabisco and Safeway Stores had gone private and tightened discipline.

Taken in isolation, each company action seemed the product of a unique blend of problems. Chief executives Robert Stempel of GM and John Akers of IBM, it was said, had failed to address the harsh market realities that enveloped their giant enterprises. James Robinson of American Express had been unable to staunch declining use of its flagship travel card. Paul Lego of Westinghouse could not extricate his company from massive property losses, and Edward Brennan of Sears had failed to fend off the Wal-Marts of the world.

Another wave of executive dismissals in 1994–95 swept away the chairman or the chief executive of Bank of Boston, Kmart Corporation, Morrison Knudsen Corporation, Philip Morris Companies, and W. R. Grace & Co. Again, no two stories are quite the same. The first corporate chief had failed to find a merger partner; the second had fallen short on a turnaround; the third had presided over a tailspin; the fourth had ignored tobacco problems, and the fifth had stayed too long.

A different kind of wave in 1994–95 brought the breakup of ITT and AT&T and the mergers of Capital Cities/ABC with the Walt Disney Company, of the Turner Broadcasting System with Time Warner Inc., of CBS Inc. with Westinghouse Electric Corporation, and of Chase Manhattan Corporation with Chemical Banking Corporation. In the breakups, the parts were viewed as more valuable than the whole. In the mergers, the combinations were seen as bringing scale economies, product synergies, and global reach that the players could not achieve on their own.

These 1990s events followed a decade that had witnessed a vast remake of the corporate landscape. Of the country's 500 largest manufacturers in 1980, one in three had ceased to exist as an independent entity by 1990. The Fortune 500 employment rolls dropped from 16 million in 1980 to 12 million by 1990. One-third of the Fortune 500 had received hostile ownership bids and two-thirds had established anti-takeover defenses. The 500 largest industrial firms had reduced their product diversity by half.

Taken separately, each event was driven by a unique combination of management personalities and business challenges. Taken together, however, the executive successions, company fissures, and corporate fusions point to a broader story. A common catalyst is to be found in accumulating investor power. Several hundred institutional shareholders—pension funds, bank trusts, insurance firms, endowment funds, and money managers—built massive stakes in the nation's enterprises during the 1970s and early 1980s. In the 1990s they have learned to convert their newfound economic dominance into political muscle. Through buyout threats, proxy fights, and quiet negotiations, investors have mastered the art of pressure politics. The CEOs of GM, IBM, American Express, and Westinghouse were among the visible early victims, and their fall delivered a message to others. Commenting on the changing shareholder world in May 1993, chief executive Lewis E. Platt of the Hewlett-Packard Company said, "I pay a lot of attention to that situation now."

The power of the changing investor landscape can be seen in the events following a disclosure in early 1995 by Heine Securities Corporation that it had acquired 6 percent of Chase's stock for $365 million, making it the bank's single largest stockholder (Rockefeller family interests had at one time been the biggest). Headed by activist investor Michael F. Price and with $12 billion under investment management in its Mutual Series family of funds, Heine Securities asserted that Chase's management "should seriously consider taking steps to realize the inherent value in its businesses in a manner designed to maximize shareholder value." Despite earlier efforts to restructure, Chase's share price had been languishing, and Price's demands seemed on the mark to many investors. John B. Neff, manager of the Vanguard/Windsor fund, had already sold off a large stake in Chase since "the company wasn't doing enough along the lines of what we thought they should. And the consistency and execution from the parent was not as paramount as we like to see it."[1]

Chase CEO Thomas G. Labrecque and his executive team were alarmed by Price's stake, fearing it could presage a contest for control, and takeover rumors were already roiling its stock. The industry was also changing fast while they deliberated: a number of other banking mergers had been announced during the year. Price argued that Chase should break itself up or sell itself off, and within several months Chase opted for a step close to the latter. It merged with Chemical, forming a new bank whose combined assets of $297 billion make it the largest in the country. The merger's outcome: $1 billion in expected savings, 12,000 employees to lose their jobs, and Price's mutual funds achieve a one-day premium of $84 million and overall a $275 million—or 70 percent—gain for their clients in the six months following the purchase of Chase stock.[2]

The catalytic role of institutional investors can be seen as well in the 1995 breakup of ITT and AT&T. ITT divided itself into three publicly traded corporations: one with the ITT Hartford insurance business; one with its Sheraton hotels and entertainment properties; and one with its automotive, defense, electronics, and technology businesses. Harold Geneen, the chief executive from 1959 to 1976, had transformed the one-time telephone company into a vast conglomerate. A successor, Rand V. Araskog, saw ITT differently, especially in light of continuous prodding from his investors to separate its diverse parts, and he finally opted to break it up. As assessed by an analyst with Salomon Brothers, "Araskog clearly responded well to all the criticism he got from shareholders," and ITT's shares soared 25 percent in the three months following the announcement. AT&T had received little such prodding prior to its historic announcement several months later. It too divided in three: the telephone business, a telephone equipment manufacturer, and a computer maker. Many factors contributed to the breakup, but here also investors were nearby, as they had been telling management that the company was worth less than the sum of its parts. "The market value of AT&T was being buried," explains chief executive Robert E. Allen. "Investors couldn't understand the strategy of the combined company." The breakup creates three "pure plays," companies that operate in narrowly defined industries that analysts specializing in industries are better equipped to appraise. As a result, Allen says, "Investors will clearly understand it now."[3]

The catalytic role of investors can be seen as well in the 1995 acquisition by Time Warner of Turner Broadcasting System. The Disney acquisition of Capital Cities/ABC earlier in the year contributed to the decision, but so too did unrelenting investor criticism of Time Warner's languishing stock price and its chief executive, Gerald M. Levin. Investors had been warning the company that they might seek to force Levin's ouster if he did not work more quickly to restructure, sell assets, and reduce debt. The principal of Gabelli Funds, a major owner, avowed in early 1995 that Levin "has twelve more months" to turn the company around; a PaineWebber Group analyst saw a "Damoclean sword hanging over Time Warner's head." While the Turner acquisition could be seen as a natural strategic fit with Time Warner's operations, it would also help keep disgruntled investors at bay. In the interpretation of one securities analyst, CEO Levin "may have felt that he had to do something dramatic to assuage the critics."[4]

Even to those not on Wall Street or in the executive suite, understanding what is driving shareholder demands has become more than a matter of idle curiosity, as turbulence at the top filters down the ranks. Hourly employees feel a squeeze on their wages; middle managers feel a squeeze in their ranks. Wave upon wave of downsizing has already forced many into early retirement, while those spared seek to make sense of a far more austere and demanding world, and to find the tools for managing and surviving within it.

The middle managers of a regional telephone company thus listen attentively as their chief financial officer and treasurer explains how "shareholder value" is now the overriding company value. The world of balance sheets, fiduciary rules, and poison pills is no longer quite so arcane. Later, at an informal dinner with managers from a major computer manufacturer, the telecommunications managers speak candidly of their concerns about market demands and employment downsizing. One telephone manager ruefully acknowledges that, after a series of early retirement programs, her company has just dismissed several hundred employees, a watershed event for the firm. One of the computer-manufacturer managers suppresses a grin. He had personally fired, he explained, more than that number over the preceding weekend. The next day, as the telephone managers hear a visiting finance professor explain how shareholder value is calculated, they seem more attentive than ever.

Understanding the animating forces behind the investor demands is of more than passing interest for another reason. The pressures for greater shareholder return are expressed by stock analysts, investment directors, and fund managers. They are further amplified by stock speculators, business writers, and electronic networks. But the ultimate foundation for the pressure comes from people like you, me, and millions of other citizens who have accumulated wealth, even if only a little bit more than the homes we live in and the automobiles, computers, and microwaves we own. Much of that wealth is in our retirement accounts. Some we have placed in mutual funds. A fraction is tied up in life insurance and private endowments. Wherever it is, we want to see it grow as fast and securely as possible. Larger assets in our mutual-fund accounts mean more schooling for our children, more travel for ourselves, and more tithing for our charities. Greater wealth in our retirement accounts means more comfortable housing, better health care, and larger estates for our heirs.

In placing our wealth in the hands of institutional investors, we have unintentionally unleashed a set of forces that is changing the face of American business. Money managers are telling companies that they must become more productive, more effective, more competitive—generally not telling them how to do it, but just to do it. A representative of one of the nation's largest investment companies explained his firm's objective in 1995 to a select audience of American and international executives: "We don't want to tell you how to run your company—we just want a well-run company." In some cases this has meant forcing executive change; in others, bust ups; in still others, mergers and acquisitions.

The emergence of what I will call "investor capitalism" had found fertile ground in the aftermath of an earlier transformation of American business: the ascendance of managerial capitalism. During the century's middle decades, a managerial revolution put professional executives firmly in control of many large, publicly traded companies. The scattering of stock among thousands of small owners had undercut the capacity of shareholders to oversee their enterprises. Save the occasional intrusion of federal regulation, labor strife, or media exposé, company executives enjoyed an era of nearly unfettered authority. The decisions they made often affected the lives of thousands of people, yet they were seemingly accountable to no one.

In recent years, however, the stock scattering reversed its course as pension plans, investment companies, bank trusts, and other institutional investors acquired significant stakes in many corporations. Managerial dominance subsided as a new set of operating principles restructured the balance of power between those who own the companies and those who run them. Managers report more; investors listen better. Directors acquire greater independence, managers greater accountability.

The developing relationships between investors and managers resemble neither markets nor organizations. Rather, they are emerging as enduring networks, a lattice of informal ties that come to guide a continuous two-way exchange of information and exercise of influence. In their strongest form, these networks can be seen in "relational investing," whereby major investors acquire large stakes in a company and work closely with top management. In weaker form, they can be seen in the routinized information exchanges among mutual-fund officials and company executives. In conflictual form, they are evident in the episodic efforts by investors to win proxy fights or oust unresponsive managers.

Financial investors turn their attention to corporate governance in part because their great holdings prevent them from readily selling their stake in underperforming companies. The traditional Wall Street rule is that an investor sells stock rather than confront poorly performing executives. As institutions become significant shareholders, however, they are modifying the rule. Now, when a large investor is dissatisfied with a company's top management, it often retains much of the holding but presses for improved performance. If results are not forthcoming, it lobbies the directors, votes against management, or even seeks new management—as the executives of the Bank of Boston, Kmart, Morrison Knudsen, Philip Morris, and W. R. Grace learned to their dismay. The disgruntled investor might still sell some of its stock in keeping with the Wall Street rule, but it is also more likely to speak up than simply cash out.

Large investors are by no means a unified bloc, and deep schisms divide the institutional field. Some investors trust management, others do not. Some hold their position and press for change; others sell their position and run for cover. Some champion activism; others deplore it. Even among those who choose the former, little agreement exists on the optimal approach. Some press for revolution, others for reformation.

Some institutional investors also take their intensifying demands well beyond the earnings statements. Many public pension funds had long urged disinvestment from apartheid South Africa, while others sought improved affirmative action or environmental correctness. When the Sun Company (Sunoco) announced its adoption of the Valdez Principles in 1993, becoming the first major company to endorse these far-reaching environmental steps, several public pension funds led the applause. These funds' persistent entreaties that companies endorse the green principles seem finally to have borne fruit.

Senior managers respond with countermeasures of their own. They view institutional investors as certainly no better qualified to run the business than they are, portraying investors' "short termism"—the insatiable demands for steadily rising quarterly performance—as one of the country's great menaces. And, in any case, management is well experienced in resisting challenges to its prerogatives, whatever the source.

The expanding influence of investors and the rising resistance of managers has served to rotate both the official and the unofficial organizational charts by 90 degrees. The law requires that shareholders be inscribed in a box at the top of the official chart. They elect directors who in turn select top executives to operate the firm. The unofficial chart portraying the de facto power relations under managerial capitalism, by contrast, looks much the inverse. In this diagram, management replaces owners in the box at the top. Both directors and shareholders are inscribed below. Under investor capitalism, both charts are turned on their side. Here, shareholders, directors, and managers coexist in an uneasy but more coequal alliance. Rather than one overseeing the other's overseeing of the firm, they oversee the enterprise together. Though the rubric of investor capitalism might seem to imply the owners are back on top, it is meant here to connote that a new kind of engaged owner is back in the picture and working closely with—though also sometimes against—company management.

Joint oversight of America's large, publicly traded companies, however, has generated a host of fresh organizational problems. How can the parties govern together? When should each resist or change in response to pressures from the other? What is the impact of joint oversight on corporate performance? Will the short-term demons of Wall Street sabotage long-term company strategies? Can the stressed managerial ranks deliver the improved results demanded? Is the voice of labor even more diminished? Are American firms likely to become more competitive against their German and Japanese counterparts?

The continuing struggle among managers, investors, and interested parties—labor, government, and consumers—is transforming the way business goes about its business. Out of the transformation are emerging a new set of rules for ownership and control of the large corporation. If the principles of family capitalism dominated industrialization at the turn of the century, and if the concepts of managerial capitalism rose to dominance by mid-century, the new rules of investor capitalism are coming to prevail by century's end.

Investor capitalism is creating a new world for those whose lives are shaped by executive decisions. It is quietly restructuring corporate organization and redefining shareholder prerogatives, reshaping business culture in its wake. It calls into question traditional theories of how corporations make decisions and operate in the United States and abroad. As owners and executives find themselves at the same table, they are operating under new rules of engagement.

This book describes and analyzes the foundations of investor capitalism, tracking its impact on managerial careers, corporate restructuring, and investor fortunes. It draws on interviews, accounts, and studies. Direct contact with this world is particularly important since, although prominent features of the landscape emerge into public view from time to time, most remain well hidden, visible to participants but out of the public eye. Of special value are a set of interviews with executives of twenty large corporations and fifty-eight institutional investors. They agreed to the discussions on condition of confidentiality and thus remain unnamed. Because events at a number of the corporations are described at length, the main firms are given pseudonyms. The company product areas and pseudonyms are:

Automobiles	Hutchins Motors Corporation
Apparel	Flora Devlin, Inc.
Beverages	International Beverages
Broadcasting	MFL Network, Inc.
Chemicals	Chase Chemical Products
Chemicals	Western Chemical Company
Commercial banking	Buckingham Bank
Commercial banking	Statebank Inc.
Computer products	Strikeline Computer Company
Consumer products	Lamont Company
Diversified products	WWK Products Corporation
Food products	Columbia Foods
Insurance	American Insurance
Insurance and property	Nelson Insurance
Metal products	National Metal Products
Paper products	Atlantic Paper Company
Petroleum products	Richards Oil Corporation
Pharmaceuticals	Stewart Drugs, Inc.
Retail services	Harrington Stores
Telecommunications	Shaw Communications

The first four chapters offer an assessment of the new power relations that have come to prevail. Chapter 1 describes the growing concentration of institutional ownership and stronger expression of institutional voice within the shareholders' ranks. Drawing on both statistical data and illustrative events at a consumer-products company and at General Motors Corporation, the chapter offers an overview of the evolving relations between owners and managers.

Specific company actions and results that trigger investor challenge are the subject of chapter 2. The divergent experiences of a major commercial bank and a large manufacturer exemplify the conditions that have led some investors to ignore certain corporations while targeting others. Conflict between investors and managers is now centered on the corporate proxy, the yearly shareholder plebiscite in which company directors are elected and governance policies are ratified. The annual company ballot offers opportunities for both sides to advance their contentions and strengthen their positions. Both place resolutions on the proxy ballot for shareholder ratification, and, on rare occasion, they also place opposing board candidates on the proxy as well. Uncommitted shareholders are lobbied as vigorously as voters during a presidential campaign.

As investors apply pressure and proffer advice to improve corporate performance, they have also mustered an ideology that justifies their intrusion into company affairs. In response, managers have erected a defensive ideology of their own that denies the validity of investor claims for short-term results and, at times, even investors' right to make demands. Chapter 3 takes up these managerial conceptions and their sometimes adverse impact on the effective flow of information and influence through the new networks.

In the face of such contrasting belief systems, investors and managers occasionally turn to the blunt strategy of simply replacing each other. Chapter 4 focuses on the conditions under which investors seek to force out underperforming management and managers seek to dispose of troublesome investors. Though rare, such strategies reveal the lengths to which each side will go and the forces they can mobilize to vanquish the other.

The subsequent four chapters chronicle the steps taken by the two sides to construct the new order in light of these altered relations. Chapters 5 and 6 describe the means by which companies listen to their investors, drawing upon their suggestions and responding to their pressures. Divisions might be sold, compensation schemes revised, and executives changed. Employment rolls and management ranks can be slashed or redeployed. Senior managers have also learned to manage their relations with investors, and to manage their own managers to better understand when resistance is necessary and when accommodation is called for. Above all, the two sides have constructed enduring personalized relations that allow them to exchange information and apply influence on one another.

The evolving conflict and collaboration between owners and managers has gradually moved up to the governing board, as discussed in chapter 7. As investors and executives have created a less hierarchical relationship, governing boards have become more engaged with both. The evolving rules have also moved into the organization of management itself, as considered in chapter 8. As investors intensified their demands for improved performance, management security lessened, executive compensation steepened, and new skills emerged.

The rise of investor capitalism and the underlying power shift has forced companies and investors to invent new rules. Few models exist, either internationally or domestically, to guide their development. As institutions continue to consolidate their influence on publicly traded companies, however, the main parties are sure to continue rewriting the rules. Chapter 9 looks at the most important forces for this continued rewriting, above all the growing assets and power of the mutual and pension funds. As institutions move outside the United States with a vengeance in search of new investment opportunities, we can also expect to see the newly invented American model for relations between investors and corporations applied abroad as well.

While the era of managerial capitalism allowed executives considerable latitude in setting their own priorities, the era of investor capitalism does not. Managerial capitalism permitted executives to ignore their shareholders. Investor capitalism does not. Managerial capitalism tolerated a host of company objectives besides shareholder value. Investor capitalism does not. In changing the balance of power between executives and owners, investor capitalism has ended an era of unrestrained managerial dominance. Overseeing the country's great companies now requires management of not only the inside troops but also the outside investors.

The revised relations between owners and managers affect institutions far removed from corporate headquarters. As large investors press companies for lower costs and stronger results, they in turn press hospitals, universities and United Ways for better service and more accountability. As stock analysts applaud corporate restructuring and workforce downsizing, communities experience the pain of closed plants and vacant offices. As companies redesign their operations for more competitive performance, some employees acquire greater responsibilities while others are pushed out of the work world altogether.

The new investor powers are thus altering both business and society. Shareholders' canons have changed. Management principles are different. Governance is no longer quite so passive. And employees, families, and communities have borne the consequences, some for the better, others for the worse. Whatever the evolving mix of the good and the bad for those inside or near the publicly traded corporation, investor capitalism is inexorably altering the face of American business.

PART I

The Investor Challenge

1

—— § ——

The New Rules of
Investor Capitalism

AT MANY OF AMERICA'S LARGEST corporations, the dispersion of stockholding and consequent weakening of shareowners left professional executives firmly in control by the early 1980s. They ruled their business empires with maximal managerial autonomy and minimal ownership oversight. Boards of directors were formally empowered by the shareholders to preside over their assets, but in practice they were more often captives of management. Dissatisfied shareholders and disgruntled directors usually found disinvestment or resignation to be the only viable options. The occasional boardroom revolt simply served to underscore management's dominance.

Corporate events of recent years, however, have signaled the end of unchallenged managerial sovereignty. Professional executives no longer hold such complete sway. They rule their business empires in consultation, not isolation. Boards are less the inside captives. Dissident shareholders and directors find protest, not just exit, to be a meaningful option. Boardroom revolts reveal management's wobbly condition and investors' confident ascendancy.

The new rules of the realm can be illustrated by two incidents. At the core of these events are struggles for company control. Underlying

15

each is a flexing of institutional muscle, and both are defining moments for the companies. The specific courses could hardly have been more different, but they reflect the forces unleashed by the rise of investor capitalism.

Mobilizing Investor Votes

A seasoned executive team verged on losing control of its company to an investor group. The firm—Lamont Company (a pseudonym)—had long held its investors at arm's length, but management's questionable actions during the mid-1980s had generated widespread dissatisfaction among the company's owners. Small holders were likely to remain loyal, but, in the event of a credible outside bid for control, would the large holders? When such a challenge did materialize, management, long the master of its own destiny, suddenly found its assumptions dangerously out of date. The fate of the company was now shared with investors, for whom loyalty often meant nothing and returns meant everything.

Lamont Company, which manufactured a broad array of consumer products, was known and represented in most American households. In keeping with the times, it had diversified into related areas, and its sales revenue had grown steadily. In recent years, its stock price and dividend payouts had outpaced both the Dow Jones industrial average and the Standard and Poor's (S&P) 500, yet a perception had developed among investors that the company could have done better with its assets—or, perhaps, that it could have done better by selling its assets. Despite this investor concern, the chief executive and his inner circle felt secure. After all, they and their predecessors had guided the company well through both good times and bad.

Such unchallenged executive control, common during the 1960s and 1970s, now proved surprisingly fragile. A corporate raider announced a hostile bid for Lamont, offering to acquire its shares at a price considerably above their current market value. Management promptly rejected the offer, its posture aided by a poison pill, an arcane financial device that made it difficult for the raider to acquire the company without board consent. Undeterred, the raider launched a fresh bid, upping the ante, and with this round the company deployed an ultimately successful defensive strategy that came to be known as greenmail. Under a negotiated settlement, the company agreed to purchase the raider's large block of stock at a considerable premium above current market value. In exchange, the raider promised to cease further takeover efforts.

This act angered other major stockholders, however. They had seen the company bypass an offer that would have made their stock far more valuable. They had witnessed a selective payout to another large shareholder. And they had glimpsed what seemed to be an entrenched management digging a still deeper trench.

The greenmail also brought Lamont's performance to the attention of a partnership of several former investment bankers and attorneys. These bankers and attorneys had broken away from established firms during the early 1980s to create their own enterprise, which I will call Capital Partners. Pooling personal funds and those from several investors, the general partners set out to take positions in troubled companies that might be turned around. The ownership stakes they sought were large enough for them to make a credible demand for a voice in company management. This "strategic-block investing" ran against the conventional wisdom of prudent money management, which dictated selling one's stake in a distressed firm. But the partnership had been making money with this tactic, and its radar screen of future targets was soon displaying a number of potentially rewarding underperformers.

Lamont was among them, and Capital Partners purchased some 6 percent of its shares, an investment of more than $200 million. Lamont Company's size placed a full buyout or hostile takeover well beyond the funding that the small partnership could ever hope to raise. Election to the board of directors, however, was well within the partnership's grasp. Once on the board, the partners could force management to improve performance by reducing the number of employees, divesting weak units, changing strategies, or replacing executives.

Getting elected to the board meant attracting a majority of the freely cast shareholder votes. Dissident nominees normally can expect to draw only a tiny percentage of the vote against board-approved, management-friendly nominees. But the atmosphere of Lamont was sufficiently volatile to encourage a viable challenger. With five openings on the board, Capital Partners prepared a proxy ballot with its own five nominees. In further defiance of convention, it gave those nominees a campaign platform. They pledged to invite outside proposals to acquire the company or its divisions, to have the company opt out of the Delaware state antitakeover protections, and to rescind the company's poison pill. The main message: end entrenchment, restructure the company, and increase shareholder value.

Lamont executives were appalled at the prospect. A challenger, in their view, would fill the board with people who had no experience overseeing a Fortune 100 corporation, let alone a firm specializing in consumer products. As the company's treasurer recalled: "The people who were after us had nothing in mind other than a short-term financial gain. They were really financial raiders whose goal was to dismember the company." It would be end of the company as he knew it. "We expected the company would be dismembered, the divisions would be sold off, and any corporate staff would no longer exist," he said. "All the pieces would belong to somebody else." Even if the changes fell short of dismemberment, the executives recognized that their livelihoods were at risk. As the company's vice chairman concluded, "It was shock treatment to the finish."[1]

Management circled the wagons with a "just say no" strategy. It found no white knight (a better alternative owner), sought no leveraging (borrowing money to buy its own stock), offered no concessions. It simply asked shareholders to vote against the dissident slate, expecting them to follow tradition and side with management. Both sides calculated that most of the company's many small shareholders were likely to remain loyal to management. The institutional holders, however, were another story. Just several hundred controlled half the company's more than 100 million shares. Institutional investors did not always determine how their proxy ballots were to be cast, since many managed other people's money, and many ultimate owners retained voting authority. Some institutions even had policies of not voting. But these were the exceptions, and the job of reaching most of the large voters would be relatively straightforward. Rather than having to solicit several thousand individual holders, Capital Partners needed only to reach several hundred institutional holders.

Working with the same list of institutional investors, Lamont mounted a nearly identical shareholder campaign. The chief executive and other senior managers dropped other business for the duration, turning their fortieth-floor suite into a command center. They met every morning, including weekends, to review and adjust their proxy strategy. They telephoned most stockholders, even those owning as few as a thousand shares. (The personal appeal inspired one female shareholder to ask for a dinner date with the male executive who called.) Several teams crisscrossed the country, one by chartered jet, to shore up institutional support.

It was not long before management knew it was in trouble. The vice chairman had recently attended a conference of institutional investors and had been stunned by their animosity: "There was no 'Let's find a way,'" he observed. "There was a lot of 'Let's go to war with these guys.'" But management also had some appreciation for the mind of the investor. The chief financial officer served on the committee overseeing his firm's own pension fund, and he understood the pressures: "We ourselves have canned pension advisers because they didn't perform up to the Dow Jones industrial average. . . . If we've got one or two of our people who consistently underperform the indices, they're going to be gone. I think the institutions are in the same situation. They have to maximize their profitability so they can report to their constituents." Yet even he was surprised that major investors seemed "so overwhelmingly in opposition to the management of this company." The company's treasurer described them as "not stockholders in the sense that I think of as an investor in the company." The typical major holder in this case was "totally short-term oriented," merely the "holder of a piece of paper."

Still, management hoped that personal solicitation might bring as many as ten of the top twenty investors back to the fold. Some of management's investor visits were to prove unproductive, at times with a touch of irony. One management group traveled across the country to meet with representatives of a large public pension fund that opposed investments in South Africa, urging Lamont to divest from South Africa as a long-term strategy. An officer of the fund told the company, in the bitter paraphrase of a company executive, "Being a long-term serious investor, deeply in love with your corporation over a period of a hundred years, always respecting the corporation's long-term growth, we ask you to kindly divest" from South Africa. Now the same executive was asking for the same fund to stand by its long-term commitment by opposing Capital Partners. "We have committed ourselves to long-term growth," argued the executive, "and to strong cash flow, to restructuring, and we're on track. We want your vote for management." An officer of the pension fund responded that a decision had not yet been made. The company manager shot back: "But what about your 'long-term investor' thing?" The fund officer replied: "Sometimes long-term can mean a matter of a few days." Equivocating to the end, the pension fund finally faxed its decision to the annual meeting just minutes before the voting was closed. It came in for the dissident slate.

Other company contacts proved more productive. One New York bank had already cast its two million shares against management. It managed a large fraction of the shares, however, on behalf of three corporate pension funds. The chairman of the targeted company called the chief executives of the three pension-fund parent firms to ask for their support, and they in turn instructed the bank to reverse its votes of their shares.

Another bank took the same action. Holding some 650,000 shares in an indexed fund, it had announced its support for the challengers, a commitment publicized by Capital Partners to bolster its campaign. But the chief executive of the Chicago parent bank subsequently received a call from Lamont's chairman. The parent bank had long worked with the targeted firm, and the two CEOs knew each other well. The bank executive ordered the subsidiary to change its vote, a last-minute reversal that was to stun Capital Partners.

On the penultimate day, company vote counters knew the outcome would at best be extremely close. "We were totally discouraged," recalled one Lamont executive, since several large blocs had just come in against the company. Company executives called the institutions whose votes were uncertain or presumably reversible again and again, pleading and cajoling well into the evening. The eleventh-hour effort may have worked. As the company's top officials pushed into the meeting hall the next morning, they had become cautiously confident. "We felt we'd just squeaked by," said one.

But the other side sensed victory, too. Since balloting was not confidential, Capital Partners tallied the votes as they were cast, and the count looked good. To nail down the victory, Capital Partners launched its own last-minute canvassing of uncommitted institutional voters. Some proved masters of obfuscation or confusion. Representatives from the trust department of one commercial bank, for instance, indicated that they were prepared to vote with the dissident challenge. To nail it down, the partners called several more times, rearguing the case and soliciting the bank's votes anew. Only later did they learn that Lamont was a major customer of the bank, and that the bank's early promises would finally prove hollow against the concerted company counterlobbying.

At a second holder, a bank trust department responsible for several million shares, an officer early on committed the bank's shares to the challengers. But again the commitment was less than met the eye. Several hundred thousand shares managed by the bank trust were indexed, a practice in which funds are invested according to a predetermined formula that requires virtually no investor attention. A separate bank manager oversaw these indexed funds, and his policy of always voting with management finally took precedence over the bank's prior commitment. The votes of another portion of the bank's holdings, some 350,000 shares managed for a corporate pension fund, were also committed to the partnership, but that too would prove problematic. The issue here was one of accounting: the bank and the corporate pension fund both told the partnership that they backed the dissident slate, but the partners did not realize that the bank was including the pension-fund shares in its total. As a result, the partners' running tallies included a double count.

At a third holder, a bank officer's promised delivery of several hundred thousand votes for Capital Partners had still not materialized on the evening before the annual meeting. The partners suspected sabotage. They were sure the manufacturing company had also called the bank, and they knew it would be easy for another bank officer "accidentally" to misplace the proxy. Working through the night, the partners frantically tracked down the banker who had committed the vote, finally reaching him in the shower at six o'clock the next morning. The banker called his office and directed that the votes be properly dispatched. Anticipating last-minute votes from outside the meeting hall, the company had installed several fax machines, and a faxed proxy for the challengers arrived from this shareholder just moments before the meeting was called to order.

The partners believed they had accumulated some 51 percent of the vote, not resounding support but enough to win. In case last-minute lobbying was still needed from within the hall, they arrived at the door carrying a set of portable telephones. As the partners pushed in through a bevy of photographers, reporters, and onlookers at the entrance to the hall, company security refused to allow their equipment inside. Lamont employees, gathered around the entry, added more hostility to the ambience as the partners went inside. Shouted one bystander, "Go back to New York!" The partners' experience on the way to the meeting was a fitting coda to the hard-edged battle. As a company executive brushed by one of the partners, the partner crowed to him, "You guys are out of here!"

Both sides anxiously awaited certification of the vote, which, because it was contested, required several days. Both sides anticipated victory. Each thought it had kept careful count of its solicited proxies. Each believed it had accumulated the necessary majority.

When the final tally was announced, it stunned Capital Partners and elated Lamont executives. Shareholders had defeated the dissident director slate by one percentage point. Capital Partners' mistaken count had reflected a double listing of several blocks of votes, and several institutions had switched their votes literally at the last minute. Some four million votes that Capital Partners had confidently counted in its column in the end simply were not there.

Though a razor-thin margin, the winner-take-all policy in proxy contests meant total victory for management. On such small moments large corporate history is often made. Lamont emerged bloodied but independent. It undertook an extensive internal restructuring, adopting many of the very changes advocated by Capital Partners. In its postmortem of the struggle, a leading business publication warned corporate managements that "you can't be too close to your shareholders nowadays." Lamont revamped its investor relations, building informed and enduring contact with its major shareholders to secure a lasting independence. In subsequent years Lamont became a star performer for its owners. During the three years after its near takeover, Lamont stock tripled in value. Capital Partners eventually dissolved.

Taking Direct Control

The investment partnership fought with management for control of the consumer products company in the proxy trenches, bidding for support from the company's uncommitted shareholders. Major investors knew the balance of power lay in their hands: the company's fate resided on their decision to vote with or against management. Yet investors, like all political actors, had learned to exercise their powers through alternative means as well. If the election of new directors was not feasible, if the annual meeting was still months away, institutions could resort to other strategies for bringing recalcitrant management to bay. During the early 1990s, unyielding executives at the General Motors Corporation (GM) led investors to try other avenues for corporate control.

GM gave daily definition to the concept of "blue chip." Its stock had been a long-standing component of the Dow Jones industrial average. Its shares were owned by millions of Americans. Its workforce was the largest of any private employer. The vast scale and pervasive reach of GM had understandably inspired the popular conception that its fortunes were somehow inextricably linked to those of the nation.

GM also ranked among the twenty largest U.S. corporations in market capitalization. This meant that GM stock inevitably found its way into many institutional portfolios. The College Retirement Equities Fund (CREF), for instance, held in mid-1992 a combined 6.9 million shares of GM's three classes of stock (valued at $278 million). In early 1991, the California Public Employees Retirement System (Calpers) owned 7.2 million shares, and the New York State Common Retirement Fund held 4.8 million. If GM prospered, so too did hundreds of thousands of retired and to-be-retired college faculty and state employees. For decades, it seemed, what was good for GM had also been good for CREF, Calpers, and New York State employees.

The American automobile market, so good to GM, reached a zenith in the early 1960s. GM's share of new car sales crested then at over 50 percent. Thereafter the trend pointed downward, with market share by 1980 sliding to 45 percent, and by 1990 to 35 percent. Worse, GM's earnings abruptly turned from black to red at the start of the 1990s. Earnings of $6.82 billion in 1988 had become losses of $4.09 billion two years later, and in 1991 the company hemorrhaged $8.85 billion—the largest one-year corporate loss in U.S. history, depressing share value and raising grave doubts about GM's future. By early 1992, GM's stock prices had fallen below their 1966 levels. An investment of $100 in Ford stock at the end of 1982 would have yielded $466 in market value ten years later; a Chrysler investment would have brought $342; and an investment in the basket of stocks in the S&P 500 would have yielded $297. The comparable figure for GM was $109.[2]

The prolonged downward slide had been evident to all, and for large stockholders that was precisely the problem. Unhappy investors could follow the Wall Street rule of selling rather than complaining only if other institutions were ready to buy the holdings at an acceptable price. Not surprisingly, few were. The aggrieved institutions were stuck; they might wait for a takeover group to appear, but GM's giant scale placed it beyond the dreams of all but the most ambitious. And by 1990, the collapse of the junk bond market and the weakening of the bank market had thwarted even the recklessly ambitious.

Their options dwindling, disgruntled institutions turned toward management itself. In early 1990, the directors of both the New York and the California pension funds asked to have a voice in picking a chief executive officer to succeed the retiring chairman, Roger B. Smith. GM rebuffed the requests, though representatives of the two funds were said to have made unannounced visits to the Detroit headquarters anyway, to discuss the process.

Despite the rumblings of investor discontent, the GM board was not ready to break with convention. In August 1990, it promoted Robert C. Stempel, a career executive and Roger Smith's chief operating officer, to the post of chairman and chief executive. And in turn, it approved the appointment of a close Stempel colleague, Lloyd E. Reuss, as president. The only bright spot for the institutional investors was GM's adoption of a bylaw in January 1991, requiring that a majority of its directors be independent outsiders. The action was largely symbolic—a majority were already so classified—but an implicit message had been sent: GM could change in response to investor pressure. Calpers' chief executive, Dale Hanson, called the reform "a breath of fresh air."[3]

As the flow of red ink at GM intensified in 1991, Calpers pressed for further action, and other investors joined the fray. And now they discovered a way to reach the board without going through management. Some five years earlier, the outside, nonexecutive directors had hired their own general counsel, the New York attorney Ira M. Millstein. He had built a network of contacts with the institutions that furnished investors with a credible conduit through which to reach the outside board members. Millstein reported that impatient investors were expecting fast, dramatic action. The channel also worked the other way: to discontented investors, Millstein reported that the independent directors were considering independent action.[4]

In the spring of 1992, GM's independent directors took action. The board forced the demotion of its president, Lloyd Reuss; demoted the company's chief financial officer, Robert T. O'Connell; removed Reuss and another executive, F. Alan Smith, from the board; and lifted Stempel from his chairmanship of the company's executive committee. "This sends a great message to other companies," offered the general counsel of Calpers, Richard Koppes. "For nonperformers, the status quo doesn't do."[5]

Yet even that shattering of the status quo proved insufficient. Just six months later, with no signs of a turnaround in the offing, the GM board forced the resignation of Stempel himself. That was soon followed by the early retirement of Reuss, O'Connell, and others. The board appointed John G. Smale, the former chairman of Procter & Gamble and a leader of the directors' revolt, to serve as the new GM chairman, thereby separating the posts of chairman and chief executive officer. The board also elevated an inside executive, Jack F. Smith Jr., to the CEO position. He in turn assembled a new team of executives with the unequivocal charge of making the changes required to restore prosperity.

It had been more than seventy years since the GM board had imposed its will so dramatically. Then again, few shareholders had previously been in a position to demand such change. In 1920, the duPont family and chemical company held a major block (23 percent) of GM stock and, working with J. P. Morgan & Co., another large holder, forced out GM's founder and president William C. Durant, ultimately replacing him with Alfred P. Sloan.[6] In 1992, the top dozen investors held an equivalent ownership position, and outside investors were once again powerful enough to force out an incumbent management group.

John F. Smith Jr., the new CEO installed by the GM board, well understood his mandate to reduce operating costs and restore shareholder value. Compared with 1991 levels, Smith slashed GM's North American workforce by 23 percent and removed an average $2,800 in costs from every vehicle manufactured. By 1993 he had turned a profit of $362 million, not much for a company with $140 billion in revenue, but nonetheless a figure in striking contrast to that of 1991, achieving, in the labeling of one business writer, "GM's $11 billion turnaround." GM shares that hit a nadir of less than $30 just before Stempel's ouster soared to $65.[7]

Ownership Rising

Institutional investors could exercise a determining voice in these incidents because they had come to hold a determining stake. Peter
Drucker had offered prescient analysis in his *Unseen Revolution* (1976),
warning that America's pension funds were rapidly growing, and that in
time they would come to constitute a major force in the securities markets. Though their quiet accumulation of assets was then little noticed,
Drucker argued that it would indeed be felt one day. The book's sub-
title warned what they might become: *How Pension Fund Socialism
Came to America.*[8]

Little in the way of "pension fund socialism" came to pass in the
years that followed. Though pension funds grew as anticipated, most
beneficiaries retained no control over the funds' assets, preventing any
collectivist worker guidance that might have given the funds a socialist
tinge. Something more akin to pension fund capitalism, however, did
appear. And with it came a parallel rise in the holdings and influence of
four other kinds of investors: commercial banks, insurance companies,
investment managers, and nonprofit endowments.[9]

This crowding of more equities into fewer hands created an economic base for investor capitalism. Institutional investors expanded
their share of publicly traded stock, while individuals contracted theirs.
In 1965, individual holdings constituted 84 percent of corporate stock,
institutional holdings 16 percent. By 1990, the individual fraction had
declined to 54 percent, and the institutional fraction had risen to 46 percent. A closer look at the 1,000 publicly traded companies with highest
market value during the late 1980s and 1990s reveals much the same
trend. Between 1985 and 1994, as seen in figure 1.1, the institutional
share rose by more than a point per year, topping the 50 percent thresh-
old in 1990 and reaching 57 percent by 1994.[10]

A political base for investor capitalism has come as a by-product of
the economic base. When shares are scattered among tens of thousands
of small holders, in the absence of an effective political mechanism,
each is relatively powerless to effect change. The situation was not
unlike the one faced by small farmers aggrieved at low produce prices
and high credit costs. In principle, small shareholders distressed by poor
company performance could exercise collective leverage, but in practice the barriers to joint mobilization were usually prohibitive. A concentration of ownership, however, lowered those barriers.

Institutional investors, as a result, singly and jointly have turned to
direct challenges of management. The predominant strategies varied by
era. During the mid-1980s, institutional holders played a major role in

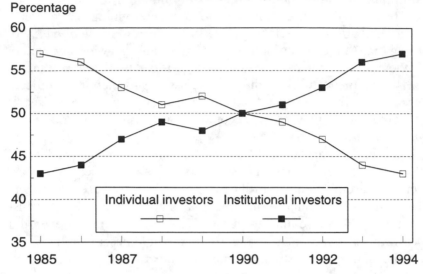

Figure 1.1 Percentage of Shares of 1,000 U.S. Largest Companies Held by Individual and Institutional Investors, 1985-94

Source: Business Week, various issues.

takeovers and buyouts. They rendered shares to would-be acquirers; they invested funds in takeover and buyout funds, and they gave votes to strategic block investors. These developments help to explain why mergers and acquisitions of publicly traded companies more than doubled between 1980 and 1988, and leveraged buyouts rose by a factor of 10 (see figure 1.2). The likelihood that a Fortune 500 manufacturing firm would receive a takeover offer also rose sharply (see figure 1.3).[11]

By end of the decade, however, the acquisition market sharply contracted, and the buyout market all but collapsed. As the door was closing on this avenue of shareholder pressure, investors have sought entry by other means. U.S. Securities and Exchange Commission (SEC) rules permit disgruntled owners to present binding or advisory resolutions for stockholder approval on matters of corporate governance. Proposed changes can range from rescissions of antitakeover defenses to separation of the offices of chairman and chief executive. Shareholders found this a promising alternative. The number of governance resolutions on company proxies proposed by shareholders rose sharply during the latter part of the 1980s, dipped in the early 1990s, and reached record levels by the mid-1990s. By contrast, the number of resolutions on company proxies concerned with social issues such as environmental protection, minority hiring, and South African investments peaked in the early 1990s and declined thereafter (figure 1.4).[12]

Figure 1.2 Acquisitions and Buyouts of Publicly Traded Companies, 1980-92

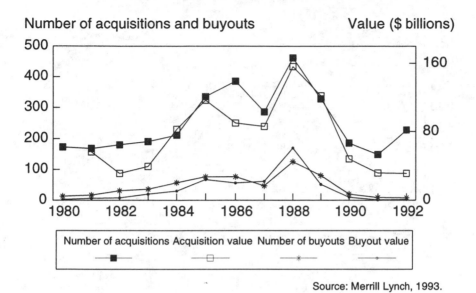

Number of acquisitions and buyouts   Value ($ billions)

Number of acquisitions — Acquisition value — Number of buyouts — Buyout value

Source: Merrill Lynch, 1993.

Figure 1.3 Percentage of Large Manufacturing Firms Receiving a Takeover Offer, 1980-91

Percentage

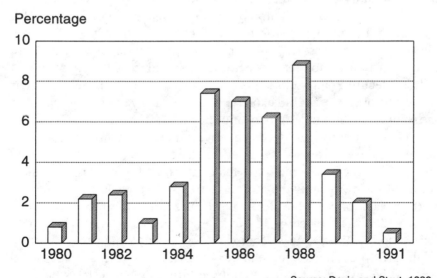

Source: Davis and Stout, 1992.

Figure 1.4 Number of Shareholder Proposals Voted on Corporate Governance and Social Issues, 1985-95

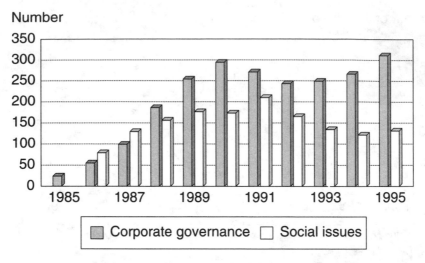

Number

Source: Investor Responsibility Research Center.
Note: 1995 figure is estimated.

During the early 1990s, investors have added a third avenue of action: direct contact with managements and boards. Directors generally rebuffed investor approaches, and many executives stonewalled. But some directors are open to the use of indirect channels, as we have seen in the case of the GM board. And most managements have instituted programs for periodic meetings with their largest investors.

At the same time, company managers have devised means for resisting or buffering investor influence. Dialogues may be informative, but they do not necessarily prove productive. Few senior managers are ready to acquiesce to greater institutional influence if the consequence is less executive autonomy. They had reached the pinnacle of their careers through the skillful exercise of power. They are not prepared to see their authority undermined, and they know how to defend it.

As protection against the takeover market, managements have adopted such devices as staggered terms for directors, golden parachutes for executives, and supermajority rules for boards. The most common—and arguably the most effective—is what came to be known as the poison pill: if a hostile acquirer purchased a firm over management and board objection, it would ingest a possibly lethal element lodged inside the acquired company. For example, the targeted firm might give pretakeover shareholders the right to purchase additional stock at below-market value, thereby diluting the stake for which the acquirer has paid a high price. So powerful is the pill for resisting shareholder pressures that its formal appellation, a "shareholder rights plan," could hardly have been more ironic. Before the mid-1980s, no firm had adopted a poison pill. As seen in figure 1.5, by the end of the decade some two-thirds of the nation's largest firms had done so.

Most managements wanted further safeguards against hostile takeovers and jointly pressed for government protection. Given the free-market philosophy of the Reagan-Bush administrations, the federal government proved doggedly uninterested, but state governments proved more malleable. Companies pressed state legislators and governors to legislate a guarantee of the poison pill. They pressed for bills allowing company directors to reject financially appealing but otherwise undesirable offers for their firms. They urged expansion of directors' responsibilities from purely fiduciary to the nonfiduciary interests of employees and communities. They pressed, in other words, for state statutes giving directors the latitude to reject an above-market offer for a firm without fearing shareholder litigation. As figure 1.5 shows, no states offered such an umbrella in 1980; by 1990, four out of five had been persuaded to do so.

From Markets to Politics

If the free exchange of company shares is a defining feature of a capital market, trading depends on the widespread availability of informa-

Figure 1.5 Number of Large Companies with Poison Pills, and Number of States with Anti-takeover Laws, 1980-90

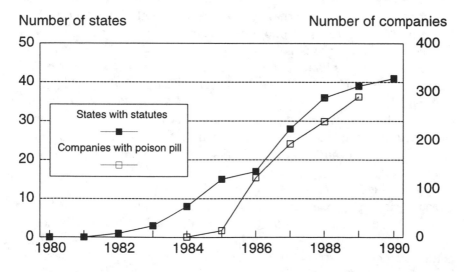

Source: Davis, 1991; Investor
Responsibility Research Center, 1992.

tion on the companies. That availability is fostered by the SEC and the several exchanges where the trading takes place. Their rules require dissemination of accurate company data and a level playing field among those who wish to receive the data. Prospective buyers and sellers can develop informed forecasts of a company's future performance, and they can readily find one another. The daily exchange of millions of company shares—sometimes more than 300 million on the New York Stock Exchange alone—offers vivid confirmation of the model

Yet the concentration of company ownership has recast such market relations. Rather than just momentarily touching one another during brief market exchanges, many investors have also sought to develop working relations among themselves and with the companies that are the objects of the exchange. And many firms, rather than limiting themselves to quarterly financial releases, have sought more frequent contact with their major owners as well. Smaller investors and firms have neither the inclination nor the capacity to move in these directions. But the largest do, and in so doing they are going well beyond traditional market principles.

Going beyond impersonal relations is risky and time-consuming, but it has also become a necessity given the partial limiting of the investor's option of selling. An institution with $10 billion or more under management is sometimes simply unable to dispose readily of its investment in a firm when it does not like what it hears about the company. Given the size of the typical institutional investment, the only potential buyers are other institutions, and they are just as likely to have been apprised of any bad news. Moreover, even when the dissatisfied seller is able to find a not-too-dissatisfied buyer, the seller can be faced with few good alternatives for reinvestment. Given the size of their portfolios, large institutions are already invested in a vast array of the country's major companies. Fidelity's holdings in 1991, for instance, were spread among some 2,300 firms, Aetna's among 2,400, and the California State Teachers' Retirement System among 3,500.[13]

Finally, by definition, indexing as a major investment strategy precludes selling. Under indexing, an investor places a fraction of its funds in a predetermined list of companies, such as the S&P 500 (the 500 large companies in the index account for about 70 percent of the market value of all publicly traded companies). Here, investing is defined as a relatively fixed asset. About one-sixth of all institutional stockholdings was indexed in 1993, much of it according to the widely used S&P 500. Mutual fund managers rarely use indexing, but in 1993 banks placed about one-third of their equity in indexes, corporate pension funds more than one-third, and public pension funds over half.[14]

Market options for large investors, as a result, are constrained.

CREF, with more than $44 billion invested in stock in mid-1992, warned of the constraint: CREF states that it "is not in a position to divest itself of a company's stock when it disagrees with the action of that company's management." The chief investment officer for the $46 billion California State Teachers' Retirement System underscores the same point: "The larger public pension funds can't just walk away when companies aren't performing well. There'd be no market. Everybody would be on one side of the trade." The chief investment officer of Calpers, presiding over 1992 investments of $68 billion, warned of the same: "We realized we don't have the option of voting with our feet. The only course available is to see [that] companies are effectively run." A pension-fund manager interviewed in 1992 summarized the shift: "Buying stock in a company is like buying a purple house. If you don't like the color, you can sell the house or you can paint it. We're doing a lot more painting."[15]

Institutional investors continually trade, increasing or decreasing their holdings by as much as 25 percent or even 50 percent per quarter. This is partly in response to changing assessments of the companies' prospects. It is also partly a product of indexing, since the identities and relative weighting of the companies in the S&P 500, for instance, are frequently revised. Quarterly changes, however, are relatively modest, with a liquidation or doubling of a major institution's position rarely encountered within a quarter. This can be illustrated by the top fifteen holders' movements into and out of the shares of MCI Communications and PepsiCo during one quarter in the early 1990s, as seen in table 1.1. Oppenheimer increased its holding in MCI by 8.6 percent, and Morgan by 18.5 percent, while Bankers Trust decreased its position by 0.3 percent, Wells Fargo by 0.6 percent. The Michigan State Trea-

Table 1.1 Shares Held and Traded by Fifteen Largest Institutional Owners in MCI Communications and PepsiCo, Third Quarter, 1991

MCI Communications Institutional Owners	Shares held	Quarterly change	PepsiCo Institutional Owners	Shares held	Quarterly change
Oppenheimer & Co.	9,404,182	811,167	Sarofim Fayez	22,252,820	665,590
J. P. Morgan & Co.	8,749,799	1,619,461	Bankers Trust N.Y. Corp.	15,399,236	46,045
Capital Research & Mgmt.	8,239,000	240,000	Wells Fargo Inst. Trust	13,800,682	−271,098
Alliance Capital Mgmt.	5,464,468	42,798	State Street Boston Corp.	11,214,907	210,225
Bankers Trust N.Y. Corp.	4,778,884	−13,262	Mellon Bank Corp.	10,436,007	−1,418,302
Wells Fargo Inst. Trust	4,395,651	−25,528	CREF	7,460,993	−287,400
Michigan State Treasurer	3,434,400	0	Lincoln Capital Mgmt.	6,809,600	−631,100
Loomis Sayles & Co.	3,080,615	−491,025	New York St. Common Ret.	6,642,702	249,881
New York St. Common Ret.	3,054,849	−130,473	Alliance Capital Mgmt.	6,047,365	−4,254,950
Miller Anderson & Sherred	2,918,427	−264,700	W. P. Stewart & Co.	5,109,027	188,145
Capital Guardian Trust	2,900,400	66,400	New York State Teachers	4,696,200	0
CREF	2,851,300	4,500	NCNB Corp.	4,196,896	−41,994
Templeton Gal. & Hans	2,303,800	−74,250	Calpers	4,850,000	−135,009
State Street Res. & Mgmt.	2,217,059	−100,300	National City Bank/Cleveland	4,775,000	94,000
Mellon Bank Corp.	2,046,067	97,126	RCM Capital Mgmt.	4,725,030	1,204,030

Source: CDA Technologies.

surer neither sold nor bought a single share. Similar movements are evident in PepsiCo stock.

Another way to see the same limited movement is to follow the quarterly holdings of a major investor in one large company. Though trades can be made at any time, information is only made public on a quarterly basis. Figure 1.6 shows the quarter-by-quarter movements of one institution in the pharmaceutical company, Stewart Drugs, over four years. While the holdings vary from period to period, the investor maintains a substantial stake in the company through all quarters.

Some institutional investors do pursue a strategy of frequent trading. In 1993, pension funds and bank trusts on average turned over one-quarter or less of their stock holdings annually, while insurance companies and investment companies averaged closer to half. The high end of the distribution, however, could reach turnover rates of 100 percent or more. Fidelity's Magellan fund, the nation's largest mutual fund in 1995, with more than $50 billion under management, turned over well over 100 percent of its holdings during the late 1970s, less than 100 percent during much of the 1980s, but again more than 100 percent during the early 1990s. Its average annual turnover for 1976 to 1995 stood at 158 percent (figure 1.7).[16]

Still, by the early 1990s, many funds have adopted strategies of relative stability. Some investors, particularly pension funds, annually turn over one-quarter or less of their assets. Rather than immediately dis-

**Figure 1.6 Quarterly Holdings of a Major
Investor in Stewart Drugs**

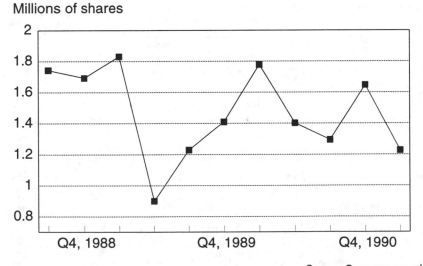

Source: Company records.

**Figure 1.7 Annual Turnover of Fidelity
Magellan Fund, 1976-95**

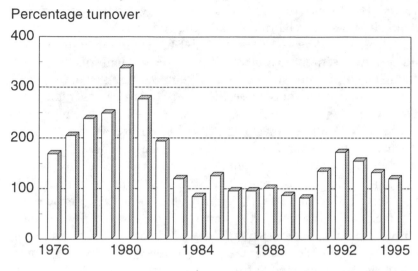

Source: Morningstar, Inc.

posing of a corporate position at the first signs of bad weather, investors
seek other means for responding to adverse conditions, including pressing managers for changes in strategies or directors for changes in management.[17]

The concentration of ownership has thus forced greater complexity
into the relations between investors and companies. To the cold mone-
tary calculus of buying and selling shares is added a personal chemistry
of negotiation and obligation between owners and managers.

A Troubled Company and a Discontented Investor

To gain further perspective on the emergent economic and political
relations, it is useful to imagine yourself temporarily placed in the office
of a top investment manager. You have been given responsibility for a
multibillion-dollar investment fund, and your year-end performance
evaluation depends on demonstrated success in its secure growth.

You hold a major stake in a manufacturing firm but the company
has fared poorly during the past several years. Its earnings have been
lackluster, the stock price lags behind the S&P 500 stock index, and the
share value and dividends average some 10 percent below those for
other firms in the industry. Wall Street analysts have issued pessimistic

reports on the company's future earnings, and several recommend that its shares be sold.

The company's governance, you suspect, may account for its faltering record. Brief study reveals that the firm is overseen by a board of fourteen directors. The chairman is also the company's chief executive, and he is joined on the board by the chief financial officer, three vice presidents, two retired executives, and a descendant of the firm's founder. The corporation maintains a shareholder-rights plan (a poison pill) but no other takeover defense. Managers and directors collectively hold less than 1 percent of the company's shares. The top five managers receive three-quarters of their compensation on average from salary and benefits (the remainder is equally divided between year-end bonuses and stock options that can be exercised in three to five years).

As fund manager, you have held some 1.5 million shares in the manufacturer in recent years. This constitutes 1.2 percent of the company's stock, and it amounts to 0.9 percent of your own equity holdings. The firm's downward spiral persuaded you to consider reducing your position, but you anticipate that there will be few other buyers for large blocks of shares at acceptable prices. As a consequence, you are considering six courses of action, several of them inspired by reading about the incidents at Lamont Company and GM described earlier:

1. Create a slate of director nominees pledged to restructure the firm.
2. Contact directors to press for changes in top management.
3. Submit a shareholder proposal to rescind the poison pill.
4. Invest a fraction of your money in a leveraged-buyout fund.
5. Contact management, and press for separation of the positions of chairman and chief executive and for changes in executive compensation and product strategy.
6. Increase your investment in the company to 4.8 percent of its shares and seek regular exchange of ideas and information with management.

Now imagine yourself on the other side, as the chief executive for the company. Here you have been granted responsibility for the security and growth of corporate assets in the billions, and your annual performance depends on continuing company expansion. While your performance is admittedly lackluster, you believe this is largely due to weak market conditions well beyond your control. Some of it also stems from decisions of your predecessors. They had entered several product markets that proved more cutthroat than anticipated. You are saddled as well with the results of your predecessors' inaction. They had failed to pare the workforce when your competitors were already doing so, and they had given too little thought to product quality or customer needs. Whatever the past, you do not think it wise to boost stock dividends despite investor pressure to do so. Slashing investment in plant modernization and product research as a response to short-term demands would mean that the outward success of the firm your successors inherit would mask a hollow shell. You need more time and more cash to restore the firm's competitiveness, a fact you hope your investors will appreciate.

Some 65 percent of your shares are held by about 350 institutions. Most rarely seek to communicate with you, but you have engaged in ongoing dialogues with representatives of the top thirty, which collectively control nearly one-quarter of your stock. During the last meeting with the managing director of the second-largest stockholder, you learned that she had become very critical of your performance and was running out of patience. Other large shareholders are signaling much the same.

Your sense of vulnerability is heightened by a 1992 change in SEC rules on investor communication. Without public notification, groups of institutions are now allowed to discuss a company in which they hold large blocks. The investment-fund managing director has implied that she has already been in touch with a dozen other disgruntled money managers among the top thirty. A *Fortune* magazine cover further fuels your alarm with a warning that "The King Is Dead," as a rash of investor-inspired boardroom revolts have recently toppled CEOs. Ignoring ownership pressures no longer seems judicious, and you too are contemplating six courses of action:

1. Bring several new directors to the board who strongly support your vision and strategy for the company, and warn the current board that shareholder hostility is widespread but misdirected.
2. Add several antitakeover defenses to complement the poison pill.
3. Order the drafting of a plan for a possible management buyout of the company.
4. Initiate an internal restructuring of the firm, focusing first on changes in executive compensation and then product strategy.
5. Recruit more individual investors, create an employee stock-ownership plan, and isolate the activist institutions.
6. Seek regular exchange of ideas and information with a core group of large investors, and encourage them to increase their holdings.

As either the investment manager or the company manager, you might seek to combine several options into a more comprehensive strategy. You might also want to move cautiously, waiting to see which actions the other side pursues. In any case, the choices on both sides are fateful. If they are correct, your organization's wealth and your personal fortunes may well prosper. If they are faulty, your organization's assets and your own career may be squandered. Identifying and evolving appropriate strategies, however, depends on an understanding of the changed environment in which you work.[18]

A Different Era

Your challenges, options, and risks as an investment manager or company manager are now decidedly different from those of your predecessors several decades earlier. No longer is the capital market quite so impersonal. No longer is the Wall Street rule the sole option for the disgruntled investor. No longer is the relationship between a money manager and a corporate executive irrelevant to the fortunes of either.

The fate of each side is now tightly bound with the other's. Presiding over capital assets or corporate assets demands a set of skills little anticipated under managerial capitalism but now required under investor capitalism. Effective management of the relationship between owners and companies has become a competitive advantage for those who do it well. It can be a costly disadvantage for those less skilled at it.

To outsiders, the struggle for corporate control might appear to be just another squabble among the rich and powerful, a dogfight of little more than passing interest to the average citizen. Esoteric talk about classified boards, leveraged buyouts, and proxy struggles would seem to have scant relevance to those who have never set foot in an executive suite or on a trading floor.

The average citizen, however, is as likely as not to be a party to the struggle. Of those who are gainfully employed, most participate in a private or public pension plan. Of those who have accumulated assets, most invest in a mutual fund or the market directly. In 1990, state and local retirement systems included 2.4 million participants, mutual funds more than 23 million households (one-quarter of all households), and private pension plans some 77 million participants. Most Americans derive a substantial fraction of their current or future livelihood from the performance of companies whose stock they directly or indirectly own.[19]

Pension and money managers are of course acutely aware that their beneficiaries and clients always want a greater livelihood. With the concentrated firepower that the millions of participants—that is, all of us—have vested in money managers, the latter now possess the clout to force companies to produce more, and they are increasingly expected to do so. As hard-pressed companies streamline operations, downsize employee ranks, move facilities abroad, and diminish low-end wages, the struggle for corporate control is of more than passing interest. Though this is not necessarily an engagement of our own choosing, under the new rules of investor capitalism we are inevitably drawn into it.

2

---- ∽ ----

When Investors Challenge Company Performance

IF INSTITUTIONAL INVESTORS ARE the new high priests, the new repositories for wealth and power, they confer their blessings on or direct their criticism at corporate managements in unequal measure. To those companies with good performance and good governance, the institutions signal hallowed status through rising holdings and benign neglect. To the weaker performers, they signal displeasure through declining positions and noisy attention. If the institutions' wealth is being squandered, if a company's performance and governance are judged inadequate, the institutions put their powers to great use. Money managers might insist on better segment and product data; they might oppose poison pills and executive compensation; they might question executive leadership and director independence. Often the demands are simply for more: more growth, more earnings, more value.

The stature that corporate wealth confers upon those recently empowered can be seen in two illustrative moments. The top officers of two of the country's largest retirement funds appeared as speakers at separate conferences on corporate ownership and governance. They moved through the crowds of prominent people with a special prominence of their own. They enjoyed the kind of deference once reserved for corporate chieftains, having joined the ranks of those to whom even the chieftains sometimes bowed. Wealth has always been a leading source of power in American society. Institutional investors had finally learned how to transform the latent power that came with great holdings into real authority. And they transformed the traditional corporate disregard for shareholders into attentive respect.

Companies and investors vary greatly in the attention and respect they accord one another. Some firms feel the angry glare of distressed investors; others barely attract a disinterested glance. Some institutions actively challenge management; others passively wait. This chapter maps those diverse actions and reactions. To illustrate the varied levels of company attention, two extremes are first contrasted: a commercial bank and an industrial firm's respective experiences with their investors, which could not have been more divergent. Here we witness one firm that garnered virtually no attention from its shareholders and another company that met with almost continuous challenges. To see the varied levels of shareholder activism, the institutional investor world is then mapped, its major divides identified. Here we observe some investors stepping forward under the new rules while others remain in the shadows.

The Power of Wealth

The chief executive, the chief investment officer, and the general counsel for Calpers, the nation's largest public pension fund, entered the 1993 New York conference on "relational investing" displaying few outward signs of the vast fortune they now commanded: more than $70 billion in assets, with $20 million added daily. When Calpers executives spoke, business listened. Their patience could allow a troubled chief executive some breathing room. Their impatience might bring the boot.

By appearance and demeanor, the three Calpers executives were indistinguishable from the executives, attorneys, and journalists filling the room. One wondered whether Michael Milken, Henry Kravis, and Carl Icahn, the high priests of the eighties, could have moved (or would have allowed themselves to move) so invisibly.[1]

By midday, however, Calpers' commanding presence became evident even to the uninitiated. The chief executive, Dale Hanson, was introduced at a ballroom luncheon as a man who required no introduction, and once he finished his lunchtime commentary on relational investing (he was for it), a dozen people pressed forward, pencils and notebooks at the ready. Their questions, however, dwelled little on Hanson's formal comments, focusing instead on the future of a single company, Eastman Kodak.

The inquisitors were a varied collection of business and financial writers, representing publications ranging from *Investor's Business Daily* and the *Toronto Globe and Mail* to the *New York Times* and *Wall Street Journal*. Kodak's chief financial officer of less than three months had abruptly resigned several days earlier. He had been billed as a "turnaround artist" for the languishing giant of the photography industry, and his unexpected departure had dismayed many shareholders. The company's stock price plummeted by more than $5 per share the next day.[2]

The business writers surrounding Dale Hanson at the conference podium wanted to know what Calpers, the holder of two million Kodak shares, planned to do. Calpers executives had met privately with the beleaguered Kodak CEO, Kay R. Whitmore, for ninety minutes the day before the conference. He "needs to be given a chance," announced the Calpers general counsel, Richard Koppes, after the meeting, and the headlines on this morning of the conference read accordingly. "Kodak's Chief Wins Support from Calpers," offered the *New York Times*. For the *Wall Street Journal*, the event was summarized: "Kodak's Chief Gains Support from 2 Holders, Whitmore Assures Calpers He Will Make Changes to Boost Productivity."[3] The journalists at the podium wanted to know precisely what Whitmore and Hanson had said to each other. The Calpers executive held the floor as an investor celebrity, a holder to be sought, a critic to be feared, a power to be reckoned with.[4]

So too had Dale Hanson's contemporaries, including the head of the $110 billion pension fund of the nation's college faculty, the Teachers Insurance and Annuity Association, College Retirement Equities Fund (TIAA-CREF). Its chief executive in 1992, Clifton R. Wharton Jr., had built a distinguished career in education and investing. Former president of Michigan State University, former chancellor of the state university system of New York, and later deputy secretary of state in the Clinton administration, Wharton rose to address a 1992 conference sponsored by the U.S. Securities and Exchange Commission on corporate governance and economic competitiveness. (The conference site, the Willard Hotel in Washington, D.C., dated to the antebellum era, and for decades it was renowned as a meeting place for "the great, the near-great, and those who aspire to greatness." Several presidents used the Willard as temporary quarters, and the hotel was favored by visiting dignitaries; but it fell on hard times and finally closed in 1968. With congressional urging, the hotel would finally reopen some eighteen years later, though not before a massive and costly refurbishing.)[5]

Wharton presented his conference remarks at a session on "the growing presence of institutions as shareholders." But he opened with a seemingly unrelated story about the hotel itself. One day in 1946, he said, a young black man had ventured into the Willard lobby. His father had just returned with his family from a diplomatic posting, and the son knew little of Washington's ways. Unaware of the widespread racial segregation in the nation's capital, he had planned to meet several associates in the hotel lobby. But on arrival he was immediately instructed by hotel staff to leave. Since he had arranged to see his associates there, he refused. Luckily, they arrived soon thereafter and spirited him out of the hotel. Years later, when the backers of the Willard Hotel renovation sought funding, they turned to TIAA-CREF. The young man nearly evicted from the Willard lobby in 1946 had been Clifton Wharton himself. Now, he was the honored speaker in its main ballroom. More to the point, it was his decision to invest $90 million from his fund in the hotel that had permitted its restoration.

The Management of Performance

The power of Calpers, TIAA-CREF, and other institutional investors remains latent for the most part despite the concentration of shareholdings. With companies that are performing well, they would have no reason to intervene. With less well-run operations, however, they would now do what major holders a decade earlier could not. They would signal their displeasure, they would say how to change, and they would replace those who failed to do so.

The ends of the spectrum are illustrated with the contrasting experiences of a commercial bank and a manufacturing firm, both among the twenty companies in our focus group. The bank remained largely untouched by investor pressures; the manufacturer found few moments of peace. The bank devoted almost no attention to its shareholders, a strategy that had seemingly worked for decades; the industrial firm directed great attention to its investors, with senior management visiting major shareholders and conducting daily conversations with the largest. The bank's aloofness was a product of years of steady, above-industry growth in earnings; the manufacturer's attentiveness stemmed from its years of underperformance in a declining industry, inviting scrutiny of almost every major decision. Taken together, their accounts confirm how varied investor attention can be. When management manages its company performance well, large shareholders rarely intercede. When companies do not manage it well, institutions are no longer reluctant to tell them how to manage it better.

The Corporate Cold Shoulder

Buckingham Bank had delivered an earnings record that would be the envy of any publicly traded company, let alone its competitors in an industry hard hit by real estate and commercial losses. This bank had somehow managed to avoid the financial debacles afflicting so many of its brethren, a success variously attributed to its conservative traditions, its strong leadership, and its strategic vision. When others were acquiring shopping centers and investing in leveraged buyouts during the 1980s, the bank's straight-and-narrow path seemed dowdy. By the 1990s, it seemed prescient.

The bank's top investors were the country's top institutions: Alliance Capital, Bankers Trust, Capital Guardian, Delaware Management, and Capital Research & Management. Four of the great activist funds—Calpers, CREF, the New York State Common Retirement Fund, and the California State Teachers' Retirement System—owned more than a million shares each. Some 400 investors jointly held 70 percent of Buckingham's outstanding shares. Although the bank's ownership structure created the potential for concerted investor protest and pressure, its performance record had managed to keep all at bay.

"We don't have a lot of time spent on shareholder relationships," said Buckingham's chairman and chief executive. "We have a much less direct relationship with our shareholders, individually and institutionally, than most companies I know." The companies he knew well included a poorly performing manufacturer, on whose board he served as outside director. Angry institutional investors had pressed for radical change at the manufacturer—and demanded the head of its chairman.

According to bank lore, the CEO's predecessors had not met with stock analysts for more than a decade, and the current CEO preserved tradition. Some analysts and a few major shareholders visited the company every year, but neither the CEO nor his senior managers ventured outside headquarters to see them. Neither were stock analysts accorded a CEO audience when they came inside. In the words of the company's executive vice president and general counsel: "We have not had a proactive shareholder or investor-relations program. We have a fairly ivory-tower attitude. We've never had an analysts' meeting as long as I can recall."

Indeed, the most recent outside event attended by Buckingham executives dated back almost two decades. The bank then, in the words of its current director of investor relations, momentarily "came out of the closet" for a meeting of an association of securities analysts. The meeting was badly run, the analysts' questions were misdirected, and the bank's presentation was vacuous—at least, that's the way it was recalled years later by many in the firm. That one disastrous outing had ended all such forays into uncharted shareholder territory.

One more exception to the stay-at-home rule only served to reaffirm the company's posture of not communicating. A meeting had been arranged during the early 1990s with another financial institution with which the bank conducted bond business. As the chief executive was ushered into the institution's offices, he was belatedly informed by his own officer that the institution was also a major stockholder in the bank. What the CEO thought had been arranged as a client visit became quite the opposite. "I went in prepared to do my client-relationship speech," he recalled, but a dozen money managers greeted him upon entry, and still others soon joined the proceedings through speaker phones. They peppered him with questions about the bank's strategy and future, with no allusions to the bond dealings that he had come prepared to discuss. It was the only investor he had ever managed to visit— and that by mistake.

Buckingham's top officers gather every Tuesday for a lengthy review of their operations. The discussion might veer toward a difficult problem with a senior officer in the bank, a problem for which the chief executive would need informal guidance. Or it might concern a new trading instrument. But shareholder considerations appeared fleetingly in such discussions, if at all.

One exception occurred in the aftermath of a new appointment to the bank's board. The name of the new director appeared in press reports, and one of the bank's top five investors called the vice chairman. Based on some unspecified prior experience with the appointee, the fund's executive asked the bank manager if he had "gone off his rocker," emphatically registering his low opinion of the new director and threatening to reduce the fund's holdings in the company. The vice chairman's reassuring explanation of the choice evidently prevented the realization of the threat. The investor's protest found its way to the weekly discussion of the executive office, but such an intrusion was rare.

It is indicative of the bank's attitude that management had adopted none of the usual takeover defenses, not even a classified board in which only one-third of the directors are up for reelection each year (preventing sudden ouster of all directors by aroused investors). Affirmative features were missing as well: no shareholder advisory committee, no newsletter for investors, no meetings between directors and owners. Despite the gap, the company had developed a well-honed vision of what it thought its investors wanted: "consistency of earnings, and a return on capital which is superior to the industry generally," according to the CEO, and "conservative management," in the vice chairman's words.

The presumed investor search for consistency had led Buckingham to diversify its sources of volatile earnings. It also pressed for asset quality, avoiding opportunities to invest in less-developed countries (LDCs) or leveraged buyouts (LBOs). Such efforts were "not without their sacrifices" at the time, the chief executive allowed. The forgone LDC earnings and LBO fees had depressed its earnings relative to other banks. But staying the course in the 1980s, working "not to confuse opportunity with strategy," proved forward looking by the 1990s. As in so many areas of company policy making, a singular vision was the key. In the chief executive's view, "If you don't quite know where you fit, you have a sort of fumbled strategy. You will either make some mistakes and end up being taken over, or you'll just become inefficient and probably be taken over" anyway.

Yet if shareholders were the assumed beneficiaries of management's chosen strategy, the strategy was management's own, shaped virtually without investor input. "If I had to say how much did the institutions affect our asset selection," concluded the chief executive, "out of [a possible] ten, I would have said about one." He was thinking about the shareholder in making his decisions, the CEO asserted, but the investor simply "wasn't telling me yet" what it wanted. Others in the company said they listened to what shareholders were saying, but not intently. The general counsel occasionally met with visiting analysts: "To some extent we can tell from their questions what they're interested in, and we can tell from sell-side reports and [Wall] Street reports what turns them on. But we have not had any systematic program to determine the goals and preferences of our substantially institutional holding."

Without investor demands for cost cutting, the disposal of divisions, and fresh products, the CEO knew he could do things his own way: "If you don't look after the client the proper way, you won't be doing a good job for your shareholders. If you don't have good staff, you won't be doing a good job for the shareholders. If you ignore the societal questions, you won't being doing a good job for your shareholders." The one constraint he understood, if not necessarily heeded, was investor wariness about new acquisitions. But otherwise he knew he had a virtually free hand: "When things are going well, [investors] pay attention to where they're not going well," which is to say, other companies. The CEO was certainly prepared to respond if investors decided to pay him more attention. He steeped himself in the company's operating details for the annual company meeting only to field no questions about them. Instead, at one recent meeting, discussion concentrated on South African investments and several dissident proposals. To the CEO's dismay, not a single question focused on the business itself.

The bank's own history undergirded the gulf between it and its shareholders. It had been privately held through most of its existence, going public only during the 1960s. The luxurious decor of its Wall Street executive floors seemed designed more to comfort affluent customers than to reassure cost-conscious investors. With a legacy of customers as sole stakeholder, the status of other stakeholders remained marginal. It was an attitude of treating the bank, offered the general counsel, "much like—I wouldn't say a partnership because that implies total disregard of shareholders' interests—but very private and focused on clients. Investors were nice to have, but it was sort of felt that they ought to recognize the attributes of our business on the basis of our public reports, and they didn't need a lot of coddling." In sum, said the general counsel, "when you're a bank and focused on your clients, you don't bare your breast to the public, and that includes shareholders."

Buckingham's tunnel vision seemed archaic in an era of rising investor power. For unrelated reasons, however, the bank did seek to reform its attitude toward investors. Product development was one reason. The bank had created a host of new trading and derivative elements, exotic enough to require patient explanation to investors. Executive compensation was another. The bank had expanded the use of stock options as remunerative incentives for its management ranks. Like many companies, it pressed stock-based compensation deep into the ranks, enlarging the pool of those on contingent compensation by a factor of ten. With a higher fraction of executives' compensation in the form of company stock, shareholder value no longer seemed so abstract to management. Political protection was a third factor underlying the new attitudes. To compete in a more head-on fashion with privately held investment banks, this commercial bank had sharply increased its compensation levels. The bank knew that investors like to scrutinize business costs, especially management compensation. To deflect investors' anticipated attention, the bank preemptively constructed a defense by better aligning its wage bill with shareholder wealth.

In keeping with the times, the commercial bank also sought to add a director with an "investor point of view" to the board. The pools of candidates here would not extend to the universe of institutional investors, only to its periphery, to those who "understand the investment world." This translated into a focus on executives of major insurance companies with large investment portfolios, but not bank competitors. Investment managers themselves, however, were off limits. "There would be a natural preference for having directors who were not representatives of a particular shareholder group," offered the general counsel. "There's no reason why a director shouldn't have a shareholder's point of view. . . . But I do not think there would be a natural tendency to pursue directors that have a particular ax to grind." In line with traditional company practice, however, a potential candidate would not be viable unless already acquainted with the chief executive, or unless the CEO found a way to cultivate an informal relationship through some other venue.

Despite modest bows in the direction of shareholder sovereignty, the bank allowed few other reminders of its investors to intrude. When asked how the shareholding concentration of the past decade had altered the bank's way of doing business, the general counsel conceded few changes. The rise of the institutions had "certainly not" affected "the day-to-day way we conduct our business and the way we think about our performance of business in our strategies and goals."

The Soft Bear Hug

If the commercial bank enjoyed virtually complete autonomy, the manufacturing firm suffered much the opposite. Its shareholders permitted scant autonomy, scrutinizing its management policies at every turn.

In the late 1980s and early 1990s, the manufacturing firm—one of America's great companies, which I shall call Industrial Products Corporation—found itself grasped in a variant of what had come to be known in takeover parlance as a "bear hug." Rarely used but instantly understood, a bear hug is applied by a corporate raider that makes a generous but largely unexpected offer to the directors of a targeted firm. The offer's terms are financially attractive, time bound, and non-negotiable. The acquirer extends the embrace with vigor and without warning. Activist investors came to apply a softer variant. The activist builds up a large ownership position in a company to ensure its message will be heard, but then, rather than making a hostile offer, the investor simply demands that management right its wrongful ways.[6]

The bear that hugged Industrial Products Corporation was a renowned (to some, notorious) practitioner of the hostile takeover. In this case, however, he stopped short, though not by far. In early 1987, the potential acquirer, Frank Zacker (a pseudonym), and his group held no shares in the company. By midyear he owned more than 2 million, and by year's end nearly 30 million, 12 percent of the outstanding stock. Several years later he peaked at 34 million shares, clearly making him the dominant object on the executives' radar. The next-largest owner during this period never held more than 7 million shares.

Industrial Products would readily fit most investors' definition of a deeply troubled firm. It had been the largest producer in one of the country's largest manufacturing fields. But new production technolo-

gies, new workplace systems, and new foreign competition had decimated the industry and the company. Its peak production ranks of well
over 150,000 employees had dwindled to a mere 20,000. As a strategy
for survival, the company acquired another Fortune 500 firm that had
long operated in a very different industry. The manufacturer sought to
make a virtue of managing product diversity, even if the synergies that
presumably came from diverse products under the same roof were
divined by few investors.

Company executives recognized that Zacker's ownership stake lent
him unique powers. "Anybody who had spent that much money investing in your stock," said the general counsel, "should be listened to. If he
thought that much of our company to think that it was undervalued and
that he could gain greater value, and he had put his money behind his
beliefs, he was entitled to a hearing." For weeks at a time, the investor
and CEO held conversations every day, ranging from a few minutes to
afternoons, evenings, and weekends.

When it first seemed that the investor was on the verge of making
an offer to buy the company, the conversation focused on the conditions under which the company would provide detailed inside information about itself. Outside events, however, cut this line of discussion
short. Zacker had been counting on Drexel Burnham for financing, but
the thinking after the federal indictment of Ivan Boesky and the subsequent unraveling of Michael Milken's empire was that one could
depend on little from that quarter.[7] With the junk-bond market spiral-
ing into disarray, Zacker simply altered course without retreating.
Poised on a 30 million-share pulpit, he bullied the company to think differently. He brought various proposals to the table, and even more
"what ifs": to list its shares on the London Stock Exchange, to reorga-
nize its operations, to break it up.

The two sides talked candidly about the investor's plans and the
company's reactions, each agreeing not to quote the other. The chief
executive nonetheless found the unsolicited advice to contain little of
real value. It seemed well tailored to the bear-hugger's benefit, but
management saw the proposals as imposing costs on other shareholders. Zacker "doesn't necessarily have the same idea of shareholder
value or the same interests as other shareholders," cautioned the chief
executive. "He's looking . . . to use the coercive powers of his position"
in our securities to get us "to do something which is of benefit to him."
Zacker and fellow raiders, warned the CEO, "always try to disguise it,
but they're really not working on behalf of all shareholders."

Not all of Zacker's proposals resonated with other shareholders,
but some did. Both he and the company knew that the ownership class
contained a significant minority, possibly even a majority, of inactive

investors loath to exert pressure but eager for short-term gains. The chief executive perceived that many institutions were ready to follow Zacker's lead because of a one-dimensional worldview: "Their idea of shareholder value is getting some air under their stock, period!" That gratification, he also believed, was required instantly. "They tend to have a very short time horizon." They are "not impressed when you talk about a five-year plan for the company and what it's going to do. They want to know what's going to happen in the next quarter." Whether or not this was an accurate portrayal of the mind of the investor, a number of holders seemed poised to back Zacker against management.

The quarterly straitjacket was especially troublesome for this company. Its two product areas experienced radical swings in prices, and thus earnings, more because of world markets than management actions. The chief executive spoke enviously of a food-products company headquartered several floors away in the same office tower. He felt sure that one of its flagship products sold for more today than it had three years earlier, and more then than three years before that. By contrast, one of his own flagship products was selling for a fraction of what it had several years earlier, making the current year a cyclical "disaster." He knew he sometimes benefited from external upswings, but he would readily relinquish any false benefit if he could also avoid false blame. The investor world, however, only partially discounted such externalities. It expected management to adapt, and this company seemed slow to do so.

Industrial Products executives continued to talk with Zacker but rejected his various unsolicited proposals. His entreaties rebuffed, Zacker turned to less personal methods. He concentrated his energies on formally imposing his priority proposal, a separation of the company's two major product lines into independent entities. To this end he placed a shareholder resolution on the annual proxy statement and solicited owner support.

Since the challenger directly controlled one vote in eight and many free riders seemed ready to ride, the company shifted into high gear. The CEO alone lobbied more than 150 institutional investors through personal visits. He wrote his counterparts at other large companies who were also members of the premier corporate lobby group, the Business Roundtable. He asked them to discuss the matter with managers of their own employee-benefit plans, many of which held stock in Industrial Products. The chief executive estimated that he devoted a quarter of his time over the course of a year to the proxy struggle and actions leading up to it. The chief financial officer wrote to a hundred of his own counterparts at major U.S. companies. He knew most of them personally and sent a handwritten note to each, finishing with a case of writer's cramp that required medical attention.

As the campaign intensified, each side successively mailed four proxy ballots to shareholders, hoping to get out the vote or to change the vote if already cast. Industrial Products knew it was starting from a deficit. Zacker had 34 million votes assured from the outset, the company none (even its pension fund was a legally separate entity). Worse, the firm learned from shareholder visitations that many blocks were already held by "special-situation investors" and Zacker "camp followers." The chief executive complained that "they're in the stock because he's in there. They're in there because they want something to happen. They don't give a damn what it is, whether it's good or bad. . . . Whatever [Zacker] stalks next they stalk." They were laying in wait, the CEO feared: "They're actively agitating for something, they want some transaction, and they're in your stock until that transfer occurs."

The company and the investor fought over every square inch of terrain. No important stockholder was taken for granted, and most were lobbied with vigor. Industrial Products established a telephone bank that contacted virtually all smaller stockholders owning from 5,000 shares down to 500, investing over $8 million in the effort.

To combat Zacker's evident appeal on substance, the manufacturer fell back on its own strong suit: preestablished relations with its more patient owners. For several years prior to Zacker's proxy fight, company management had regularly visited its primary holders. Three executive teams also traveled the country to meet with virtually all major investors during the four months before the annual meeting. They even visited large institutions that did not hold the company's stock. The purpose, said one team leader, was "to talk to them to find out why they didn't and try to describe what the company was and why we felt it was a good investment." The contact also served as intelligence gathering. "The more we keep in touch with big investors," offered the chief operating officer, "the better off we'll be in terms of knowing how they see us." To ensure investor interest in the meetings, each team included a top officer. With three vice chairmen at the time, one for the two sides of the business and one for financial affairs, the firm usually placed one or two of its four senior managers in most institutional meetings.

The company executives wisely built their relationships around the principle of reciprocity. Unabashed in their efforts to sway investors, they arrived with a willingness to be swayed as well. Investors "especially like to know that you want to hear what they want to say," found the vice president for finance and a frequent team traveler. The teams often focused conversation on how the company might best dispose of a large discretionary cash flow that it had been enjoying at the top of one of its earlier product cycles—$1 billion a year. The teams asked investors to rank their priorities for disposal of the money through debt reduction, stock buyback, or dividend increase. Management preferred the first course, since the company's bond ratings were at the minimum for investment grade. Several money managers urged higher dividends, but the company was pleased to learn that most concurred with management's expressed priority.

Some meetings, however, were more ominous. At a breakfast meeting with a major institution in Los Angeles, several analysts peppered the team with technical questions. Later, a more senior analyst turned the questioning to company strategies and priorities. It became clear early on that the company's diverse product mix and its potential bifurcation were already much on this investor's mind. "We were talking about three priorities for creating better value," recalled the company's chief operating officer. But "they were screwing around with the idea of some kind of breakup [of the company] without actually coming out and saying that they would like to see you do that." Some of the analysts' later write-ups included estimates of the value of the company if divided into two stand-alone entities.

Though cultivating investors was viewed as a necessity, the executives never came to see their labor-intensive contact as a virtue. It ranked among the least pleasant of their executive tasks. "It's wearing, and you don't look forward to it," concluded one team member. "The problem is you end up saying the same damn thing to four or five different groups the same day." One complained of forgetting whether he had already made certain points at a given meeting or at earlier meetings that day. And since virtually all the meetings were held at the institutions' offices, travel added further to the already burdened executive schedules. After so "damn many" meetings covering the same ground, confessed one participant, "you really burn out." Other senior managers wondered how the firm's executives could be away so much. "Shouldn't somebody be minding the store?" was the question implicit in colleagues' occasional comments. One executive complained of management by triage. Upon returning from an investor trip, he would spend a day or two taking care of urgent matters and then depart for the next round of investor contacts, leaving all but emergency issues shelved for later.

This strategy of intense forays into investor territory stood in stark contrast to the firm's no-contact strategy of two decades earlier. Until 1970 the company never met with brokerage-house analysts (often termed the "sell side"), let alone money managers themselves (the "buy side"). For the occasional telephone query, the pat response had been: "Read the annual report; that's what we make it for." In the early 1970s the company assigned an assistant comptroller as sell-side analyst liaison, but the buy side would be ignored for another dozen years. The chief operating officer had overseen the development of the investor relations operation from its inception: "The change in [the early 1970s] was a recognition that the market was going more to institutional holdings through the growth of pension funds and money-management funds. So we ought to have a little more respectable effort to communicate."

The turning point for company relations with the buy side followed the acquisition in the early 1980s of an unrelated business, a move that management recognized as requiring explanation and more intensive investor contact. The company also began to churn out reams of quarterly statistics, giving analysts and investors the financial data they had long sought.

Whatever the avowed purpose of the company campaign to meet with large investors, the executives also understood they were building a network whose full value might only be revealed on a rainy day. The company's chief operating officer had played a central role in those meetings for years. "One of the values [is] getting to know personally a lot of these people who are in the determining position in terms of whether to hold, sell, buy more, or reduce their position." As investors come to know management personally, "we have to think that's a positive—as they saw you perform and heard your ideas, that warmed their hearts." When presented with a list of all of his company's institutional holders, he could claim personal familiarity with 80 percent to 90 percent of those in most shareholding size classes, whether million-share owners or those holding just 20,000.

The personalized relations proved an asset for influencing analyst reports. When an analyst story seemed off track, an officer would sometimes call, on a first-name basis, to set the record straight. But the ultimate payoff for the years of network building came during the company's fight to extricate itself from Zacker's bear hug. Industrial Products' credibility with its major shareholders proved an invaluable asset. Concluded the company's chief operating officer: "We had a base of goodwill and understanding and knowledge and acquaintanceship with these [investors] that enabled us to go in and deliver our message."

The showdown came in 1990 when a formal spin-off measure, the crux of Frank Zacker's campaign, appeared on the company's annual proxy statement. Though garnering widespread investor support, it fell short of the simple majority required. Some 45 percent of the vote came in for the resolution but 55 percent against.

Since the company enjoyed nonconfidential voting, it knew precisely who had stood with it and who had not. Senior managers were pleased to discover that virtually all the public pension funds, which it had assiduously cultivated, had sided with the company. One dissident, however, presided in a state where the company operated major facilities. The chief executive still fumed at the fund's misbehavior: We "had a virtual sweep of all of the public institutional investors, except for the goddamn [X] State Teachers, which really burned me up because of this company's presence and investments in the state. . . . If any group of teachers had any reason to vote with this company against a goddamn raider, it would be the [X] teachers, and they voted against us."

The chief executive was so incensed over the vote that he sought to "raise hell" with the pension-fund trustees. He demanded a meeting and thrust the fund's own publicity brochure back in its face, noting that it styled itself as a long-term investor. He urged the fund to turn back its clock, to reembrace the Wall Street rule: "If you can't support the damn management, if you really feel that bad, you ought to sell the damn stock."

The fund's chief investment officer defended his decision to the trustees, reasserting that the breakup would have achieved greater value. The CEO conceded afterward that he did little more than vent his own frustrations. Yet he watched with perverse satisfaction soon thereafter as the fund resoundingly rejected his advice to sell, instead raising its investment from 2 million to 3 million shares. They "must have liked *something* that they heard," said the CEO, with a smile.

Zacker had mobilized many investors in search of higher stock price, and others in search of better performance, but the high-water mark was not high enough. Having failed at the polls, Zacker sought a "settlement" and finally backed away, disposing of his entire block of shares. Having done considerable time together, the two principals shared a kind of prisoner's remorse after being released. The investor said he would miss the daily conversations. Yes, the chief executive added, but their end would also bring a windfall bonus of time.

In the victory's postmortem, Industrial Products managers attributed the outcome in part to the relational foundation they had formed with major investors several years earlier. The mid-1980s initiative had been critical, in the words of the chief operating officer: "The chairman figured we'd better get out there and try to make some friends. No more complicated than that. We just ought to get to know who the hell our investors are even better than we already do."

While management agreed on the general value of the dialogue with its investors, it divided on whether Zacker's bear hug had made a real difference in company operations. In the view of several managers, the company did what it would have done anyway, only at greater cost in terms of management time. Others believed the active investor and his fellow travelers catalyzed desirable changes that might otherwise never have come to pass. "On balance," concluded one, "he helped us to focus better on our relations with our major shareholders." Investor meetings, in his view, became more pointed, better prepared, and more regular. The company also better structured them to ensure a two-way flow. "We became more sensitized to the idea of getting more feed-back.... Even though at times having somebody like [Zacker to contend with] can be an irritant, sometimes it's a positive irritant and I hope that we've all learned enough from this that we don't backslide."

Which Investors Challenge Companies?

Zacker had led the charge against Industrial Products Corporation. Many others quietly followed. Still others supported incumbent management instead. The diverse stands and responses are symptomatic of the varied postures among institutional investors. The shades of activism are many, the boundaries faint. At the inactive end of the spectrum are investors who avoid all intervention and pay no attention to governance issues—often a matter of choice, sometimes a matter of convenience. In the middle are investors who cast proxy ballots against management and provide passive support for the activists while refraining from overt action themselves. On the active end are the fund managers who make conscious efforts to influence companies through noisy campaigns against managements or quiet consultations with them.

These divergent positions within the activist spectrum are held by distinct investor species. The activist wing draws public pensions, the middle attracts investment companies, and the inactive wing pulls private pensions.[8] The differences are not hard-and-fast: representatives of each species appear at all points of the activist spectrum. But the differences are pronounced. This can be seen in surveys on governance questions, where the species line up in much the same fashion on issue after issue. Consider six antimanagement resolutions frequently appearing on proxies during the 1990s. Placed on company ballots by disgruntled shareholders, the resolutions called for dismantling company defenses against takeovers or strengthening shareholder rights over management:[9]

1. company self-exclusion from a Delaware statute that makes it easier to thwart unwanted takeovers;

2. repeal of board classification, a corporate means of staggering director terms that prevents wholesale replacement of a board;
3. adoption of cumulative voting that makes it easier to elect dissident directors;
4. adoption of confidential voting that insulates investors from company lobbying;
5. rescission or voting on a poison pill;
6. prohibition of golden parachutes for company executives.

Table 2.1 reveals that majorities of the public pension funds favored each of the antimanagement measures, majorities of corporate pension funds opposed the measures, and investment managers fell in between. The chasm between public and corporate pension funds can be yawning: more than four out of five public pension plans in 1994 backed confidential voting, rescinding or voting on poison pills, and prohibiting or voting on golden parachutes, while less than half of the company pension plans so agreed.

Activist Investors from the Ranks of the Public Pension Funds

At the leading edge of the owners' mobilization are a relatively small number of activist institutions. They articulate the grievances, formulate the strategies, and launch the assaults. In the face of widespread company resistance and substantial investor skepticism, they also construct a worldview, a culture of rebellion, for sustaining action. They envisage themselves as engaged owners, not passive holders. In their view, the Wall Street rule is not golden, nor is the boardroom sacrosanct. Companies could and should benefit from their advice. To err in strategic decisions goes with modern capitalism, but to reject corrective suggestions runs against investor capitalism.

The activist funds play a role akin to that of political leadership in social movements. When a group of individuals or organizations faces distressed conditions, many may feel aggrieved but few are called to challenge. Leadership typically falls on the shoulders of a minority, a subgroup whose special conditions facilitate and inspire rebellion. Often this small cadre is composed of those who are most secure in their status and least subject to reprisal; so, ironically, those least aggrieved are sometimes most in the forefront: affluent peasants, middle-class taxpayers, and large organizations have frequently spearheaded movements on behalf of their less fortunate brethren.[10]

At the core of the investor movement leadership is a small set of public funds. During the height of the 1993 proxy season, for instance, dissident shareholders had formalized 388 corporate governance pro-

Table 2.1 Percentage of Investors Supporting Antimanagement Proxy Resolutions, by Type of Investor, 1990–94

Year of proxy resolutions	Public pensions	Invest. mgrs.	Corp. pensions	Public pensions	Invest. mgrs.	Corp. pensions
Opt out of Delaware takeover law				**Adopt confidential proxy voting**		
1994	NA	NA	NA	95%	74%	43%
1993	61%	28%	14%	88	57	50
1992	72	23	20	94	64	60
1991	84	45	29	100	66	43
1990	75	37	50	95	61	50
				Rescind or vote on poison pill		
Repeal classified board						
1994	80	62	42	85	57	43
1993	78	66	38	79	74	28
1992	78	61	20	78	76	40
1991	79	70	29	78	76	28
1990	80	55	33	NA	NA	NA
				Prohibit or vote on golden parachutes		
Adopt cumulative voting						
1994	60	45	14	88	54	0
1993	67	38	14	70	60	29
1992	56	30	20	88	45	20
1991	58	32	14	61	45	14
1990	60	32	50	65	32	33

Source: Investor Responsibility Research Center, *Voting by Institutional Investors on Corporate Governance Issues*, 1992, 1991, 1990, 1993, and 1994.

Note: The numbers of investors upon which the percentages in the three columns are based are, respectively, 24, 39, and 12 for 1990; 19, 38, and 10 for 1991; 19, 34, and 6 for 1992; 24, 35, and 8 for 1993; and 20, 24, and 7 for 1994.

posals for the proxies of 217 companies. Of these proposals, 42 had been prepared by a handful of public pension funds: 2 from California funds, 4 from New York pensions, and 1 from a Wisconsin fund. Several also came from CREF, and the remainder from investors with small stakes but large messages. These included unions (such as the Amalgamated Clothing and Textile Workers Union), church groups working with the Interfaith Center on Corporate Responsibility, members of the United Shareholders Association (a Washington lobby group of some 65,000 small holders), and several individuals who had made a career of dissident resolutions. Most notable were those that were entirely absent. No proposal came from any of the investment companies or private pension funds.[11]

Public and private pension funds follow divergent political paths because they march to such different drummers. Simply put, public pensions respond to elected officials, private pensions to company officials. They operate in distinct worlds of authority.[12]

The public character of the public pensions is displayed in their governing structures: elected officials and their appointees exercise a commanding presence. The sole trustee of the New York State Common Retirement Fund is the state's elected comptroller. The manager of the California State Teachers' Retirement System is under a board that is three-quarters appointed by the governor. The chief executive of Calpers reports to a board composed of the state comptroller, the state treasurer, four appointees of the governor, one appointee of the legislature, and six members elected by state employees. A 1993 survey of 291 state and local systems, representing 451 pension plans, finds that the typical governing board includes three elected members, three appointed members, and two ex-officio members.[13]

The political oversight of public pensions encourages antimanagement rhetoric, especially when directed against big business. Since the pensions and their overseers are never far from the voters' minds, pounding on the private sector for public gain can be an appealing political course. The concept of public gain from pressuring management is more than rhetorical. Though the public-fund managers' perceptions are generally not derived from research, such managers intuitively grasp what academic studies tend to confirm. Proxy contests for control, for example, yield positive share price gains ranging from 5 percent to 30 percent, depending on the specific outcome. The defeat of a dissident shareholder effort, by contrast, can yield negative changes of 15 percent. The successful mobilization of investors to reject management proxy proposals containing antitakeover provisions increases share value by some 9 percent; failed efforts depress the value by 8 percent.[14]

While it makes good sense for public pension systems to press private-sector managements for higher returns, such actions also contain downside risks for the funds. An activist profile can subject a pension fund to unwanted pressures from both the targeted companies and the business media. It can also undermine access to corporate executives, threatening the informal flow of information upon which money managers have come to depend. The fact that public exposure cuts both ways helps explain why some public funds remain on the sidelines. The manager of one public pension thus justified her largely inactive stance: "We prefer to do it on a low-key basis, to review things ourselves, to basically make our determinations and stay out of the spotlight as much as possible. We are not a political entity, and I think the more you become a part of the activist movement, the greater are the political risks you run."

Nonetheless, a small cadre of large public pension funds has taken up the cudgels, performing the catalytic role that is the sine qua non for any political movement. While neither investment managers nor private pension funds are at its side, some are close behind along with other public funds, providing the essential firepower that the cadre of activist funds could not muster on its own.

Inactive Investors from the Ranks of the Private Pension Funds

Though private pensions are no less interested in maximizing their own returns, private-fund managers know that their bosses look unkindly on overt challenges of other corporations. Though competing vigorously against one another in the marketplace, corporate executives quickly close ranks when it comes to national policies or shareholder power. This is due to both higher principles and pragmatic politics. Top managements still share the traditional belief that they, not shareholders, should run their companies. They know, in any case, that allowing their pension funds to vote against the managements of other firms is to invite retaliation the next time their own enterprise is under shareholder challenge. Companies constantly compete with other companies for customers, but they seem constitutionally incapable of challenging one another on governance.

Corporate control of private pensions is evident in their governing structures, where company executives and their appointees retain ultimate authority. Top management typically designates a company pension manager, often from the financial side of the company, to oversee the fund. The inside manager either invests the assets directly or manages one or more outside institutions that in turn invest the assets on the company's behalf, or both. A 1987 survey of 127 large firms found that 80 percent relied entirely on outside investment managers, 3 percent on inside staffs, and 17 percent on both. Although federal pension regulations require that both inside and outside pension managers advance the financial interests of retirees even when they clash with company interests, both kinds of fund managers nonetheless remain under the shadow of company management.[15]

The resulting absence of activism among private pension funds is rarely the result of an executive's decree. More commonly it is a natural product of company operations. This can be seen in an employee pension fund of the Hutchins Motors Corporation. The company operates both a defined-benefit and a defined-contribution pension plan (the first specifying how much is given out, the second identifying how much is paid in). A small fraction of the funds is managed in-house, but the remainder of the $20 billion in assets is administered on the outside. Under the guidance of a three-person company staff, thirty-five separate outside money managers invest the money in doses ranging from $10 million to $2 billion. The company specifies how the investments are to be divided among equity, fixed income, and real estate, and none of the money may be placed in the company's own stock (on the premise that employees already have enough of their futures tied up with the firm). Otherwise the outside money managers are free to pick their specific investments.

In selecting outside managers, Hutchins' internal guidelines call for choosing money managers who do broad-based rather than niche investing (specializing in leveraged buyouts, for example), who are able to invest a large amount of assets over long periods of time, and who are likely to beat the indexed funds. Investors are left free to seek growth stocks (companies that are expected to show strong growth in revenues or earnings) or value opportunities (companies that have underperformed financially or are out of favor with others holders), small or large companies, domestic or international securities. The company plays out a long leash, using five-year returns as a principal measure of outside fund performance. "Because of the size of the assets that we have and the small staff," observed the inside executive, "we want to have managers who can manage sizable amounts of assets. We want to feel comfortable with them, and we want to allow them to manage those over long periods of time." The typical outside money manager has worked with the company for ten to twenty years, with one enduring relationship dating back four decades.

Hutchins Motors sets neither instructions nor guidelines on voting proxies, leaving the decisions entirely to the outside managers, though it does require that all proxies be voted. Since "the investment manager is the one who purchased the stock," offered the company executive, "we feel that he is most familiar with the investment decision, and that the proxy vote is closely aligned with that." These policies are in keeping with common corporate practice. A 1987 survey of 127 large companies found that only 5 percent voted their own pension proxies; the remainder delegated the responsibility to outside money managers. Although the inside-voting fraction had risen to 28 percent, according to a survey of 72 major firms in 1991, it is evident that most companies still prefer to have others exercise their voting rights, albeit within general guidelines (such as "votes should be cast in the best interests of plan participants").[16]

With its investments spread among three dozen money managers who in turn place the funds in an estimated 2,000 companies or more, Hutchins' tiny in-house staff could not itself begin to evaluate the annual proxy flow. The administrative necessity of contracting out the voting is further reinforced by a fear of buyer backlash: "As a consumer-products company, there's a lot of political pressure that can be brought to bear by outsiders," warned the company official. The chairman often received letters from other companies asserting that they had purchased many of the company's products in the past and that they now sought the manufacturer's vote in a proxy fight of their own. The company's policy of out-sourcing fund management provides an immediate buffer against such requests. It also insulates the pension from union challenge. Nearly half of the money in the defined-benefit plan is invested for unionized employees. "If the company was to suddenly want to take a fairly activist role in voting proxies," said the company manager, "I don't think there would be too many nanoseconds before the [union] would be at the door saying, 'We want to get involved in this decision too.' " Externalizing the money management and proxy voting thus helps solve several problems. But an implicit outcome is also to divide and divorce the assets from centralized company control. This has the effect of removing any implicit clout the company might exercise if it sought to throw its weight around. The pension fund could not have acted like an activist had it wanted to do so.

For companies that retain fund management and proxy voting on the inside, even stronger disincentives for activism are evident. Few inside managers are inclined to challenge managements of other companies, if for no other reason than the fear that chickens can sometimes come home to roost. When challenged by a takeover bid or proxy challenge, archcompetitors turn into blood brothers. Private pension managers, as a result, tend to fall back on the familiar nostrum that investors should be in the business of picking companies, not turning them around.

One private pension-fund manager reflected the summary view of many: "I'm old-fashioned. I like the way the capitalist system works. I think the auction system for rationing capital around the world works pretty well. That is, good managements and good businesses get capital; bad managements and bad businesses lose capital. I'm not caught up in the romanticism of shareholder-rights groups." For him, the Wall Street rule still prevailed: "Our country is really built on a free marketplace, the free exchange of capital and ideas and people. . . . We vote by selling stock."

Semiactive Investors from the Ranks of the Investment Companies

Investment companies—mutual-fund and money managers—generally occupy the middle ground between the public and private pension funds. No shareholder governance proposals during the 1993 proxy season had come from them either, but compared to private pensions, they more often cast their votes with the dissidents.

Most money managers single out their diverse clientele as a primary reason for avoiding activist visibility. They must represent a wide range of client interests, they note, and clients rarely agree on the potential rewards for activism. In addition, since many company pensions place funds with outside money managers, a company targeted today for activist intervention might be a potential client tomorrow. In the words of one investment manager, they face numerous conflicts that "limit [our] ability to be too active. [We] represent too broad a constituency." On the other hand, since they are competing with each other for customers, pressing companies in their portfolios for better performance can be seen as a competitive advantage. These two factors together help explain why investment managers tend to occupy the spectrum's middle ground.

As a case in point, CBS Inc.'s second largest stockholder, Capital Group Companies, quietly protested what it considered mediocre performance by withholding its 3.8 million votes in 1995 from the television company's slate of directors, including Chairman Laurence A. Tisch. While CBS had posted a relatively strong performance in the eyes of some investors, this was not the Capital Group's assessment, which held 6.2 percent of the company's stock. The largest institutional owner, J. P. Morgan, with 4 million shares, sided with the management-approved director slate. But Capital Group concluded otherwise. Its principal investment manager for the media and entertainment industry was said by like-minded investors to be unhappy with the chairman's long-term dismantling of what had been a successful communications empire, and with the company's more recent setbacks. CBS had lost local affiliates and football rights to the Fox network, and its earnings had dropped by more than two-thirds during the quarter just prior to the directorship vote. Unlike activist public pension funds, Capital Group did not broadcast its decision; but unlike the nonactivist private pension funds, it expressed its disapproval.[17]

Indexed Investors

The widespread use of indexed investing adds a peculiar logic to these political winds. Indexing comes in many forms, but among the most prominent is use of the Standard and Poor's (S&P) 500. Indexing practitioners using the S&P 500 receive a continuously updated list of the 500 largest companies by market value (outstanding shares times share price), and they invest their funds in these companies according to the weight (relative market value) of each in the index. Hutchins Motors Corporation places about one-third of its equity assets in indexes, but other funds go as high as three-quarters or more.

An indexed fund by definition alters the composition of its portfolio only as the composition of the index changes. A largely indexed fund can thus only improve its overall returns by improving the management of the companies in the index. Eschewing the option of selling, such funds might be expected to be the ultimate activists. Yet they face a double-bind: a major reason for indexing in the first place is to reduce the costs of money management. Lean operations and large indexes mean little staff for sustained attention to any company. Calpers employs only two inside managers to oversee its $20 billion internally managed indexed funds. Vanguard's Index Trust–500 Fund, one of the oldest and largest (more than $20 billion in 1996) indexed mutual funds based on the S&P 500, annually charges customers a mere 0.19 percent of their assets under management. By contrast, the typical stock mutual fund annually charges 1.35 percent.[18]

Indexed fund managers thus often back activist initiatives but can devote no time or money to their causes. Some indexed funds are so lean that they are reluctant to vote their own proxies for lack of any staff analysis. A manager at a highly indexed fund doubted her own fund's qualifications to do more than buy and sell: "There are analysts [elsewhere] who are better prepared to make judgments than we are."

A Field Divided on Investor Activism

Large investors not only differ greatly in their behavior toward corporations, but they also vary greatly in how they view one another's behavior. Investor activism creates nearly as much dissent within the investor ranks as opposition by the corporate ranks. Movement leaders are only as strong as their ranks are united, and this internal division is one explanation for the fact that activist investors must still struggle to mobilize proxy votes or otherwise apply pressure on management. It is also one reason why company executives can sleep easier than the institutions' aggregate holdings might otherwise suggest.

The Critical Wing

Anchoring the most critical wing of the investor community are funds for which any investor voice constitutes a backward measure. Echoing managements' own complaint, these institutions see more harm coming to corporate performance than good. One investment manager disdained the "frivolous shareholder activity" that "is not in the interests of all shareholders." Another questioned the activists' vision: "Public pension funds push for corporate governance ideology without clear economic rationale." A public pension manager worried about the capacity to make informed judgments: "Personally, I'm not in favor of [activism]. It's difficult for an organization to make judgments on many of the issues that are raised. The analysis that is necessary is well beyond the scope of most institutional investors." A foundation manager complained that "when state and municipal pension funds get overly involved in the corporate governance issues, that is negative for [our] fund and negative for society." An investment manager flatly rejected the "we can't sell" argument often used to justify the activism: "If you can't give management a vote of confidence," then you should get out of the stock. "There are a lot of stocks out there. If you don't like this one, there is another one."[19]

Some investors even question the activists' motives. The manager of a large private fund observes that public fund activism "creates great publicity, gives power to certain people, and allows them to play a big game they couldn't enter except for being big proxy voters.... It is clear that a number of public officials are using their power with these proxies as a way to enhance their public image." Many managers see public activism as a luxury afforded by public guarantees. "My role is to manage these employee-benefit assets for the benefit of [the company] and the employees," notes one private-pension-fund manager. "If the assets are not sufficient to fund the liabilities, [the company] has to 'kick the kitty.' That's my first concern." By contrast, "in California, if there isn't enough money to fund the liabilities, the state can raise taxes."

Doubts abound, even among supporters, about the purported benefits of activism. One major activist, for example, claimed credit for a substantial improvement in a particular company's earnings. A second investor said with equal conviction that he could see no causal connection between this activist's intercession and the company's turnaround. One fund manager expressed the pragmatic doubts of many: "Whatever we do in the area of proxy initiatives or voting proxies, there has to be fundamentally an economic motivation behind it. Before we devote resources to something we really have to be able to say that this is going to leave our participants better off than if we hadn't done it."

The Ambivalent Wing

In the middle are institutions that are noncommittal; they do not necessarily support specific activist efforts, but they do support the right of investors to take action. Here one also finds a certain gratitude toward activists for drawing attention to management problems, though it is sometimes still mixed with skepticism about activist motives and their expertise in righting the wrongs. The investment manager for a large foundation observed: "We take the proxy process very seriously, but we're not out trying to lead some sort of revolution. We're really here to maximize the return on investment. We're not here to change the world."

The Fellow-Traveling Wing

Among the activists' supporters are funds that applaud the activists' work but often so quietly that neither the activists nor their targets hear much clapping. The director of a large though inactive private pension fund thus suggested that the active public funds are playing a natural leadership role, with his own fund ready to follow. The public pensions "may be the legitimate, rightful leaders in governance issues. They may be fulfilling a very valuable function, and they're the right people to do it." The director of a major public pension fund saw the political risks as too high for his own fund to act, but he backed others: "I actually have a lot of admiration for [the activists]. I think they are saying things that should be part of the public dialogue." In the summary words of another silent supporter: "Institutional investors may save corporate America from itself."

For the silent supporters of the activists, it is the risk of high-profile opposition to management that serves to keep their support quiet. And they stand to gain in any case as free-riding beneficiaries of the activist-induced changes. Even institutions that wholeheartedly back the activism in principle are often unwilling to commit their own resources to any activist drive as long as some other institution is doing so. The managers of these funds quietly support the intervention of the activists and routinely vote with them, but devote neither time nor money to the cause. One director of a large private pension fund, for example, cited the troubles of a major financial services company, yet expressed a belief that change would surely occur without his input. He was aware of and quietly supported the activist funds that were pushing the company's management for change but remained otherwise unwilling to expend his own resources to help. Another private pension was so leanly operated that it had no resources to give. Though a supporter of investor activism in principle, the fund manager said that "for us it boils down to economics, not politics."

Which Companies Are Targeted?

Some investors seek across-the-board changes in governance provisions such as abolishing poison pills and instituting confidential voting. Activist investors thus target companies that have implemented anti-takeover devices or failed to adopt shareholder protection devices.

Remarkably few takeover defenses succumbed to the broad-based rescission campaigns, however, and few shareholder safeguards gained. Three out of five large companies had adopted a poison-pill strategy by the turn of the decade, and this fraction even rose slightly during the early 1990s. Of the 1,000 largest market-value companies, 495 carried the pill in 1989 and 643 in 1992 (figure 2.1). Another measure often opposed by shareholder advocates, golden parachutes (rich severance packages for top executives in the event of a change in control), were in place at 495 firms in 1989 and in 535 three years later. Classified boards, also viewed as an entrenchment device by many investors, rose from 550 to 594. Investor pressure for confidential voting, however, claimed at least a small beachhead: in 1989, 35 companies of the top 1,000 had adopted the measure, and three years later 94 had done so.[20]

Despite the activist emphasis on governance devices, the main issue for many institutional investors remains actual company performance, not its oversight. The identification of poor performers requires some care, of course, since institutions know that a company's record must be judged against market trends and within an appropriate time frame and market sector. Activist investors accordingly have developed fine-honed methodologies for locating the worst offenders in their large portfolios, and this typically led to a focus on the extremes.

The New York City Employees' and Teachers' Retirement Systems thus singled out eleven "focus" companies for special attention in 1995 because of their weak long-term performance. Similarly, Calpers identified the fifty weakest companies in its portfolio in 1992, selected because of their poor long-term performance compared with industry peers and the market as a whole. By much the same criteria, Calpers

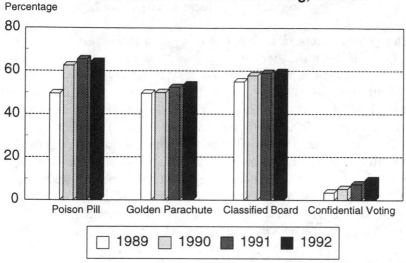

Figure 2.1 Percentage of 1,000 Largest Companies with Three Takeover Defenses and Confidential Voting, 1989-92

Source: United Shareholders Association.

chose in 1995 to concentrate on nine especially poor performers, including Boise Cascade, Navistar International, and Kmart. The latter, not coincidentally, dismissed its longtime chief executive, Joseph A. Antonini, in March of 1995, not long after Calpers' targeting. "Kmart's Embattled CEO," read the *Wall Street Journal* headline, "Resigns Post Under Pressure from Key Shareholders." Explained the company chairman in justifying the CEO's forced exit, "Large shareholders said, 'Joe has to go.'" The Council of Institutional Investors—whose 100 members preside over combined assets of $800 billion—targeted its own list of twenty underachievers in 1995, including Morrison Knudsen Corporation, Toys 'R' Us Inc., and Salomon Inc. The latter, like most on the "focus list," is anxious to remove itself. "This is a list that we don't want to be on," responded Salomon's CEO, Robert E. Denham, "and we're doing everything we can to get off of it."[21]

For some investors, the stress on company performance came to displace any concern with governance and related executive practices. A symptomatic case is investor reactions to the Coca-Cola board's compensation of its chief executive in 1991 with more than $80 million. The off-scale annual income attracted critical media commentary but drew little institutional fire because the company had done so well for its shareholders.[22] Its exceptional performance left one private pension manager utterly unperturbed. Coca-Cola is one of his largest holdings: "The stock has compounded at 35 percent a year. I don't care what they pay him."

The general premise is that a firm's governance should be challenged only if the firm's performance has plummeted. "An ineffective governance system is never exposed if a company performs well," offered one investment manager. "If their performance is up there, I don't think anybody cares." The procedures of two investors for identifying their weak performers are described in table 2.2.

Still other institutions choose to ignore governance questions on the premise that a company's superior or inferior governance policies are already reflected in its share price. The director of one private pension fund that delegates its voting rights laughed when asked how he monitors the outside manager's voting record: "Why would I want to do that?"

For many investors, however, the emphasis on a company's performance has complemented, not displaced, a focus on governance. Accordingly, the annual proxy remains a potent point of review, and most major institutions set forward formal voting policies regardless of company performance. Of large investors surveyed in 1987, three in four had already developed written proxy voting guidelines, and by 1991 some nine in ten had done so.[23] CREF's 1993 policy statement, for instance, offers ten pages of detailed guidelines for evaluating company governance and proxy proposals.[24] Investor policies generally recommend antimanagement votes when resolutions clearly serve to entrench executive power or reduce shareholder value. Summaries of the written guidelines of an investment company, a public pension fund, and a private pension fund appear in table 2.3.

Seen from the company side, exceptionally weak performance can attract exceptional investor attention. The chief executive of Industrial Products Corporation certainly appreciated this point. Exceptionally good performance can also deflect most investor attention, as Buckingham Bank's CEO learned as well. Exceptional means exceptional: to qualify, the performance at either end must fall in the highest or lowest 10 percent to 20 percent, if not even narrower bands. At the low end, only the worst performers manage to attract the kind of sustained attention experienced by Industrial Products. The Calpers campaign against its bottom dwellers, for example, ensnared less than 5 percent of the companies in its portfolio. And, at the other end, only the consistently high performers manage to obtain the kind of immunity from investor scrutiny long enjoyed by Buckingham.

Exceptionally defensive governance, however, can attract investor notice regardless of performance. Managements know that building the barricades too high invites investor efforts to dismantle them entirely. Executives learned that their targeting by disgruntled investors follows the first rule of investor capitalism: financial adversity is the mother of attention. They came to know it followed a second law as well: governance perversity is the father of intervention.

Corporate performance and governance, then, constitute the crosshairs with which investors target companies under the new rules of investor capitalism. Dual application of the two criteria can be seen in the United Shareholders Association's annual rating of America's 1,000 largest companies. Short- and long-term financial performance carries half the weight in calculating the rankings. A dozen shareholder-rights issues (confidential voting, a poison pill) and the executive-compensation record constitute the other half.[25] To avoid the ranking's bottom requires both reasonable performance and reasonable governance; to

Table 2.2 Two Institutional Investors' Procedures for Identifying Poorly Performing Companies

Public Pension Fund: "We identify between fifty and one hundred companies at the beginning of the proxy season which are underperformers. We give that list to our investment staff of portfolio managers to cull down to a much more manageable number. We usually whittle that down to about twenty companies. Then the proxy staff and investment staff meet to discuss the twenty companies to decide at which, if any, based on poor performance and whether management has been responsive to questions, we're going to file a shareholder resolution. We also look at antitakeover mechanisms in place and our level of ownership and the ownership of other institutional investors. So, there are about six things we look at in making a final decision as to whether to target a company."

Private Pension Fund: "What shareholders want is rate of return, so let's work with our portfolio and look at companies which failed on rate of return compared to market return over a sufficiently long period and ask what happened. It goes from stock performance to looking at certain key fundamentals, and then having one of our analytical staff look at it who is familiar with the company to put together a little picture of what has been going on. This creates a list of candidates. Then we prioritize the list and get management and boards to talk to the investment committee. If their strategy sounds rational to us, we'll say, 'Okay, we'll give you a chance.'"

Source: Investor records.

Table 2.3 Policy Guidelines of Three Institutional Investors for Voting Company Proxies

Public Pension Fund

Detailed guidelines describe the fund's position on a long list of issues, ranging from confidential voting and antitakeover measures to matters of a "financial nature only." The lengthy document requires the maintenance of detailed proxy records and active voting: "It is expected that there will be no abstentions on issues that may affect the economic value of shareholdings." When "pertinent information is unavailable" or legal requirements conflict with a fund principle, however, the proxy caster is given considerable discretion, and, more generally, the guidelines frequently defer to the final "judgment of the responsible party."

Investment Company

General policy: "Proxies must be voted in the best interests of the shareholders."

Routine Issues: "We will vote with management. Routine issues include election of directors, approval of stock option plans, and ratification of auditors."

Social and political issues: "Unless instructed by a client, we will usually vote with management. Included here are restrictions on business activities in certain countries and limitations on controversial products."

Governance issues: "We will usually vote against proposals that limit shareholder sovereignty. Such proposals include elimination of cumulative voting and approval of poison pills."

Nonroutine business issues: "We will vote on a case-by-case basis. These matters include restructurings, acquisitions, and divestitures."

Private Pension Fund

A brief statement guides the fund's investment managers. The two-page outline requires that "proxies are to be voted exclusively for the benefit of participants." And they are to be exercised. Proxies "are considered assets" to be "voted on by the investment manager." Avoiding guidance on specific governance issues, the document instructs staff to vote with management "on routine matters," though routine remains undefined. The proxy voter is to report the votes annually to the pension-fund director. However, plans to vote against management are to be communicated, whenever possible, to the director prior to the vote. The fund is to notify the corporate parent of all "controversial votes" as well.

Source: Investor records.

hit the ranking's top requires both great performance and great governance.

This joint emphasis on company performance and corporate governance is a central motif of the new investor capitalism. Shareholders have always been concerned with performance. That, of course, defines modern capitalism. It is the investors' response to weak performance, their abrogation of the Wall Street rule, that adds the contemporary twist.

3

$§$

Cultural Resistance to Shareholder Insistence

IN THEORY, EACH CORPORATION belongs to its shareholders. They are entitled to give whatever direction they would choose for the use of their equity. Yet the outward acceptance of investor sovereignty coexists with private rejection of investor advice. In management's view, investor ownership does not carry with it the right to give direction as to how to enhance shareholder value. It remains management's right to set strategy, acquire divisions, market products, promote executives, and fix salaries.

This chapter is about management conception of investors' rights and its own responsibilities. It concerns management perceptions and prescriptions, or what we commonly take to be the fiber of corporate culture. In the dominant ideology of managerial capitalism, professional executives viewed themselves as firmly and justifiably in control. They had been groomed, promoted, and finally elevated to the executive suite because they were the best at their profession. It was their ship to pilot to the best of their professional abilities, and it was theirs to pilot alone. In the dominant culture of investor capitalism, by contrast, top managers recognize that they are no longer so firmly in control. Like their predecessors, they too had reached the top of the company pyramid because of their demonstrated leadership. But unlike their predecessors, they discovered that it was no longer their ship alone to sail. Investors, it seemed, insisted on serving as copilots.

Though now cognizant of the new shareholder power, professional managers nonetheless construct grounds to keep investor hands off the tiller. They do so by disparaging the would-be copilots. Demanding investors, company executives would say, are too narrowly focused and too unqualified as managers to have any real standing.

The awkwardness of resisting what is not formally yours to reject is made to appear less so through an innovative cultural lens. As seen through this lens, several investors' flaws together result in an institutional cadre that, in the view of company executives, cannot consistently promote the best interests of either its shareholder constituencies or the companies they own. Institutional investors know so little about how to guide a modern enterprise that they would have to be ignored for their own good.

Whatever the validity of the criticism, it offers senior managers a self-protective rationale for ignoring the advice they would prefer not to hear. Their critique of investors is akin to the denigrating criticism that government authorities sometimes hurl at political protesters whose grievances the state wishes to ignore. Of course such forms of self-justifying defense can be of limited practical use against powerful protest groups. But short of the revolution, a protective ideology can usefully shield public authorities or private managers from facing what would otherwise become an unacceptable contradiction: the democratic state ignoring the will of the people—or, in this case, the public company ignoring the will of the owner.

Since top executives are the elected agents of the company owners, overt rejection of shareholder advice is awkward if not dangerous. Defiance runs against the cultural grain of American capitalism, and it invites retaliation. Acts of resistance are therefore rarely explicit. Executives seek instead to appear responsive without necessarily being so. The art of politics is saying no without appearing to do so, and company managers have become adept practitioners.

Features of the new culture of investor capitalism can be seen at virtually any security analysts' meeting or quarterly gathering that a major company hosts to review its results. We begin by visiting two such meetings, one at Capital Cities/ABC, the other at ITT Corporation. We then turn to the rationale behind management's resistance to such shareholder insistence, and here we explore the general contours of executive perceptions. The purpose is to understand the managerial mind-set under investor capitalism, the spectacles through which executives have come to view the far more powerful world of their shareholders.

The Analysts' Meeting

Though ostensibly an occasion for companies to brief their major stock-holders on recent developments, the analysts' meeting has also become an occasion for investors to press their own views on company managers. Their pointed questioning often delivers a message as clear as any declarative urging. Yet, while management listens, it rarely accedes. It is open to all questions but unresponsive to most suggestions.

Capital Cities/ABC

Wall Street denizens have filled ABC's Prime Time studio. Clustered in an off-camera area, the row upon row of conservative business suits seems at odds with the unfinished walls, half-facades, and open cables of a television production facility. Those arriving on the set explain the analysts' presence. Filing in to the set are ABC's chief executive, chief financial officer, general counsel, and three division heads.

It is the end of a fiscal quarter in late 1991, and the management of Capital Cities/ABC (as the company has been formally known since the former acquired the latter in 1986) has invited large institutions and brokers to learn the results. Daniel Burke, the chief executive, is making his way into the studio, and he greets many along his path, a kind of celebrity working a familiar constituency. The nearly 140 constituents in this case are made up of those who hold ABC shares, sell its stock, or rate its bonds. Six of the top ten owners are present: Ruane Cuniff & Co. (536,000 shares), Oppenheimer & Co. (448,000 shares), J. P. Morgan & Co. (428,000 shares), First Manhattan Co. (348,000 shares), Bankers Trust (299,000 shares), and Fidelity (286,000 shares). Nobody is present from Berkshire Hathaway, the top owner, with 3 million shares (worth over $1 billion at meeting's start), but its chairman, Warren E. Buffet, already knows the results since he serves on the company's board. Virtually all of the largest brokerage houses are there, including Merrill Lynch, Kidder Peabody, and Salomon Brothers. So too are staff members of the two main credit raters, Moody's Investor Services and Standard and Poor's.

An informal buzz fills the room. Several of those near the back are musing on their visit yesterday to a class at the Harvard Business School, where a management case on Johnson & Johnson was discussed. At the time of the case, the pharmaceutical giant had been headed by Daniel Burke's older brother, James Burke. The latter's son, it seems, was a student in the class, and when asked about the differences between his father and his uncle, he had reportedly offered a kind of Yogi Berra response: Daniel's sideburns are longer; otherwise their outlooks are the same.

Daniel Burke and his immediate predecessor, Thomas Murphy, were known for a disarming style that had misled many a new analyst. Today Burke lives up to his reputation. He opens with the suggestion that nobody should take notes, "since there's nothing important that we say anyway. We will take all your questions and then do our best to avoid answering them." He reviews ABC's results, noting that its revenues had been flat over the past year and its net income down by 21 percent. A share-repurchasing program is on track. And ABC has invested in several European television companies (though one of these was currently in an "investment phase," self-admittedly a "euphemism for the fact that it is losing a lot of money"). In summary, Burke says, "the last six quarters have been difficult, in part because of the Gulf War and in part because I became CEO. We stepped into an open manhole. But now we are cautiously optimistic."

The assembled analysts are given their shot. One asks about television program ratings. A second analyst questions the impact of the upcoming 1992 winter and summer Olympics on ABC earnings. ABC had held the franchises in 1972, 1976, 1984, and 1988, but now the summer games were in the hands of NBC and the winter games were in the hands of CBS. It will be hard to be on the sidelines, Burke confessed, but he added that he would watch the Olympics this year "without all the agony that I've had in the past." A third asks about developments in ABC's publishing arm, another about current network costs, and others about federal regulations, advertising revenues, and affiliate relations. Some challenges are broad: "Do you think, Dan, of new strategic directions for creating growth in the 1990s?" (Burke responds that he does not want to get into details.) Other challenges are narrow: "Why don't you repeat some of the best daytime programs at night?" (Burke concurs that the network will have to find ways of showing successful shows more often.) After ninety-five minutes of give-and-take, he finds an optimistic exit: "As proof of our continued prosperity, we will buy you a drink."

Burke's upbeat note despite the day's downbeat financials resonates with the analysts. As they move toward the door or bar, one comments to another, "This is such a money machine. They keep making cash when business is bad. Imagine what it will be like when the business gets good." A dozen analysts soon surround Burke on the set. "What would happen," one asks, "if the other two networks got out of the network business?" ("It would create a great opportunity for us," he responds.) Another queries why ABC does not drop Monday-night football since it is losing money ("We don't have peanut butter to spread on seven slices. . . . We just don't know if we have enough good programming to fill the gap.") Nearly a half-hour after the meeting's formal conclusion, an analyst asks, "When you look ahead ten years, what do you think about programming?" Still no nearer the cocktails than when he had formally closed the meeting, the sixty-two-year-old Burke begins to pull away from the crowd: "Look at me—do I look like a man who will be worrying about these kinds of things in ten years?"

ITT

Several months later another group of analysts is gathering in the ballroom of a Sheraton Hotel in Manhattan. On stage here is ITT's chief executive, Rand Araskog, along with his chief financial officer, comptroller, and two executive vice presidents. They are about to face the analysts who specialize in ITT, a distinct crowd from those who follow ABC and the television industry. They are, however, wearing much the same subdued attire. To an outsider accidentally stumbling into the room, the ambience might suggest that either a private memorial service or a big money discussion is about to begin.

The chief executive opens the meeting with a formal review of ITT's quarter and year, and then questions from the 175 analysts come in rapid-fire succession. As at a presidential press conference, the chief executive calls on many of the questioners by first name, and some in turn open their questions with "Rand, . . . ":

Q: *Would ITT be willing to repurchase 30 to 40 percent of its shares, and is Sheraton [the hotel system owned by ITT] up for sale?*
A: No to the second question. On stock repurchases—we don't get the funds [from a large divestiture] until later. The board would not approve, I think I can say, borrowing money to repurchase.
Q: *What about the Hartford [ITT's large insurance arm]?*
A: I can say that during my time as CEO, we will hit 15 percent return on equity.
Q: *Aren't Sheraton and Rayonier [ITT's forest-products division] highly cyclical?*
A: Our hotels are doing well. Rayonier is significantly down at the moment.
Q: *You say you have many cyclical businesses. Does this mean you will divest or make some changes?*
A: We will do some divestitures and acquisitions along the way. But we don't want to buy assets cheap that turn out to be cheap.

Q: *Could you comment specifically on the incentive compensation system?*
A: It will be in our proxy statement. The new program shifts from earnings per share to return on equity. The new system is set by the compensation committee, all [of whose members are] outside directors.
Q: *Would you consider a one-time special dividend for shareholders?*
A: We haven't really thought about it.
Q: *You mentioned earlier that new and striking things will be happening at ITT. Can you elaborate on what those things can be?*
A: No.

As the meeting breaks up, several analysts (including one who had asked about executive compensation) privately grouse about ITT's administrative costs, citing Araskog's recent flights to Paris on the Concorde. Last year the analysts had been angered by a large grant of restricted stock options to the chief executive. Now they will sullenly wait to see what the ITT proxy statement has to say.

A group of reporters attended an ITT press conference with Araskog just before the analysts' meeting, and they are invited to join the analysts but to refrain from questioning. The next day's financial headlines suggest that they discerned little affirmative news from either the press conference or the analysts' meeting: "ITT Unlikely to Spin Off Hartford," offered the *Financial Times* of London; "Shifts Hinted by ITT," said the Associated Press story in the *New York Times*.[1]

An Irresistible Force Meets an Immovable Object

The analysts offer up their advice. For the ITT chief, their questions placed compensation, dividends, and divestiture on the table. For the ABC chief, they put earnings, regulation, and programs on the table. Yet the rules of exchange are not those of a town meeting. The authorities are not duty bound to honor anything said or not said. Unlike town officials, managements retain the prerogative to ignore the grass roots, and they often do. Like politicians everywhere, however, they value the art of saying no to constituents without appearing to do so.

The stock analysts attending such meetings have become a force onto themselves. The number of stock analysts is enough to fill most town halls. The top twenty domestic investment-research firms employed 901 analysts in 1992, up from 883 in 1991 and 751 in 1990. Merrill Lynch alone employed 100; Lehman Brothers, 68; Smith Barney, 62; Goldman, Sachs, 61; and Salomon Brothers, 58. The total number of analysts at all firms following U.S. stocks in 1992 stood at nearly 2,400, a rise over the previous year but down from slightly more than 3,000 just before the market crash in October 1987. At larger investment companies, the multitudes ensure a fine slicing of the market, with some following single industries or even just select corporations.[2]

From their own point of view, executives of major companies face a bevy of specialists tracking and analyzing their every move. PepsiCo, with annual sales of some $25 billion and a market capitalization over $30 billion at the end of 1993, is actively followed by 35 sell-side analysts and 115 buy-side analysts. The vice president for investor relations is in continual telephone contact with more than 100 of the analysts.[3]

The analysts constitute the active voice of the large investors. It is they who most often and most directly express the shareholders' whims and wants to company management. It is they who communicate what executives should consider doing differently. It is they who question all strategic moves. It is they who represent the newly concentrated wealth of the great owners.

Company managers say they appreciate the analysts' rights of expression. Yet managers equally maintain their own right to hear the voices selectively or to ignore them altogether. This flow of investor advice—and company resistance to it—can be seen in the reactions of the broadcast, automobile, and petroleum firms to their shareholders.

MFL Network receives a continuous flow of unsolicited investor advice, ranging from suggestions for specific programming to recommendations for the acquisition of other companies. From time to time, for instance, the company invited five or six analysts to meet privately with the CEO and other top managers, and after a company presentation and general questioning, the challenges typically became more pointed. In the investor-relations director's paraphrase, one question was: "'You know what you guys really ought to do? You know what I think you should do? I think you should buy the Acme Manufacturing Company.'" Others analysts pressed for the broadcasting company to buy a major film studio or cable company. The corporate response here was often a kind of deflecting nonresponse: "Putting $92 million down on the table for *Terminator 2* is something the [CEO and COO] are unlikely to do."

MFL's investor-relations director viewed the inflow philosophically. The investors "all think they can run your business today, and certainly they have a right to their opinion. I think it sort of comes with the territory." Still, he occasionally worried about the analysts' advice to their clients. In preparing their reports, some analysts had taken to personally previewing new programs that the broadcasting firm would be launching. The director of investor relations found the prospect appalling. "I think they're coming in primarily because they're television viewers more than anything else," he observed. "God help us if a [stock] buyer's sole recommendation hinges on *Twin Peaks.*"

Hutchins Motors Corporation, with products that analysts could also judge as consumers, receives a similar flow of unsolicited—and insubstantial—advice. Investors would sometimes call to complain about an undesirable feature on a vehicle they had just purchased. Analysts often insisted on seeing future auto designs, grumbling that they were not being allowed to see far enough ahead. Company managers privately complained that when the analysts were allowed to see the products and plans, their reactions, often appearing in their subsequent reports, were more a matter of personal predilection than in-depth understanding. Company executives occasionally exploded on seeing the reports, especially when the products were placed in what was viewed as ill-informed pejorative comparison with those of the other automakers.

However dubious the investor advice or sensitive the issue, company managers typically feel obligated to seem responsive. At times sarcasm or humor fills the void where substance cannot. When an MFL Network executive was asked by investors whether the company would be interested in acquiring a particular enterprise, his unresponsive response became, "Do you have any other stocks that you're underwater with that you'd like us to take off your hands?"

At rare moments, and preferably no more often, the companies offer blunt retorts. Richards Oil Corporation, for example, received unrelenting counsel from its analysts, in part because it had undergone a wrenching restructuring, several proxy battles, and a takeover threat. Some analysts had come to terms with the company's reality, allowing it to go its own way. But others persisted in proffering advice. They criticized its $20 billion capital investment program, attacked the absence of a stock-repurchasing program, and challenged a host of other policies. The vice president for investor relations finally dug in her heels. There is no buyback plan, she said, simply "because we can make more investing for you than we can buying back stock." Exasperated over the incessant demands, she said she finally blurted out what she had hoped to avoid: "If you don't like it, go buy someone else."

Management Culture

Linda Hill, John Kotter, and Jeffrey Pfeffer, seasoned observers of corporate politics, note that the capacity to get anything done in corporations arises from mastering the exercise of power and influence within.

The act of managing organizational resources, they argue, is really the art of managing power. Those who are effective in doing so rise to the top. Senior executives can thus be seen as the ultimate winners of a career-long tournament, each stage a contest over who is best at wielding authority. If investors are to exercise power over the firm, they would have to take it from those who are very used to having and holding it.[4]

When confronted with investors asking for more power, top management's blank stare is thus unsurprising. Still, the executives are dogged by the fact that the advice givers are not disgruntled company employees or troublesome regulatory officials but representatives of the firm's owners, the executives' ultimate boss. With this conundrum much in mind, company executives have constructed a self-justifying culture, a set of insulating beliefs that serve to protect them from owner interference if not oversight.

At the core of the management culture is a rationale for resisting certain investor demands. Like any ideology, it is by no means universally shared, it carries numerous variants, and it frequently fails as a behavioral guide. Still, the culture of management has become consistent, animating, and common enough to constitute a worldview, a template giving shape to the continuing contact between companies and investors. It reaffirms the right of management to resist, and it questions the right of shareholders to demand.[5]

At the center of this managerial resistance to shareholder insistence are three lines of argument. One concerns the length of investors' time horizons for evaluating company performance; a second concerns the qualifications of investors to speak on management issues; and a third concerns the authority of investors to speak on behalf of their ultimate owners. Investor horizons are purportedly too short for effective corporate management; investor backgrounds too limited for informed counsel to management; and investor voices too unrepresentative of their own constituent owners to render legitimate advice.

Executives implicitly turn the principal-agent conundrum against investors. When it comes to applying the right time frames and managerial principles to the operation of the firm, executives presume that they themselves are far better prepared than investors to make such judgments. Since sound management now should generate more investor wealth later, company executives reason that their own judgment calls represent owner interests more completely than any investment manager's articulation of them. In the words of the CEO of National Metal Products: "I think there is a lot of mystique and misunderstanding out there amongst institutional investors as to what the hell is in their best interest." In the same vein, the chief executive of Champion International, a large forest-products company, saw following the equity market's preferences as a sure prescription for disaster, the opposite of good management. "There is intense pressure for current earnings, so the message is: Don't get caught with major [long-term] investments." In other words, they are telling executives to "do all the things we used to consider bad management."[6]

These ideas are seldom expressed openly. To the ear of the investor they can sound like one more sign of entrenchment alongside a poison pill and staggered board. But within the privacy of the executive suite, they find frequent expression. There, capitalist correctness yields to managerial candor.

The technical accuracy of these views is not at issue here. Some aspects of the claims find support while others do not. What counts is their persuasive capacity and their behavioral utility in furnishing a convenient cultural insulation against encroachments on managerial prerogatives.

Investors' Short Time Horizons

Company managers appreciate one of the universal laws of physics: to define any object or event in the universe, one must specify the time of its observation. To define corporate performance, then, requires an appropriate temporal yardstick. The problem arises, in its simplest form, from the fact that managers see investors as using too short a yardstick, gauging company performance yearly, quarterly, and even daily. Managers, by contrast, see themselves as applying the right measuring stick, producing company value not by the quarter but over the years. In this contrasting perception, executives find both personal solace and the will to resist.

To see how these conceptions emerge, we start with the experience of one company in facing an extraordinary demand by a large investor for a cash payment. We then turn to the more routine daily imperatives faced by managements everywhere. All demands pointed in the same direction: more value for the shareholder now. Much of this component of management ideology, then, is borne of practical experience.

Chrysler's Impatient Investors

Chrysler Corporation's management discovered the hazards of having a powerful but very impatient owner. The investor Kirk Kerkorian had held nearly 10 percent of Chrysler's shares since the early 1990s. With that kind of stake, an investor could readily make his or her voice known, and Kerkorian did so. In 1992 he sought a seat on the company's board, but management immediately said no. He also fought a move by management to diminish former chairman Lee Iacocca's role on the board. "Recent events have made me concerned about Mr. Iacocca's continued leadership role in the company," warned Kerkorian in a letter to the directors. Company moves to reduce Iacocca's role had led him "to question whether the interests of the shareholders now require strengthened representation on the board." Again management said no.

Two years later Chrysler felt the same thorn in its side. Still owning more than 9 percent of the company's stock in 1994 (some 32 million shares worth $1.7 billion), Kerkorian now demanded a massive dispensing of dollars, since, in his view, the company had become cash engorged. Chrysler had managed to amass $6.6 billion as a result of internal restructuring and a rebounding car market. In management's view, retaining the cash was essential if it was to be prepared for the next rainy day. It was a circumstance of more than hypothetical interest since Chrysler had nearly run out of funds in 1979 and only a $1.5 billion guarantee by the U.S. government finally rescued the firm. Chastened by having once looked into an open grave, management now said it planned to gather $7.5 billion to $10 billion as its own guarantee against the next recession. Its worldwide competitors did much the same: Japan's Toyota Motor Corporation maintained a rainy-day fund of more than $25 billion. Chrysler wanted to break from the vicious cycle of boom and bust, to transcend what a General Motors executive had once described as Chrysler's bouncing between "disaster and mediocrity."[7]

Despite management's strategic concerns, Kerkorian insisted on his short-term agenda. He complained that his own ownership stake constituted "30 times as many shares as the entire board of directors taken together," and unless Chrysler immediately sent some of its hoarded cash back to the shareholders, he would consider additional actions, including a proxy fight or legal action to void the company's poison pill. Ira Millstein, outside counsel to the directors of GM and other corporate boards, saw the moment as "a clear case of short-term shareholder value vs. the long-term health of the company."[8]

Against its avowed better judgment, Chrysler management capitulated seventeen days later. Though Kerkorian was still very much the minority holder, he had aroused other investors, and management sensed that impatient holders smelled blood. The company announced that it would raise its dividend by 60 percent, repurchase $1 billion of its own stock, and relax its poison pill. A spokesperson for Kerkorian's holding company, Tracinda Corporation, applauded the decision: "We believe what the Chrysler board has done represents an appropriate balance between the need for stability in the company and the enhancement of shareholder value." Chrysler asserted that it would continue to build its cash holding and expand its capital spending, raising the latter from $21 billion to $23 billion over the next five years. But Kerkorian, the company's largest and most vocal shareholder, had forced company management to give shareholders more value now despite management's preference for returning more later.[9]

The investor's insatiable appetite for cash today reappeared with a vengeance in 1995. Still dissatisfied with Chrysler's response, Kerkorian finally sought to do through outright control what he could not achieve through informal influence. His Tracinda Corporation proposed to purchase the 90 percent of Chrysler's shares not already held by Kerkorian at a price 40 percent above market price, an offer valued at $20 billion. The company promptly announced it was "not for sale," but other investors saw a pending opportunity to reap windfall profits. Some viewed it as a referendum on management performance. "The market is the ultimate arbiter on how Chrysler's being run," offered one stock trader, "and the market is saying it's sorely mismanaged." Perhaps, but many in the market were also saying that they would take their certain profits now even if it made Chrysler more difficult to run later. One observer mistakenly assumed that it must be Jack Kevorkian—the physician known for assisting suicides of Michigan's troubled elderly—who must now be assisting the troubled Michigan automaker. Management repeatedly asserted that a cash reserve—now targeted at $7.5 billion—was a matter of prudent judgment, the near-term cost of insulating against what could otherwise be far-term suicide. Kerkorian and investor allies obviously thought otherwise.[10]

Knowing that the company's fate resided in the institutions' decision to back management or cash in on the takeover, Chrysler's management met with its largest investors to explain itself and appeal for loyalty. For the moment it succeeded. The state treasurer of Michigan, a holder of 7.3 million shares, reported that he preferred a higher divided but only if management freely approved it. He avowed, "I'm not trying to micromanage Chrysler." With other investors ambivalent and most investment banks reluctant, Kerkorian and Tracinda Corporation quietly retreated from their direct challenge. At the same time, Chrysler executives asked their dozen largest holders, excepting Kerkorian, whether to increase the share dividend or buy back more stock. The company did both, doubling the dividend and repurchasing $2 billion of its shares.[11]

Though the hostile bid dissipated, the spur to action served to confirm managements' worst fears. Without care and coddling, shareholders, it seemed, could be a most impatient lot. Continuous attention would be needed, as Kerkorian was soon to increase his Chrysler holdings from 9 percent to 14 percent, and Fidelity jumped into the fray, doubling its stake to 13 percent. Chrysler and Kerkorian finally arranged a truce in 1996. Kerkorian agreed not to initiate a takeover or a proxy challenge, or increase his holdings for five years. Chrysler agreed to place a Kerkorian associate on the board, seek buyers for its nonautomotive operations (such as its car rental companies), compensate directors in stock rather than cash, and repurchase an additional $2 billion in shares.[12]

Chastening Experience

Other companies have learned much the same through their own near-death experiences. The large institutions, complained the vice president and treasurer of Lamont Company, "are very short-term oriented. They're not an investor in the company, they're just a holder of a portfolio of paper. They're like a commodity trader or a foreign exchange dealer. They're really not interested in the company." The concepts of investor loyalty and longevity did not readily come to mind; investor fickleness and lack of staying power did. In the treasurer's summary: "The only difference between an [arbitrageur] and an investment manager was half a point."

The chief financial officer for Harrington Stores, the retail-services company, offered much the same assessment, a perspective shaped by a takeover threat during the late 1980s. A group known for attempting hostile acquisitions had abruptly purchased a large number of the company's shares. Although no formal tender offer ever materialized, speculation was rife, with many perceiving a bid in the offing. The company's share price and stock holding gyrated wildly in the weeks that followed. Institutional commitment wobbled badly. "We continue to see their job as making money for their beneficiaries," offered the CFO. "Most of them are not directly beneficiaries of the funds they manage, and some of them don't know and have never communicated with or asked their beneficiaries what objectives they have." As a result, he had concluded, the institutions unfortunately "continue to have the short-term, total-return objective as their primary objective."

Such views also pervaded the executive suite of Industrial Products Corporation, the manufacturing firm that had thrown off Zacker's bear hug. The company's chief executive heard it this way: "These guys [the fund managers] feel the pressure. In turn, you sense it. They don't come out and say, 'We don't give a damn about the long term.' Their question is, 'What do you think the earnings are going to be in the next quarter. Are you going to be able to get a lift? Do you see the stock going anywhere by the end of the year.'" The chief operating and financial officer observed the same: "Their thinking is shorter term than ours would be. Without articulating it—but you knew it—they're thinking shorter term."

The manufacturing company had invested in several projects that were not expected to yield products for five or six years. Handsome results were then expected, but this long-term investment seemed to draw almost no attention from the analysts. One year—maybe two—was about as distant a horizon as the investors could muster, and upon which they recurrently focused. The investors' questions followed a familiar groove:

- Are inventories [for a major summer product] too big?

- Are your production facilities [for a summer product] going to be full tilt?

- Is the third quarter going to be an up-earnings quarter, compared to the third quarter last year?

- How much could you take out of your capital investment budget this year?

- Are you going to be able to have a dividend increase this year?

The investor questions, whether rendered during investor meetings or visits to headquarters, constituted a chastening education for the managers, especially for those who had spent comparatively little time with their shareholders. Industrial Products' vice president for investor relations reflected, "I used to think three to five years [was long term]. I guess one year seems pretty long to me now." For the company's general counsel too, extensive investor contact had the effect of enriching his understanding: "Even though we had a long-term strategy, some of the messages were that . . . you don't need to manage from quarter to quarter, but you ought to be more cognizant of trying to get results in a quicker time frame." He had learned that "we better try to shorten up because sometimes in the long run we're all dead." The company had wanted to tell the investors that it had developed a grand strategy for the coming decade, but the general counsel and others learned to focus on what the investors wanted to hear: what the company would be doing over the quarter, the year, or the next year. Beyond that, they knew investor eyes would glaze over.

Daily Experience

A takeover threat in the name of shareholder profit taking is likely to convince almost any management that its time horizons were at odds with its investors'. Faced with takeover or proxy threats, management had seen its fate hang in the balance, and on close inspection found large institutions at the fulcrum. When high stakes concentrate the attention and clarify the positions of both sides, managers are shocked to find the horizons of many institutions radically foreshortened from their own.

Far less threatening experiences achieve much the same for other company managers. From daily contact with big investors, virtually all managements have come to conclude that the institutions' clocks tick faster than their own. In almost any executive suite, as a result, a strikingly consistent commentary on investors' limited time horizons can be heard. The perception of abbreviated investor attention spans is most vigorously held and most vividly expressed by managers who have suffered near-death experiences. Yet even of those never close to a near miss, virtually all profess to think in long waves while Wall Street acts in short ones.

The chief financial officer of WWK Products, the diversified company, diagnosed his shareholders. "While many of them are long-term holders," he said, "they're also looking for short-term fixes. When the stock is selling below book, they'll always have an idea. 'Why don't you sell this and use the proceeds to buy back stock?'" The analysts continuously pressed the executives, complained the CFO: "An analyst wants you to move the stock, and if he thinks a divestiture or buying in stock would move the stock, that's what he's going to recommend to you—or at least ask why you're not doing it." The divisional president found that, alarmingly, "the analysts' time frame has been contracted the past four or five years." Too many of the analysts, he complained—and most typically the younger ones, are more interested in, "are you going to buy back some stock tomorrow to boost your stock?"

Some company managers complain of the fickle behavior of investors, of the "day-trader mentality," of "running to the hills at the first sign of bad news." Institutions are seen as acting on personal whims, information fragments, and false rumors. To company executives, this fleeting ownership in the company, jarred by the scantiest information, casts further doubts on the investors' right to reign. To illustrate the point, the vice president for investor relations of the MFL Network waved his hand at the roster of his company's major investors: "There are institutions here on this list who read their *USA Today* and find out that the anchorwoman on [a well-known national program] has a cold. 'Oh my God, that's going to affect their second-quarter earnings!' "

Some investors appeared to devote substantial time to understanding this broadcasting company before acquiring its stock. Several representatives would visit MFL Network, sometimes three or four times, asking for an extensive review of its operations. If they liked what they saw, they would then take a substantial position in the company. The due diligence, however, provided little guarantee against early defection. If the company's rating slipped, some of the new investors would scurry for the exit. "Their loyalty," complained the investor-relations manager, is "almost nil."

Like all orthodoxies, this one has its dissidents. Dissenting executives are often located in companies with few near-term crises and many long-range plans. To these managers, it seems that if the shareholders are well informed of the company's risks and cycles, they will consequently see well beyond the quarter. The chief executive of Columbia Foods presided over a record of growth and prosperity. He found himself presiding as well over a shareholder base of peace and tranquillity. "You're never going to hear from me that, 'Oh God, these security analysts are so short term,'" said the chief executive. "They are as short term as you make them short term."

Two steps by Columbia Foods had served to make its investors less short term. First, company executives set out its corporate plans and sales objectives—not just for the immediate future but for the next eight to ten years as well. They pressed investors to assess both their momentary accomplishments and their promised achievements. Second, company executives continually reminded investors that long-term growth would best come with short-term risk taking. They pressed investors to see that a no-mistake culture could steady earnings now but undermine growth later. The chief executive would remind investors on almost every occasion that his company failed more often than its competitors. But, he was quick to add, his company also succeeded more often than its competitors. "We don't believe in being average around here," explained the CEO. Being above average included, he believed, "screwing up from time to time." He felt the message had stuck. His investors seemed more tolerant of the ups and downs of the company than most.

Though learning to understand and occasionally change the mind of the money manager, few company executives accept the investors' precepts. Their principles are recognized, but they are rarely internalized. Investor time frames should be rejected, company managers imply, because they do not accord with good management axioms. The chief executive of Industrial Products could appreciate the investors' preference for orderly growth. But he also knew that he could not run his company on that principle. "Our shareholders want some demonstration that, over time, preferably over a short time, things are getting better." But the company's two main product areas are highly cyclical, and both required costly long-term investments. "We're not that kind of a vehicle," he complained. "We're in two erratic, crap-shooting type of businesses that are prone to rather violent cycles. . . . We're in two big commodity businesses, and prices just knock the hell out of us from time to time. Therefore we have a more difficult time achieving success under the [investors'] rules." With a polite bow in the direction of the investors, he continued to operate his business as best he knew how.

A 1987 survey of 400 chief executives from among the nation's 1,000 largest firms revealed the breadth of management criticism of investor time horizons. When asked to identify the leading sources of short-term pressures on them, CEOs singled out two culprits: institutional shareholders and securities analysts. A 1989 survey of 760 company managers of investor relations revealed much the same. Asked about their leading concerns regarding the company's relationship with the financial community, they replied that one factor overshadowed all others: the "short-term perspectives of sell-side and institutional holders." A 1994 resurvey of 585 company managers of investor relations showed an equally critical appraisal. The number-one concern in the company's relations with the financial community remained Wall Street's short-term perspectives, with more than half of the company managers citing this as their chief worry.[13]

Investment managers themselves confirm some of company managers' greatest anxieties. Of 135 responding to a 1990 survey, half affirmed that short-term performance was overstressed by those who evaluate and control their career prospects. Seven out of eight asserted that the market (which they help make) overreacts to setbacks in short-term earnings even when the earnings reports do not adversely reflect on a company's long-term prospects. A survey of pension-fund managers and outside money managers contracted to invest the pension funds confirmed much the same. Half to two-thirds stated that their investment performance is reviewed on a quarterly basis.[14]

The Tyranny of Expectations

In a universe of short-term expectations, unexpected fluctuations become an enemy. Not so in a world of long-term confidence. Whether quarterly earnings fail or exceed analysts' forecasts is of little moment if shareholders are there for the long run. The Japanese tradition of cross-holdings of stock among sets of firms united in *keiretsus* such as

Mitsubishi or Sumitomo has meant that periodic shortfalls—or wind-falls—in company profits are of no great concern. The investing companies in Japan are committed to one another through thick or thin. In the American tradition, by contrast, investors are not so committed. Vows must be continually renewed, and they are thus continually tested. Unanticipated swings in a company's quarterly performance call the vow into question. In this universe, a surprisingly good quarter can paradoxically be worse news than a predictably bad one.[15]

Shareholder expectations are now a standard baseline for a firm's three-month or annual performance. The firm's actual performance is judged more as a variance around the expectations than as an achievement in itself. "Compaq's earnings double, surpassing expectations," reported the *New York Times* in summarizing a set of quarterly results for the major computer maker. Compaq's share price surged 3 percent. "Lower-Than-Expected Loss Posted in Quarter by AMR," the *Times* reported the same day for the parent of American Airlines. Despite the loss, its shares rose 2 percent. Intel Corporation, said the *Times,* "far exceeded the most optimistic of Wall Street analysts' expectations." The analysts had expected $1.65 per share but the company reported $2.04, and in after-hours trading its price rose nearly 3 percent. "Kodak's results," reported the *Wall Street Journal,* "beat analysts' per-share earnings estimates by about 20 cents a share," pushing the stock up by almost 9 percent.[16]

For a major software maker, by contrast, a successful quarter proved unsuccessful because it was not successful enough, falling short of what investors had anticipated. To the untrained eye, the next day's headline could hardly be more ironic: "Shares Plunge 12.2% Despite 74% Profit Increase." Conversely, for Boeing Company, a failing quarter proved successful because it had not failed as much as analysts expected. Boeing reported a quarterly earnings decline of 38 percent—but its stock rose by 2 percent because analysts had expected worse. The USAir Group savored even greater countermovement. The airline lost $97 million during one quarter, and in reaction 3.5 million shares changed hands the next day compared to a daily average volume of only 0.5 million. But since the airline had lost twice that amount a year earlier—$197 million—Wall Street sent the stock not down but up—by 21 percent.[17]

Digital Equipment Corporation rode the roller coaster in the other direction. Digital had been atop the earnings crest of rising demand for midsize computers during the 1980s. It had also sunk into the losses trough of declining demand during the 1990s. Various restructuring plans, including the creation of autonomous business units and the deletion of some 28,000 employees, failed to stanch the financial hemorrhaging. Digital managed to produce a profit in only a single quarter out of twelve between early 1991 and early 1994. The stock had seen a high-water mark in 1987 of $199 a share. By contrast, a day before the quarterly earnings announcement in April 1994, it languished at less than $29 a share. The 1994 announcement proved a stunner: revenue fell by 6 percent compared to a year earlier, and losses widened from $30 million to $183 million. Most stock analysts had forecast a loss, but many had expected only one-quarter of the actual. "This is a disastrous quarter," offered an analyst with Brown Brothers Harriman, a "third straight surprise and this was the worst of all." To a Dean Witter analyst, the quarter was "a real shocker." Investors reacted with fury. Some 5.8 million shares changed hands, making Digital the day's most actively traded stock, and at market's close the share price had lost almost $6, more than 20 percent of its value. Speculation intensified that Digital's chief executive, Robert B. Palmer, successor to Kenneth H. Olsen, the founding CEO who had been dismissed in 1992, might himself be shown the exit.[18]

Company executives thus learned that investors abhor short-term surprises as much as anything. Study of top management turnover reveals that company shortfalls in meeting analyst forecasts are better predictors of executive dismissal than are shortfalls in the actual earnings. Put differently, you are more likely to lose your job if you shock investor sensibilities than if you dock company earning. Meeting investor expectations—or revising them, when possible, to meet those of the company—is thus prudent management.[19]

"My conclusion is this," declared the Industrial Products' CEO. "Institutional investors . . . are most comfortable with orderly progress. . . . If you could wake up every portfolio manager in the middle of the night and say, 'What do you like best,' he'd probably say 'orderly progress.' He can buy something, he can assume a little dividend increase annually, or every other year, and a price that moves upward in an orderly fashion."

The chief financial officer of Chase Chemical Products reached the same conclusion. For nearly a decade his company had reshuffled its portfolio of businesses to reduce cyclicality and volatility. Enough variability remained in its product lines that they "still can eat your lunch periodically." But despite the occasional flare-ups, the company had strived to achieve a "steadiness and predictability" in earnings. When asked over what time period regularity was expected, he replied, "year after year after year after year." The company's experience-based working premise, observed the CFO, was that "the market seemed to reward those companies that had a little more control over their own destiny," meaning their quarterly results.

Are Managerial Time Horizons Really Longer?

Management's disparaging view of investors' penchant for near-term gains and short-term overreactions has become so widespread that it is now a virtual truism. Yet enough ironies surround the short-term thesis to raise doubts about its factual foundation.

The short-term theorem states that corporate managers look to horizons far more distant than do their large investors. But, first, consider the inside operation of the firm. While it is true that good executives are visionaries, it is also true that they usually hold their own subordinates to tough performance standards measured annually, quarterly, or even monthly. Presidents of strategic business units are frequently expected to meet predefined earnings and spending targets on a quarterly basis. They are almost always expected to measure up in tough annual performance appraisals and compensation reviews. While the chief executive may be casting a strategic gaze over the next five years, when it comes to managing those who are expected to produce the results, the vision is not so far-sighted. As investment managers pass their near-term judgment on those who are expected to produce results for them, they may be doing little more than what any good company manager does.

Consider, second, the underlying drivers of executive compensation. Illuminating data here come from a firm that annually surveys the total compensation packages of the top seven or eight officers of some 45 large manufacturing concerns. In 1993, long-term incentives, primarily share-based plans such as stock options, constituted less than two-fifths (38 percent) of the top managers' total compensation. While this may seem large to readers whose income contains no long-term performance incentives at all, it is useful to remember that the glass is more than half-empty: three-fifths of the executives' income depends not on the company's multiyear performance but on only this year's.[20]

Even more to the point, the proportion of management compensation packages predicated on achieving multiyear objectives was lower a decade earlier when shareholder pressures were far less intense. In 1982, for instance, only one-sixth (17 percent) of the top managers' total compensation derived from long-term performance. As investor demands for short-term performance seemingly intensified, managerial compensation moved in the opposite direction, reaching more than one-third by 1993. It is less ironic than one might first suppose, since investors also generally applaud multiyear stock-based incentive plans. Still, in an earlier era when senior managers were presumably freer to indulge in long-run planning without investor interference, their own more self-determined compensation schemes allocated only one-sixth of the total to multiyear criteria.[21]

Consider, third, the time frames evidently employed by investors and managers when they focus on research and development (R&D). This is the company area where long-term gains most clearly require short-term losses. If institutional investors place greater value on near-term results than do managers, then they should be less drawn to companies whose management allocates more for R&D. Yet when companies announce increased R&D spending or capital investments, their stock prices tend to move up, not down. Other studies reveal a positive correlation between ownership concentration and R&D investments. While the causal relationship could go both ways, and probably does, the fact remains that large investors are not necessarily allergic to companies that are conspicuously spending on distant, downstream products.[22]

Conversely, other evidence suggests that executives themselves balk at long-term investments when such spending does not fit well with their own career time lines. CEOs are found to spend above average levels on R&D during the first years of their tenure, but then to spend below average levels during the final years, when they no longer can expect to realize personally the fruits of such long-term actions.[23]

Compared to their Japanese and German counterparts, American managers and investors clearly operate within more compressed time frames, as various studies document. No American company comes remotely close to the strategic planning cycles of Japan's Matsushita Electric Industrial Co., which plans 250 years ahead in twenty-five-year segments. But it is not unequivocally clear that, compared to one another, American managers and investors operate under distinct temporal regimens. The widespread acceptance by management of the two-time-frame thesis thus suggests that it furnishes a useful, if not necessarily factual, construct. Alleged time disparities would seem to have as much to do with a creative managerial buffering against persistent investor badgering as with the actual clockworks.[24]

This cultural precept was not simply invented as a convenient defense. Instead, it gradually emerged over the course of numerous exchanges between managers and investors. Investors' recurrent questions and responses, repeated in analysts' forums and management meetings from ABC to ITT and beyond, conveyed a message on the shrinkage of time. Stockholding trends added credibility to the message. The New York Stock Exchange reported, for instance, that the average holding for stocks dropped from seven years in 1960 to two years in 1990. Takeover threats at Chrysler and elsewhere further reinforced the perception.[25]

Once corporate consensus deemed investor demands to be excessively near term, managers classed shareholder insistence with a host of other shortsighted pressures that executives are well trained to discount. Focusing on the far horizon is, after all, one of the premier tasks of senior managers. Strategy manuals advocate that executives set clear objectives for where the company is going. "A corporate vision articulates top management's strategic intent," asserts one widely used text. "It focuses the attention of the firm's managers and channels their energies toward a common purpose." Leadership studies similarly urge executives to formulate compelling visions for the long run. Executives are pressed by James MacGregor Burns in his Pulitzer Prize–winning *Leadership* to resist the continuous demands for near-term compromises if their strategic leadership is to be effective. In John W. Gardner's seminal treatment of the subject, *On Leadership*, we learn that a mark of personal greatness is the ability to instill a sense that "the achievement of long-term goals requires a willingness to defer gratification." For John Kotter in *The Leadership Factor*, "overcoming short-term economic" forces is one of the paramount tasks of corporate leadership. Urged and rewarded for the art of seeing ahead, general managers are well schooled in rebuffing diversionary pressures for the here and now. From this vantage point, investor demands for quarterly or annual results are just one more set of pressures to be resisted.[26]

Ultra Short-Term Investors Are Not Owners

Another management means for comfortably denying the most vigorous investor pressures is through a kind of linguistic legerdemain. With a simple act of relabeling, executives declare the shortest of the short-term investors not to be "owners" at all. Though not universally shared, this act of exclusionary judgment draws on a long history of excommunication, whether by religious, political, or racial groups. Here, the logic goes, temporary investors are not truly owners since they acquire the stock only for quick gain, not as an act of "genuine" ownership.

The treasurer of Lamont Company, when presented with a ranked list of the firm's institutional investors, drew the line: "I don't think many of them *are* shareholders. Not the way I'm defining a shareholder anyway." He preferred a narrow definition: "Someone who is an investor *in the company*, rather than an investor *in the shares* of the company." A former president of several large companies had reached the same conclusion: "Money managers are not owners. When the computer kicks in, they sell their shares."[27]

The vice president of investor relations for Industrial Products, examining his list of major holders, agreed: "To me the best [owners] are the long-term holders." He singled out the top fifty: "All of these I would classify as good." Other, smaller holders who were known to move in and out of the stock, however, were not. "It's when an investor comes in, he hears a rumor that somebody's going to do something, and he jumps into it. The next week he jumps back out of it when something doesn't happen." They are the ones whose ownership claims can legitimately be ignored. "Those are the sort that I don't have much patience for."

Viewed as pariahs by managers, quick profit takers constitute the truly excommunicated. But an even wider group of investors than the speculators is suspect too. Doubts are cast on the corporate patriotism of almost any short termers. Their ownership rights do not, in the minds of many managers, entitle them to any say in the property they own. If "profit takers" can safely be ignored, then it follows that the executive has an active duty to ignore them.

Limited Investor Qualifications for Advising Companies

A second major line of managerial defense against owner intrusion focuses on the qualifications of investors to speak on management issues. Here attention shifts from their future horizon to their past experience. Investors may be expert at managing moneys, goes the argument, but they are novices when it comes to managing companies. They bring little to the table in the way of experience-based understanding of the pressures and problems faced by management. By virtue of this deficit, investor advice can be discounted, if not safely ignored.

The depth of executive hostility toward uninformed and unprofessional investor intervention in company affairs can be seen in the commentary of the chief executive at WWK Products. The firm had defeated three hostile raiders during the turbulent 1980s, and now the CEO served on a presidential commission that included several pension-fund executives. It was, in his view, a sobering experience. "We've got these guys out there saying how corporations ought to be organized, what boards ought to do." His assessment of the unsolicited advice in light of the status of its giver: "This is nonsense!"

The managerial critique of investors' managerial incapacities even found echo among some investors. A managing partner of a major money firm observed, with reference to the activist public pension funds, that he has a "problem with their expertise." The public funds "seem to want to run companies," he noted, but they wanted to do so with virtually no special credentials other than their status as government "bureaucrats."[28]

Like well-trained professionals in most settings, company executives question the authoritativeness of anybody rendering "cross-boundary" judgments without the appropriate credentials. In corporate management the best credential is line experience. This is one reason that companies arrange for the rotation of young managers who have high potential through a range of line positions to ensure that they can appreciate each before they later come to preside over all. It is also why companies prefer to appoint managers of joint ventures who have worked with both parties.[29]

As seen from a corporate executive's vantage point, institutional investors bring very little of the right stuff, since most of them have never set foot across the divide. The background of money managers is strikingly bereft of direct company-management experience. Consider the prior work experience of the top managers of three of the best-performing stock mutual funds in 1993. The managers for the stock funds with the highest returns during the past quarter (American Heritage Fund), past year (Oakmark Fund), and past five years (Vista Growth and Income) carved their careers entirely within their world of current employ. The manager of the first fund, aged forty-nine, had previously worked at Wood & McKenzie (a British brokerage firm), White, Weld & Co. (an investment bank), and the Deutsche Bank Capital Corporation. The second, aged thirty-five, brought earlier experience with the State Teachers Retirement System of Ohio. The third, aged thirty-seven, had previously worked with Citibank and Chase Manhattan Bank.[30]

For a broader cut, consider the background of the top managers for the nation's fifty largest pension funds (thirty-two public, eighteen private), forty largest investment managers (fund managers, insurance companies, and bank trusts), and ten largest foundations. Drawing on publicly available sources and direct contact with the investors' offices, table 3.1 reports a picture of minimal personal exposure to nonfinancial company management, with the partial exception of those who oversee corporate pension funds. The latter typically hold master's degrees in business administration and have come up through the company. Relatively few of the other money managers, however, bring either an M.B.A. or tangible experience in nonfinancial corporate management. Nor can most money managers point to a stint as a nonfinancial corporate director.[31]

The career divide between managing investments and managing companies thus runs deep. A few transcend the line: a chief executive of the College Retirement Equities Fund, Clifton R. Wharton Jr., served as a director of the Ford Motor Company. His successor as CEO of CREF, John H. Biggs, served on the boards of McDonnell Douglas Corporation and Ralston Purina. Another CREF executive, B. Kenneth West, served as a director of Motorola and had previously served as

**Table 3.1 Percentage of Money Managers with Nonfinancial
Management Experience, by Type of Institutional Investor**

	Private pensions	Invest. cos.	Public pensions	Founda- tions
Holds M.B.A. degree	91%	50%	33%	13%
Company management experience outside of finance	50	0	0	14
Serves as director of a major nonfinancial company	0	20	0	20

Source: Author's analysis.

chief executive of Harris Bankcorp. The chief of the Vanguard Group, John C. Bogle, also served as a director of a major manufacturer, Mead Corporation. But they remain the exception. When investors lack direct experience in the managers' terrain, the latter find it easy to question the former's advice on virtually any issue. Hospital executives without medical degrees face continuous credibility problems in presiding over their medical doctors, and cultural administrators without creative backgrounds face analogous problems in overseeing performing artists. Institutional investors without stints in corporate management face much the same credibility question.

Though such thoughts are rarely allowed to slip beyond the executive suite, former executives sometimes feel less constrained, giving public vent to what their successors privately harbor. The observations of Charles Wohlstetter, vice chairman of GTE Corporation and ex–chief executive of Contel Corporation, are symptomatic: "Fund managers have no history to justify the exercise" of increased influence on corporate management, he charged. "I do not know of a single state or municipal pension fund that employs personnel who have a background in major corporate management. . . . [W]e have a group of people with increasing control of the Fortune 500 who have no proven skills in management, no experience in selecting directors, no believable judgment in how much should be spent for research or marketing—in fact, no experience except that which they have accumulated controlling other people's money." Robert H. Malott, chairman of FMC Corporation's executive committee and its former chief executive, is equally unequivocal: "I do not think that shareholders have a constructive role to play in compensation or in selecting consultants. I struggle to see how institutional investors can play a constructive role in what basically, in my judgment, is a managerial decision." In short, investor intervention is "crazier than a hoot owl."[32]

Executive criticism of investors' management abilities is also expressed through formal associations where there is some safety in numbers. The Committee of Publicly Owned Companies, an evanescent group of the early 1990s, issued a call to arms: "We must not . . . permit a few noisy activists to intimidate us from entrepreneurial risk taking or succeed in micromanaging our companies." The more enduring Chief Executives' Council, composed of a dozen retired chief executives, carried the call forward with equally alarmist rhetoric: "Micromanaging a company from outside" can "be terribly counterproductive" and may be no less than "the road to *corporate socialism*."[33]

Corporate Executives as Pension Managers

Exacerbating the investor credibility problem is the absence of a corresponding cross-boundary experience among corporate managers. While company executives generally bring diverse corporate experience to the office, virtually none report any background in managing institutional investments. Most senior managers reached the apex of their firms after long careers in industry. Some emerge from the manufacturing side of the business; others from sales and marketing; and still others from finance. Whatever the functional origin, it almost never contains a stint as an investor.[34]

A rare exception to the rule came in the occasional company executive whose career had begun as an investment manager. A case in point is Robert A. Bowman, who in 1995 became president and chief operating officer of a reconstituted ITT Corporation. He had served from 1983 to 1991 as treasurer for the state of Michigan, and in that position had managed the state's public-employee pension fund. Another partial exception to the rule can be found in the service of company executives on internal committees that oversee their own company pension funds. As formally designated trustees, they of necessity come to appreciate if not mimic the mind of the investment manager. The vice president of investor relations for PepsiCo in 1994, for instance, had joined the company in 1973 as an analyst in its treasury department. Among the positions she held during the ascent to her present post was oversight of the money managers responsible for the company's pension funds. This past experience of investing in the securities market instilled a lingering appreciation for the mentality of the investor.[35]

While the résumés of most company executives list no direct experience in investment management, many executives help oversee their company's own pension assets, and in this role some come to use the short-term yardsticks that they have criticized in others' hands. The chief financial officer of Lamont conceded that he had come to be of two minds on the matter. He was highly critical of the limited investor time horizons that had led to the near takeover of his company. But because he serves on the committee overseeing his firm's own pension fund, he also understood and contributed to short-term investor pressures on other companies: "We ourselves have canned pension advisers because they didn't perform up to the Dow Jones industrial average. . . . If we've got one or two of our people who consistently underperform the indices, they're going to be gone. I think the institutions are in the same situation."

In some instances, however, the reverse also holds. Harrington Stores manages its pension fund with a traditional, and thus relatively short, time frame for evaluating performance. As is the case at many companies, it scatters its pension moneys among a set of outside investment firms (in this case, fifteen of them). The money managers are naturally eager to produce reasonable near-term gains, lest they find themselves sacked. Rather than learning to appreciate the time-constrained mind of the institutional investor, however, this company asked its money managers instead to appreciate the less time-constrained mind of the company manager. The impetus for the change had been the company's own brush with a hostile suitor. A takeover group had abruptly amassed a substantial stake in the company after the firm reported an unexpected drop in earnings, and short-term holders flooded into the company's stock. The firm estimated that within the following four weeks 30 percent to 35 percent of its shares changed ownership, placing one-third of its stock in the hands of those who held it for less than a month. After sounding out investor sentiment, management concluded that the rapidly entering arbitrageurs were not the only ones prepared for rapid trading. Many of the investors with more than a month's stake—including various private pension funds—confessed that they would also be gone tomorrow if the price were right.

Harrington Stores launched an aggressive counterstrategy, ultimately defeating the ownership challenge. But the near miss constituted a chastening experience. In the aftermath, the chief executive sought to personalize his relations with the firm's major investors. And he also instructed his own outside pension-fund managers to rethink their practices. The company general counsel acknowledged the prior inconsistency: "People say 'corporate America' is being two-faced. They're telling raiders, 'stop thinking short term,' while at the same time they're imposing exactly the same standard on their own pension fund managers."

Now cognizant of its own double standard, Harrington Stores pressed for consistency. The company executive responsible for the pension fund dispatched a letter to the outside pension managers to report that the company's investment guidelines had been revised: "No manager shall invest in LBO funds or other funds whose primary purpose is to put companies in play or make them the object of hostile takeover attempts." Moreover, "if a stock that is held by a manager becomes the target of a takeover attempt, the manager need not tender the stock into the offer immediately." The official also reminded the outside managers of a guideline in the 1989 joint statement by the U.S. Department of Labor and Department of the Treasury on pension investments: "It would be proper to weigh the long-term value of the company. . . . [and] the long-term business plan of a target company's management would be relevant." The company would not be hoist with its own petard.

Investor-Relations Directors on the Front Line

Company directors of investor relations are nearest the boundary with the investor world, and it might be expected that at least they would bring direct experience on the other side. Like directors of corporate public affairs, many of whom are recruited from the world of business journalism, directors of investor relations should be as likely as any company managers to have had some personal experience in the world of institutional investing.

The investor-affairs manager for Strikeline Computer Company, for example, had served in an investor-relations capacity with the company for more than a decade, and viewed the divide firmly from that side of the wall. Yet prior to entering the company he had worked the investor side. Over a five-year period he had served as a buy-side trader, then a securities analyst, and finally as a portfolio manager. He no longer represented investors, but he could still appreciate the mind of the owner.[36]

Yet even among directors of investors relations, this is the exception, not the rule. Prior work experience on the investor side remains a rarity. This can be seen in a 1989 survey of 760 such managers by the profession's main association, and in repeat surveys in 1991 and 1994. Table 3.2 shows that the vast majority have come up through corporate finance or communications. Only one in twenty can claim major experience as an analyst, trader, or broker.

Investors Reject the Rejection

Virtually all investment managers reject the right of companies to tell them what time frames should be used in managing their money. Most also defend their own right to advise companies on how to make

**Table 3.2 Primary Past Experience of Company Directors of
Investor Relations, 1989, 1991 and 1994**

Primary Past Experience	1989	1991	1994
Corporate finance	38%	42%	50%
Communications/PR	28	29	24
Analyst/trader/broker	**6**	**6**	**6**
Journalism or law	5	5	2
Operations	3	3	4
Other	20	15	14

Source: National Investor Relations Institute.

money. And many assert their right to question the capacity of company executives to run their own enterprises. While familiar with how company managers portray their alleged shortcomings, money managers are not cowed by it.

Dale Hanson, when he was chief executive of the California Public Employees' Retirement System, defended his prerogatives: "While institutional investors' real expertise is in investing money, this does not mean they are moronic about all other issues." So, "even though investors may not know how to make better widgets, they can certainly find somebody who does."[37]

Still, some investors are cautious about exercising their newfound influence, questioning their own capacity to render useful advice. "The dilemma is," mused the managing partner of a large money-management firm, "do you have the expertise to get involved in running a company?" Given the ambivalent answer to his own question, he had steered his firm toward a select activism, normally saying nothing about company management but occasionally demanding change. "There is something between doing nothing and being in there like the big public funds."

Can Investor Qualifications Be Changed?

While company managers viewed the qualifications of many investors to speak on management issues with some disdain, the investors' inexperience can be viewed in more than one light. It may be seen as an immutable fact. But it may also be characterized as a rectifiable shortcoming. Many company managers veer toward the former interpretation, finding grounds therein for the dismissal of investor suggestions.

Yet company efforts to educate investors inexperienced in the ways of company management could be pursued. Several avenues are feasible. Inviting investors to serve on the company's board, albeit a method that is fraught with other problems, could foster such experience. So too could sustained and open consultation with investors. The comparison with management consultants may be apt here. Management consultants often bring little prior personal experience in senior management positions. They nonetheless add value to corporate management by virtue of their extensive prior consulting work with a range of other companies. If provided more opportunity for sustained and informed consultation on management decisions, investors could presumably learn the same way.

Cases in which the advice of investors was sought by management suggest that such arrangements are feasible though difficult to create in practice. The executives of MFL Network routinely consulted with its largest outside investor. The investor had opposed the formation of a strategic planning office, and the company backed off from creating one. Similarly, the investor had doubted the merits of a major programming decision, and though he joined management's deliberations in their late stages, he nearly convinced the chief executive to delay the decision. Confided the CEO: "We don't do anything important that we don't discuss with him."

Some investors have acquired majority ownership positions permitting them to render authoritative advice to management at will. Kohlberg Kravis Roberts and a number of lesser-known buyout and venture-capital specialists offer continuing consultation to the companies they have acquired through leveraged buyouts. Warren Buffet's Berkshire Hathaway prefers a large minority stake to outright control, but its position has been large enough at such companies as Salomon Inc. (16 percent of the ownership) to ensure that its voice is heard. As a case in point, in 1991–92, when Salomon nearly collapsed in the wake of a bond-trading scandal, Warren Buffet gave himself the reins of power, serving as interim chairman.[38]

One investment firm, Allied Investment Partners, explicitly built a stable of principals who bring management expertise to the table. This, the firm said, aided not only in picking companies that were soundly managed but also in directly overseeing its investments once placed. Like KKR, Warren Buffet, and a handful of other investors, Allied's partners serve on the boards of companies in the portfolio, and it believes that the quality of the directors' service is enhanced by their management backgrounds.[39]

Such arrangements are more prevalent in Europe. In Sweden, for instance, what have been termed "managerial strategic investment companies" take positions in companies and then actively advise management. Their staffs include those who have had active operating experience in company management. In the United States, however, such investor practices remain the rare exception.[40]

Scattered experiences do not constitute a trend, but they do illustrate the potential for involving investors in management decision making, thereby creating the hands-on experience in corporate management that executives criticize them for lacking. In this sense the absence of investor qualifications is cause for concern but does not constitute an unalterable fact.

Illegitimate Investor Authority

The third major line of management critique of its investors questions the very foundation of their authority. Most money managers invest other people's money. In making investment decisions, investors are, in principle, exercising legitimate, delegated authority. In practice, however, they often exercise a counterfeit authority, according to company managers. The money's ultimate owners appear to have virtually no influence over the money managers' decisions. As a consequence, goes the critique, institutions that are tightening company screws are taking such actions without even the tacit approval of the final beneficiaries. The ultimate owners did not approve the actions and, if asked, surely would not back them.

In the view of company managers, then, investor demands sometimes come from a self-perpetuating cadre that fails to represent the best interests of its own constituents. Shades of elite theory are much in evidence here: those in power are portrayed as exercising unresponsive and even illegitimate authority. Shades of agent theory are also evident: those delegated to make the investment decisions are characterized as wayward agents for their owning principals.

The implication of this cultural axiom for company management points in the predictable direction. If the preferences of the ultimate owners are so poorly articulated by those who, in principle, represent them, company managers are again entitled to resist money manager demands.

This managerial critique of investor authority is most persuasive when applied to pension systems offering employees no choice. For other funds, wealth holders retain the option of exit. If dissatisfied with the investment record of a bank-trust department or mutual-fund manager, owners can simply take their assets elsewhere. In many public and private pension funds, however, the beneficiaries are completely captive. Some employers now offer retirement choices, but others still follow a simple formula: if you work here, you join the single sponsored system. If money managers such as Fidelity and Vanguard anchor one end of the beneficiaries' freedom axis, pension funds anchor the other.

The managerial critique of the authority of pension-fund managers could be heard in the executive ranks of the Lamont Company. Its treasurer took issue with all of those investors who voted against his firm during its extended proxy fight, but especially with the public pension funds. The company treasurer and his colleagues had vigorously courted the votes of the public systems, including one in California. The company had a large operation in the state, and its schoolteachers were represented by the California State Teachers' Retirement System. It had voted against the company, and the disfavor still stung. "There are schoolteachers represented by that pension fund. They're teaching kids that are represented by employees of our [X] division in California. If they asked those teachers and employees how they should vote, would it have been the same as the professional manager's vote?" His answer to the rhetorical question was an obvious no. "Does a corporation have a responsibility only to its shareholders? Does it have any responsibility to its community or to its employees?" His answer here was equally obvious: "*We* always thought so."

Pressed to explain how pension managers could veer from their constituents' expected path, some company managers embrace a classic corollary of elite theory. In their view, those who preside over the funds are guided less by their beneficiaries' concerns than by their own professional or political concerns. They constitute a self-perpetuating elite whose selection and socialization is guided by those already in the club, not by those whose fortunes they are pledged to advance. Public pension funds "look at themselves as a profession in their own right," offered Lamont's treasurer. "They don't represent the employees of the state of California, they represent a 'discipline.'"

Company executives identify the discipline as the profession of pension management, noting that some money managers build careers by moving from fund to fund. Executives also see it as the profession of politics because some pension managers appear to harbor political aspirations. Asked why Calpers had played such a visible role in pressing for corporate change, the response of the manager of investor relations at Richard Oil Corporation is typical. "I think it's political," he said. Simply put: "Dale Hanson would like to run for political office eventually."

Company managers hope for but do not soon expect a depoliticized investor world. They appreciate the political constraints and incentives that come with operating a public pension fund. They are sometimes bemused or angered by the behavior that follows.

The chief executive of Richards Oil had been invited to meet with the head of a New York public pension fund. In the midst of a proxy fight such invitations could not be turned down, nor, he found, could the agenda be controlled. As the chief executive arrived at the fund's headquarters, the money executive announced that he would like a "press opportunity" and immediately invited in a bevy of photographers. During the closed-door meeting that followed, the pension executive and several associates asked a few desultory questions of the oil CEO but quickly adjourned the private meeting. The pension executive then walked the company executive out to a prearranged press conference. In the firm's private view, the meeting achieved little more than furnishing the pension executive, an elected official, with an opportunity for the voters to see him with a captain of industry, "hat in hand."

Many company managers expect better. "You've got to hope that the investors live up to their end of the bargain," offered the oil company's investor-relations manager. "If you're willing to share all of this information, then they should have the quality people in place who can understand it and be responsible." But the continuing irresponsibility remained an irritant. As perceived in company headquarters, some of the public funds served their beneficiaries last by following their political instincts first. "These public funds really have to struggle . . . to keep [investment decisions] away from politics," concluded the Richards Oil manager. "It's not going to do them any good in the long run [to be political]. If I were a beneficiary, and I knew the way some of the [pension managers] operate, I would be very upset."

The United Shareholders Association, a frequent sponsor of proxy resolutions and self-designated promoter of the shareholder, especially the small holder, was viewed in an equally disparaging light by company executives until its closing in 1993. Its founder and chairman, Boone Pickens, was deemed more self-interested than cause directed. "Pickens early on was critical of us," observed the chief executive of National Metal Products. "He was outlandish in what he was trying to do. . . . We've always regarded him as a self-promoter who really isn't interested in anything but Boone Pickens' welfare." The hypocrisy seemed evident: "He does it under the cover of trying to be a positive influence for shareholders."

Again, managerial portrayal of this investor deficit has more plausible persuasiveness than factual basis. Management critics possess scant detail on either the funds' internal operations or their unprofessional behavior.

Supportive evidence is there to be found. Consider just one area where a substantial research literature has developed—the quality of management of state and local retirements systems. On two grounds, company executives could acquire scholarly ammunition to bolster their view. First, of the public retirement systems, a substantial fraction—about one in six—is underfunded. State and local pensions on average are squirreling away less than $9 for every $10 they will need for future payments. Second, the public pension funds are less than paragons of administrative virtue. A detailed analysis of 197 funds in 1992 reveals, for instance, that on average they operated with only 65 percent efficiency, signifying that they themselves have fallen short in applying the principles of cost reduction and return optimization to their own houses.[41]

Research evidence, however, does not constitute the foundation of company critiques of investor qualification. Much of the criticism is rooted in the conflict, each side constructing a post hoc rationale for denigrating the motives and behavior of the other. Company managers required little hard evidence before drawing the basic conclusion that money managers are themselves in glass houses and should not be throwing such big stones at executive mansions.

Resistance Allies

Company executives are not the only opponents of unbridled investor influence. Their culture of complaint finds unlikely but ready allies in small shareholders, government officials, labor unions, displaced workers, even popular culture. Such allies contribute little direct aid, but in siding with management they are a source of comfort.

The alliance of small stockholders stems from their differences with large holders. Though united in ownership, individual and institutional investors sharply diverge in their perceptions of how the stock market operates and who benefits. A 1993 survey of 680 individual investors by Louis Harris revealed widespread suspicion among small shareholders regarding their larger—and seemingly privileged—brethren. Two-fifths believed that stock-market rules gave large holders better access to company information, and three-fifths asserted that the market generally favored big investors over small.[42]

Small holders also ally with management in rejecting the right of big holders to influence company policies. Only one in five of the surveyed individual stockholders agreed that institutional investors should have major influence on companies. They also sided with management in questioning the ability of money managers to represent the ultimate owners. Three in five of the small investors said money managers should seek the counsel of the true owners before voting company proxies. A similar majority said that institutions should cast their ballots in accord with true owners' preferences rather than fund managers' predilections. The latter distinction is of no small moment. Studies of proxy voting on poison pills and company prerogatives show large differences, with small holders far more often backing management.[43]

The alliance of government officials with company management stems from other differences with large holders. Neither insider information nor institutional favoritism is a driver here. Rather, it is the loss of jobs, the unseemly downsizing, that vexes the public servant. For elected officials whose fortunes rise and fall with the mood of the electorate, investor-inspired cutbacks offered little comfort. Institutional investors, they believe, promote and applaud the reduction in personnel. "Enthusiasm for corporate downsizing is particularly strong among large institutional investors like pension funds," charged the U.S. Secretary of Labor in 1993. "Pension-fund managers are quick to defend their new appetite for corporate downsizings," but, he warned, "investors—especially large institutional investors like pension funds—[should] reconsider their assumptions. Rather than pressure firms to cut payrolls, they may do better to insist that companies invest more in their workers."[44]

Congress also targeted investor myopia. The Excessive Churning and Speculation Act of 1989, a bill introduced in the U.S. Senate, pressed institutional investors to move beyond their short-term mentality. The legislation's sponsor offered the rationale: "Production and innovation require long-term commitments. Corporate America, however, is increasingly being acquired by institutional investors having only a transient interest in the companies that they own and control."[45]

Organized labor finds common cause here as well. In 1994, when AT&T announced a layoff of 15,000 of its 100,000 long-distance workers, the Communications Workers of America, one of its major unions, pointed its finger at large investors. "Here's another example of a healthy company," complained a union vice president, "playing to Wall Street and looking for a quick cost-cutting fix."[46]

Company employees who had been ousted by downsizing themselves also see the shadowy hand of shareholder impatience in layoff decisions. "It's quarter-by-quarter management," complained one employee of a contracting firm. Said another, "We have these long-range strategic plans, but they seem kind of pie-in-the-sky because we are always focusing quarter by quarter." The implications of short-term shortfalls seemed evident to all: "If we don't make a profit at the end of the first quarter," warned a third employee, "more people . . . are going to be cut, and they'll just keep cutting and cutting until they make a profit."[47]

Aggrieved professional groups join the chorus. With industry positions for scientists and engineers in decline, and industry R&D in eclipse, research scientists could detect Wall Street's evil hand. "Corporations are concerned with tomorrow's stock value and the next quarterly income statement," complained one of the nation's leading physicists, "and have lost interest in promoting applied research."[48]

For individual investors the rising institutional power is seen as worsening their own disenfranchisement. For government officials, the rising institutional activism is viewed as compounding their political problems. For labor unions and affected employees, investor influence is held responsible for much of the corporate downsizing. For scientists, big shareholders are undercutting the nation's research. These groups, often critical of company management, on this issue had become its odd bedfellows.

This culture of complaint has entered our popular culture. Dismay over investor-driven shortsightedness has become such a commonplace that it could serve as a convenient conversational filler akin to weather, family, and sports. The criticism even appears in popular films, which are often an arbiter of what will become axiomatic.

In Clint Eastwood's 1993 film, *In the Line of Fire,* a would-be presidential assassin, played by John Malkovich, is meeting with the chairman of the president's California campaign fund. Protecting the president is Eastwood himself, a veteran Secret Service agent still haunted by the fact that years earlier he was on duty when John F. Kennedy was assassinated. The agent knows of a plot but has failed so far to identify the would-be assailant. The assassin and the California fund-raising chairman are taking a few moments in a hotel lounge to warm up their acquaintanceship when Clint Eastwood breaks into the conversational circle to take the chairman aside, not realizing that Malkovich, the assassin himself, is a part of the circle. Moments before Eastwood's close but unknowing encounter with the assassin, Malkovich had been engaging the fund-raising chairman with one of the clichés that had come to fill such moments: "Your average American businessman," he mused, "looks at a product, a marketing scheme, what have you. He sees the length and width of it. The Japanese see the depth, the long-term effect. We look at the next fiscal quarter. The Japanese look at the next quarter-century."[49]

Further Protection

While corporate culture and its popular support give management a persuasive rationale for resisting shareholder pressures, the power of positive thought is not always sufficient. Companies have added both standard antitakeover measures and more customized devices. Some companies find special protection, for instance, in the continuing presence of founding-family fortunes. These families retain large blocks of stock in the companies, maintain a presence on their boards, place members in senior positions, and let it be known that tender offers for their companies would be decidedly unwelcome. Other corporations create the equivalent by bringing in a large outside investor pledged to resisting a takeover challenge. The outsider acquires such a dominant position that efforts to unseat incumbent management or force policy changes would almost surely require the outsider's acquiescence. To unequivocally signify that such an acceptance would not be forthcoming, the investor and chief executives at one company went so far as to sign an agreement granting management voting authority over the investor's stock. The investor formally conferred for a decade "an irrevocable proxy to vote any shares" on the CEO or his successors.

Such governance devices prove popular management tools. They are rooted, however, in a management ideology that views them not as cynical mechanisms for executive entrenchment but rather as affirmative mechanisms for shareholder advancement. In this way, management culture serves as an encompassing framework for rebuffing investor demands. It redefines what might be deemed narrowly interested acts of managerial resistance as broadly oriented acts of ownership advancement.

A generation of managers had come to high office through the exercise of power over the corporation. A generation of investors now believes with equal conviction that it should rightfully share in that power. Major shareholders are no longer shy about expressing their opinions on many such matters, especially when companies falter. But company executives are still prepared to use their advice selectively, if at all, because investors have yet to prove themselves fully worthy of attention.

4

$\mathcal{S}$

Vanquishing Opponents

STOCKHOLDERS RETAIN ULTIMATE AUTHORITY over company directors and managers. While managers and directors come and go, owners remain. After all, executives are only the owners' hired management agents, temporarily placed in high office to build shareholder fortunes. And directors are, of course, the owners' appointed monitoring agents, momentarily assigned to ensure that fortunes are indeed built. If either directors or managers falter, if company value declines, shareholders can invoke their legal right to discharge either or both. If ownership means anything, it means the right to remove those who fail.

Though the theory here is straightforward and is encoded in both corporate culture and law, the practical reality is less clear cut.[1] Executives sometimes do just the opposite of what theory allows. Rather than accede to owner demands, they seek new owners. Instead of sharing their power with active owners, they recruit inactive ones. The replacement chain, as a result, resembles less an authoritative hierarchy and more a business variant on the child's circular game of scissors–paper–rock. Shareholders can replace directors, directors can replace managers, and managers in turn can replace shareholders.

The relationships between owners and managers thus bear a certain symmetry under investor capitalism. Organizations are better aligned to meet shareholder interests. But shareholders are also better aligned to meet organizational interests. Investors sometimes throw out underperforming managements, and managements sometimes jettison overly controlling investors.

The displacement of opposing parties remains an infrequent event. Though executives are fired, directors retired, and investors displaced from time to time, these are the moments that punctuate rather than define equilibrium. Still, implied but unapplied threats, akin to strategic deterrence during the cold war, can serve the contending parties well. Even if never finally deployed, disciplinary value is to be found in their potential use. Replacing opponents is therefore a weapon of last resort under investor capitalism, a useful threat but one rarely enacted and then only after the last best alternative has clearly failed.

During the late 1980s and 1990s, contending parties concluded on occasion that the better alternatives had failed. Shareholders developed a new arsenal of strategies for pressing executives, yet managements had also constructed a counter-repertoire for resisting, with each new investor challenge met by an equally effective company defense. With the contending parties deadlocked, replacement emerged as a weapon of final choice. Thwarted in purpose, adversaries pressed to remove their rivals from power, and eliminate all they stood for.

Replacement initiatives emerge into public view on occasion. Company directors dismissed their top executives at General Motors, Digital Equipment, IBM, Eastman Kodak, Westinghouse, American Express, and Borden in 1992–93, and at Morrison Knudsen, W. R. Grace, Bank of Boston, and Kmart Corporation in 1994–95. Yet these publicized events constituted only the most visible edge of a more widespread development. Investors and directors more commonly pursue their replacement initiatives behind the scenes, quietly forcing what later comes to be portrayed as purely voluntary, a decision to pursue "one's interests elsewhere." Even less visible are the quiet campaigns by companies to replace activist investors with more passive owners. Corporate managers exercise strategies—rarely seen but often practiced—for attracting "good" owners and avoiding the bad.

Exploration of this terrain begins with an illustrative change in the membership of one company's governing board. It then turns to the broader contours of the replacement landscape, exploring how and when executives displace their shareholders, shareholders replace their executives, and both remove their directors.

A Fateful Replacement

The chief executive of Capital Cities/ABC had warned the analysts that, through no fault of his own, his company had stumbled into an open manhole in the aftermath of the Gulf War. If the claim he offered was persuasive, stock analysts might be forgiving. In this case, it was, and they were. Richards Oil Corporation was not so fortunate. It too had stumbled into an open manhole, but one clearly of its own making. Shareholders may discount a company's plight when it is occasioned by a slack economy or a quirk of history. They can be unforgiving when the company's distress is brought on by its own leadership.

So deep was the petroleum company's manhole and so clearly was top management responsible for it that the firm's share price plummeted and takeover prospects mounted. One of the major buyout figures stepped forward, and incumbent management followed the well-trod path of bolstering its incumbency by securing support pledges from its largest shareholders. Richards' chief executive and his associates pleaded with the major institutions. One of the largest, most active, and most influential holders offered a quid pro quo. It would back management against the raider if the chief executive would replace one of his directors with a nominee of the investor's own choosing. The company agreed, and the investor furnished a list of twelve acceptable candidates.

By fortuitous circumstance, one of the twelve candidates also appeared on a list of five director prospects that an executive search firm had already prepared for the company. The coincidence furnished company executives with a win–win opportunity. The firm could select a candidate it had privately wanted anyway, and public credit could go to the activist investor. In management's view, the activist investor had little real interest in having somebody on the board who "represents their interests." The symbolic motive, as the director of investor relations saw it, was for the fund to be able to say, "I forced [the company] to have a director of my choosing on the board."

The investor's noisy victory and the company's quiet gain, however, did not come without costs. "What do you mean he's going to be the public funds' director?" came the angry (though privately expressed) objection from a nonpension money manager. "I don't want any director there representing those characters." Executives of other corporations also privately voiced their reservations to the company. The outside director's publicized appointment, they feared, would soon be used as precedent to compel them to do the same. The petroleum executives responded that they had planned to select the person anyway.

Richards Oil looked to fill two directorships as it prepared its proxy statement for the annual spring stockholders meeting. One position on the board was open due to a retirement, the other created in response to the investor's demand. To ensure that the nominees were fully aware of their legal responsibilities and liabilities, the chief executive dispatched his general counsel to meet the two leading candidates, including the individual suggested by the investor. One of the candidates resided in London, the other in New York City, and the general counsel arranged to see them in that order a few days before Christmas.

Richards' attorney visited the first candidate, in London, and then telephoned the chief executive in New York. Their conversation turned to the next day's scheduled meeting back in New York between the attorney and the second nominee. (On learning that the recent pace of events had prevented the general counsel from any holiday shopping for his family, the CEO suggested that the attorney delay his return flight and spend the afternoon shopping at Harrods. The general counsel called Pan American to rebook his flight, number 103, for the next day. Later that evening he learned that flight 103 had vanished somewhere over Scotland.)

On returning to New York City the following day, the general counsel briefed the other director nominee. In the months that followed, shareholders duly elected the new directors to the board, the takeover threat eventually dissipated, and the oil company gradually restored itself to financial health. Through numerous steps large and small, including a restructuring of the board, Richards Oil managed to climb out of its own manhole. Its general counsel appreciated the decisions large and small that his CEO had taken.

Displacing Investors

Much of a corporate executive's day is consumed by requests, proposals, and problems. In the course of a morning, the executive may meet with a divisional manager seeking a new capital investment, another divisional manager asking approval for a strategic alliance, and a third warning of a sales battering in a weak market. As the afternoon progresses, the executive learns that a senior manager is being wooed by a competitor, a regulator is challenging company compliance, and a production manager wants approval to build a facility abroad. When investors add their concerns to the executive's day, whether these concerns involve the downgrading of the stock or the threatening of a proxy proposal, their problems are appended to an already lengthy list. From the executive's standpoint, investor entreaties cannot be entirely ignored. At the same time, they come as only one among a diverse array of demands to which the executive must daily listen if not always respond.

One avenue for managing the investor pressures is by removing their source. Stilling ownership demands by changing the owners would seem to contradict capitalist orthodoxy. For the unorthodox, nonetheless, it can serve as an appealing solution. Management by mitigation—the outright elimination of the most meddlesome elements—could be viewed in the same vein as a dismissal of a disgruntled manager of a plant or office. The manager who finally challenges or criticizes the home office once too often, the long-standing thorn in the side, can simply be removed. So, too, at times, can the most meddlesome investors.[2]

If changing shareholders is conceptually an unnatural act, for most companies the practical steps for doing so are not. Companies had already built sophisticated offices for orchestrating their relations with a host of external constituencies, ranging from the White House to charitable funds and environmental activists. By the early 1980s, most of the nation's largest companies had established full-time public affairs offices. Professional staff, under the direction of a senior manager, often reporting to the chief executive, had mastered the use of media contacts, political action committees, company foundations, lobbyists, and other devices for controlling and shaping the company's public environment. Extending the management of public affairs to the management of shareholder affairs was therefore a natural extension of power that companies had already learned to wield elsewhere.[3]

Attracting some shareholders over others, however, cannot be achieved through executive fiat. A company's ability to reshape its shareholder base is inherently constrained by the owners' open choice of whether or not to invest. Within certain limits set by U.S. securities regulations, unwanted owners are free to acquire or retain any stake they wish. And company-preferred replacements are under no compulsion to buy. Moreover, individual and institutional preferences for a company's stock, and their final decision to buy or sell it, are shaped by market trends, analyst recommendations, and other factors well beyond management's reach.

Restructuring the shareholder base thus depends upon a successful promotion of company shares among preferred groups, and a studied avoidance of others. Here, too, companies can draw upon an accumulated organizational expertise—in this case, the marketing of products and services. Promoting shares should be seen, in the words of a consultant, as "a marketing function that employs public relations tools to further the financial goals" of the firm. And to achieve those goals, offers another consultant, "marketing stock can be more important than marketing a product." Many of those in the business have come to see shareholding in part as a marketing issue. The chief executive of Richards Oil views investor relations as part of a more general management of the competitive fray: "We compete for shareholders just as we compete for customers at the pump." The investor-relations man-

ager for the Strikeline Computer Company is fond of telling people
that he is a "salesman" just like the other 7,500 salespeople on the
company's payroll. The only difference is in the product. They sell computers for the company, he sells the company "as an investment vehicle." For him, the competition is not other companies in the same industry competing for the same customers, but other large companies in
several industries competing for the same investors. To some, marketing shares has become as significant as market share.[4]

Companies employ a range of actions to reconstitute their ownership base in what is often known as a "shareholder mix" campaign. The
tactics include meeting with some shareholders and not others; selectively working with brokers whose clients are among the preferred
groups; splitting the stock to lower the price per share (thus making it
more attractive to small investors); tailoring the company's communications to match shareholder concerns; expanding stock-based compensation among managers; facilitating shareholder reinvestment of
stock dividends in additional company shares; providing for the direct
(nonbrokered) purchase of company stock; and creating employee
stock-ownership programs to build inside ownership.[5]

More Individual Ownership, Less Institutional

In the minds of many company officials, institutional owners are
often too meddlesome, while individual owners are almost always vir-
tuous. A company strategy for altering the relative mix of the institutional and individual holding thus promises relief if dissident investors
can be eased out in favor of more "patriotic" owners. Short-term
investors can be pushed aside in favor of more patient owners. When
successful, the firm will have reduced shareholder pressure without
appearing to compromise the integrity of ownership supremacy.

Companies most commonly embrace the general strategy of replacing institutional holders with individual owners, especially company
employees. Because of their modest holdings, most individual investors
are generally not in a position to pressure a firm directly. When given a
chance to vote on company policies, they side with management far
more often than do institutional investors. And if small holders tend
toward passive loyalty, employee holders tend toward active support of
management. This is in part because their personal livelihood is tied to
incumbent management, and in part because they are more vulnerable
to direct persuasion from top management.[6]

The managerial conception of the employee owner is thus one of
implicit alliance, especially during contests for corporate control or
when activist institutions are pressing a proxy challenge. The chief exec-

utive of National Metal Products applauds the steadfastness of his inside owners during several bruising proxy struggles. "Our retirees and employed individual shareholders are much more stable owners," he says. "They don't face the kind of pressure that the institutional investors themselves face." He knows that the employee holders will remain loyal when others are not, and he knows he can count on their proxy support.

For similar reasons, the chief executive of Richards Oil laments a loss of small holders from his shareholder roster: "Individuals are a proportionately smaller presence for us now [and] this is unfortunate, since they tend to be loyal, long-term holders." He offers the observation from hard experience. During the company's several proxy fights, the institutions had split down the middle. By contrast, 99 percent of the individual holders had voted with the company. Compared to other groups of shareholders, employee stockholders, then, are generally considered management's staunchest allies when a company's roof threatens to collapse.[7]

The extent to which employee and other "safe" individual ownership can be enhanced through concerted intervention can be seen in McDonald's Corporation actions during the 1986–94 period. The company expressed fears about excessive volatility in stock price that it believed came with high institutional ownership. "The risk of high institutional ownership is the risk of the herd mentality," warned McDonald's vice president for financial communications and investor relations. "I don't know how [investor-relations] people can sleep at night with extremely high institutional ownership." The company encouraged employee, supplier, and franchisee shareholding through a variety of programs, wrapped, as is typical of such initiatives, in the ideology of general benefit. "[W]e believe," the company asserted, that employee "share ownership encourages performance that serves the long-range interests of shareholders." Between 1986 and 1994, the company doubled the fraction of ownership—from 7 percent to 15 percent—in the hands of its individual employees, suppliers, and franchisees (figure 4.1).[8]

Stewart Drugs achieved a comparable change in its shareholder base. Institutional holdings had reached 70 percent by 1986, and that had triggered an internal examination of why large investor holdings had grown so much in recent years. The rise of institutional holdings in the market at large was of course recognized. But the company also concluded that its own practices had unwittingly contributed as well. As a result, to reverse the mix, Stewart refocused some of its attention away from the institutions—which had previously received virtually all of it—to smaller holders. The executive responsible for investor rela-

**Figure 4.1 McDonald's Corporation's Share of Ownership
by Employees, Franchisees, and Suppliers, 1986-94**

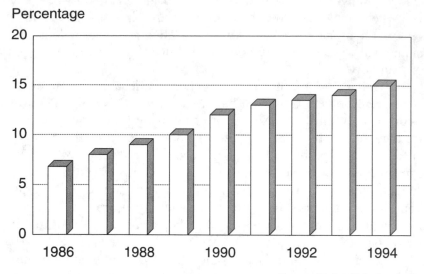

Source: McDonald's Corporation.

tions launched a round of visits to retail brokers across the country. The visits required patience. Institutional holders generally knew the company and industry well, but with the retail world, it was another story. "They kind of scratch their heads," he complained. "They don't even know if aspirin is the same or different from Advil" (it is different).

The campaign's launch also proved propitious, since Stewart Drugs was about to bring out a new hair-growth product expected to reach large numbers of consumers. "We figured that with this [product] coming out . . . it was a perfect opportunity," observed the executive. "Every bald head in America is going to buy this product, and [we might expect them] to buy a couple of shares at the same time." Consumers, he concluded, "want a little piece of the rock."

Stewart Drugs drove its shareholder-mix program by first splitting the stock. The company had been advised that individuals often acquire shares in blocks of 1,000, and the share's current price near $80 put the purchase out of the reach of many. Following a three-for-one split, individuals came back in droves, as predicted, and the company managed to restore individual holdings to a majority of its shares within four years (figure 4.2). The number of shareholders also doubled. Concluded the executive (now president), who had engineered the change: "It was miraculous."

While individuals steadily moved into the stock of McDonald's and Stewart Drugs through concerted company action, company action can

Figure 4.2 Percentage of Stewart Drugs Shares Held by Individual Investors, and No. of Holders, 1986-91

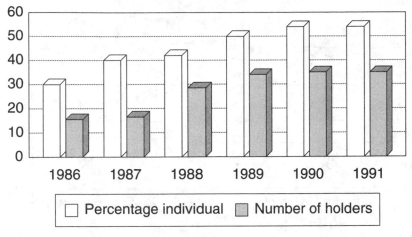

Percentage of shares held; thousands of holders

□ Percentage individual   ■ Number of holders

Source: Company records. Note: Holder number and % data
for 1991 are for 1st quarter; other data are for 4th quarter.

also lead individual holders to move out. One of the manufacturing companies in this study had teetered on the edge of financial disaster in 1987. As shown in figure 4.3, individuals sold off their shares in droves, with institutions picking up the slack (at bargain prices). Individuals held 55 percent of the shares a year before the disaster, 35 percent a year after.

The manufacturing company set out to undercut this institutional hegemony. Beginning in the early 1990s, the firm actively cultivated the small holder, instituting a direct purchase program that allowed individuals to buy company stock directly without going through a broker. "We try to encourage individual investors by making it easy for them to buy shares," offered the CEO. The "philosophy" underlying the program, reported the director of investor relations, "is that registered individual shareholders are loyal. They don't trade stock, so they reduce the volatility in the stock." In 1991, the individual percentage rose by three points, and in 1992 by two more points. Despite the modest trend reversal, the CEO confessed that he could only partially buck the market's growing concentration: "I'm realistic," he concluded, "that large holders will continue to increase."

Other companies have also concluded that, in the absence of well-known consumer products of their own, a shareholder campaign will be uphill. "We're not an individual-household word," complains the chief financial officer of Chase Chemical Products. The company neither sells

Figure 4.3 Individual and Institutional Shareholding in a Large Corporation, 1986-90

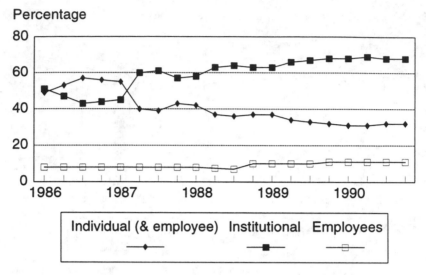

Source: Company documents.

nor advertises to the general public, depriving its name and stock of any general recognition. With individuals increasingly turning to mutual funds rather than direct investing and thus even less drawn to less well-known stocks, "We don't have the natural fit for retail ownership," the CFO concludes.

Companies with household products, however, often do seek increased individual holdings by playing on their name recognition. A productive avenue for doing this is through the thousands of small-investor clubs that have formed across the country in recent decades, clubs that go directly to the grass roots. These are tiny associations created to help members better manage their personal holdings. The typical club in 1994 had but 12 members and a portfolio valued at a mere $89,000. But the number of such associations is enormous. Clubs affiliated with the main national organization, the National Association of Investors Corporation, doubled from 1984 to 1994, reaching more than 11,000 nationwide. Membership more than doubled as well, cresting at over a quarter-million small holders.

Club members love the stocks of prominent consumer companies. Product familiarity evidently gives comfort to small holders. In 1994, McDonald's shares are the number-one pick of club members, with Wal-Mart Stores, PepsiCo, Merck, AT&T, and Walt Disney close behind. Sensing a natural market for the sale of even more shares, companies directly market their stock through such grass-roots groups. *Better*

Investing, the association's monthly magazine, reaches some 175,000 readers, and major corporations regularly tout their stock there. A 1993 issue of *Better Investing* brought McDonald's plea to these micro-worlds of the small holder: "Wouldn't you like to be part of our world?" asked a colorful advertisement for the company's global expansion into Beijing, Budapest, and Buenos Aires. If so, the company is at the ready to provide information to those who see "McDonald's as a global investment opportunity." So too is Texaco looking for the investor who wants to "own your share of America through Texaco." Still other companies extol their performance records and their programs for direct stock purchase and dividend reinvestment.[9]

Some companies seek more institutional ownership generally but studiously avoid visits to potentially troublesome institutions. Chase Chemical, for instance, has developed a list of fifty targets, investors whose holding profiles include similar companies but not itself. It sends company information and reports to the targeted buyers, and a manager then places cold calls to them. But such calls are not placed to all logical targets. We "want to be very careful about institutions who might be viewed as overly activist in a negative way," cautions the vice president for financial communications. The company does not discourage their ownership, and it would certainly host a visit to the company by any of these institutions that requested one. But it also takes no steps to encourage their ownership.

Others companies sharpened the blade by playing on the international boycott of South African business. Many public pension funds were prohibited by state and local law or regulation during the late 1980s and early 1990s from investing in companies engaged in South African business. In 1993, near the end of apartheid, a third of the nation's nearly 300 state and local public pension funds could not invest in companies dealing with South Africa, and it was among these that many of the most active funds are found. Several companies remaining in South Africa thus fortuitously benefited in their minds from the fact that their South African presence tended to repel activist funds, a kind of poison pill against the unwanted.[10]

Most companies have reconciled themselves to a future in which a majority of their shares are held by institutional investors. But many nonetheless seek to dilute the fraction held by any single institution through expansion of the number of institutions. Slightly more than 400 institutions hold stakes in Columbia Foods, controlling nearly two-thirds of its shares. The company does not expect to reduce the overall fraction, but it does want to see more institutions a part of it, each with a smaller slice. To that end the manager of investor relations regularly examines the ownership profiles of all major competitors, searching for those institutions drawn to the food business but not yet drawn to his own company. They become his primary targets for stock marketing.

Odd Lotters Can Be Too Expensive

To appreciate the individual shareholder advantage, however, is not necessarily to act upon it. It also has to be feasible and cost effective. Despite an evident vulnerability to institutionally backed takeover threats, National Metal Products actually moved in the opposite direction. It sought to repurchase its "odd lots," individually held shares in sets of less than 100. The chief financial officer concluded that handling accounts that only numbered in the double digits had become too expensive. "We recognized at the time that we would be chasing out some people who would be loyal voters for us," observed the CFO. But the magnitude of the holdings even in the aggregate, he concluded, would be "lost in the rounding anyway."

(A certain nostalgia colored National Metal Products' loss of its odd lotters. During several proxy battles, managers had often relished their lobbying calls to small holders. Among those reached were life-long holders in their nineties, including numerous ex-employees. Many expressed delight on receiving a call from the top management of the corporation that they had long known but rarely, if ever, heard from personally. After listening to the company's appeal for proxy support, some insisted on turning to such topics as their families or gardens. Others plaintively closed, "Why don't you call again?" Personal loyalty and the novelty of contact with nonagenarians aside, however, the company deemed the odd-lotters' numbers too small to justify the continuing expense of managing them.)

The broadcasting company has arrived at a similar conclusion. Some two-thirds of MFL Network's shares are already in institutional hands. Its stock trades at a price of several hundred dollars, a level considered prohibitive by many individual investors. Several brokerage houses had been pressing the firm to split the stock to make it more attractive to their retail customers. Even employees found the shares prohibitively expensive. A twenty-five-year veteran of the company reminisced that one of his fondest early memories was of finally saving enough to buy *one* share. The company, however, expresses no interest in the possibility of a split. Its tea leaves suggest that the small number of remaining small holders are relics of the past. Says the director of investor relations: "There are those who say there are no individual investors left. That's a gross overstatement, but there is a kernel of truth there. To spend your time wooing individual investors is really not cost effective." The company understands that in following the corporate trend it is also relinquishing a security blanket. The director knows that small holders often lock their shares in safe-deposit boxes, creating an immovable ownership foundation "that might come in handy one day." The company has nonetheless concluded the costs outweigh the benefits. So confident is the company in its strategic formula that it calculates it had little to fear in any case since, the director avows, those "rainy days don't come around" here.

Harrington Stores also concludes that although individual shareholders are certain loyalists, the costs of recruiting and retaining them have come to outweigh the advantages. Executives have discussed the possibility of an individual-shareholder campaign for several years. Individuals are known for their commitment (desirable), but also for their remoteness (undesirable). "Even though they're long-term holders," says the manager of investor affairs, "they have very little impact on any decisions or proxy issues" because of the extent to which their numbers have dwindled: only 15 percent of the company's shares remain in individual hands. The company sees the small shareholders as faithful but simply too expensive to manage.

Matching Company Strategy with Shareholder Mix

Companies also seek to rework their shareholder base if the mix does not match the firm's strategy. If a corporation expects slow growth, patient investors are required. If it plans global expansion, international investors are needed. If it anticipates cyclical earnings, understanding investors are essential.

Companies know that money managers adopt highly varied investment strategies. Some investors pursue a growth strategy, others want steady earnings. Fidelity's Equity-Income Fund, for instance, stresses stocks with income records, placing capital appreciation as a secondary objective. Fidelity's Magellan Fund, by contrast, prefers stocks with potential for capital appreciation, making income a lesser goal. If a company alters its strategy, perhaps thereby moving into a period of faster expansion but slower earnings, it will also sometimes seek to catalyze a corresponding change in the investor base, bringing in more Magellan-type holders and fewer Equity-Income–type holders.

The chief financial officer for the pharmaceutical company Stewart Drugs sees investor relations in much this way, a matter of strategic alignment: "We want to manage for the long term, and we want owners who are long term." Unfortunately, his current owners think otherwise. Rather than bring enterprise strategy in line with owner preferences, however, Stewart managers have chosen to bring their preferences in line with its strategy. "Our objective now," says the CFO, "is to align the

ownership of the company with where the management wants to go."
To serve that objective, he concludes, there was no alternative but to
"change the shareholder base."

To identify those institutional investors who are a better match for
management objectives, companies often turn to databases that track,
analyze, and classify the nation's 2,000 major investors. Institutional
investors are required to file 13F reports on a quarterly basis with the
U.S. Securities and Exchange Commission, statements detailing the
money managers' investment portfolios. Several commercial services
(such as CDA, Contrac, Technimetrics, and Vickers) compile the data in
convenient databases that come with user-friendly software for pin-
pointing both desirable and undesirable institutional holders.

Consider, for instance, a company that views itself as subject to too
much pressure from short-term investors given the longer-term growth
strategy it has adopted. A first step is to sift through one of the databases to identify the firm's present long-term holders, those institutions
that have held large blocks of stock for many quarters. The company
then studies the investment strategies of these patient owners. The
analysis might characterize the patient investors in terms of the weight
they place on such criteria as growth (versus value), market capitalization, proxy policies, and economic trends (some investors move holdings from industry to industry in response to macroeconomic forecasts).
With that profile in mind, company managers then comb the data for
other investors that have similar profiles but which are not yet invested
or are relatively underinvested in the company. They are natural targets, and if the investors are large enough, top management will then
arrange a personal visit to pitch its stock. "Companies are learning how
to see themselves as investors see them," offers a seasoned observer.
They have learned how to zero in on the targets that best fit their corporate strategy. This kind of data-based market intelligence permits
companies to remake their shareholder base to more precisely match
the mix they want.[11]

Many institutions recognize on their own when a company has
made a strategic shift, and they need little prodding by the company to
buy in or sell out. For institutions slower to appreciate the change, however, managements are prepared to provide a personal reeducation.
Harrington Stores, for example, has found that the mix of its shareholder base has moved away from growth-oriented investors toward
value-oriented holders. But its managers worry, given their plans for the
future, that the shift has gone too far. The loss of the growth investors
has been particularly evident during periods of stock-price decline, and
it is then that the company has intervened to dampen the exodus. Its
largest growth-oriented investor, for example, disposed of some 750,000

shares during one brief period. The company as a result initiated monthly contact with this and other growth investors, urging them to slow or reverse their defection.

Unstable holdings constitute a downside of a growth-focused base. Investors move in and out of the shares, depending on whether the company's growth looks robust or anemic. The resulting profit taking is well understood by company managers if never much appreciated. Some growth-oriented holders even warn the company of their impending outward movement and explain, with a shrug. "Hey, it's not a reflection of how I feel about" Harrington Stores, one investor explained to an company executive, "but I'm taking my profits."

But other things being equal, most companies prefer stability over fluidity. To this end, some devote more time and attention to longer-term investors, whatever their investment strategies or proxy activism. Harrington Stores follows such an approach, for reasons of both push and pull. "It's in our better interests to continue to cultivate these people who are willing to hold us and show some stability," offers the manager of investor affairs. "They are the ones who generally tend to show more interest" in talking with the company. Such investors contact the company more often than others. They more frequently share their financial models for the company's earnings. And they call more often to discuss what they have heard or read from sell-side analysts. Company managers readily embrace the dialogue. It constitute one means for retaining a shareholder base rich in long-term investor presence.

Still, companies recognize that most of their major holders inevitably adjust their holdings from time to time. Examination of virtually any quarterly listings for virtually any company holdings reveals that most institutions have bought or sold some stock during the previous three months. The indexers change little, as do a few long-term holders. But most institutions change some. A university endowment fund, for instance, which is one of the two largest investors in Columbia Foods, has maintained an almost unchanged position in the company for years. So too has a private pension fund. Two large commercial bank trust departments with indexed funds also make only minor adjustments from time to time. But most of Columbia Foods' remaining institutional investors find reason to make major adjustments frequently, sometimes exiting altogether only to reappear a year or two later. The chief executive has become philosophical about an evolving shareholder base over which, at best, he could exercise only modest control. He knows that on hitting certain targets or following certain criteria, many investors will cash out. But he also expects many to reappear later on, and he does what he can to facilitate their return. "People rotate in and out of [our] stock," he says. "This myth that 'once a shareholder, always a shareholder' is crazy. Anybody that's managing their money that way should be shot."

Selling Products to Shareholders

A company's marketing of its shares to customers contains the potential for a related application as well. Why not sell products or services to one's individual shareholders? After all, they are already familiar with the firm, they presumably believe in its products or services, and they are certainly interested in its prosperity. They are also on a time-tested mailing list for quarterly communication. The ready-made opportunity to reach this unique set of natural customers is something that certain firms cannot pass up.

A limited number of companies developed formal programs for selling goods or services to their individual shareholders by the 1990s. According to a 1993 survey of 111 large companies with brand-name recognition in such areas as food, telecommunications, financial services, and automobiles, one in five had actively taken to promoting its products or services through this kind of cross-marketing. Such programs typically include the insertion of advertising materials in shareholder mailings, additional direct-mail campaigns, and discounts for shareholders on products or services. Some even tout product discounts as an incentive. IBM offered its stockholders a 10 percent discount in 1994–95 on personal computers and printers (10,000 took advantage) and a $30 discount on software.[12]

As should be expected, reverse "shareholder marketing programs" tend to go hand in hand with shareholder-base strategies emphasizing individual and employee investors. A Midwestern bank, for instance, asks shareholders to consider becoming customers through direct deposit of dividend checks, and it asks account holders to consider becoming investors through direct purchase of company shares.[13]

Conditions of Company Action

Companies vary in their stances and strategies when dealing with the shareholder world. Some firms remain unconcerned with the composition of their shareholder base, devoting no time to changing its demography but a fair amount to shareholder relations. Others, however, invest time in both. A deciding factor here is management's preference for autonomy and whether it perceives that autonomy as vulnerable. When managements feel secure and without challenge, shareholder composition is of little concern. When managements experience or anticipate challenge, however, that composition emerges as a genuine concern.

An examination of the origins of variations in company strategy is useful since these origins suggest the dynamic relationship between investor actions and company reactions. Five factors drive companies to seek to alter their shareholder base in the direction of smaller institutional holdings and larger employee positions.

A first driver is direct shareholder pressure on the company in the form of a takeover threat. The importance of unwanted acquisitions in motivating companies to restructure the shareholder base is evident in a 1989 survey of 761 companies. Asked whether the company's investor-relations program is "influenced by takeover considerations," more than half of the companies asserted that it is. For managements threatened by hostile challenge, altering the shareholder mix can be an appealing path to a safer haven.

A second driver is shareholder pressure for short-term results. More than half of the companies singled out "short term perspectives of sell-side and institutional holders" as a major company concern. Since institutional owners are generally perceived by management to be more concerned than individuals or employees with short-term company performance, decreasing the institutional presence is thus also a way to attenuate the drumbeat for near-term results.

A third driver is an existing shareholder base in which institutional holdings are highly concentrated. As the McDonald's vice president warned, an extremely high institutional presence can portend trouble and sleepless nights. Reducing this presence even in the absence of any immediate threat may therefore constitute prudent management action.

A fourth driver stems from the extent to which companies view the shareholder mix as a condition that can be changed. Traditionally, most managements have passively accepted their mix of investors as a market condition largely beyond their control. While virtually all major companies have created professional investor-relations staffs for tracking and informing their shareholders during the past decade, a smaller fraction has integrated the investor-relations function into top management. Such integration allows for continuing strategic focus on shareholders and the commitment of the resources necessary to alter the shareholder mix if executives find it necessary to do so. Altering the mix may entail investing more executive time with retail analysts, and less with institutional investors. It may also involve deciding to promote employee stock ownership through in-house newsletters, compensation policies, and employee stock-ownership plans. Whatever the actions, they require top-level commitment. Without it, the shareholder base is more likely to remain a fixed feature of a company's environment, even when a company is confronted by ownership challenges.

A fifth driver is the firm's size. Larger companies have greater resources at their disposal for reshaping their environment, including the shareholder base. They control more unobligated cash to invest in investor relations, and more senior managers are available to work with shareholders. They have also had more experience in reworking their environment. Those who preside over large corporations view other organizations less as fixed features of an immutable world and more as malleable features of a changeable universe. Larger companies should therefore be more inclined to seek greater individual and employee shareholding and lesser institutional holding.

Indicative of the scope of management concerns about its shareholder composition, the survey of 761 companies found that only one-third regarded their ownership base as satisfactory. One company in six sought to increase its institutional holdings, but one in five sought to enlarge its individual ownership and one in three its employee holdings. A 1994 repeat of the same survey questions, now to 585 companies, revealed persistent dissatisfaction: only one-third found their current shareholder mix acceptable, with greater individual and employee holdings the preferred solution. A substantial fraction of the nation's major companies have thus sought during the late 1980s and 1990s to redesign their investor landscape.[14]

Statistical analysis confirms the impact these five factors have on a company's decision to restructure its shareholder base. The evidence indicates that companies facing takeover threats or short-term institutional pressures are indeed more likely than others to seek a greater presence of employee shareholders. A commanding presence of institutions in a company's portfolio leads to similar actions. Senior managements that treat investor relations as a strategic function are also more likely to seek additional individual holdings and reduced institutional holdings, as are larger companies.[15]

Corroborating evidence comes from analysis of the formation of investor-relations offices among the Fortune 500 manufacturers. In 1984, one in four operated such an office; by 1994, three-fifths did so. Typically, the companies that created such offices over that decade were those with large institutional holdings of their shares, those that had faced shareholder proxy resolutions—and especially companies with large institutional holdings that had lagged financially.[16]

Some managements thus not only defend against unwanted ownership intrusion in their affairs but also go on the offensive. They replace demanding or potentially threatening shareholders with those that are less so. Instead of submitting to investor discipline or threats, they rid themselves of those imposing the discipline or making the threats. These executives have learned to bow graciously to appease the new princes, but they have also learned how and when to take countermeasures to vanquish the princes.

Dismissing Managers

Like company executives, money managers also face a host of pressures that must be addressed. A money-manager's boss may have signaled displeasure with the quarter's results; a client may have communicated an intention of moving its moneys elsewhere; a company may have lobbied for a favorable proxy vote. Compared to the demands on company executives, the concerns here are more narrowly and clearly focused on the client base and portfolio performance. But the pressure for results can be just as keen.

If a company in an investor's portfolio is not producing results, for some money managers it makes little difference who is presiding over the company. The executive suite is a necessary but little-examined organizational means to a financial end. But for others, the identity of top management does matter. This is especially true of institutions whose great size or investment style makes swift exit from an ailing company difficult. Then the investor's radar is pointed at the executive suite itself. If the reading is exceptionally adverse, and if previous efforts to force company performance to improve have failed, aggrieved institutions may seek to force offending executives out. Vanquishing an opponent remains a weapon of last resort. When a company is troubled, "the tradition was to vote with your feet," offered John Neff, long-time manager of Vanguard's Windsor fund, America's fourth-largest mutual fund. "But you can't do that anymore. The size of our positions is such that it's hard to get out of some of our positions." As a result, "the policy of sometimes trying to alter management is sometimes necessary."[17]

Investors communicate their displeasure with management, when they do so at all, in two ways. Traditionally and most commonly, investors sell or buy shares in response to high-profile management changes. Less commonly but far more now than in the past, investors render direct advice on what the succession should be or should have been.

The rise and abrupt fall of a chief financial officer at Eastman Kodak and the subsequent fall of his boss are illustrative of both. Christopher J. Steffen had been hired in January 1993 to help turn around a company whose earnings and stock price had been sluggish.

He was characterized as the "white-knight chief financial officer who could save stodgy Eastman Kodak." Investors applauded his much-publicized arrival. The company's stock price soared in the days that followed his hiring, adding more than $3 billion to the company's value. It seemed, however, that the board had imposed Steffen's appointment on a reluctant chief executive, Kay Whitmore, and despite the use of antirejectionist therapy, the transplant failed to take. The CEO warned that "he will not last very long" if he "comes in here assuming he's the Lone Ranger." Steffen indeed did not last long. The "three-billion-dollar man" resigned ninety days later, leading investors to forward a message. They dumped Kodak shares with vigor, driving the company's value down the next day by $1.7 billion.[18]

The message, however, seemed to fall on deaf ears. Whitmore remained in office as CEO and the company persevered. Calpers and other public funds rendered public counsel, as Dale Hanson had revealed at the New York conference on relational investing in the days following Steffen's departure. He and other investors offered private advice as well, reminding board members of the displeasure already expressed in the sell orders. Three months later, the board finally forced the resignation of Whitmore himself. Large brokerage firms, including Lehman Brothers and Prudential Securities, immediately raised their stock recommendations to buy, and the company regained much of the value it had lost when Steffen resigned. "Getting Kay Whitmore out of there was a critical step in getting this company going in the right direction," offered a Prudential analyst. Now, as a result, added a Dean Witter analyst, "the board's position and investors are . . . in alignment."[19]

Eastman Kodak's experience is symptomatic. A study of 480 large publicly traded companies in the early 1980s reveals that meeting analyst expectations is an act of CEO survival. When annual company earnings per share fall below analyst forecasts, the likelihood of CEO dismissal rises significantly higher. And, in the aftermath of an under-performing CEO's dismissal, other research suggests, investors send a confirming note. Study of CEO succession at 235 large companies during the late 1980s reveals that stock prices generally react favorably to board-initiated replacements when company performance is poor.[20]

The board of American Express dismissed its long-time chairman and chief executive James D. Robinson III in 1993, and investor reactions here are also illustrative. Robinson had presided over one of America's blue-chip financial-service companies since 1977. During Robinson's fifteen years at the helm, the company's performance had gradually declined and its stock price followed. American Express shares traded for more than $40 in 1987 but less than $20 by 1992. "Many on Wall Street are howling for Robinson's head," offered one business writer, since, in the bald assessment of a partner of Brandy-wine Asset Management, a million-share owner, "American Express stands out as an embarrassment for corporate America."

Frustrated investors finally took their grievance to company directors. "Directors were lobbied directly to get this guy out of here," said one person familiar with the board. Some investors told the board that they would vote against the company's slate of directors at the forthcoming shareholders meeting if Robinson were not forced out. In response to the demands, Robinson initially agreed in late 1992 to step down as CEO and chairman, and company stock soared 6 percent the next day. Shortly thereafter, however, he momentarily maneuvered to retain his chairman's title; because of this move and an adverse report on the earnings of one of the company's units, the stock then plummeted 9 percent. When investors and directors finally forced him out altogether several weeks later, American Express stock rebounded, and by mid-1993, five months after the boardroom coup, it reached $32 a share, a 40 percent recovery of value.[21]

Not surprisingly, CEOs installed in the wake of investor-inspired coups seek not only to calm shareholders' fears but also to control their aroused expectations. Harvey Golub, Robinson's successor at American Express, therefore asserted on taking office that he would be "deeply involved, and lead" his operating units to recovery but it would take time. The new chief executive of Eastman Kodak, George Fisher (formerly CEO of Motorola), asserted in late 1993 that Kodak would come in well below the analysts' earnings forecasts for 1994. The new chief executive of IBM, Louis V. Gerstner Jr. (formerly CEO of RJR Nabisco), cautioned his investors soon after taking over in early 1993 that he would need time to correct the many problems he had inherited. The new chief executive of Westinghouse Electric, Michael H. Jordan (formerly an executive with PepsiCo), said on taking office in mid-1992 that he wanted to reestablish credibility with his disgruntled shareholders "through consistency of financial results, avoiding major surprises and major disasters."[22]

When Do Investor Demands for Executive Dismissal Work?

Clamoring for a CEO's head, whether through stock sell-offs or direct entreaty, is not the same as having it, or even coming close. Management by plebiscite, a corporate variant on government through perpetual town meetings à la Ross Perot, might be preferred by some constituents. Like the federal bureaucracy, however, executives can shield themselves well from direct constituent rule.

A study of sixty-seven semiconductor producers from 1968 to 1989 suggests that the chief executive's power within the firm is critical in such matters. If the CEO was well ensconced—whether because of large stockholdings, status as a founder of the firm, or having hand-picked the directors—the likelihood that he or she would succumb to investor pressure was lower. Another study of sixty-seven board-forced retirements between 1988 and 1992 of chief executives at the nation's 1,000 largest companies had similar findings: poor performance drove the firings, but dismissal was much less likely if the CEO was also serving as board chairman, if the directors came on the board during the CEO's reign, and if the CEO's outside board appointments were more prestigious than those of the directors. A third analysis of targets of unsuccessful takeover efforts between 1983 and 1989 found that a third of the CEOs stepped down within two years of the threat. This is double the normal rate, but among poorly performing companies the event is less likely if no major investor acquired the firm's stock during the contest for control.[23]

If power politics often prevail in the struggle for control of the executive suite, a smart but ineffective CEO would therefore be well advised to pack the board with company executives whose paychecks he or she signs. Such executives are directly beholden to the chief executive and should consequently be the chief's strongest defenders if investors begin calling for the chief's head. The study of the semiconductor industry revealed that practice followed theory in this case: more inside directors on a board reduced the likelihood of a CEO's dismissal.[24]

Ironically, however, the placing of more inside directors on a board does not always furnish the chief executive with the desired security blanket. A study of 114 large industrial firms from 1960 to 1990 found just the opposite: companies with more insiders on their boards were more, not less, likely to oust a troubled CEO. This counterintuitive result points to the importance of succession dynamics over executive loyalty. It seems that a board is more prepared to replace a faltering CEO if it is confident that it has an experienced replacement ready to take over. If board members have already had the opportunity to work closely with a potential inside replacement, they can be more confident of a replacement decision. By giving able lieutenants the visibility that comes with a director's seat, a chief executive is more likely to be replaced by one of them.[25]

Dispersion of a company's stock ownership is also found in these studies to reduce the likelihood of dismissal. This research confirms one implicit objective of corporate campaigns to alter the shareholder mix. When ownership is less concentrated in the hands of a small number of powerful institutions, executives have more leeway to act and are less likely to find themselves out of work. Though executives require no such studies before launching their programs to bring more individuals into ownership of a company, the research-based conclusions corroborate their experience-based perceptions.[26]

An executive can only be dismissed by the board of directors, and other evidence indicates that unhappy investors are likely to find many boards reluctant to lower the boom on a poorly performing executive. A survey of 726 directors of Fortune 1,000 companies in 1992 confirms that shareholders are the constituency to which directors feel most accountable. Shareholders loom larger in the directors' minds than do customers, employees, management, communities, and lenders. The directors also assert that the long-term financial performance of the company is their paramount criterion for evaluating and compensating the chief executive. When it comes time to consider dismissing a CEO, however, other criteria come to the fore. Financial or ethical malfeasance lead the list. Far down are five-year financial returns. At the bottom of the list are unsatisfactory one-year and three-year returns, declining market value, and shareholder unrest. Fewer than one-fifth of the directors would use these criteria in deciding whether to force a chief executive out of office.[27]

Does Executive Dismissal Work?

The presumption behind investor-inspired executive dismissal, of course, is that the new executive will be an improvement over the old. Perhaps, but much depends on how the successor is selected. The turbulence occasioned by a forced departure can undercut performance improvements, and the dismissal of a poorly performing chief executive can also lead to the resignation of loyal subordinates who are performing well. Thus, shareholder campaigns to alter the management mix may not necessarily work.

Research evidence casts some doubt on the dictum that forcing out the bad will necessarily usher in the good. A study of ninety-six acquisitions from 1980 to 1984, for example, revealed that the resignation and firing of executives of the acquired firms led to a drop, not an improvement in their subsequent performance. Similarly, study of 102 acquired companies during the late 1970s found that able managers in the targeted companies were more likely than less capable managers to depart after the merger. The former may chafe more under new ownership, and they may look better to a headhunter. Whatever the cause, the fact remains that able managers more often leave—not the managerial "deadwood" that is a presumed target of a takeover.[28]

The experience of one retail company's acquisition of another's chain is illustrative. Ames Department Stores took over the discount department stores of Zayre in late 1988 at a purchase price of $778 million, believing that it could turn around the then-languishing chain. To Ames' chief executive, it appeared to be a good match. He knew Zayre well, since he had earlier worked for the company. It would also be a personal vindication since his earlier managerial stint with Zayre had ended in dismissal. In any case, improved performance of the ailing Zayre chain was expected to follow the takeover. In practice, however, as Ames management took over the Zayre operations, replacing the incumbent management, it committed a series of blunders. It renamed the stores Ames, even though Ames was little known in most regions where Zayre operated. It ended weekly mailings to Zayre shoppers, changed the apparel mix, and altered pricing policies, alienating regular customers with each move. Despite the management-improvement theory behind the takeover, "Ames stumbled because management didn't run the Zayre stores properly," observed one investment banker. From early 1989 through early 1990, sales at former Zayre stores dropped an average 15 percent. Though the acquisition and management changes were done in the name of improved operations, in April 1990 Ames' mismanagement of the Zayre stores dragged the whole company into bankruptcy.[29]

Though forced CEO resignations or company acquisitions in the name of better performance do backfire, such changes should generally be followed by improved company performance. Indirect evidence is suggestive. A study of sixty-seven forced CEO exits from large firms between 1988 and 1992 reveals that replacements are far more often drawn from outside the company than in the case of routine executive succession. Less than one company in five recruits new blood when a CEO steps down voluntarily, but more than two in five of those that fire a CEO go for outsiders. In seeking new approaches to old problems, boards, it would appear, are acting to restore firm performance.[30]

Direct evidence confirms that a firm's performance is often restored. A study of 908 changes at the top-executive level in 1985–88 reported by the *Wall Street Journal* focused on sixty-three forced resignations among them. Unlike firms experiencing unforced turnover events, those where forced exits occurred had seen their income decline over several years. More to the point, the forced resignations were followed by substantial improvements in operating and net income, while unforced executive changes were not. Investor pressure was on: during the two years following the turnover, firms that forced out top executives were more than twice as likely to be the target of a takeover, leveraged buyout, or new block investment. Restructuring is a common response. New top executives who came in after the firings were far more likely than other newly appointed executives to reduce employment and capital expenditures.[31]

The fresh powers of institutional investors have thus overwhelmed management on occasion, forcing early departures from the executive suite. The precipitating elements are languishing performance and poor prognosis. Few executives and even fewer directors are successfully forced out, but the frequency with which their impeachment is sought signals the rising power of investors to challenge management entrenchment. The fact that underperforming executives and directors are not always the ones forced out is also indicative of the occasionally ineffective application of that power.

Supplanting Directors

The party of the corporate triumvirate experiencing least daily pressure to perform is surely the nonexecutive director. Investors and managers are continuously pressed for more results, for better growth, for higher returns. By contrast, outside directors face only episodic demands, and then mainly for their time. They must attend board meetings and seek to be well versed, but between meetings and outside of crises they are relatively free to ignore both company affairs and shareholder interests.

For large companies, the typical board convenes nine times annually, and the average meeting lasts three hours. Directors invest another ten hours per year in board committee business and some thirty to forty hours preparing for board and committee meetings. Taken together, a typical director invests seventy to eighty hours per year on company business. Most executives, by contrast, devote more than 2,000 hours annually to the job.[32]

During moments of company crisis or prospective change of control, however, directors can invest huge blocks of time and experience wrenching conflicts. Board members at Paramount Communications, for instance, devoted long hours, worked under intense time constraints, and were harshly criticized during the company's 1993–94 friendly takeover agreement with Viacom Inc. and hostile rejection of a counter-bid by QVC Network Inc. So too for those involved in the 1993 ousting of the chief executive, James Robinson, at American Express. At a moment when the board still supported Robinson despite vigorous demands from investors to oust him, major holders, Robinson's friends, and company executives aggressively lobbied directors Rawleigh Warner Jr. (CEO of Mobil Corporation), Frank P. Popoff (CEO of Dow Chemical Co.), and Henry A. Kissinger (former U.S. Secretary of State), among others. But these are exceptional moments that punctuate otherwise relatively uneventful and not unpleasant meetings. More than three-quarters of a typical board's discussion is devoted to preplanned agenda items prepared entirely by management.[33]

As one might expect, inside directors normally step down from the board when they leave the firm. On occasion they go off the board before that point to make way for additional outsiders. Both insiders and outsiders tend to depart from the board in the aftermath of a company's ownership change, especially following a hostile takeover or a leveraged buyout. A study of ten of the largest leveraged buyouts of public companies during the late 1980s, for instance, finds that the typical board is cut in half and most of the outside directors are replaced by the new owners and owner-managers. Similarly, a 1992 survey of 512 directors of Fortune 1,000 firms revealed that two-fifths had left at least one other board, and, of these, half had departed because of a change in control following an acquisition, merger, or buyout.[34]

Still, even without an ownership change, directors are involuntarily replaced from time to time before they reach a mandatory retirement age (set at seventy to seventy-two at nine out of ten large companies in 1989). Top management rarely forces out its own directors since it normally proposed them for the board in the first place. Mistakes are occasionally made even here, as evidenced by CEO Roger Smith's ouster of Ross Perot from the board of General Motors several years after having brought him on the board when GM acquired Electronic Data Systems in 1984 (which Perot had built). Such actions, however, are rare exceptions to an otherwise relatively fault-free appointment process.[35]

Investors, by contrast, enjoy little access to the nomination process and are thus more likely to quarrel with the outcome. Indicative of their exclusion is the fact that they almost never recommend nominees to serve on the board that nominally represents them. Of 375 major firms surveyed in 1992, only 6 percent had received even a single director nomination from an institutional investor. Equally indicative of investor exclusion is the absence of electoral choice in director selection. Virtually all proxy ballots include a set of nominees precisely equal in number to the number of board openings.

With little direct capacity to affect the director entry process, investors have found they can nonetheless influence the exit process. Shareholders occasionally stage rear-guard actions to oust directors they do not like. The near victory of Capital Partners in replacing five incumbent directors of Lamont Company is a case in point. So too was a 1991 proxy fight by Tiger Management Corporation, a money manager, to displace five board members of Cleveland-Cliffs, Inc., an iron-ore producer. Shareholders had become disgruntled over Cliffs' uneven performance, problematic diversification, and insular board. Tiger launched a campaign to elect five of its own nominees to the company's twelve-person board, and it convinced investors to cast a majority vote for Tiger candidates. Five directors of Tiger's choosing were elected to the board, displacing five incumbents.[36]

Just Vote No

A rear-guard strategy of replacing unwanted directors, however, is expensive to mount and difficult to carry out successfully. An inexpensive alternative is to vote against incumbents without actually replacing them. While this can communicate much the same bark, it does not produce quite the same bite. Since 1967, U.S. securities regulations have required that proxy statements include a provision permitting shareholders to "withhold authority to vote for each nominee" for the board, even if unopposed. In the hands of shareholder advocates and a few pension funds, this gave rise during the 1990s to "just vote no" campaigns in which holders withheld their vote from some or all nominees.

"Just vote no" campaigns remain entirely symbolic, as the percentage of proxy votes they attract rarely rises above single digits. During the 1992 proxy season, for instance, 9.3 percent of Champion International's holders voted no in such a campaign, and 5.8 percent of Sears, Roebuck holders did so. During the 1993 season, 3.2 percent of American Express holders withheld their vote. Even if the minority protest vote had somehow mushroomed into a majority, however, the nominees would still have taken office. Director candidates require only a plurality of the votes cast, and "no" votes are considered not to have been cast at all. Though symbolic politics, the "no" vote for directors is nonetheless viewed by advocates as sending a potent message for change. "'Just vote no' can responsibly prod boards to step up their oversight of corporate performance," argues Joseph A. Grundfest, a proponent of this tactic. It can also "discourage well-managed firms from resting on their laurels."[37]

The chief executive and chief financial officer of the diversified company WWK Products confirmed the assumptions of the "no"-vote theory. When asked if institutional investors had expressed complaints about the composition of their board, the CEO said that the "best indications we get are when the vote comes in for the annual meeting." Both he and the CFO express pride in the fact that less than 1 percent of the vote is typically withheld from their directors, including themselves. Still, they worry about campaigns that can turn out substantial "no" votes. "What really bothers me," says the CEO, "is that you've got big groups of people voting against" companies now, and "it's going to hurt confidence in a company." Despite an element of personal bravado about his own "no" votes, any public rejection, he confides, proved "embarrassing."

Whatever the theory behind replacing directors, actual director turnover appears to display relatively little relationship with their performance. This can be seen in an analysis of which company directors go on to join other boards. The study focused on the directors of 456 large corporations in 1986 and 1990 and asked which 1986 directors had acquired additional directorships among this set of firms in 1990. Several factors yield predictable results: those who held two board positions in 1986 were almost two-fifths more likely to be invited onto a third by 1990; those who sat on well-connected boards in 1986 (whose others directors served on many other boards) were also significantly more likely to receive an additional later appointment.

Less predictable, at least from the theoretical premises of efficient markets for corporate control, are the findings for two other potential predictors. If a director sat on a board in 1986 that had adopted a golden parachute for top management, the director was more likely to receive an additional appointment by 1990. Since golden parachutes, a potential sign of management entrenchment, are viewed with some skepticism by investors, it appears that directors who favored managerial over shareholder interests will flourish. Even more to the point, the companies' financial performance in 1986 had no bearing on whether their directors received additional board appointments in 1990. In other words, despite occasional exceptions to the contrary, directors' careers bear little or no relationship to their performance on behalf of shareholder returns.[38]

PART II

Constructing Investor Capitalism

5

—— ⌇ ——

Restructuring the Corporation

WHILE COMPANIES RESIST some investor pressures, they accommodate others. The belief in shareholder sovereignty is, after all, part of the gospel of American capitalism, even if unruly shareholders are sometimes denied participation.

The executive suite still calls the shots, but how they are called is less a purely managerial decision than it was at the height of managerial capitalism. The tilting toward shareholder concerns is fluid, varying from firm to firm and issue to issue. Company executives nonetheless pursue strategies and foster designs not entirely of their own making. Naturally, they rarely concede this publicly. To do so would diminish the facade of managerial autonomy and embolden investors. In private, however, managers acknowledge the new shareholder reality.

Institutions are pressing for more and better information on company products and divisional performance. They seek personal contact with top management and ask to tour production facilities. They express opinions on executive compensation and management succession. They favor further acquisitions by some companies and discourage other companies.

Management has been responding. In revising executive compensation plans to make them more contingent on company performance, general counsels often review the plans privately with activist pension funds. When considering the timing and even desirability of an acquisition, chief executives turn to investor specialists for a prediction of how the market would react. Whether in setting strategy or selling divisions, investor preferences now unite with regulatory constraints and legal risks as part of the operating environment that executives no longer ignore.

Companies introduced many changes during the late 1980s and the 1990s for reasons entirely unrelated to shareholder entreaty. Some of today's restructurings can be traced to the adoption of better information systems and new production technologies. Others can be traced to the introduction of process reengineering and improved work systems. Still others can be linked to domestic deregulation and global competition. But the hand of the institutional shareholder can be felt in much of the remaking. Rarely, however, is the causal chain unambiguous. Few instances come to light in which a shareholder demands X and the company does X. More commonly, investors have encouraged the restructuring in conjunction with other drivers. If not always in boldface or black ink, large investors' catalytic signatures can nonetheless often be detected.

In chapter 3, we saw executives refusing shareholder demands, and in chapter 4 we saw them removing demanding shareholders. In this chapter, by contrast, we see them embracing shareholder demands. On first glance, such behavior seems inconsistent, even schizophrenic. Companies appear to be intransigent one moment and acquiescent the next. Yet closer inspection reveals a picture of partial resistance and partial concession, of avoiding what cannot be done, equivocating on what might be done, and adopting what has to be done.

The chapter begins with an illustrative account of investors' harsh reactions to a company's surprising acquisition, reactions so strong that the firm eventually made several midcourse corrections in its organization and strategy. It then turns to investor-driven changes observed among other companies in six main areas: (1) shareholder voice inside the company; (2) workforce size; (3) redesign and reengineering; (4) company strategies; (5) executive leadership and succession; and (6) corporate governance. As always the picture is uneven, with some companies accepting extensive change while others refuse all change. Still, these are the areas where investors most concentrate their firepower, and where managements most often change in response. Taken together, the six areas constitute a large component of the restructuring that has swept through so many corporations by the mid-1990s.

An Unaccepted Acquisition

Western Chemical Company entered a new line of business in the early 1980s. It bought one of the major players in another industry, an act that overnight made it one of the nation's premier producers in not only its original industry but also the new industry. Management viewed the two business lines as a strategic fit. The ups and downs in one were likely to be countercyclical with the downs and ups in the other. They shared many of the same industrial customers. And the output of one was a major input for the other.

The stock analysts and fund managers, however, never warmed to the acquisition's rationale. Before the purchase, Western Chemical had been touting a posture of focusing on its core business, and the analysts' reports naturally reflected what they were hearing. The company's secret negotiations around the acquisition had remained just that: its announcement came as a stunning reversal, an embarrassing shock to those who had been led to believe the core strategy could never be otherwise. For the analysts who then had to explain to their bosses and customers why they had not seen it coming, the company's handling of the diversification move—or, more precisely, the handling of the analysts—would not soon be forgiven.

With the passage of more than a decade, the analysts' irritation seemed unrelieved. During the early 1980s, when investors were barely on management's mind, their irritation could be ignored at little peril. By the 1990s, however, investors were taken much more seriously, and the company installed a senior line manager to direct investor relations. He had run a $2 billion division of the company, had presided over the firm's strategic planning, and had the confidence and the ear of both divisional presidents and top executives. Senior managers knew the fuzzy outlines of investor thinking, but when the investor-relations director brought analysts into the company for the first time to talk with management, it proved an eye-opener. Management learned that investors expected earnings growth rates far higher than its own. Management's personal dialogue with the investors clarified its perceptions of shareholder expectations, and management soon factored these expectations into its internal benchmarks for divisional and firm performance.

The agenda worked the other way around as well, with Western Chemical executives also using the meetings to improve investors' understanding of the firm. When asked what an ideal company relationship with the investment community would look like, the investor-relations manager avowed that it would come when "our investors understand our strategy as well as we do." Yet, despite the company's efforts to make its acquisition strategy better understood, the diversification measure remained *misunderstood* more than a decade after its consummation. Executives fielded unending variations on the same basic questions: Why had they acquired the other business, and when did they plan to dispose of it? Since the acquisition had long been completed and there were no plans to revise it, the endless questioning had long since become tiresome. Still, in that era of more powerful investors and more responsive managers, executives suppressed their aggravation.

An investor's contact with Western Chemical in 1993 displayed the new give-and-take. An analyst who followed the company for a major institution listened to the chief executive at a general briefing. The analyst expressed misgivings about what he heard and already knew, and asked if he might contact the CEO privately. He had already met personally with the newly elevated chief financial officer, but that had failed to allay the analyst's general concerns. Encouraged by the investor-relations director to pursue the higher request, the analyst wrote the CEO, raising questions anew about the company's management of the business line acquired more than a decade earlier. In preparing the letter, the analyst conferred with his counterpart at another institutional investor, though the latter held no stock at the moment in Western Chemical. The lead analyst concluded the communication with a request that he and the conferring analyst come for a private meeting with the chief executive.

The lead analyst faxed a copy of the letter to the director of investor relations, giving the latter several days to lay the groundwork within the firm before the letter's formal arrival by mail. The director warned the CEO and the president of the acquired business unit about the letter's imminent delivery, advising them to give serious attention to the analysts' concerns. The chief executive agreed to a meeting, and the two analysts were soon ushered in for a planned forty-five-minute dialogue with the CEO. Warming to the discussion and delaying other business, the chief executive kept them for twice the scheduled time.

The analysts' critical message came in two parts. The first concerned market signaling. With two business lines protected by one umbrella, the analysts argued, neither could fully sense when rain was falling or the sun was shining on the other. If either line fell from Wall Street's grace, a depressed company stock price would incorrectly send an adverse signal to both. If either rose in favor, a heightened stock price would send an equally flawed affirmative signal to each. Neither would have an accurate reading of where it stood in the eyes of the owners.

The second challenge concerned Western Chemical's management of the acquired business. With a divisional president who prided himself on running an autonomous operation, the acquired line issued a separate financial report for investors. Outsiders could thus judge its operations against other stand-alone companies in the same industry, and the two analysts sitting in the CEO's office suggested that the disputed division did not measure up. Compared to its competitors, they asserted, the division was spending too much. Its use of capital was too loose, its organization too big, its reactions too slow. Why, for instance, was the company still using one particular source of raw material when everybody knew that it had become too costly? In short, the company was not managing the business line as well as its industry competitors. In closing, the lead analyst warned that if the hurdle rate for new capital investments in the division were not soon raised to industry standards, the market will simply take it off the company's stock price. The other analyst added that this was a major reason why her own organization had so far withheld any investments from the company.

The messages in this instance had exceptional credibility. The messengers were among the few buy-side analysts who knew well both the parent company and the acquired business. Most analysts who followed the firm specialized in Western Chemical's original line of business and still could not fathom the new line—even a decade after its acquisition. The visiting analysts, by contrast, were among the few who were familiar with both product areas. While company executives are often suspicious of the motives of sell-side analysts—since it is not their own money on the table—executives see buy-side motives as more credible. The analyst who had taken the lead was also well known to company management. In his immediately previous incarnation, he had run the firm's pension fund. Though his decision to leave the corporation was still viewed as an act of disloyalty, none would dispute his intimate knowledge of how the company operated.

Company executives were chastened by what they heard, but they were also constrained in what they could do. Selling the disputed division was not an option since its value now appeared to be considerably lower than when it was purchased, indirectly confirming the analysts' fears. The alternative of partially spinning off the division through an issue of stock to the public was considered, but that idea too was rejected because management was unprepared to relinquish any control. Other actions, however, were not ruled out. Soon after the CEO's meeting with the analysts, the company announced that it was dropping its use of the disputed source of raw material. The company also raised the minimum return requirements for investing in the division. Finally, the executives reminded themselves that surprise acquisitions in little-related industries often entail costs far beyond the purchase price itself.

The day after the analysts met with the company chief executive, the noninvested institution bought several million shares in Western Chemical. The chief executive was immediately informed of the purchase, which came as welcome news in the midst of seemingly unrelenting criticism from Wall Street. Company management learned not only that it could no longer avoid listening—but also that being responsive could yield tangible benefits.

Bringing in the Investor

The first of the six areas where companies most often listen and respond to investors is the creation of organizational mechanisms to carry investor voice into the firm. These are formal and informal devices for ensuring that the perspectives of major investors are brought to those who run the firm. The devices are similar to those used to bring customer perspectives to the attention of top management.

Company managers sometimes allude to "bringing the market into the firm." This is not an effort to turn a firm into a market. (Some companies have also moved in that direction, building a "networked" or "virtual" organization through an array of contracts among suppliers, producers, and sellers, a kind of minimarket within the firm.) It is, rather, an initiative to channel customer concerns directly to management. A range of devices help achieve this. Market surveys and focus groups are standard tools, but companies have also sought to admit customer concerns to other decision points. AT&T, for example, evaluates its senior managers on three criteria in their annual performance appraisals: EVA, or "economic value added" (their contribution to company earnings); PVA, or "people value added" (their effectiveness in managing and developing subordinates); and CVA, or "customer value added" (their effectiveness in the eyes of major customers). Similarly, Southwest Airlines, in forming a committee to hire flight personnel, includes customers who are members of its frequent-flyer club. Such "market-in" efforts are based on the organizational premise that routinized management contact with customers, the creation of customer advocates inside the firm, and the inclusion of customer criteria in decisions can help ensure company responsiveness to shifting market demands.[1]

In response to investor pressures, companies have designed the investor-relations function to achieve much the same. The shifting market demands here come not from the consumer market but from the capital market. Yet in analogous fashion, the thrust is to ensure that the firm's investor concerns are well understood by top management.

Hutchins Motor Corporation has developed an elaborate program for reading its investor environment. The program evolved from a posture of presenting information to a means of learning what information should be presented. Its philosophy is "customer driven," said the financial executive who oversees the company program; the customers in this instance are not auto buyers but institutional investors: "Our mission is to serve our customers"—that is, institutional investors—and "in order to do that, we've go to listen to them. We can't do what *we* think is right. We've got to go out to *them* and ask them what kinds of information they want, how they want it presented to them, and pay attention to what their needs and what their desires are." This marks a significant departure: "I think in the past we haven't listened enough," he confessed. "We've done too much of what we thought was right."

Some firms, predictably, have not yet embraced the premise, remaining largely impervious to direct investor input. Buckingham Bank's chief executive maintains personal contact with virtually none of his investors, nor do the investors see any of his senior managers. Senior management recognizes the underdeveloped state of its relationships. "We raised the issue amongst ourselves," says the CEO. "Should we see more of these people?" Yes, he decides, but the appointment book fills very slowly.

More typical is Columbia Foods' practice of routinely arranging for institutional holders to meet not only with its top executives but also with those running major divisions. Investors learn more, but so do the line managers. "Shareholders don't have as good a view [of the company's operations] as we do," notes the chief executive, "but they have a separate view, and every now and then . . . I've learned things by listening," he says. "They will worry about something and they'll get my attention." By having the investors meet with his line managers, he also intends for the investors' worries to reach them. "It's a continuous feedback thing," concludes the CEO, "just part of the market."

Bringing the investor in does not negate the equally valued reciprocal functions of bringing the executive out. Many institutions certainly want their own voice heard, but they want to hear the executive's voice as well. The view of one money manager expresses that of many who take active interest in the companies in their portfolio. He follows an investing strategy of depth over breadth, taking a stake in twenty-five highly select companies. He consults with the chief executives of all, but he also spends much time with the director of investor relations and other senior managers in order "to know them, to have a feel for them." He insists on kicking the tires. "I want to have a lot of contact with the company," he asserts. "My attitude is to keep the portfolio small so I can know the company well. So I want to have as much contact as possible, to know what makes the company tick, to know the culture of the company."

Architecture as Emblem

Bringing investors physically into the home office creates an unanticipated pressure for architectural change. Cost-conscious investors now see the company's flagship building, not just an earnings statement. They are still unlikely to see the corporate "air force" or other hidden perquisites, but for them the headquarters edifice is emblematic of company values. In an era of lean budgets and cost constraints, an opulent home office sends them the wrong message.

The long-standing headquarters of IBM occupied a sprawling architectural masterpiece in Armonk, New York. With a 50 percent contraction of IBM's central staff following the 1993 investor-driven ouster of CEO John Akers and installation of Louis Gerstner, much of the 400,000-square-foot building had become superfluous. But perhaps more to the point, the building's lavish interior and immaculate landscaping represented a colossus that shareholders no longer (or perhaps never) valued. With an extensive restructuring of the firm underway, IBM placed one of the preeminent symbols of its formerly preeminent position on the selling block. The architecture of a company's headquarters signals its mental architecture, and IBM sought a fresh signal.[2]

As one money manager visits companies in which he has invested, he takes careful note of what he sees on the way to the executive suite. Sometimes he approves, other times he does not. "I like to see cost consciousness," he offers, and "I don't like to see a company's management building a monument to themselves." Visits to the headquarters of two retail companies in identical product areas illustrate the difference. As the money manager enters one that had undergone a leveraged buyout four years earlier and much restructuring since, he observes an ordinary building with seasoned desks and well-worn carpets. The other, by contrast, he discovers to be a glittering edifice, fine for those who worked there but one that, in his view, "didn't go to the bottom line." Comparison of the first company's headquarters before and after the buyout is also revealing. Before the leveraging, the home office had been a "colossal monument," but now that monument had been sold (along with a fleet of corporate jets). "It's really hard to put the company culture into words, but I know it when I see it."[3]

Shrinking the Workforce

The second of the six areas of company change in response to investor pressure is contraction of the workforce. Large shareholders take little interest in the employment totals per se. But they take much interest in what the totals say about the organization's management.

For most large shareholders, workers are viewed as only one of many means to an end, and one they know little about. Investors have virtually no direct contact with employees below the executive level, and they can draw on almost no expertise or experience in human-resource management. Analysts and money managers themselves rarely oversee more than a handful of associates. The chief executive of Calpers presided during the early 1990s over a staff of some 700, most of whom were concerned with distributing pension benefits rather than managing investments. Those who preside over union pension funds, such as the funds of the International Brotherhood of Electrical Workers and United Brotherhood of Carpenters and Joiners of America, are sensitized to employment security and staffing issues. But many large investors bring little experience in managing people to bear in judging firms whose employment numbers typically began in the thousands and sometimes reached hundreds of thousands. They are far removed from the organizational turbulence and personal turmoil occasioned by massive layoffs. For more than a few, human-resource management means a course they skipped as finance majors in an M.B.A. program.

Still, the size of a company's workforce and that of its major divisions can serve as a convenient yardstick for the investor, a visible proxy for management quality and cost containment. To some institutions, employment numbers at times seem far out of sync with a company's revenue trends. For others, lean operations and employment downsizing have become virtually synonymous with good management.

It sometimes seems that corporate managements behave as "good" managements should. During one three-month period in late 1993, for instance, Philip Morris announced a layoff of 8 percent of its workforce, Xerox of 10 percent, Eli Lilly of 12 percent, U.S. West of 14 percent, and Warner Lambert of 16 percent. In all, some 30,000 employees were to lose their jobs, but large shareholders expected more: not necessarily more workforce cuts, but certainly more comprehensive changes. They rarely saw downsizing as an end in itself; rather, they viewed it as a necessary step toward becoming more efficient. GTE announced the layoff of 17,000 employees and Delta Airlines cast off 15,000 in 1994; Chemical and Chase Manhattan banks had space for 12,000 fewer employees after their merger in 1995; AT&T announced the termination of 40,000 employees in 1996.

The market reaction to Xerox Corporation's announcement of the 10 percent cut in its workforce in 1993 is illustrative. Xerox had been decentralizing its divisions and streamlining its work for several years, and investors perceived the 10 percent reduction as the latest installment in a prolonged remaking of the company, not panic masquerading as a plan. In announcing the cutbacks, CEO Paul Allaire reminded shareholders that the downsizing was part of a long-standing agenda designed "to make the company more productive, more customer oriented, and bring products to market more quickly." Given the company's recent history, the message carried credibility. On learning of the layoff announcement, a First Boston analyst spoke for many: "We are just starting to see these types of restructurings. These guys are ahead of the curve." Despite a charge of $700 million to complete the restructuring, on the day of the announcement stock buyers outnumbered sellers, and investors drove Xerox stock up by 7 percent.[4]

Investors delivered a similar message to the pharmaceutical firm Merck & Co. Amid a wholesale reconfiguring of the health-care industry during the 1990s, Merck announced a cut of 2,100 positions with a charge of $775 million against its pretax earnings. The company had been performing well, and this was not a crisis-driven announcement. The arbiters of investor wisdom approved the preemptive action and pushed the stock price up by 4 percent. "They are aggressively moving to reduce head count and streamline manufacturing to increase efficiency," offered a securities analyst at Alex. Brown & Sons. Any "obits for Merck appear to have been premature." Market consistency, however, is not a luxury always enjoyed by the executive suite. When GTE announced in early 1994 a plan to reduce its workforce by 13 percent, its share price barely moved, despite an extensive reengineering effort of its own.[5]

Still, the predominant message from the "Street" is to downsize the company as part of a larger scheme to make a firm competitive in an era of domestic deregulation and international challenge. Analysis of share-price reactions to a number of company layoff announcements in 1979–87 corroborates the point. In the days immediately following layoffs announced as part of general restructurings, stock prices rose an average 4 percent. Downsizing announced simply as a cost-cutting measure, however, depressed stock prices an average 6 percent. Wall Street likes restructuring *and* job shedding but disdains cutbacks that are not part of broader plans for improved results. Though some large investors seek quick returns and expect to gain from immediate payroll reductions, more expect enduring gains from layoffs that are part of a general revamping of the firm's organization.[6]

The ouster of Eastman Kodak's chief executive in 1993 offers a lesson on the hazards of inaction. The CEO had already shed some 18,000 employees from the troubled firm, but he had failed to explain the downsizing—at least in the view of attentive investors—as part of a bolder reconstruction of the firm. It was not even clear to investors in what direction the chief executive wanted to go. Several of his large holders had pressed him to "benchmark" Kodak's performance against its competitors', an increasingly common corporate practice for gauging success and establishing goals. In their frustration with the CEO's evident lack of a strategic vision or plan of action, investors called for his head despite an extensive downsizing record.[7]

Redesigning and Reengineering the Firm

Redesigning and reengineering the firm constitutes the third of six areas where investors have become vigilant on corporate change or the lack thereof. Redesigning the firm consists of altering its decision making, operating divisions, and management culture. Reengineering entails changing the procedures by which the work is accomplished and products are delivered.[8]

Process restructuring, as championed by Michael Hammer and James Champy in their *Reengineering the Corporation: A Manifesto for Business Revolution*, can deliver cost reductions of 50 percent or more. Lean production and flexible organization, as portrayed by John Womack and colleagues in *The Machine That Changed the World*, also suggest a law of "halves." Womack and his colleagues intensively studied the Japanese automobile industry, and their research revealed that Toyota and other makers—by applying the principles of teamwork, quality control, customer focus, minimal buffers, and continuous improvement—had cut product defects by half, factory space by half, work time by half, and development time by half. Since quality improvements and cost reductions of this magnitude drop to the bottom line, investors are naturally attentive to initiatives elsewhere that promise the same.[9]

The impetus for organizational redesign and process reengineering does not explicitly come from large shareholders. It is again left up to management to find its own path for improving performance. Still, once the company has embarked on a redesign and reengineering path, alert shareholders take note. They appraise the likely impact of the redesign and reengineering, and, if it is favorable, commend management resolve.

Western Chemical Company embarked on such an effort. During the early 1990s, the company found that intensifying competition and customer resistance imposed price ceilings upon many of its products.

In the past, rising costs could be met by raising prices. The competitive field and, especially, the product market, however, had altered: company customers were primarily other large firms, and their own programs to bolster quality and constrain costs had now extended into their supplier relations. The chemical company was left with little real choice but to seek improved earnings through quality improvements and cost reductions.

Western Chemical launched an ambitious, multiyear remake of both its formal organizational and its production process. To identify how far the improvements should go, the company departed from the customary practice of benchmarking itself against other firms in the same chemical industry. It chose instead such firms as Motorola, Hewlett-Packard, and General Electric, all well known for their lean and innovative designs. Using these firms to set new standards for performance, the company found itself badly lagging. Its central-office administrative costs, for example, constituted some 15 percent of its total expenses. While Western Chemical was on a par with IBM and General Motors, senior managers were appalled to learn that its comparison companies had reduced such costs to 5 percent.

Removing two-thirds of Western Chemical's administrative overhead would require radical surgery. The company accordingly instituted far-reaching redesign and reengineering programs. It combined more than sixty business lines into a dozen strategic business units. It moved strategic planning, human resources, and research and development into the business units. It streamlined its production schemes. As one tool for persuading reluctant managers to embrace the streamlining, the company takes them through "one day in the life of a molecule" to see how it is transformed from raw input to finished product. Following that process step by step offers new insight into which links in the production chain add value to the molecule. Whatever does not add value would have to go.

Despite widespread resistance and much chaos during the improvement campaign, the effort by Western Chemical Products displayed tangible gains. It curtailed headquarters operations, reduced management layers, sold operating units, and streamlined business process. A statistical summary by the fourth year would be enough to turn many investor heads. The firm had taken out more than $1 billion in fixed costs and nearly the same in capital expenditures and company debt. It cut central staffing by half. It reduced office and production space at four major locations by half (some 1.5 million square feet). It slashed total employment by 18 percent and middle management by 26 percent.

Several institutions with holdings of four million to five million shares took special interest in the redesign and reengineering, visiting

Western Chemical monthly. One of them had characterized the company as a "sleeping giant," and though the phrase rankled the chief executive, it reminded him that shareholders believed hidden value remained to realized. While stopping short of telling the CEO specifically what to do, investors vigorously reinforced management's efforts to reveal the hidden value. On observing the company early in the process of shaking off the slumber, money managers peppered the chief executive with questions: "How far are you going?" (meaning you haven't gone far enough) and "When will you get there?" (meaning we expect big results soon). The company was especially sensitive to questions from mutual-fund managers among its largest holders. "They have so much money," the CEO observed, that "they *are* the *new* financial world." The company acted on their message. Over the four-year period of the company's restructuring, the firm doubled its earnings per share. Investors in turn doubled its price per share.

Corporate Strategies and Business Lines

Company strategy is the fourth major area of management responsiveness to investor pressure. A firm's vision of where it is going, the general road map of how to get there, and clever means for ensuring that the competition does not arrive first are the first principles of company management. Strategy should drive structure and all that goes with it, from divisionalization to incentive compensation and performance appraisals.

By textbook prescription, company strategy should be the sole prerogative of senior management. Directors must approve and review strategic thrust. But if government agencies, labor unions, and especially shareholders are able to dictate what strategies to pursue, their parochial self-interest will surely misdirect the otherwise efficient allocation of capital. Senior management should appreciate the special concerns of all constituencies, but it should also buffer itself against the undue influence of any to ensure that its judgments are rendered in the best interests of all.

The governing board is in principle management's chief buffer against shareholders. Directors officially stand between investors and managers, and they avow that their first obligation is to protect all owners. A 1992 survey of 726 directors of Fortune 500 companies illustrates their mind-set. When asked what most deserved board attention, these directors pointed to strategic planning and shareholder value. If investors seek to alter a company's strategy, the traditional governance model should therefore point them first toward its directors, whose obligations are generic and whose perspectives are catholic. Yet the official authority chain is rarely honored. Investors almost always bypass the board, taking their case for strategic change directly to management.[10]

Directors account for much of their own problem. They generally present themselves to the investor world as unapproachable, resisting any direct contact with shareholders. A 1992 survey of 600 corporate directors serving on the boards of the Fortune 500 found widespread approval of investor contact with executives—and equally widespread *disapproval* of contact with board members. Four-fifths of the directors stated that top managers should meet periodically with major stock-holders. Three-quarters asserted that board members should *not* do so.[11]

Leaving directors out of the loop, investors are not shy about informing management of its strategic mistakes and unrealized oppor-tunities. Their specific communiqués correspond closely to the com-pany's recent performance and future promise. If a company's stock has fared well, and if incumbent management inspires confidence, the mes-sage is simple: stay with the strategy. In the absence of either condition, the message is blunt: get a new one.

The experience of Buckingham Bank provides an example of the kind of strategic advice investors offer when they view the company's course as correct. The bank had created a successful focus, and it heard only rarely from its owners on matters of strategy. What little contact executives did have with investors, however, contained a recurrent point: do not modify the strategy. When he had met with representa-tives from one of the largest holders, the chief executive observed, they "made it clear to me, by the questioning and afterwards, in case it was-n't clear, that they hoped we will not change the business strategy that we have been following." The investor's questions had focused on whether the bank was considering an acquisition in a related area. The CEO inferred that the queries were posed in the "hope that I would say no," that "we were not going to buy something in the financial-services business somewhat unconnected with the business that we have man-aged so well." The CEO reassured his investors that he was committed "not to confuse opportunity with strategy." He stressed an unswerving emphasis on "focus." He pledged that the "thrust of our strategy [is] to continue as we have always done in the past—to service a select group of clients around the world and try to provide them with the changing array of services they need." He said he would not rule out an acquisi-tion if it were required to meet his clients' changing needs, but such an action would be clearly justified within the company's existing strategy. "We knew what we were doing," and that, he learned, is precisely what his investors wanted to hear.

The experience of the Industrial Products Corporation was at the opposite pole. The firm received an unending flow of unsolicited strategic advice from an array of anxious owners. The message here came in several parts, each unequivocal. First, in light of the company's languishing earnings, the institutions pressed for a fresh strategy. Second, in light of evident problems in managing a recent acquisition, the institutions urged a moratorium on all future purchases. Third, in light of the company's depressed stock price, investors also called for the creation of separate classes of stock for the several lines of business, a move also fraught with strategic implications.

The last point recurrently appeared in discussions that Industrial Products' chief operating officer held with major holders. "There was a tone by a number of major investors that we really ought to do something" about the diverse lines of business. Many of the investors, it seemed, wanted to be "in" one of the lines and not the others. Privately, investors criticized the breakup proposals of Frank Zacker, the raider who had applied a bear hug to the company. But they shared Zacker's basic concerns and pressed the company to find a better solution. "I agree with the defects that you point out in his proposal," said one, "but can't you figure out some way to do it right?"

Proxy fights over both Industrial Products' governance policies and its board membership added urgency to management efforts to find the right strategic path. The company successfully rejected the would-be suitor and defeated his alternative board slate and most of the other proxy measures, but as a matter of political expediency it concluded it would have to meet other investor demands, including the creation of several classes of stock.

Even the separation of the company's stock did not go far enough for many investors. They continued to be harshly critical of the earlier acquisition that had moved the company into such unrelated lines of business. They were "mad as hell," reported the director of investor relations, and "they made their opinions very, very well known" during his many visits to the company's major holders after the acquisition. One of the company's former top holders made it abundantly clear that it had exited entirely in the wake of the acquisition and refused for several years to repurchase any of the company's stock. The investors had not been forewarned, and they remained unforgiving.

The investors' violent opposition to the acquisition delivered its message. "You have to say in hindsight they were right," conceded the manufacturing company's director of investor relations, since it had "become obvious that the . . . acquisition was a very bad acquisition." Management vowed to avoid all "bad" acquisitions in the future, which in the near future for this company translated into *any* acquisition. With investors paying close attention to every strategic development, executives became gun-shy. Executives worry about "the reactions of institutional investors," offered the investor-relations director, "and they won't make any acquisition or any major change" without consulting them.

Chase Chemical Products reported much the same experience. It had taken the step of aggressively communicating to investors its long-term strategy and expected growth. This was a risky gambit, but the company's forecasts helped bring in and retain long-term investors comfortable with the strategy. By explaining its plans, the company had built a more consistent fit between general strategy and ownership base. But the company also learned that, once the fit was achieved, the plan acquired its own inertia: the congruous investors insisted on strategic continuity. Institutions would challenge, for instance, any acquisition that appeared to deviate from the company's professed direction. Investors consistently criticized inconsistency, observed the company's chief financial officer. Their main refrain: "Are you sticking to your strategy?"

Even when a company pursues a strategy that is accepted by the major holders, institutions remain alert to tactical errors. Investors can be quick to target potential missteps, not just grand fallacies. Columbia Foods, for example, evolved a strategy that few investors challenged. But the chief executive heard continuous queries about his specific actions. He maintains an open door for institutional investors. "We are very responsive to anybody who wants to come and talk to us," he asserted. Of course it has to be "somebody of some note as opposed to a single shareholder," warned the CEO, but "any institutional person . . . is very welcome." His largest single shareholder appears often on the welcome mat and focuses his questioning on how the strategy is being implemented, where the competitive environment was generating new problems, and whether retail customers were themselves changing faster than the company. "Like all big money managers," observes the chief executive, this shareholder obsesses whether "problems will come up that will interfere with our strategy."

At times, companies feel a tyranny of the new. Some investors seemingly look for signs of fresh directions regardless of content. This is especially evident among companies with spotty performance records and in industries with much restructuring. WWK Products had felt the heat for both reasons, leading executives to consider new actions purely in response to incessant investor questions about why the company had not taken more actions. The manager of investor relations offered a summary assessment: "It's often not so important what you do—it's just doing something."

De-Diversification and the Analyst Industry

While diversification had been a hallmark of good management during the 1960s, shedding unrelated business had become the measure during the 1980s and 1990s. De-diversification, back to basics, and a return to core competencies have emerged as management ideologies for good reason. Wall Street generally applauds divestitures of unrelated business lines. A study of sixteen refocusing announcements by highly diversified companies between 1980 and 1988, for instance, finds that they add some 3 percent to 4 percent to the value of the company's stock. Similar announcements by less diversified companies, by contrast, produce virtually no price change. Some owners also applaud before the fact. A tracking of a set of Fortune 500 companies between 1981 and 1987 reveals that companies with large blocks of stock in a few hands in 1981 more often reduced the diversity of their product areas by 1987 than did other companies. Investors make an exception for General Electric, whose products range from jet engines and consumer durables to television programming and financial services. Its performance had been so good that its unorthodox strategy draws little criticism. For those whose performance is less than stellar, however, diversity can be the object of unrelenting criticism.[12]

Whatever the operating value of de-diversification—and much research does confirm the value—some of the move away from conglomeration has as much to do with the organization of the analyst industry as with the organization of the firm. Brokerage analysts generally specialize in industry groups, ranging from tobacco, drugs, and steel to airlines, telecommunications, and banking. The annual selection of an "All-America Research Team" by *Institutional Investor* magazine displays the industry divides. It surveys the research directors and chief investment officers of the 300 largest institutional investors, directors of investor relations of some 150 corporations, and others who are deemed major clients of the sell-side analysts. It rates the analysts in sixty-five industries on their stock recommendations, estimates of corporate earnings, written reports, and client service. In 1993, for example, Teena Lerner of Lehman Brothers tops the analysts' rankings in biotechnology, and Joel Price of Donaldson, Lufkin & Jenrette leads railroad analysts; in 1994 Lerner again tops the biotechnology field and, with Price's retirement, Gary Yablon of Wertheim Schroder emerges at the top of the railroad analysts' list.[13]

Using a competing methodology, the *Wall Street Journal* offers its own rankings of the "best stock pickers and profit prophets" in forty-three industry groups. It evaluates the analysts' stock recommendations against the stocks' actual performance, and also compares the analysts' earnings forecasts with the companies' subsequently reported earnings. Meirav Chovav of Salomon Brothers tops the 1995 *Journal* rankings for earnings estimates in biotechnology, and Craig Kloner of Goldman, Sachs in railroads.[14]

Wall Street brokers, investor users, and company managers share much the same cognitive map of who specializes in what, indicative of the well-established industry niches that analysts have carved out for themselves. Given the enormous amount of information and analysis required to master a whole industry, let alone its major companies, the division of labor is natural. But the analysts' specialization in turn has had the effect of discouraging companies from unrelated diversification.

Executives at companies active in divergent product sectors grumble that specialist analysts continually complain about their firms' complexity. Industrial Products Corporation, for instance, witnessed the problems directly during its meetings with analysts. The company's two major divisions were almost never covered by the same securities specialists, and analysts gatherings thus drew two separate groups into the same room. The chief financial officer was bemused by their mutual incompatibility. "The [industry A] guys didn't know what the [industry B] guys' discussion was, and the B guys didn't know what the A's side was. Every once in a while some A guy would ask a B question, and there'd be guffaws on the other side. 'Dumb bastard doesn't know anything about it.'" The company later divided its stock between the two product lines, and the CFO applauded the move because it separated the analysts. "One of the reasons that I think this split of the stock is good is because you'll [now] have the analysts' meetings for A, you'll have the analysts' meetings for B, and everybody will know what the hell they're talking about."

Executive Leadership and Succession

To the outside world in search of immediate impressions, the persona of the chief executive plays a role akin to that of the architecture of company headquarters. The image of the CEO and of the building's facade speaks of the quality of the organization on the inside. Both the executive and the architecture are symbols of the firm's values, visible signs of whether the firm is shareholder friendly or self-indulgent.

While the choice of the CEO is exclusively that of the board, investors are prepared to voice their preferences, the fifth area of investor-influenced change. If investors believe that a succession event is imminent, by virtue of either the CEO's rising age or declining per-

0

formance, they redouble their scrutiny of the firm's leadership. They study the reigning executive's style and the potential successors' qualities. They send signals to headhunters if the firm is seeking an outside replacement. A credible executive with a compelling vision and effective follow-up implies not only good leadership at the helm but also good organization below. If his or her successor promises the same, so much the better. In the absence of either, investor questioning turns critical.

A case in point is RJR Nabisco's 1995 elevation of John Greeniaus, head of its food business, to the position of vice chairman. In giving him responsibility for the firm's operations in both food and tobacco, it effectively promoted him to chief operating officer and heir apparent to the position of chief executive. Since the company's market share in tobacco had been languishing, Wall Street took keen interest in the appointment. A tobacco analyst with Paine Webber detected new strategy in the tea leaves: the company is "trying to tell the investing public that they are trying to focus very heavily on domestic tobacco." Since Greeniaus had no background in the tobacco side of the business, however, investors questioned the qualifications he would bring to the table for turning the company around. And, by putting both operations in his hands, was the company saying that a hoped-for breakup of the company was now less likely? Investors drew negative conclusions on both counts. "I find it hard to see any positives in the change," offered a food-industry analyst at Goldman, Sachs. Said a tobacco analyst with S. G. Warburg: "I'm shocked—the tobacco industry isn't the food industry."[15]

Investor reactions to the abrupt resignation of Michael A. Miles as chief executive of Philip Morris Companies in 1994 are also symptomatic. The New York City pension fund—a holder of 5.7 million shares —Calpers, and other activist investors had been pressing the company more aggressively to address looming litigation and legislative problems with tobacco. The board named Geoffrey C. Bible, a veteran executive of the tobacco business, as new chief executive, but institutions split on whether this signaled a charge or retreat. Miles' "removal is a rebuff to the big shareholders," offered a pension manager for the International Brotherhood of Teamsters. An analyst with Sanford C. Bernstein, holder of nearly 10 million shares, concluded by contrast that before Bible's appointment "nobody was fighting back," but now "you will have a company that is much more open and much more aggressive."[16]

The experience of Buckingham Bank with one of its major investors is indicative of how intrusive active investor interest can become. Its largest holder, an investment company, is particularly attentive to the bank's executive turnover. Whenever Buckingham fills any of its dozen top positions, a senior money manager of the investment company requests a personal meeting with the newly appointed executive. The senior money manager has followed this practice for years, always going through the bank's vice chairman whom he has come to know well. The investor's purpose is to acquire a personal impression of the new officer, and, hopefully, to confirm that the newcomer would uphold the bank's proven policies. The investor and his fund colleagues are "interested in conservative management," observes the bank's vice chairman. "They are interested in management that looks at risk intelligently and are not taken by whatever is in vogue. They like to meet new people coming along because they want to understand their consistency and thought process."

Upon arrival, new chief executives often receive a round of visits from large shareholders. Like powerful constituents paying their respects to newly elected officials, investors seek to learn more of a new executive's intentions and to impress their own concerns upon the new appointee. The moment the CEO of WWK Products took office, he found two major owners on his doorstep. They both sniffed the air for his plans and shared their opinion of the firm's performance and stock price.

The owners' interest extends little beyond the chief executive at some companies, especially at firms with a strong leadership tradition. MFL Network is among the latter, and investors look little further than two individuals who have long dominated its decision making. Together, they have served as stewards of their company for over a decade, and both enjoy high profiles in an industry already known for its celebrity personalities. One had even made several cameo appearances on one of the network's daytime soap operas. In keeping with the principles of modern investor-relations theory, the executive had also arranged for the company's largest shareholder to appear on camera with him. Emmy nominations are in store for neither, but both enjoyed the moments that enlarged their already larger-than-life reputations.

As the chief executive of MFL Network approaches retirement age, large investors express great interest in the succession outcome. They obliquely sound their opposition to certain successor candidates. "I would be surprised," some would say to the director of investor relations, if a certain executive were under consideration. More generally they implicitly press for a clone of the current CEO. The company's performance record has been good for large investors, and they make it clear that leadership continuity is a priority. MFL's chief operating officer fits the bill well and he is already well known to the investment community. The chief financial officer, several divisional presidents, and others whose positions might make them logical candidates should, in the view of many holders, simply not be in the running.

Investors express little interest in other senior managers beyond MFL's chief executive and heir apparent. Once convinced of the quality of the person who makes "the final spending decisions" and his evident successor, the particulars are assumed to follow. The company would soon announce that the chief operating officer was indeed being promoted, ensuring continuity and easing investor anxiety. Only then did their attention turn to the next in line.

Even Industrial Products Corporation found that although investors developed vigorous opinions about the chief executive, they developed few opinions about others in the executive ranks. Some investors had conveyed a low regard for the previous CEO because of his controversial remaking of the firm, including the foray into the unrelated business. Investors took great interest when his successor, the current CEO, assumed office, looking for signs of discontinuity with the past. Other senior appointments, however, barely attract notice. The head of one of the company's major business lines, for instance, moved up to the vice chairmanship. Neither his promotion nor that of his own successor drew any attention. Investors asked few questions, offered scant comment, conveyed little anxiety.

At other companies, however, the shareholders' gaze extends well beyond the chief executiveship. Company power structure usually explains the difference. If the CEO operates a strong executive committee or otherwise shares power with a top management team, investors take interest in all. If the company has formed strategic business units or otherwise decentralized its operation, investors also focus on powerful line managers. Analysts concentrate on those in whose hands the company's fate is believed to reside.

For some investors, however, the story is entirely in the numbers, not the managers. Who occupies the highest corporate rung is of no more relevance than who fills the lowliest. Investors who index their holdings, for instance, look at only two criteria in deciding to invest, neither having anything to do with incumbent management: is a company in the index and, if so, what is its weight? For others, earnings momentum, price/earnings ratios, and market forecasts are everything. But for many, the quality of the company's senior management, an intangible but invaluable asset, carries great weight.

Investor Qualities for Corporate Leadership

Several qualities among prospective executive successors stand out. The person's prior performance record naturally tops the list. This can be tangibly gauged if the manager has served as the head of a large operating unit whose results are already well known to the investment community. If the successor has come up a financial or other functional career, however, personal performance is less transparent.

A second quality is the strategic focus that the manager will bring to the executive suite. Harrington Stores, for example, receives numerous queries about its management-succession plans that reflect this second criterion. The first consideration remains paramount, but it is not the end of the story. "The institutions are more interested in management today than just the financial results," observes the chief financial officer. "They're trying to find out what we're doing strategically, and manpower is an important cog in that strategy."

A third leadership quality is the extent to which the executive successor is likely to bring a shareholder focus to high office. The observations of a vice president at a major money-management firm illustrate the litmus tests often used by active investors. The money manager carefully evaluates companies, including their executives, before investing. "When you find good management," he says, "you go for it." The yardstick for him is management's preoccupation with company value. "You look to see a management working for the shareholders. You hate to see a company working for itself."

Unusual Succession Events

Unusual succession events draw special notice. An unusual event is one that exceeds convention or violates expectations. If an executive is too young, too old, or too otherwise exceptional demographically, investor questions flow. If an executive is a descendant of a dominant owning family, still other questions follow.

One of our companies had appointed a forty-five-year-old chief operating officer. This would not be unusual for a startup company: Craig McCaw, CEO of McCaw Cellular Communications with $500 million sales in 1990, was at the helm at age forty-one; William Gates, CEO of Microsoft with $800 million sales in 1990, was there at thirty-five. But the average age for CEOs of America's 1,000 largest companies stands at fifty-six. To be far afield from the mid-fifties is to raise investor eyebrows.

In the case of this $7 billion company, the new COO lay well outside the expected age range, and a flurry of investor questions followed. Isn't the company afraid that the COO might leave (his visibility at such a young age would make him a candidate for a chief executiveship elsewhere)? Has the company become unhappy with the present CEO (why else take such an unusual step)? Company answers to both are an emphatic no. Why then had he been appointed now? The simple response: succession planning. "This is going to round out his development in an area he hasn't had experience with," the CFO said, and "we're trying to get him more involved in the broader decision making."

Scions of founding and still-owning families often attract investor notice even if their current careers are still far removed from the executive suite. Their personal futures are too intertwined with investor fortunes to escape scrutiny. Institutional holders of Ford Motor Company are thus mindful of the special powers that come with family holdings, since descendants of the founder, Henry Ford, still control two-fifths of the voting stock (though the family owns less than one-tenth of the company's total stock value). Investors are also mindful of the presence of two fourth-generation descendants, cousins Edsel B. Ford II and William C. Ford Jr., in the upper-middle ranks. With Edsel in his mid-forties and William in his mid-thirties, they are still a dozen years and several rungs from the executive suite. But with the family fortune a powerful propellant, the relative obscurity of their positions cannot obscure their presence. Noting that investor pressure had led General Motors to oust its chief executive in 1992 for record losses, one business writer wonders if the Ford cousins will measure up in the tougher performance climate that institutional investors had helped create in the auto industry. "Edsel and Bill Ford have the right last name," observes the writer, "but do they have the right stuff?"[17]

Stewart Drugs' executive suite includes a prominent member of the founding and still-owning family. He has moved high in the company and appears to have a reasonable shot at the chief executiveship. He knows that his pedigree lends him a visibility far exceeding that of his peers. Investors frequently ask other executives about his performance and his prospects. Institutional investors "want to kind of size people up, especially when you get a family member," he says. This executive descendant is understanding if not entirely accepting of the shareholder scrutiny. "By all rights, I ought to be in Florida cutting coupons. . . . They're always suspicious of family members: 'Are they capable? Are they bright? Are they there just because they're blood?'"

Corporate Governance

Investors also take a company's governance policies as a sign of what is inside. In this sixth area of corporate response to shareholder pressure, companies have remodeled the board, sometimes as a concession, other times preemptively.

The record is uneven, with companies unyielding on some fronts and accommodating on others. The crosscurrents can be seen in company actions or inactions on three of the most visible governance devices: staggered director terms (the "classified" board), confidential proxy voting, and independent board committees. The classified board is usually opposed by investors, while confidential voting and independent committees are typically favored. CREF issued a policy guideline on corporate governance in 1993, and its posture is illuminating. Though it adopted no stance on classified boards, it favors confidential voting —"the corporation should adopt confidential voting for the election of directors and all other matters voted on by shareholders"—and backs formation of three board committees "consisting entirely of independent directors": audit, compensation, and nominating.[18]

Swimming successfully against the shareholder tide, more companies have adopted classified boards than dropped them. Between 1989 and 1992 the fraction of the nation's 1,000 largest firms with staggered terms for directors rose from 55 percent to 59 percent. On the other hand, because of investor urging, more companies have also adopted confidential voting. The fraction of the top 1,000 firms with such protection rose from 4 percent to 9 percent over the same period. The number of companies with audit, compensation, and nomination committees also grew (figure 5.1). Virtually all had adopted an audit committee by 1992, though much of that change was the result of a requirement by the New York Stock Exchange that listed companies have an independent audit committee. Less than one-tenth of the companies operated an independent nominating committee in 1972, but nearly two-thirds did so two decades later. In 1972, 70 percent maintained a compensation committee, but 90 percent had one by 1992.[19]

Company decisions to adopt or abandon governance policies in response to investor insistence are rarely abrupt and never simple. Rather, they often emerge over a lengthy period characterized by considerable jockeying between the two sides. This is evident, for instance, in Stewart Drugs' decision to adopt confidential proxy voting. In the view of institutional investors, the secret ballot protects investors against both lobbying before the annual meeting and reprisals afterward. Company managers, by contrast, are permitted by nonconfidential voting to reargue their case with investors voting against management. Stewart Drugs had successfully fended off three efforts by a public pension fund, with the support of a church group, to force confidential voting on the company through proxy resolution. The challengers attracted only one-sixth of the votes cast. By the fourth proxy challenge, however, the company had lost its will to resist. "This year, rather than fight it any longer," observes the company's general coun-

Figure 5.1 Percentage of Large Company Boards with Three Committees, 1972 and 1992

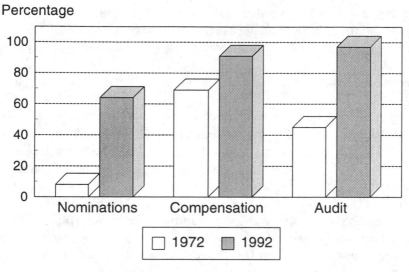

Percentage

□ 1972   ■ 1992

Source: Bacon, 1993.

sel, "we simply went ahead and agreed to do it." Management feels it could readily defeat the proposal again. But it also believes, in the general counsel's words, that the activist fund "probably represented the general feeling of investors." The company's CEO sits on the board of another company that had adopted confidential voting, and his experience there made it easier for him to accept it at home.

Stewart Drugs never talked directly with other investors about the confidential-voting proposal, but simply entered into a telephone dialogue and then negotiations with the pension fund. They soon reached agreement, with the company instituting confidential voting and the pension fund agreeing to withdraw its proxy challenge. The conclusion to the long campaign was anticlimactic. The company sent a brief note to the pension fund stating that its board had just adopted a policy of confidential voting on proxies, "contingent upon withdrawal of the shareholder proposal" calling for such a measure. It was withdrawn, and the company's annual proxy statement mentioned, without reference to the negotiations, that the company had adopted confidential voting.

Again, investors convey their preferences not only through direct discussions but also via buy and sell orders. The adoption of governance measures disliked by shareholders, such as poison pills, or the elimination of measures shareholders like, such as cumulative voting (a policy increasing the chance of electing dissident directors to a board), invites a modest drop in share price. Favored actions, such as appointing a new outside director, elicit a modest rise.[20]

Of some companies, however, institutions demand nothing at all. Harrington Stores learned this as it responded to what it believed was heightened investor interest in governance affairs. In the aftermath of a nearly successful hostile takeover, the chief executive and general counsel speak often with investors about their governance policies. "Governance is an issue that we spend a lot of time thinking about," said the CEO to a meeting of investors, "and it is one that we are constantly striving to improve." The chief executive reports that he is "eager to discuss how this one system of corporate governance works for us." He stresses the company's adoption of confidential voting, the directors' active review of divisional strategies, and the board's annual review of his own performance. He proudly notes that twelve of his fourteen directors are "completely independent." Yet he finds little real audience. The company considers adding shareholder forums that would focus on governance, but on testing the waters, the manager of investor relations forecasts that forty-nine of the top fifty investors would fail to attend. "The message we got back," says the general counsel, is "if you threw a party, nobody would come." Concludes the general counsel: "For the most part the people who come" to the analysts' meetings "don't have any idea what we're talking about. . . . They have no interest in corporate governance."

Changing All the Parts to Fix the Whole

These six areas of change constitute much of the restructuring that affected so many firms during the late 1980s and 1990s. Redesign and reengineering had spread far and wide. Corporate change emerged as the norm, stability the exception.

The scope of the restructuring is evident in any number of company surveys. A 1991 study of 406 large firms revealed that one-third had significantly reduced management staff, half laid off a substantial number of workers, half sold a business unit, and two-thirds shut down some company operations. A 1992 survey of 530 reported that three-quarters had downsized during just the preceding year, nearly the same fraction reorganized, and one-quarter divested, merged, or acquired (figure 5.2). An annual survey of large corporations during the first half of the 1990s found that a near majority or more had downsized their employment annually, and that they had knocked out one-tenth of the workforce on average when they did so (figure 5.3).[21]

The impact of restructuring is evident in other studies. Firms have

Figure 5.2 Percentage of Large Companies
That Restructured in 1991 and 1992

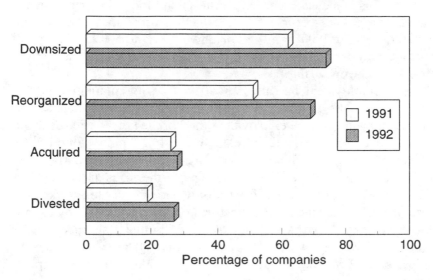

Source: Wyatt Co., 1993.

Figure 5.3. Percentage of Companies
Downsizing, 1990-95

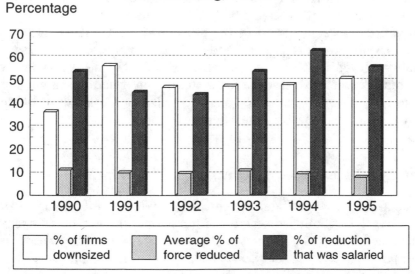

Source: American Management Association, 1995.

stripped away unrelated business areas: by 1990, the typical firm among the Fortune 500 industrial companies manufactured in only half the product areas of a decade earlier. At the same time, "high performance systems" have also spread far as companies introduced new job and work schemes: by 1990, half the Fortune 1,000 (the 500 largest manufacturing and service companies) had introduced quality circles and self-managed work teams. [22]

Lean employment has also spread widely, its cumulative effects squeezing millions of workers out of the traditional high-wage sector. After cresting in 1979, the employment total of the Fortune 500 declined annually over the next fifteen years. Some 16.2 million found work there in 1979, but only 11.5 by 1993 (figure 5.4). During the early 1970s, the Fortune 500 employed one of every five Americans in the nonagricultural workforce; by the early 1990s, only one of every ten worked for those firms. The decline of manufacturing is partially offset by expansion of the service sector. While the 500 largest industrial firms shed 2.9 million employees between 1982 and 1993, the 500 largest service companies added 2 million. Still, even the service 500 display no employment growth during the first four years of the 1990s. [23]

Restructuring actions taken in each of the six areas singly tend to achieve few enduring gains. Downsizing the workforce generates short-term cost savings, but in the absence of a broader reorganization, it brings only temporary relief. Reengineering business process creates immediate gains, but the gains are short-lived without changes in performance measures, compensation incentives, information technologies, employee skills, and organizational structure. [24]

Restructuring, then, should be seen as a multifaceted revamping of the corporation. A layoff of 5,000 employees—in and of itself—will not obtain what investors are demanding and competitors are already achieving, even if the cost savings are tangible. Neither will a newly revamped executive compensation system, even if tied to shareholder value. Nor will a turnover in top management or a reconfiguring of the board, even if the new occupants hear investors better.

The Two Faces of Restructuring

The extensive changes catalyzed in company organization by investor pressures have both worsened and improved the lot of company employees. Lean redesigns, cost reductions, and repeated downsizings have terminated careers and decimated communities. At the same time, process reengineering, flexible work, and streamlined hierarchies have improved employee productivity and product quality. Some employees

Figure 5.4 Total Employment of Fortune 500 Manufacturers and Fortune 500 Service Firms, 1979-93

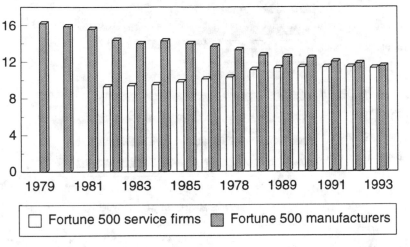

Employment in millions

Source: Fortune, various issues.

found they had lost all—or stood on the precipice of losing all. Job security, pension income, and health insurance were at risk or gone altogether.

For those who survive the restructuring, the aftermath often brings long work weeks and high stress levels, but also greater autonomy and more challenging assignments. A survey of the restructuring experience of 530 corporations in 1992 revealed heightened loads, diminished morale, and reduced employee commitment. Yet the survey also found companies reporting enhanced quality, customer service, risk taking, workforce competence, and productivity. The reorganized office or plant has often come to be a more challenging, more creative, more engaging place (figure 5.5).

A detailed study of one of the regional Bell telephone companies is illustrative. A survey in the early 1990s of employees revealed that the company's extensive restructuring, an agenda that had included a flattening of hierarchy and enlarging of control spans, had led to increased work loads and reduced job security. But it had also led to expanded work responsibilities and job discretion.[25] The two faces can also be seen in a journalist's 1993 portrait of a downsized General Electric manufacturing plant. The employment ranks at this jet-engine factory had been cut by half, and those still on the payroll feared additional rounds of layoffs. At the same time, they found the reorganized work

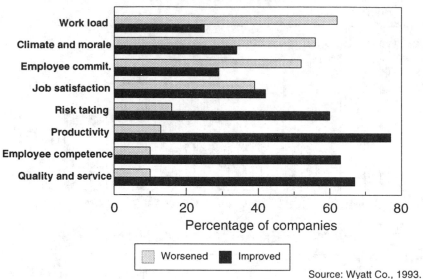

Figure 5.5 Company Assessments of Impact of Restructuring on Work and Employees Among Large Companies, 1992

Source: Wyatt Co., 1993.

system more engaging and collegial. People were "working scared," concludes the journalist, but they were also "working smarter, harder, more flexibly and more cooperatively."[26]

The dual impact of corporate restructuring on those who experience and manage it accounts for some of the schizophrenia toward restructuring. Devastated communities and ruined careers abound. So too do work environments characterized by high anxiety and low morale. At the same time, however, the work quality often improves, introducing a sense of variety, responsibility, and teamwork that survivors have never before experienced. Executives experience extraordinary stress as they manage the transformation. But in doing so they are also laying a foundation for improved company performance, richer compensation packages, and enhanced shareholder return.

While private investors applaud the gains, the public hates the losses. *Parade*, the nationally syndicated Sunday news magazine, asks rhetorically, "You're 49, and the boss just told you to empty out your desk . . . who will hire [you] now?" The *Wall Street Journal* observes on its front page that "jobless males proliferate in suburbs" and "survivors of layoffs battle angst, hurting productivity." The *New York Times* observes on its front page that "more are forced into ranks of self-employed at low pay," and later drives the message home with a photograph of dismissed IBM executives and their spouses who have gathered for prayer. A *New York Times* series on downsizing opens with the headline, "On the Battlefields of Business, Millions of Casualties." *Newsweek* runs a cover with photographs of the CEOs of four downsized companies—Digital Equipment, Scott Paper, AT&T, and IBM— under the caption, "Corporate Killers: Wall Street Loves Layoffs. But the Public Is Scared as Hell."[27]

Humorists find their mark as well. A *New Yorker* cartoon depicts a small delicatessen that is all that remains of IBM; the caption reads: "The Downsizing Continues." A newspaper drawing displays a makeshift sidewalk stand selling "Lemonade and Computers." On the front of the stand appears the IBM logo, and behind it a salesman mutters, "Well, the stockholders must be happy with the downsizing now." The accompanying human stress also generates its upbeat fantasies, exaggerated realities, and dark humor. A *New Yorker* cartoonist portrays the edge of a desert town with a sign warning motorists: "No layoffs next 200 miles." A personnel manager in a newspaper cartoon tells an applicant, "The job comes with a thirty-day guarantee." The caption of another *New Yorker* drawing, in which an executive throws a manager out of a high-rise office window reads, "This is why I get the big bucks."

Several days after the investor-driven ousting of Eastman Kodak's chief executive in 1993, financial journalists could already see the coming trade-offs: "If you're one of Eastman Kodak's 170,000 shareholders," wrote one, "rejoice. Stock analysts say your company is about to become more profitable. But if you're one of Kodak's 133,000 employees, get nervous. Analysts say there is a 1-in-6 chance you will lose your job."[28]

6

Managing the Shareholder

COMPANIES NOW MANAGE their investors in much the same way they manage any constituent group, whether inside or outside the firm. The tactical repertoire includes education, cultivation, and communication. It comprises informal briefings, private tours, and daily calls, executed with the professionalism befitting any executive action. Companies reward the large and loyal investor with privileged access; they punish the critical or inaccurate analyst with the cold shoulder.

Investor relations (IR) have moved high on the corporate organizational chart. Most IR managers report directly to the chief financial officer, and they have come to travel in the company's innermost circles. With a unique window on the world of investing, the IR manager knows as much about the company's position in the capital markets as anybody in the firm. Few restructuring actions are taken without looking through this window. Few strategic moves are made without consulting its manager.

Managing institutional investors also necessitates managing company managers. Executives must extract the right information from the ranks of the latter in order to be as fully informed and forthcoming as investors have come to expect. When company executives convey an incomplete or incorrect story to investors, both their personal credibility and stock price are sure to suffer as the real story later emerges. Executives must also patiently explain investor concerns to their own managers. Without an understanding within the company of Wall Street's engines, executive actions may seem incomprehensible, the demanding focus on shareholder returns a curious obsession.

The concept of a company managing its investor agenda stands in stark contrast to the image of proxy challenges, takeover battles, and executive firings, events in which investors appear to be managing the company agenda. If proxy challenges thrive on conflict, managing investors survives on cooperation. If proxy challenges bring tumult, managing investors fosters stability. If proxy challenges depend on momentary confrontation, managing investors builds on enduring relations.

The pitched battles and stable alliances are the Janus faces of investor capitalism, and they are rooted in the inherent but ambivalent dependence of large shareholders and company executives upon one another. They need each other—yet they are sitting in different corners. Investors and executives share mutual interests in the generation of wealth but divergent interests in how to create it and what to do with it. The partially opposed interests make perfect alignment an illusory goal; the partially shared interests make continuous conflict an ineffective means.

Though conflict and collaboration between investors and executives are inherent in this interdependence, the collaborative side has become more dominant as investor capitalism has matured. Open struggles for control draw attention but also mislead. They are but the tip of the iceberg, with most of the traffic between managers and investors transpiring out of sight. This was less true during the 1980s, when executives and owners were constructing the new foundations of investor capitalism in fits and starts. But it is far more true during the 1990s as the foundations have settled and relations become routinized. Investors and executives seek informative dialogue in place of proxy battle. They opt for dispassionate alliance over heated struggle, for quiet collaboration over defensive resistance.

To understand the evolving company management of investor affairs, it is useful to think about the evolving corporate management of human resources. While strikes and strife had characterized labor-management relations during the early rise of industry, dialogue and negotiation have become more dominant as each side has learned to work more effectively with the other. The interests of labor and management may be no more convergent now than before, but they pursue their respective interests with more collaborative and less costly strategies. Similarly, the interests of investors and managers may be no more alike during the 1990s than a decade earlier, but both sides have learned to apply less conflictual means for achieving them. To stretch the analogy, modern investor-relations management is to shareholder activism what modern human-resource management is to union activism. Put differently, shareholder activism is a certain feature of investor capitalism, but investor-relations management is the surer and ultimately the more dominant feature.[1]

This chapter characterizes the collaborative relationships that have emerged between investors and their companies, mapping the world that company executives must now regularly manage. The chapter, which begins with one company's agenda for managing its shareholders, examines how executives build relationships with investors, manage the complex and ever-changing array of relations that results, share information with their investors or withhold it from them, and use the investor network to sell the company's strategic story to an always skeptical audience.

Building a Relationship

Supplier relations, joint ventures, and strategic alliances are of necessity built from the ground up. They are constructed step-by-step through repeated contact over extended periods. In building shareholder relations, companies move in much the same fashion. They seek to create enduring, personalized contacts with those who oversee their shares, to move beyond the fleeting, impersonal contacts that have traditionally characterized their relationship to the capital market. In halting fashion, with frequent setbacks and occasional failures, companies have constructed an investor network that facilitates regular exchange of information and influence. The encompassing web is built on a thousand actions, some visibly grand but most the prosaic work of everyday management.[2]

The investor-affairs strategy of Statebank illustrates the micro work required to forge the macro network. A centerpiece of the bank's investor management is its annual analysts' meeting, which is held at a luxury hotel near headquarters. At one point the bank had scheduled the two-day gathering for the end of a fiscal quarter, and at another point for the end of the fiscal year. But bank executives found that the analysts' preoccupation with anticipated or past earnings undermined the meeting's purpose, and they moved the event to a period of no news when the analysts' minds could be most concentrated and least distracted. The bank initially filled the event almost entirely from the sell side. By the 1990s, however, it recognized the shift of ownership and power and extensively recruited from the buy side as well. The eighty-or-so analysts who attend the annual meetings are now drawn almost equally from these two wings of the investor community.

The analysts arriving on the first evening of one annual gathering find no fewer than forty members of senior management joining them for cocktails. The company has arranged each of the ten dinner tables to seat four company executives and eight analysts. The match is deliberate: analysts known for certain interests are seated with managers known for certain answers. After dessert, the bank's chief executive offers an extended—and upbeat—assessment of the company's past performance and future prospects. The following morning, the chief financial officer, the director of mergers and acquisitions, the head of the trust department, and other company officials offer more specialized assessments. The formal dialogue, however, is less important than the informal relations the company designed the gathering to foster.

To ensure that the right kind of relations develop, Statebank carefully scripts the event. It sends the forty senior managers a one-hundred-page briefing book with biographical sketches of each of the investor analysts and summaries of each one's current views of the company. The briefing book tells them that one buy-side analyst has been on *Institutional Investor's* "All-America Research Team" for the banking industry; another has recently placed a buy recommendation for the company's stock; a third jumped from two previous employers before working for the present firm. The briefing book includes a two-page profile of each represented institutional owner, a profile that characterizes the owners' investment strategies, portfolio turnover, and current holdings (one, an owner of nearly 2 million shares, is described as a "classic value" investor with low turnover).

The bank concludes the second day's formal program by noon. From experience, executives know that the analysts' technical attention will taper off by then. The analysts' recreational attention will not, however, and the company arranges golf and tennis for the afternoon, again with company managers and investment analysts carefully matched for more than their handicaps or serves.

The orchestrated informality seeks to personalize the bank's investor network at every turn. Statebank's chief executive inaugurates a mid-1990s gathering with a warm embrace: "It's great to see so many people here, a lot of familiar faces." Opening the next morning's program, he continues: "We're very pleased to have such a strong group and so many good friends join us on an annual basis." He applauds the expanding investor interest in the bank: "It's also nice that there are a few new faces each year. This gets to be a bigger and better group." As the CEO introduces the morning's first speaker, he observes that "most of you know" the bank's chief economist, and, "I think most of you know as well" the bank's head of retail operations. When the formal sessions later in the morning are about to give way to clubs and rackets, the CEO suggests to the analysts that "as those of you who have been here over the years know, you'll get lots of shots during the rest of the day—if you haven't had a chance to ask your questions—on the golf course or tennis court."

Small missteps that might be ignored or would never have occurred in the impersonal world of the past, however, are now magnified by the microcosm the company has created. Nuances are salient, their impact instant. During one of Statebank's annual analyst meetings, the program proceeds well for the bank until an executive's presentation on its recent string of acquisitions. The firm's merger and acquisition chief has just concluded a detailed defense of the actions when an analyst asks about their impact on shareholder value. The executive readily answered previous questions from the analysts, but here he offers only a cursory response and one that implies the acquisitions would have little effect. Some in the room believe very much otherwise, and afterward several call the vice president for investor affairs to complain about the dismissive response. While the program has achieved its purpose of renewing the personal chemistry between management and ownership, the vice president worries whether the passing comment has done enduring damage to a shareholder-responsive image that the bank has long been striving to create.

While bent on keeping the familiar faces returning each year, Statebank also seeks to widen its investor network, to add fresh faces to a secure institutional roster. Fear of excessive institutional influence is not high on its list of anxieties; fear of too little demand for its stock is. Therefore, the bank commissions a survey of investment analysts by a well-known polling organization. The 200 face-to-face interviews completed by the pollster reveal that the company is under-recognized. Compared to a set of similar banks, Statebank was less often on the surveyed analysts' computer screens. Only one-third are able to name any specific strengths or weaknesses of the company (a few praise the bank's conservative management, others criticize its acquisitions strategy). But among those analysts who are well aware of the company's operations, the bank' strengths outweigh its weaknesses, and their overall perceptions are more favorable than those of less-informed analysts. If familiarity makes the heart grow fonder rather than breeding contempt, the company sniffs opportunity. By aggressive presentation of its strategy story through personal contact with potential investors, it can stimulate new holdings.

The chief executive accordingly misses few occasions to meet with large shareholders and their advisers. In a reaffirming instance, the campaign clearly pays off. One of the nation's leading investment companies had perplexingly left Statebank out of its portfolios. Noting that the investment company's holdings include a leading competitor of the bank, Statebank executives invite the fund's managers to visit company headquarters. The bank also solicits an invitation for the chief executive to visit the investor's headquarters. The targeting works. The investor soon purchases some 2 million bank shares, gratifying confirmation of the theory of network building. Additional golf and tennis partners are expected at next year's meeting.

Managing an Array

Management formation of a shareholder network is like building any system intended to transcend spot relations. Stable, predictable, and personalized ties among the major parties constitute the crucial ingredients. Before the rise of institutional investing, companies seeking to create such relations with the shareholders faced a prohibitively large array of them. The concentration of corporate wealth in relatively few hands, however, has opened the way for the cultivation of a more limited set of enduring ties.

Company executives are generally well aware of the macro trends, but their practical concerns are primarily shaped by micro trends in ownership of their own firm. For the vice president of investor relations at National Metal Products, the shareholder array had finally shrunk to manageable size. "We have something like 150 institutions that own our shares," he observed. "They hold about 60 percent, and so you have a relatively small number of institutions that own a large amount of our stock." The consolidation permits his office to engage in a host of relationship activities, all focused on the large holder. "It's easier to concentrate on them than to try to do something with the 135,000-or-so individuals that own the other 40 percent."

Like the management of any resource, network investing requires an organizational foundation. Two aspects of the relationship between companies and investors give special shape to the foundation. One, *spans of influence*, concerns the number of relations that investment managers and company managers oversee. The second, *information for influence*, concerns the quality of the information flowing through the network. Both components are already familiar to those who travel the higher circles of corporate management, for they have long managed relations and exchanged information within the firm on their own way to the top. Managing an outside network is informed by a lifetime of managing an inside network.

Spans of Influence

When company executives take a moment at the end of a busy day to glance at their current list of shareholders, few find themselves staring at a roster topped by several dominant owners. For most executives, the register is a familiar but lengthy list of institutions, none claiming more than a thin slice of the company's equity. Fidelity, Calpers, Bankers Trust, and Prudential appear on the upper ranks of many lists, some running to 500 or more holders. Whatever the number, rare is the company executive who finds a single outside owner with more than a sliver of the firm's stock, typically no more than 2 percent or 3 percent. Even rarer is the executive who faces the same dominant owner more than several years in a row.

Conversely, when investment managers review their lists of large holdings, few see a roster topped by just one or two dominant companies. For most investment managers, the list is a safe but extended array of publicly traded firms, none accounting for more than a small fraction of the investor's equity. Topping many portfolios are the nation's blue-chip corporations, General Electric, Exxon, General Motors, and Philip Morris high among them. While some portfolios are limited to just several dozen companies, others run to 1,000 or more. Whatever the number, few money managers place more than 1 percent or 2 percent of the fund's equity in a single stock. Even fewer are the investors who maintain the same large position for more than several years.

True, the lists bear faint resemblance to what company executives and money managers had seen several decades earlier. The top ten or twenty investors now comprise a far more potent force in many firms' futures. Compared to their counterparts in Germany and Japan, however, American company executives and money managers still gaze upon thick forests with few standout trees. As a case in point, consider the holdings of the largest automobile makers in each of the three countries. The top five shareholders of Germany's Daimler-Benz (maker of Mercedes Benz) in 1986 held 74 percent of the stock, and the top five of Japan's Toyota Motor Corporation in 1992 held 22 percent. But the top five shareholders of America's General Motors in 1990 held less than 6 percent (the Michigan State Treasurer owned 1.4 percent, Sanford C. Bernstein 1.3 percent, Wells Fargo 1.2 percent, CREF 1 percent, and Bankers Trust 0.9 percent).[3]

Or consider the ownership structure for the ten companies with greatest capitalization as of the end of 1990. The top holder averaged 2.6 percent, and the next four ranged from 2.1 percent to 1.2 percent. Or focus just on those firms whose shares are already more than half institutionally owned. Of the 100 largest companies in early 1991, 58 are so held, and here the fraction of the company's shares owned by the single largest investor averaged 5.9 percent. A number of these largest single holders are not outside investors but rather the company's own employee stock-ownership plans or pension funds under outside management. The average fractions for the second through fifth largest holdings, more indicative of the outside ownership structure, range from 2.9 percent down to 1.8 percent.[4]

When viewed as a management issue, the still thin fractional presence of even the largest investors necessitates company oversight of a very broad span of influence for investor management. Inside the company, the span of control refers to the number of subordinates a given boss oversees. Outside the company, a span of influence refers to the number of institutional investors that a given company seeks to inform and influence.

To see the challenge faced by a company seeking to manage its investors, it is helpful to compare the spans of influence outside the company with the spans of control inside. Textbooks have traditionally asserted that an average of seven to eight "direct reports" (that is, employees who report directly to each manager) is a sign of good management. A study of 105 units of twenty-five large North American firms in 1989 reveals that a manager on average directly oversaw eight subordinates. Span width varies by industry, with oil firms preferring narrow spans and automakers broad ones. It also varies with the number of management layers, the vertical links in the reporting chain from front line to chief executive. Companies with many layers tend to have narrow spans, while those with few layers tend to have broad ones. Recent restructuring campaigns have led many firms to expand their spans and reduce their layers, but even in the leaner and flatter world of the 1990s, few corporate executives oversee more than a score of directly reporting managers. The typical organizational chart is a five-by-eight—five management layers with eight direct reports per manager.[5]

By contrast, the comparable chart for the relationship between companies and their investors is far flatter and far wider. A company's investor-relations office typically oversees the relationship, and its staff is tiny. Surveys of 531 firms in 1992 and 585 firms in 1994 found four-fifths of the companies had two or fewer professional staff members concerned with investor relations, and a majority had budgets under $0.5 million. True, the full-time attention of the investor-affairs specialists and the part-time attention of top executives concentrate on just the fifty to one hundred largest holders. Even so, the width of their span of influence—one or two company managers for fifty to one hundred major investors—stands at an extreme.[6]

On the other side, it is also useful to examine the spans of influence managed by institutional investors, the number of firms over which they may seek to exert some sway. These firms too preside over a very wide array of companies. Consider the 1,107 institutional investors that had filed a 13F form with the U.S. Securities and Exchange Commission (SEC) at the end of 1991. Institutional investors that exercise "investment discretion" in managing at least $100 million on behalf of others must file quarterly 13F listings of their individual holdings, and the filings offer relatively complete identification of institutional holdings. About one-quarter (246) of these institutional investors hold stock in fifty or fewer companies (figure 6.1). Even with a tiny staff, these funds should have ample opportunity to kick the tires of most of their firms. At the other end of the spectrum, however, 119 investors each hold stocks in more than 500 companies, and their combined assets constitute half (52 percent) of the assets of all 13F filers. Thirty-three investors hold more than 1,000 separate stocks, eight more than 2,000 (table 6.1).

In diagramming a network chart for the relations of the nation's largest industrial firm, Exxon Corporation, with its some 700 institutional holders in 1990, the architecture looks very different from a typical organizational chart. The network chart comprises two layers and a 700-width span (figure 6.2). This stands in contrast to oil-company organizational charts, where the norm is some six layers and four-width spans. The analogous chart for the administrators of one of Exxon's top five investors, CREF, looks much like Exxon's outside network chart

Table 6.1 Institutional Investors Holding More Than 2,000 Stocks, 1991

Institutional Investor	Number of Stocks	Market value ($ billions)
Wells Fargo Inst. Trust	4,801	61.7
Mellon Bank Corporation	3,851	56.9
Bankers Trust New York Corp.	3,635	59.5
American National Bank & Trust Co.	3,581	12.8
California State Teachers Retirement	3,550	16.1
Dimensional Fund Advisors	2,979	4.3
Aetna Life and Casualty	2,420	7.7
Fidelity Management and Research	2,300	48.6

Source: Blume and Zeldes, 1993.

Figure 6.1 Number of Common Stocks
in Portfolios of Institutional Investors, 1991

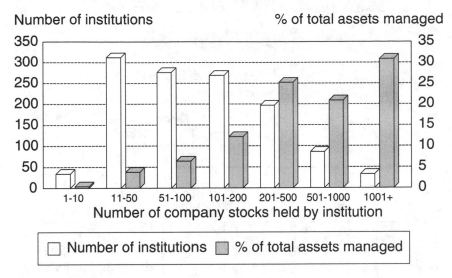

Source: Blume and Zeldes, 1993.

and little like Exxon's inside organizational chart. Here the parameters are two layers and an 1,800-width span (figure 6.3).

Investor Drift

The typical network chart, which differs radically from the typical organizational chart in its construction, is also different in terms of stability. We know that the chief executive of a large company typically holds office for nine years. We also know that company leadership acquires special strength when enduring executive teams are formed at the top. Opportunities for constructing analogous long-term working relations between companies and investors, however, is limited by what might be termed "investor drift."[7]

Investor drift can be illustrated with the top stockholders of WWK Products Corporation. Table 6.2 displays its ten largest investors on a semiannual basis over a five-year period. Imagine that you are appointed by the chief executive to manage relations with the company's top ten holders. Your charge is to work intensively with them to form a deep and enduring relationship such that both sides are thoroughly familiar with each other. But within a year, two of your top ten investors have left. Within two years, half have turned over. Within five years, eight of the original ten have dropped out. Another fourteen

Figure 6.2 Span of Influence of Exxon Corporation, 1990

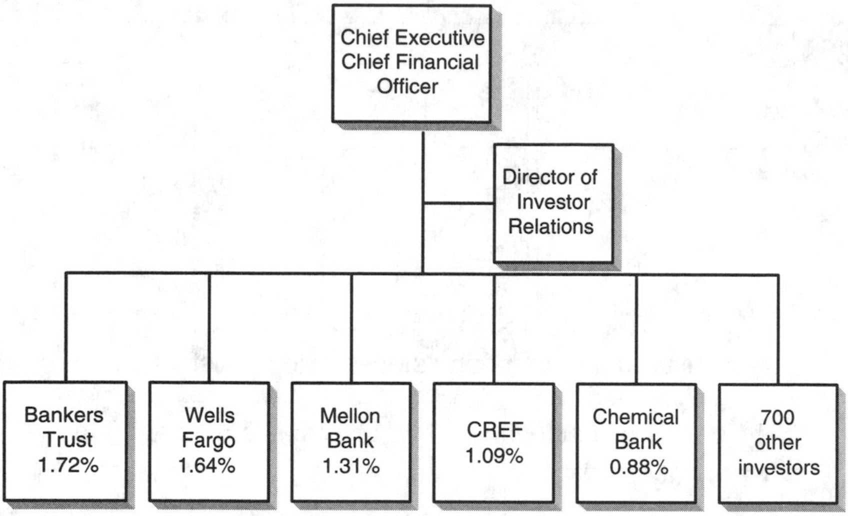

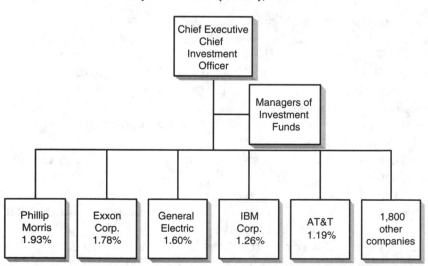

Source: Disclosure, Inc.

Figure 6.3 Span of Influence of College Retirement Equities Fund (CREF), 1990

Source: CREF.

investors are ranked among the top ten at some point during this five-year period. While your original charge was for intensive contact with the top ten, you actually have had to manage relations with a total of twenty-four. Only a single investor, a commercial bank that indexes—and thus has no interest in meeting with you—remains top ranked throughout the five years.

It is also notable that most of the relations you are able to form for WWK Products are with investment companies, home of mutual-fund and money managers. Of the twenty-four investors that are the focus of your attention, seventeen are investment companies, including Merrill Lynch, Fidelity, and Putnam. Among institutional investors, they are known to turn over their portfolios often. In 1993, mutual funds on average replaced over 48 percent of their stock holdings. Thus there is a fifty-fifty chance that an investment company in which you invest great time and energy will no longer be a major holder just twelve months later.[8]

Only three pension funds, all public, appear on WWK Products' top-investor list. Their small number is disappointing since, of all institutions, public pensions turn over their stock least frequently—just 13 percent in 1993—and you had hoped that a number of pension funds would constitute a stable core around which to build your investor network. Many pension funds, you learn, have turned the bulk of their equity over to outside money managers for investment: in 1993, pen-

Table 6.2 Ten Largest Shareholders of WWK Products Corp. as of June 1988, and Semi-annually through June 1993 (millions of shares)

	1988		1989		1990		1991		1992		1993
Investment company	4.13	4.98	4.75								
Investment company	2.65	2.68	2.30	2.54	2.39	2.70	2.35	2.09	2.40	2.36	
Investment company	2.50	1.92	1.71								
Commercial bank	2.15	2.09	2.07	2.11	1.98	1.95	2.05	2.13	2.15	2.11	2.70
Investment company	2.11	1.72									
Investment company	2.00	2.07	1.66	1.65	1.59						
Commercial bank	1.71	1.81	2.00	2.03	2.05	1.96					
Public pension	1.66	1.59	1.55	1.47							
Public pension	1.60	1.66	1.60								
Investment company	1.59			1.37	1.60	2.12	2.01	2.18	3.00	3.04	2.36
Commercial bank		1.49	1.70	1.74	1.77	1.93	2.02	2.07		2.06	
Investment company			1.82	2.28	1.64	2.08	3.14	2.74			
Public pension				2.11	2.54	2.94	2.94	2.94	2.74	2.74	2.74
Investment company				1.30	1.55	1.72					
Investment company					1.85	1.51					
Investment company						1.81	2.19	2.66	2.93	2.91	
Investment company							2.57	1.99	2.34	2.59	2.79
Investment company							2.32	2.14	3.10		4.20
Investment company							2.08	2.16			4.07
Commercial bank										3.49	3.27
Investment company									2.33	2.52	2.63
Insurance company									2.32	2.43	2.35
Investment company											2.39
Investment company											

Note: Holdings of investors not ranked among the top ten in a given year are not shown. The first column for each year is for holdings at the end of June; the second column is for the end of December.   Source: Disclosure, Inc.

sions held 50 percent of all institutional assets but directly managed only 22 percent. The potentially patient presence of pension funds is thus lost to your relationship program because of their widespread use of intermediary—and more fickle—investors. In short, your management work is cut out for you.[9]

Cultivating a Transient Familiarity

The investor drift and broad spans of influence generate a managerial challenge for both sides. If stability fosters attention, drift instills neglect. With investment managers responsible for relations with hundreds of companies, and with company managers responsible for relations with hundreds of investors, it comes as no surprise that denizens of both sides sometimes find their counterparts remote, unfamiliar, and unresponsive. In a market world, this is no problem; in a network world, it is. Mechanisms for establishing and nourishing contact between the two diverse and ever-evolving arrays of organizations are required.

The process of constructing these mechanisms is one of tediously building up from hundreds of custom-designed micro-foundations that were cultivated through personalized, painstaking, oft-repeated contact. Even the decision to foster such networks is often taken implicitly, a product of numerous smaller actions over years. As new investors enter the picture, companies repeat the process, routinely reaching out to cement ties with them. As in the case of company executives and military officers transferred to fresh venues, it is understood that familiar relations must be quickly established, even if they are to endure only briefly. It is a web of transient familiarity, always evolving and recurrently personalized.

Though no single model prevails, companies employ a host of techniques for orchestrating investor contact. Most bring major investors to headquarters for private discussions with top officers. Many arrange for the chief executive and financial officers to visit investor offices. A few invite select institutions to meet with company directors. Virtually all maintain an open telephone line for investor queries. Financial officers often lead the charge—a survey of CFOs in 1992 reveals that two-fifths met with their major investors at least twice a year—but company strategies usually entail redundant and multiple contacts at many levels. Several company examples illustrate the rich diversity.[10]

National Metal Products has established routinized contact with its major investors by taking its chief executive to them. The office of the CEO makes ten to fifteen days a year available for visiting institutions. His vice president for investor affairs arranges two or three meetings for each of those days in cities around the country, about half with holders currently among the firm's top 100, and the other half with prospects. One of the CEO's itineraries from the 1990s is shown in table 6.3. In arranging the meetings, the company seeks to sit with the fund's key decision makers, both those who make the investment and those who cast the proxy. In some instances that proves challenging since a number of individuals and committees have a hand in the decisions at some of the larger institutions. A consulting firm and the company's own informal queries, however, usually identify the key players well in advance. On this trip, the CEO met with representative of institutions that jointly hold more than 30 million of his company's shares, about one-eighth of the total. One of the stops was the headquarters of Calpers, the premier activist shareholder, where, the chief executive believed, he came to appreciate the minds of its money managers.

Though personalized relations between executives and investors are in some instances long-standing, they are rarely taken for granted. A university endowment fund, for instance, has ranked among the top investors of Columbia Foods for nearly two decades. Company executives often visit the fund's offices, typically meeting with the university treasurer, the principal investment officer, and the consumer-sector analyst. "We're talking to people that we have been talking with periodically for the better part of the last twenty years," observes the company's manager of investor affairs. Managers of the university fund, which is a long-term investor, express little interest in the company's momentary concerns or price swings, preferring to concentrate on its strategic plans. As one discussion draws to a close, the university treasurer reminds company management of his special stake in seeing a steadily rising dividend from a steadily executed strategy. The endowment supports faculty research, and continuing dividend growth, he says, permits the university to grow its research budget annually without dipping into endowment principal.

Companies also aggressively encourage top investors to visit headquarters, where they are given the red-carpet treatment. As they would in hosting any visitor in the upper reaches of the corporate pyramid, company staff prepare executives to make their important guests feel warmly welcome. Large corporations also tend to arrange for investors to travel well beyond the executive suite. With an assemblage of products, an assortment of divisions, and business in many countries, they recognize that the detailed data sought are known by no single manager.

As a case in point, the Hutchins Motors Corporation operates worldwide, and it provides a wide consultation base for investors. It insists that all investor contact come through a single finance office at headquarters. "We are paranoid here," explained the responsible man-

Table 6.3 Meetings of the Chief Executive of National Metal Products with Institutional Investors During a Seven-Week Period, Early 1990s

Date	City	Institutional Investor	Current Holdings
March 21	New York City	Dreyfus Management	50,000
		Lehman Ark Management	4,618,390
		Neuberger & Berman	53,997
April 4	New York City	Merrill Lynch	132,040
		Buckingham Research	4,993,995*
April 9	San Francisco	McCullough, Andrews & Cappiello	0
		Dodge & Cox	0
	Sacramento	Calpers	1,175,379
		California State Teachers Retirement	898,130
April 10	Los Angeles	Trust Company of the West	0
		Capital Group	315,000
		First Interstate Bank	513,107
April 19	Columbus	Ohio School Employees	0
		Ohio Public Employees	0
		Ohio State Teachers Retirement	1,587,997
April 24	Boston	Fidelity Management & Research	5,099,382
		Wellington Management	818,550
		Putnam Management	4,054,908
May 1	Philadelphia	Newbolds Asset Management	0
		Delaware Management	10,068,600
		University of Pennsylvania	575,000
May 7	Houston	Texas Commerce Bank	0
		American Capital	435,000

*Organized meeting with eleven institutional investors: Salomon (Lehman) Investment Management (0 shares); Knights of Columbus (0 shares); Harvard Management (0 shares); Alliance Capital (1,163,099 shares); Oppenheimer Capital (15,000 shares); Prudential (315,896 shares); American International Group (0 shares); Delafield Asset Management (0 shares); Hudson Capital (0 shares); Jarmusz Asset Management (0 shares); and the company pension fund (approximately 3,500,000 shares).

Source: Company records.

ager, "about making sure that the institutional investors come through" his department. This is no small concern, since the flow is large—twenty-five sell-side analysts regularly track the company and fifty buy-side people are in active contact—and since some investors seek to form special relationships with top executives like those that journalists cultivate with well-placed sources. But once ushered through the right office, the company opens access to a dozen executives and another two dozen managers in operations around the world.

Hutchins Motors carefully customizes the visiting investor's itinerary. The customizing is a matter of both power and precision. "Based on our assessment of the analyst and his importance ... to us and the investment community," says the investor-relations manager, "and based on what his desires are, what subjects he wants to discuss, we set up an agenda." Analysts seeking broad information might be sent to a vice president for finance who serves as the company's primary spokesman to the investment community. Analysts seeking information on the company's European operations, by contrast, might be directed to a manager in finance whose full-time responsibility is to track the European division. They might also be handed off to the finance office in the European headquarters for a personal visit there. For those who are insatiably curious about product development, the company dispatches the hearty to a nearby test track for a spin in the latest prototype. Those whose holdings are enormous the company sends upstairs for an audience with the chief executive.

Richards Oil Corporation pursues a similar course but adds personal contact between investors and directors as part of the network glue. It invites about a dozen major shareholders to meet over lunch with company directors near the time of the company's annual meeting, giving them free rein with company directors and officers.

A consumer-products company, not among the focus firms, elevates the director contact to formal company policy. In what it terms an "owner's program," it periodically arranges for separate meetings between several outside directors and key investors. The meetings draw twenty to forty representatives from both investment companies and pension funds. Often attending is the investor that had pressed the company to begin such forums (upon their establishment, the investor had agreed to withdraw a proxy resolution calling for the establishment of a shareholder advisory committee). Two of the company's more seasoned directors participate in the first meeting, and others participate in subsequent semiannual forums. The company's general counsel prepares the directors for the encounter, stressing that the "ground rules are no new disclosures." Within that framework, the first meeting's dialogue concentrates on the board's criteria for nominating directors and evaluating executive performance, the company's long-range plans for both domestic and international expansion, and the firm's policies on stock dividends and share repurchases. To management's satisfaction, the discussion focuses little on the next quarter, much on long-term strategy. To investors' satisfaction, the chief executive withdraws from the board's nominating committee soon after the first meeting.

This program is but one strand of a complex blend of efforts used by the consumer-products firm to expand its band width. During one twelve-month period, for instance, the company arranged for more than one hundred institutional investors to have direct conversations with its senior managers. The chief executive and general counsel themselves met privately with a public pension fund that had been pressing for policies that were more shareholder friendly (such as confidential voting) and improved company performance (the company had been known for its strong defenses and weak earnings). The company routinely forwards analysts' reports and earnings estimates to all members of the board. The underlying philosophy, according to the company's IR director, is "to move away from a 'we-they' relationship." As the investor contact expanded, the chief executive learned that shareholder input could be as important as management output for avoiding adversity: "In the almost three years that I've been chairman," said the CEO, "I've discovered that owners are looking for more dialogue than presentation. In a word, what they want is communication."

Most companies have moved well beyond passive reaction to active engagement. Rather than responding to queries, they initiate the calls, not only to current holders but also to those that ought to be. One large financial services firm (also not among the focus companies) displays the constructive strategy common to many. The company has come to track its institutional shareholders on a daily basis, and a "relationship manager" and a backup manager are assigned to work with each of its fifty largest investors. This stands in contrast to the recent past when the largest were not even fully identified, let alone stroked: "Five or six years ago we didn't know for sure who the top fifty were," confided the senior vice president for investor relations. It "was a reactive approach: the phone rings, you answer it." That is past history. "Because we have aggressively gone out to determine who our shareholders are, we now have a much better idea both of who our shareholders and who our potential shareholders are." To pinpoint the best potentials, it shadows more than 2,000 institutional investors. "We always have a targeted list of investors," explained the financial-services manger. "When you match their appetite against the [actual] holding of us, we identify those who we should be a logical holding for, but aren't." It is those that the company then seeks to draw into its web.

Chase Chemical Products follows a similar proactive strategy with what it considers a core set of investors. It defines the core by the investors' size and length of holdings, and its analysis reveals that sixty-six institutions held at least 100,000 shares during every quarterly reporting period over the past eight years. Their holdings varied from quarter to quarter, sometimes exceeding 3 million shares but never dropping below 100,000. Together, the sixty-six controlled more than two-fifths of the company's shares at any given time. And it is to them that the company directs its energies, viewing communication with smaller or vacillating holders a "waste" of time. "We're trying to create a fair value over time, and the long-term holders will spend some time understanding our fundamentals and not just black-box analysis," offered the chief financial officer. "We want them to know our company. We think that if people understand our company, they'll put a fair value on it."

Crisis Construction

While most companies construct their investor networks gradually, in some instances companies jump abruptly into the business of relationship building. A shareholder crisis is usually the spring behind the leap.

A case in point is Harrington Stores following the takeover threat during the late 1980s. As a raider accumulated shares and arbitrageurs came in close behind, management discovered to its horror that many long-term holders displayed fleeting loyalty at best. If the takeover group offered an attractive price, investors were prepared to tender their shares. "Some of our largest investors seem more interested in obtaining short-term gains than standing by a company that had provided them with excellent returns for many years," complained the chief executive.

Prior to the crisis, Harrington Stores' chief executive had made few of the increasingly conventional moves that signal shareholder attentiveness. Like a politician never on the stump, the CEO's invisibility created the impression, recalled the general counsel, that he "wasn't particularly interested in financial analysts or the institutional shareholding community." The company learned in retrospect that its executive ranks were not only unknown personally but also of unknown quality. As a result, when the company's earnings dropped and the raider came in close behind, many investors were quick to conclude that the company "doesn't have fundamental management strength."

Through a series of unusual antitakeover maneuvers, Harrington Stores finally prevailed, but management concluded that it would have been in a far stronger position to resist the threat if it had already known its owners. "We really hadn't done a good enough job in talking with institutions," confessed the general counsel. "We did a pretty good job getting information out. What we weren't doing enough of with the institutional shareholders was reaching out to communicate with them directly." Since personal presence symbolizes personal interest, its absence signaled impersonal disinterest.

In the wake of Harrington Stores' successful defense, the chief executive arranged meetings with virtually all of his major holders. He had been known for his "hands-on" managerial style inside the firm, and now he applied the same outside the firm. He appeared at an owners' watering hole, the Council of Institutional Investors, to explain the new philosophy he had learned: "My experience during this takeover threat ... has taught me the value of a strong corporate governance policy—and it has taught me the importance of an active program of communication with investors."

Harrington Stores designed its program to overcome the impersonality that management felt to be a fundamental weakness upon which the raider had capitalized. "It's a little tough to walk in on ten minutes' notice," concedes the general counsel, and say, "Let's develop that relationship over the next four or five minutes." A principled commitment also drove some of the company initiative. Major shareholders simply deserve a better relationship, the general counsel asserts, and they are "entitled to hear from us." But energizing the principled behavior is the self-interested purpose of ensuring that investors can be seen on short notice.

Reaching the right people on the investor side to create the relationship usually—but not always—proves straightforward. At some of the largest institutions, the functions of the portfolio manager, stock analyst, and proxy voter have evolved into separate roles. Proxy and investment committees occasionally exercise a final judgment as well. During a proxy fight it is thus important to have a relationship with the proxy voter, while the portfolio manager and analyst are the right people when the company is promoting its shares. The chief financial officer for Harrington Stores expresses the preferences of many executives: "We'd like to communicate with the decision makers, especially when there's a change going on at the company, to make sure that we've got their attention and that they are informed."

Companies create their investor networks on premises similar to those behind the fashioning of their political networks. Gifts by corporate political action committees (PACs) to candidates for office are seldom intended to shape a particular policy or vote. Rather, companies offer their PAC contributions to candidates primarily as a way of later ensuring a reception on Capitol Hill, of guaranteeing a chance to present their case on legislation that really matters. Harrington Stores' general counsel sees similar payoffs in management's relations with investors: "We at least want to have, at a minimum, a neutral, open hearing when an issue comes up."

But Harrington Stores' general counsel also confirms that his company seeks more than that. Companies also build their investor networks on premises similar to those of their charitable contributions to nonprofit organizations. Much corporate giving is designed not so much around either philanthropic or narrow self-interested ends, but rather to create an aura of public respectability for a company and its management. In the words of the general counsel, this too is a major objective of the investor networking: "We would like, if something breaks, to have our institutions say, 'Oh ... that's a good company, it's a well-managed company, they plan long-term, and they do listen to their shareholders.'"

Information for Influence

The second management challenge concerns the quality of the information pulsing through the company-investor networks. Without accurate and timely information about each side flowing to the other, any mutual advice giving is sure to be error ridden. Misled investors have long memories.

A first principle echoes the concept of the efficient market: enough information about the company should be in the hands of the investors for a fair pricing of the stock. The chief financial officer of Chase Chemical Products describes it this way: "Our objective is to try to keep a fair evaluation of [the company's] stock price out there. We're not trying to hype the stock, we're just trying to provide the investors all the relevant information we think [they need in order] for them to put a fair value on the stock." Solid information should yield evenhanded treatment. "If we get a fair value on our stock, I don't think we can expect any more."

The company executive most responsible for ensuring effective dissemination of the information is the manager of investor relations. His or her task is to assemble, distill, and articulate the company's account of itself. The investor-affairs manager for Strikeline Computer Company pulls information together from a host of divisional managers: "I get the pieces of the operating men's part of the puzzle," he says, "and if they have an important story to tell" the investors, "I'll help them tell it."

To convey the information, managers of investor relations require both the information and a perspective for interpreting it. Acquiring the information depends on effective internal relations with the executives who generate the data. Acquiring the perspective depends on detailed study of the company and its market, competitors, and investors. In the words of the IR manager for Columbia Foods: "You must have access to information, both financial and market-type data. You must also have access to people because it is the perspective that you get that goes beyond the numbers that is important in describing the business and giving investors the confidence that they understand the company and what it's trying to do." He asks rhetorically, "How can I discuss in a meaningful way with investors our cereal business without understanding the dynamics of our industry? How can I discuss our prospects without really understanding the dynamics of what makes this business work?"

To understand how the business works, the Columbia Foods IR manager meets almost daily with the chief executive and chief financial officer, routinely calls division presidents, joins corporate planning and budgeting meetings, and attends management presentations to the board. When he lacks information in response to an investor query, he has the levers to quickly obtain it. One analyst, for instance, had asked what the firm was doing in response to a competitor's use of new information technologies for faster delivery of inventories to a group of retail stores. "Instead of making some flip answer that may or may not be right and may in fact be misleading," the manager says, he called through his well-oiled network and soon delivered a well-informed response.

Some IR managers further cultivate the network through the time-honored practice of simply walking around. At Strikeline Computer Company, for instance, the IR manager delivers more than seventy presentations a year to groups of company employees at a variety of plant locations. The employees' questions about the stock market and the company's image betray a more than passing curiosity. The company has extended stock options widely to its employees as an incentive scheme, but since the company's stock price has been in decline for several years, most of the options were well "underwater" (that is, the current stock price had fallen below the option exercise price). Until investors could see a brighter future for the company, employees would be forced to forgo their option-based compensation. After addressing their questions, the manager of investor relations makes his appeal: Investor perceptions depend on what investors learn from the company, and, as the chief communicator, "I'm only as good as my information flow. If you have interesting vignettes, if you have an interesting story, or some important data, tell me. Help me tell the story." Though few people spontaneously follow up, the walking around facilitated their responsiveness later, when they were called with specific requests.

Once the function of the IR manager is well established within the firm, executives contact the IR office before taking virtually any action likely to pique shareholder curiosity. "When something hits the *Wall Street Journal*," said a divisional president at WWK Products, "none of us wants" the IR manager "to be embarrassed by not knowing what's going on."

Occasionally the company's representative to the investment community is deliberately misled by the company's own managers. Such a moment came in the wake of the development of a high-profile product by Strikeline Computer Company. The responsible product manager had a good track record both in the technical development of new products and in appraising market demand for them. As his latest product is nearing completion, he informs the IR manager and the latter, in turn, informally discusses the forthcoming introduction with many investors. Though not formally disclosed by the company, the anticipated product and its expected impact in effect become a matter of public record. In this instance, however, the IR office is given overly optimistic forecasts, and the product falls far short of company—and investor—expectations.

When later confronted by investors disappointed by the product's limited success, the IR manager finds himself awkwardly trying to excuse what he had inadvertently led investors to expect: "Upon further tests," he confesses, "it didn't quite materialize the way we thought." The real mistake, he believes in retrospect, was not to have double-checked the product information with his deep-throat sources, secret sources he had cultivated long ago because he had been burned several times by management misinformation. In this instance, despite a confidential source in the product-development section, the IR manager had not bothered to double-check the product manager's claims because of the latter's stellar reputation for reliability.

The manager of investor affairs for Strikeline Computer knows from hard experience, confirmed once again, that inaccurate information is its own worst enemy. "You eat it because Wall Street's just going to throw it right back in your face." He vows to take even less for granted in the future. He never again invites the product manager to meet a securities analyst, either individually or in a group of company managers. And he subjects all further information from the product manager to detailed double-checking. He also begins to pose the fictional questions of a "mystery analyst," a device he had earlier developed for use elsewhere in the company. "An analyst said to me . . . " he begins, and then asks probing questions that allegedly have been posed by a tough but unnamed Wall Street source.

Broadening the Flow

The flow of information from companies to investors improved during the 1980s and 1990s, at least as assessed by the investors themselves. In annual surveys of more than 500 investors by Greenwich Associates since 1981, the institutions report continuous improvement in the quality of company data. Institutions affirm every year that the amount and quality of corporate information provided to them has improved, and that the number and willingness of companies to meet with them has also increased. A 1993 survey of stock analysts and portfolio managers found three-fifths reporting contact with their companies several times a month, and one-fifth with contact several times a week.[11]

On the other side, most companies also report that they are expanding their dissemination of information to investors. The channels are many: analysts' meetings at the end of every quarter; conference calls open to all interested investors in the wake of major company events; newsletters for shareholders; commercial services for faxing or interpreting company announcements or news to interested parties; and informal telephone and personal contact between managers and investors. Numerous multicompany forums add to the reach. Columbia Foods, for example, participates in an annual four-day meeting in New York with consumer analysts. More than a dozen major firms offer their visions before an audience of 300 representatives of both the sell and the buy sides, including a number of major international investors. The chief executive and his three divisional presidents attended one recent event, offering seventy-five minutes of formal assessment at the podium and more informal commentary in the hallways afterward.[12]

New technologies expedite the dissemination. The U.S. Postal Service and Federal Express had carried much of the news during the 1980s, but by the 1990s several commercial services (for example, First Call, Bloomberg Business News, Streetlink of ADP's Investor Communications Services, and the Dow Jones News Service) and fax and Internet facilities had turned overnight service into instant delivery. Within several hours of an earnings release or special announcement, detailed company news in the form released by the company—rather than interpreted and summarized by a third party—reaches most major analysts and institutional investors. Through the same channels companies learn equally fast about revisions in analyst stock recommendations and earnings estimates. Companies also use the channels to learn about one another. Columbia Foods, for example, subscribes to a daily service that provides all analysts' reports on its competitors as well as the competitors' reports about themselves to their investors.[13]

Many companies and investors turn to the even more instant link of electronic mail. The automation of public reporting helped as well. The SEC's Electronic Data Gathering and Retrieval (EDGAR) mandates that all publicly traded U.S. firms file all documents electronically by the end of 1996, allowing for instant retrieval by interested investors. Several organizations (for example, Dow Jones, NBC, and Bloomberg) offer video coverage of company analysts' meetings and interviews with company officials. Conference calls have also become a staple, both for quarter's end and for special events. When Computer Associates International announced a $1.7 billion acquisition of Legent Corporation in 1995, Computer Associates' chief executive, Sanjay Kumar, immediately held a morning conference call with some 300 investors and analysts to explain its merits (Computer Associates' stock price dropped two points during the first hour of trading on the day of the announcement—but rose five points later that morning by the end of the seventy-five-minute conference call). New telephone technologies allow companies to predetermine which analysts are given priority when company officers finish a presentation and invite questions. Without knowing it, the unfriendly analyst is relegated to the end of a queue that seems never to move forward. Small investors, of still less interest to company managers, never even learn of the conference call.[14]

Companies have also increased their band width, pumping far more information through the communication channels. They are expanding their breakouts of company sectorial and regional results. They are adding parameters that analysts seek for their investing models. They are describing key products in more detail. Company executives know, however, that they have to set their own new limits on the information flow. The analyst appetite for information is insatiable. Companies also know that the more open they are with data, the more the competition knows about them. Managers assume that any information channeled to analysts will reach their competitors.

Richards Oil's information strategy is typical. In response to investor requests, it had been expanding its public reporting for over a decade. By the early 1990s, it had added a quarterly supplement for its analysts that included many of the parameters they had sought, consistently comparing the quarter with its counterpart in the previous year. The report includes the quantity and price of crude oil and natural gas; oil and gas production by world region; refinery inputs and refined product outputs; U.S. and international product sales; and capital and exploratory expenditures by region. "Why they want that [data]," said the company's IR director, "I don't know. But they want it." So illuminating are the figures that top management concluded the report should also be distributed to all employees. Some analysts seek still greater detail on the regional and product breakouts, and while this detail is not formally reported, the company provides it as soft data upon request. Still, the information pit is not bottomless. When the company was asked by one analyst to provide revenue figures for every company product for every country in Europe, the simple response was, "No!"

Companies have also established ways to reach their owners almost instantly when major developments call for it. Statebank, for instance, had announced several major acquisitions during the early 1990s. The purchases had not been fully expected, nor had they been entirely welcome. The company scheduled open conference calls with analysts immediately after each of the announcements to maximize the information flow and minimize the damage. Richards Oil had pursued a similar tactic in the wake of a fire at one of its major refineries. Within minutes, the company communicated what it knew of the refinery disaster—and why the event should not be seen as an earnings disaster—to both the financial media and the analyst circuit. The company's stock initially lost $1.50 as news of the refinery fire came over the wires, but the intervention helped calm the market and by day's end the price had rebounded.[15]

Restricting the Flow

Occasionally companies move in the opposite direction with respect to certain aspects of company performance, withholding rather than disgorging more information. These instances usually emerge in the wake of dissemination initiatives that backfire. A case in point is Hutchins Motors' disclosure of data on its capital expenditures. Executives discovered that what they viewed as good news is sometimes twisted into bad news. If project expenditures came in below budgeted levels because of cost savings and new efficiencies, executives found themselves accused of cutting back on capital investments when they should have been doing the opposite to meet the Japanese challenge. Even though it was patiently explained, the interpretation was lost in reporting, and the new efficiencies were somehow recast as an appraisal that the company was "running out of money." In the assessment of the vice president for finance, the analysts "were trying to latch onto something, whether it's positive or negative doesn't matter, but something that's different that they can put in their report and get some notoriety." With interpretations of trends in this area hard to control, the company discontinued the release of any such information.

Companies also temporarily withhold information from time to time when disclosure can roil the market. Harrington Stores' response to its rumored takeover offers a case in point. As trading volume hit record levels and stock speculators accumulated positions, the smallest quantum of information could move mountains. Executives received a spate of calls from new, speculative holders, most of which were thinly disguised efforts to smoke out management's next move. "Managing a lot of money, we own a significant piece of your stock," would be an opening line. Then: "We've been buying more and we have confidence in the company." The listening executive silently scanned the company's shareholder list to check the caller's holdings. More often than not, no trace could be found since the "significant piece" was but days old.

Oblique but transparent questions would follow. "What does [the company] think about LBO activity in the marketplace today?" "We're buying your stock now, what are you going to do to help it go on up?" "Is the board going to do a poison pill?" The slightest positive response could send the stock north, as the holder inferred that management might fight back with a leveraged buyout; the slightest negative hint could send it south. Executives mastered the art of no response.

Trading Information

Improved company dissemination of information is also valued for the reciprocity it engenders. Experienced analysts are often viewed as walking encyclopedias, repositories of tangible, current, and textured data on both the industry and its key competitors. Those who have followed the sector for years are sometimes perceived as knowing more about the company than its own recently appointed executives. "It always amazes me," offered the vice president for investor relations at National Metal Products, how analysts "seem to know so much about your company when there are so many other companies out there." Many also know the industry in detail. The chief executive of Columbia Foods savored his frequent contact with the food analysts. "I find out things about our industry that I wouldn't necessarily find out in quite the same way," he confided, since "they talk to our competitors." Naturally, as a result, "we think having good relationships with them is a very good thing."

So too do executives with Richards Oil. The rival Exxon Corporation had held an analysts' meeting in Dallas, and Exxon management's main points at the meeting were quickly conveyed to Richards Oil's management by a petroleum analyst who covers both companies. In describing Exxon's exploration and production projects, an Exxon executive had reportedly asserted that Exxon was ahead of the competition. An analyst asked what rates of return are expected on the projects, and the executive answered 12 percent. When the 12 percent figure is later communicated to the CEO and CFO of Richards Oil, both chortle. The chief financial officer quips, "a project that only earns 18 percent probably won't even get looked at here." If Exxon thinks that 12 percent is a good target, he gloated, "they are in deeper trouble than I thought."

Chase Chemical executives always value visits by experienced analysts. "The very best analysts will not only talk to us," observes the vice president for financial communications, "they'll also talk to our competitors, customers, our suppliers, [and] they will very frequently learn things about the marketplace that we may or may not know." Among the most prized nuggets are insights into the thinking of the competitors. Chase Chemical had long dominated one U.S. product market but feared fresh challenge from abroad. A European maker had been considering an American plant as manufacturer of the product. But a visiting analyst, just back from a European tour that included a stop at the prospective competitor, reported from his personal discussions that the European maker is unlikely to enter the U.S. market.

So large is the information pipeline through the analysts that Chase Chemical had evolved a rule of thumb: if you don't want a competitor to know something, don't tell it to an analyst. The flip side to the rule is: if you do want to send a message to a competitor, telling it to an analyst is a convenient, aboveboard means for doing so. Chase Chemical had developed new technologies for a product market it still dominated, making the product both better and cheaper. To dissuade would-be competitors from jumping into the fray, the company informed its analysts of the breakthroughs, confident that the information would quickly reach and discourage other firms.

Information trading is one way for management to pry loose some of the analysts' store of knowledge. "I view it as two-way communication," said the Chase Chemical vice president, "that benefits the two parties involved." A tactical corollary follows: better-informed analysts receive better company treatment. As top managers juggle tight schedules, they find ample time for analysts whose knowledge and intellect they respect, less for others. The vice chairman of Buckingham Bank speaks for many executives when he offers this explanation of how analysts win his respect: "It's [a question of] how up the [analysts] are on what's going on in the industry. If they're coming in and asking a bunch of inane questions, I'll give them answers to the questions, *but* . . . " By contrast, he singles out the "bright" managers with several investment firms "who ask very tough questions." The key criterion, he says, is the quality of the information and thinking that goes into their queries. In the absence of quality in either area, admitted the vice chairman, they "don't get in to see me any more because it's a waste of my time and theirs."

Companies, of course, say publicly that they treat all analysts equally, as indeed they are obliged to do. Formal compliance with the principle of equality before the law generally finds few better applications in American life than in the area of corporate disclosure. But company managers also draw a distinction between passive equity and active equity. They seek to provide the same response to the same question from different investors, but they also know that some analysts ask far better questions than others. "There's nothing that says that we have to go out and tell this guy what the right question to ask is," explained Buckingham's vice chairman. In compliance with an alternative principle—to those who have, more shall be given—some analysts receive better information because they begin with better information.

Well-informed analysts are also welcome visitors for operating managers in search of fresh intelligence. Divisional heads often come to know them well and readily make time on their busy schedules to meet with them. Sometimes the analysts' visits provoke companies into further analysis. During one visit by several analysts to a consumer-products company that had recently reorganized its global operations, two senior officials for international operations were asked who was responsible for Poland. The first responded that it was the other executive. The second said no, it was the responsibility of the first executive. Only then did they both realize that Poland had somehow fallen between the cracks.

So good is the high end of the analysts' ranks that one company executive said he had even thought of hiring first-rate analysts for the company's strategic planning office. He also confessed that the thought was entirely hypothetical since the company could never hope to match the million-dollar salaries of the best.

As another indicator of the enduring relationships that have emerged, managers and investors have evolved informal understandings on the use of "off-the-record" information. Once a sense of two-way trust has emerged, some managers are willing to share additional information for limited use. Two restrictions can apply: the source may not be identified, nor may the data be published. The company's stated position on the first restriction, in the words of one executive, is: "We don't want anything in print that attributes this back to the company, but here's the background information, and if you want to draw your own conclusions then you're free to do so." The company's phrasing of the second restriction is: "Look, this is strictly background so that you understand the context of the situation—but I don't want to see anything like this in a report." The latter line allows companies to disclose what they consider proprietary information yet prevent it from reaching the competitors, a kind of partial plug in an otherwise leaky sieve. Honorable relations are of course required for this to work, but the two sides have come to recognize that they need and know each other well enough to operate on that premise.

Chase Chemical Products understands that some analysts base their models on sales levels of key products. Though Chase would not formally reveal such levels, it does provide off-the-record "guidance" on them. "Don't attribute this back to the company," offers the vice president for financial communications, "but if you would be roughly in this kind of range, you wouldn't be too far off." The chemical company also believes that some analysts make a more informed assessment if they understand how the company contracts with two large business customers for one of its largest products. Contract pricing information is highly sensitive since its prices differ not only between the two major customers but also among other purchasers. "We can't have you discussing anything regarding the specifics of our contracts with our customers," said the vice president, "but just so you understand the kinds of issues that we're talking about. . . ."

With the norms of reciprocity established, company managers acquire access to relatively good informal information on emerging concerns among their major investors. Companies often receive early warnings of proxy challenges and shareholder resolutions. They usually learn quickly of the hands behind unusually large stock movements. On occasion their intelligence gathering even permits them to anticipate major trades in advance.

Though radically improved in the last decade, the flow from investors to companies is still uneven. Some topics have yet to be discovered by the so-called information superhighway. Most large investors, for instance, have written voting policies on shareholder and management proxy resolutions, yet few investors make their policies publicly available, nor do many announce their proxy decisions on governance resolutions.[16]

A company's discrete questions to its investors produce such information on a case-by-case basis, but even then company executives are hard pressed to discern the outlines of a policy. (Public announcements of proxy policies by Calpers and CREF remain the exception, not the rule.) One measure of the public scarcity of such information is its commercial availability. The services of one major proxy solicitor include access to a proprietary database of previous proxy decisions by a large cross section of major stockholders. The data come not from public records, which are uneven at best, but from the firm's own contractual work. Since the firm solicits proxies on both shareholder and management resolutions for a broad range of corporate clients, it draws on an insider's accounting of how major shareholders voted on a number of previous governance questions.

Conversely, companies do not place large sections of their own information bases on the table. In nearly all directorship elections, for example, companies still limit proxy information on their nominees to the minimum required by the SEC: the candidate's age, principal business experience, first year on the board, and shares held in the firm. Information about the nominees' governance views or prior performance virtually never appear.

In the experience of some companies, the quality questions and information come more from the investment company side, less the public pension side. The difference can be seen in their divergent concerns. Strong money managers and mutual-fund managers pay much attention to strategic directions, product performance, and prospective risks. Strong pension managers, by contrast, seem more preoccupied with the formalities of governance. Because of the evident difference, the latter group left the chief executive of Columbia Foods cold. For him the challenging—and useful—questions lay in product strategy rather than board policy. The investment company managers, for instance, had been aggressively questioning his company about a knockoff product that a major competitor had just introduced in Europe. This was where the company should be questioned, confided the CEO, but public-pension managers tended to ignore the issue. The latter's minds, he said, had locked on form over substance, mechanical prescription over thoughtful interpretation. He mocked what he viewed as their view of the company's strategic dilemmas: "'That's not our issue. We don't want anything to do with that issue. We want to know about *really* important stuff, like staggered boards and cumulative voting.'" For this CEO, little constructive challenge came from one side of the investor divide while much came from the other, and this guided how he divided his time.

The absence of an exchange makes the governance pressures from the heavily indexed pension funds, in the eyes of some managers, especially galling. In 1993, institutions on average placed 16 percent of the equity in indexed funds. Investment companies and insurance companies indexed virtually none of their portfolios; banks on average indexed 33 percent, corporate pensions 36 percent; and public pensions, 52 percent. Calpers' indexing stood at 59 percent, CREF at 64 percent, New York State Teachers at 85 percent. The chief executive of WWK Products expresses the considerable animus harbored by many toward such indexed funds, especially public pensions whose indexing fraction runs so high. "The problem with the indexers is that historically the people who owned our stock in an index didn't want the treatment that we give to other large stockholders." A proffered handshake had been rejected. "They don't have an analytical staff necessarily; they don't want us to come out and talk about the business." [17]

From the executive perch, public pensions offer disparate faces. "You get the feeling that you're dealing with two separate groups," complains Chase Chemical's general counsel. "There's the political cadre, if you will, almost in the old Marxist sense, that runs around making these shareholder proposals, making speeches, and thumping the drum on all the governance issues." At the same time, the "political cadre" expresses little interest in the company's economic fundamentals. The pension funds' investment officers, who make up the other group, express at least some interest in the firm's economic performance. Yet even that is irritatingly tepid at times since they had parked so much of their money in indexes.

Information as Instrument

Both sides have learned that if information exchange is to work in their mutual self-interest, it must remain within certain implicit guidelines. The information cannot betray the competitive position of either organization. The giving and receiving cannot be inequitable. And the content cannot be inaccurate. On the latter point, the vice chairman of Buckingham Bank summarizes his own marching order for a forthcoming meeting with six key bank analysts: "Don't mislead them in any way, shape or form." Most of the flow conforms to the new norms. That which does not leads to subtle and then not-so-subtle reminders of what the implicit network contract has become.

While information reciprocity implies mutual dependence, it also opens the way for information weaponry. From time to time companies are aggravated by an analyst's report, sometimes for doing little more than downgrading a stock recommendation, more often for not having the facts right or for having the estimates wrong. IR managers often call the offending analysts, suggesting that they correct a factual misstatement or ease an earnings misforecast. The latter requires elegant circumlocution since companies do not announce their quarterly results until the quarter is over, and any suggestions to investors prior to a public announcement are viewed dimly by market regulators.

Certain elliptical expressions have come nonetheless to be well understood by both sides. When MFL Network perceives that an analyst is too optimistic, the IR manager, "rather than laminating the report and hanging it on our office walls," resorts to familiar code. He calls the analyst to warn of several developments that could break either way for the company, "and things must go in our favor in order to meet your expectations. That's going to take a bit of luck." When the company believes an analyst too pessimistic, similar interventions occur, hints then pointing north instead of south. Strikeline Computer follows much the same model. Fearing uneven disclosure, the IR manager is reluctant to take explicit preemptive moves. He waits instead until an overly optimistic analyst calls him or, short of that, he finally invents some excuse to call the analyst. Then, following a discussion with the analyst on the unrelated matter, the manager slips in, "I looked at your model. I know you're feeling pretty good about the company. I really appreciate the support, but you know the economy's tough, it's a bitch." By the implicit code, he knows he has delivered the message.

Numbers in the messages cannot be too precise, however, since that verges on selective disclosure. To ensure that the numbers are suitably imprecise, companies typically communicate acceptable ranges for earnings per share, not target points. Strikeline Computer has introduced a fail-safe measure against even the inadvertent disclosure of specific data. The IR manager arranges to remain well informed of the ranges for the quarterly results—but to remain willfully ignorant of the specifics. When a quarter is near closing, the company comptroller develops an increasingly precise fix on the period's results. But by prior agreement, the comptroller only reports a range to the IR manager. So long as the comptroller's figures are consistent with the IR manager's working range, the comptroller, reports the IR manager, does "not yank his chain." But if the company's results are moving outside the expected range, the comptroller takes corrective steps to ensure that the IR manager corrects his own message to investors.

If companies are unsuccessful in subtly correcting what they see as overly pessimistic analysts' assessments, they are not above using less subtle measures. The offending analysts are "still going to get invited to our meetings, and invited to our luncheons, and we're still going to speak to them," offered a MFL Network manager, noting that other companies are often not so generous. Corporate magnanimity, however, is not evident even at this company if analysts' factual misstatements are not corrected quickly, if "they put out a sell recommendation on us where they distort the facts." In such cases, the manager first calls the analysts. But if their response is "inappropriate," he is not reluctant to go over their heads. He places the second call to a superior: "I just want to let you know, I've been on the phone and I will continue to be on the phone with your clients and our shareholders saying that what your analyst wrote in that report was just dead wrong."

Analysts could find their access cut off if management judges their style to be too aggressive, too far outside the implicit norms. Hutchins Motors for instance, has identified a half-dozen analysts whom it perceives as posing "rude" questions. With such preambles as, "Your last two-door sports car was a complete flop," these analysts forcefully present their queries. But norms of information sharing proscribe such gambits, and company executives fielding such queries react indignantly to the violations. When "someone comes on telling [company executives] how dumb they are," they predictably lose interest in further discourse. Violations are also sometimes provoked by company stonewalling. It is well known that executives refuse to disclose information on certain subjects, yet some analysts bluntly persist, angering and alienating the executives. Yet most analysts, company managers observe, have mastered the art of repeating questions in oblique fashion when first rebuffed, and then backing off—without getting "snotty"—when twice rebuffed. "For the most part," says another finance manager, "the real pros are really good."

Overly aggressive investor behavior generally leads to less executive candor. This can be seen at Hutchins Motors' annual two-day gathering for investors and executives. Some forty senior managers typically join some one hundred sell- and buy-side analysts for review of the company's performance. Seating is carefully arranged to place the right analysts with the right managers. The company arranges to seat analysts who "really cause problems" with more junior managers or, alternatively, with well-briefed senior managers ("you're going to meet with this person who can be very antagonistic—be ready for it, just stay calm, keep control of the meeting, don't let them set you off"). One of the automaker's finance managers offers: "Certainly the people that we're comfortable with, that cooperate with us, would tend to get a little bit better service than some of the people that really cause us problems."

At the same time, some companies and analysts have evolved a symbiotic working relationship with business journalists. Executive succession or company mergers draw writers from dozens of publications and the electronic media, and the writers often turn to analysts for comment. The writers have instant, on-the-record assessments; the analysts place their firms in front of readers. When directors of the Bank of Boston, under investor pressure, forced CEO Ira Stepanian to resign in 1995 for failing to broker a merger, an analyst with Brown Brothers Harriman & Co. confirmed to a reporter that, yes, Stepanian "has bypassed some opportunities." When directors of W. R. Grace & Company forced its longtime chairman J. Peter Grace Jr. into retirement in 1995, an analyst with Smith Barney observed to a writer that "shareholders realized they had a certain amount of influence, and they utilized it" against Grace, who had "wanted to remain chairman of W. R. Grace as long as he lived." When Chase Manhattan Corporation and Chemical Banking Corporation announced their investor-encouraged merger in 1995, an analyst with Salomon Brothers told a journalist, "I think it's a great transaction."[18]

Business writers for the *Wall Street Journal,* the *New York Times, Business Week,* and other publications draw on their own contacts in the analyst community, but writers for publications that cover business or the firm in question less frequently have less of a head start on such sources. At the end of calls to the public-affairs office of a company to discuss a story, some request names of knowledgeable analysts, and the public-affairs manager, no surprise, values the steering opportunity.

Telling the Strategy Story

The information symmetry of the investor network yields to strict asymmetry in one area. Many executives believe that if shareholders better understand and appreciate the company's strategy, they will invest more. A persuasive story is expected to bring in those who are not currently holders. Getting the strategy story across thus becomes a critical function of executive outreach to the investor community. Some companies change strategic direction after learning that their traditional story is not being well received and a new one works better. But others, more confident of their mission, simply seek to state and restate the strategic vision. To do so requires frequent, personalized selling. The customary opening in almost any meeting with investors has come to be an executive summary of the firm's strategic direction.

For those most responsible for relating the story, the account's acceptance has become an important criterion for judging themselves and their work. When business writers, financial analysts, and money managers all seem to understand the company's main directions, its strengths and weaknesses, one of the executives' jobs is getting done. Damning but accurate appraisals of company strategy are preferred over favorable but inaccurate reports. "I don't care if you don't get all your facts right," said the IR manager for Strikeline Computer, "but are you at least focused on the significant issues?" For him, the best measure of what he is seeking to accomplish is whether he has told the story correctly, whether it is absorbed well, and whether the journalists and analysts write it up "fairly and accurately." To ensure the absorption, he and his senior colleagues, he says, repeat the strategy "ad nauseam" until those following the company have finally, in his words, "succumbed" to it. The company, for example, had early entered the field of computer networking. Its potential was little known or appreciated by stock analysts in the early years. But the company repeatedly told investors of the robust growth prospects for the market and company. Because this message was stated often enough, analysts eventually came to cite networking as a unique edge for the firm, a competitive strategy with expected payoffs in the years ahead.

The strategy story cannot be told too often. Buckingham Bank's account is well understood and accepted, yet bank executives constantly retell it. The vice chairman describes the agenda: "It's communicating to the investor out there what your strategy is in a way that they understand it." When quarterly and annual results are announced, if the communication has been effective, he continues, "we can explain enough about what's happened [during the reporting period] so that they can put it in their information box and learn from it."

Columbia Foods takes a similar tack. The strategic chronicle is already widely disseminated, but it always bears reiteration. The chief executive aggressively seeks out shareholder contact, going out to investors' offices, inviting investment managers in, and appearing before analysts' groups. "The more they know about us, whether we're doing well or poorly, the more they'll understand where we are," explains the CEO. "Lack of information and surprises are the enemies of high stock prices." Of course it helps to have high confidence in those who are executing the strategy. "We've probably got a better depth of management than most companies in our business," says the chief executive, "so we trot our managers out" to meet the investors and reaffirm the company's account of its future.

Telling the strategic story entails continuous smoothing, downplaying windfalls and discounting setbacks, explaining actions that might otherwise undermine investor perceptions of company direction. It also entails describing how seemingly contradictory tactics actually fit with the strategic direction. Harrington Stores, for example, had positioned one of its divisions as a stable earner, telling investors that it would expand steadily but slowly. Without warning, however, the division acquired two dozen stores from another company. "Well, what do you mean it's not a growth company?" several analysts cried. "You just doubled your number of stores!" The company said, yes, but it is still not a fast growth business. The acquisition should be seen, executives argued, as a "strategic gift" that "we had a once-in-a-lifetime opportunity to put together." The debt-financed purchase was large enough, however, to detract from earnings over the next one to two years because of start-up costs and new interest payments. Senior management asked investors here to see the action as a momentary aberration in an otherwise steady growth strategy, and they pleaded with owners to wait two years for the investor benefits to come on line. Most did.

Richards Oil Corporation's strategic vision is less well accepted since the company is still recovering from a disastrous setback. The firm has restored its earnings, but investors remain wary. In the face of unrelenting skepticism, self-confidence is essential. "You just have to get to the point where you believe in your own program," counsels the vice president for investor relations. "If you communicate it openly and honestly, then [investors] can make the choice." Convincing the skeptics of the company's goals has become a major agenda for the chief executive, and success in doing so means no pulling back: "Several years ago, investors began to ask more about our strategies, less about our results," he explains. "Articulating our strategies in public has been a valuable experience because it imposes a certain amount of discipline on the company. If you put your plan out to the public, by God you better do it."

Once the strategy is well understood, companies believe they can better weather the episodic downturns that would otherwise drive investors away. Put differently, an effectively communicated strategy constitutes another foundation for the investor network. The IR director for Richards Oil describes the impact of her boss's educational agenda: Our managers and shareholders "are on the same track. We view it as a partnership. . . . [The shareholders] can help us too, because if the shareholders understand your strategy, they'll bear with you. If you have a down quarter, they are not going to be worrying about it, because they know what your future plans are."

Stewart Drugs faces cyclical problems whose lengthy periods create special problems for executives seeking to sell the story. Some of its best-selling drugs are slated to lose their patent protection, and some of its future best-sellers still require years of testing and government review. The research-and-development pipeline delivers major products in fits and starts, producing flips and flops among unconvinced investors. Building a secure investor network therefore requires creating an informed network, one that comprehends not only how the pharmaceutical industry operates but also how this company sees its future. To this end, company executives seek to foster understanding of the cycles, especially of an anticipated dip several years ahead. Their challenge is to move investors not only beyond day-trading and quarterly mentalities, but also beyond annual and even biannual benchmarks. For the chief operating officer, "The story that we're trying to tell is: 'Look, this company is going to have some interesting challenges in the middle part of this decade, and here is how we're going to address that period.'" The goal is investor patience: "We're trying to get the analysts who just look at the next five years to look a little bit beyond that in our company." The president presses investors to stretch in the same direction. He bluntly states the choice: "If that's what you like, stay on. If you don't, you know you can walk."

Analysis of the impact of executive briefings of stock analysts corroborates the executive agenda. One study examined more than 2,800 presentations in 1984–88 by chief executives of some 1,100 firms, to meetings of security analyst societies affiliated with the Association for Investment Management Research. At the meetings, which were held in New York, Los Angeles, Chicago, Boston, and other metropolitan areas, substantial numbers of both sell-side or buy-side analysts were present. During the three months following the company CEOs' presentations, their firms benefited in two ways. The number of analysts following the typical firm at the time of the event had been a little over fifteen. In the wake of the event, the analyst following for each firm increased on average by another half an analyst. Also, during the quarter that followed, institutional holdings in the typical firm rose by over one-half a percentage point. Analyst presentations thus tended to booster both analyst interest and institutional investment. The magnitudes are modest but the results tangible.[19]

Getting out the company's account is also valued for the "air" it can put under a company's stock in the absence of a crisis—assuming of course that the story is compelling. The manager of shareholder relations for one of the nation's largest consumer-products firms (not a focus company) said his office's raison d'être is to ensure that the market has enough data to value the company "fairly." "We're in business to make sure that the stock is valued where it should be. Normally, that means it should be higher. 'Fair' is usually higher than what the stock is trading now. When the stock is below that, we believe that there is insufficient information in the market." This widely shared self-definition of the investor-affairs function has an instructive if ironic edge. Efficient capital markets are built on the premise that sufficient information about a company's strategy and performance is already in circulation for fair stock valuation to occur. The assertion that the company is now doing with information what in theory it should always have done signifies how far the emergent nonmarket relations have helped achieve what the market itself had not.

No Turning Back

Most company managers elevate information exchange into an abiding corporate principle. Whatever the occasional downsides and exceptions to an open, two-way flow, the concept seems sound. And there can be no turning back.

The chief executive of Richards Oil had served as management liaison to investors earlier in his career, and he contrasts his relations then with what he wants as CEO now. "I learned more from security analysts than they learned from me. But that was a commentary on the times, since we were not very forthcoming. . . . Now we liken [investor relations] to an open window, with things flowing in and out." The company's IR director echoes the principle: "It is my job to be the company's day-to-day liaison with the investment community, and the liaison is two ways. I am a conduit for information out, and I am a conduit for information in." The vice president for finance of Hutchins Motors carries the company's results and plans to the firm's analysts, but he also brings much back from them. "These people are dedicated," he observes, and "they often understand things more thoroughly than we do."

By the early 1990s many investors were seeking to move beyond control struggles and proxy fights, and company managers found a receptive field. The general counsel of Harrington Stores observes that the institutions "were beginning to reach the point where they were controlling all of corporate America," yet they "really haven't figured out what to do with all this power yet." But they have, in his experience, figured out what to do in one area: "The one thing that they do understand they want is communication." As the attorney urges the institutions, "If you've got a director nominee that you think we ought to consider, let us know." His company is more than ready for the input: "Pick up the phone and call us."

The formula, then, is mutual openness. The spans are vast, and companies of necessity have developed complex devices to manage personalized relations with great arrays of investors. But the principle is simple, and it promises mutual gains. As summarized by Harrington Stores' chief executive, "Open communication between management and investors can be very effective in achieving maximum shareholder value over the long term."

The Strength of a Weak Network

In analyzing economic phenomena ranging from finding jobs to forming alliances, the researcher Mark Granovetter found that relations among people and organizations can be usefully classed as strong or weak. Strong ties are characterized by their depth and permanency, weak ties by their breadth and impermanence. From many studies of such networks in operation emerged a seemingly ironic phrase, "the strength of weak ties." By virtue of their greater diffuseness and flexibility, weak ties are often observed to offer a better medium than strong relationships for the widespread dissemination of information and the diffuse exercise of influence.[20]

The relationship between shareholders and companies in Japan stands close to the strong end of the network axis, a system that researcher Michael Gerlach has aptly christened "alliance capitalism." The relationship between the two parties in the United States, by contrast, stands closer to the weak end of the spectrum.[21]

Aspects of what has developed in the United States have been characterized as "relational investing," a set of strong ties between a few major stockholders and a few large companies, ties premised on extensive dialogue. Warren Buffet's investments in Coca-Cola and Capital Cities/ABC are often cited as paradigms for what relational investing should or could be. So, too, are several special funds, such as Corporate Partners and Lens, Inc., that were created to serve the explicit strategy of working closely with management. Yet such paragons remain little more than that, models of virtue that few could or would emulate. What has developed instead is a set of weak ties between many large stockholders and many major companies premised on far more limited, but not zero, dialogue.[22]

Not zero means not zero. The purely impersonal market relationship with shareholders, at least several score of the largest, is a relic of the past. Some investors had previously relied entirely upon sell-side analysts for tracking the companies in which they would place their funds. They had no need themselves to meet management. Now, however, they insist on kicking the tires. "The buy side has over the years increasingly bypassed the sell side," observed the IR manager for Strike-line Computer Company. "They use them, they sift them, they read them, but when it comes to putting your money or your client's money on the table, they want to come here and make eyeball-to-eyeball contact with us." The contact is not necessarily frequent. Nor is it redundantly personalized through memberships in the same exclusive clubs or on the same nonprofit boards. But executives and investors have acquired a first-name familiarity, a working acquaintanceship that adds personal identities to the otherwise cold calculus of stock reports and program trading.

Where strong ties are occasionally formed, they tend to have great importance for managers, investors, and observers alike. But the attention they attract can also be misleading, for their form and impact are the exception, not the rule. What predominates instead are webs of weak ties. Diagrams of ownership of Japanese companies often portray several dozen lines among the lead banks and member companies of a major *keiretsu*, such as Sumitomo, Mitsubishi, or Mitsui. Such lines capture much of the shareholder reality within which a Japanese company executive must work. The analogous diagram of ownership for many American companies requires far more, and far thinner lines to capture the same reality.[23]

The relations that have emerged between investors and managers in the United States resemble neither a market nor a hierarchy. Rather, they look more like an enduring network: nonhierarchical, semi-stable, and personalized. They have become the optical fibers of investor capitalism, replacing the limited-capacity copper wiring of managerial capitalism. They guide and transmit a more intensive, continuous two-way exchange of information and influence. Their formation serves to achieve what takeover threats, proxy battles, and other blunt forms of "communication" between owners and companies failed to do in the past.

Elements of the organizational foundation for investor capitalism have thus been well established. They are not built from some theoretical template or available model. Neither Japan nor Germany offered much guidance, for their ownership systems are too different to be a source of exemplars for the United States. When U.S. company executives describe the relations they have established with investors, few cite other company experiences and none allude to non-U.S. models. Companies have, of necessity, invented their own solutions to the problems of managing a far more concentrated yet still remarkably diverse ownership base.

Formal "principal-agent" relations—the master owner versus the hired manager—have given way to negotiated relations between coequals. Primacy could be claimed by none; neither shareholders nor companies could assert unlimited sovereignty over the other.

The continued development of such a system depends on continued interest on both sides in creating the network, one that is symmetrical, with each well informed of and influenced by the other. The chief financial officer of Harrington Stores calls on the institutions and other companies for joint construction of the network, saying, "The institutions and most companies [should] recognize that there really is a partnership here, that we are allied with each other [but] that we have different points of view." Each side requires the other: "The institutions are necessary in our capital system because they manage money for most individuals as well as most individual retirement funds, and it is the only vehicle we've found to put together lots of money to focus on equity." And the relationships should endure: The institutions, by virtue of their vast holdings, "must be long-term shareholders in one company or another. I believe they will choose [companies] that seem to be willing to consider their agenda . . . not solely their agenda, but their agenda as a long-term partner in it."

7

S

Engaging the
Company Director

INVESTORS HAVE MASTERED TECHNIQUES for challenging, cajoling, and controlling companies, while executives have mastered techniques for resisting, accommodating, and managing the pressures. Both have learned that webs of enduring relations are management devices far superior to cycles of recriminations. These early foundations of investor capitalism have been established, however, with little leadership from the body most central to the relationship—the governing board of the company.

On the face of it, this is odd, for the board of directors is formally portrayed as *the* place where investors and executives meet, where owners' elected representatives instruct their agents. The board is charged with voicing shareholder interests, and it is through the directors that shareholders instruct management. As the official bridge between the two worlds, the directors, one might expect, would be the first to sense investor unrest, the first to press for shareholder value, the first to build a web of relations. In theory, traffic across the bridge should reflect the quiet revolution under way.

Yet the board remained a kind of backwater during the 1980s, sometimes the target of takeover efforts, occasionally the executor of executive dismissal, but most often little more than a bemused bystander. Disgruntled investors rarely contacted company directors; directors even more rarely responded, let alone initiated contact. As investors and executives built their information and influence channels, directors remained out of the loop, uninformed and unengaged. Their bridge carried virtually no traffic.

The rise of investor capitalism is ending that disengagement. For shareholders, an actively independent and empowered board is doing what shareholders cannot: keeping management's feet to the fire. For executives, an actively independent and empowered board does what executives cannot: keeping investors at bay. The failures of early institutional efforts to force corporate change—together with the high costs of management efforts to resist shareholder intrusions—have led both sides to rethink the role of the board. For each, the governing board could and should play a more forceful role, one more channel for the two-way dialogue. For both, the issue has become relatively straightforward: how to change the board's structure to bring its reality in line with theory.

While investors propose, managers dispose, and reforming the structure of the board remains a management function—of course with investor guidance. This chapter focuses on how companies have redesigned the organization of their governance systems to support the new rules of investor capitalism. It begins with a discussion of the nominating committee of one corporate board as it considered bringing investors directly onto the board. The chapter describes the traditional disconnection between directors and investors, and then turns to the steps companies are taking to reconnect the two parties, ranging from showering information on directors to reconstituting rosters of directors and redesigning rules for them.

Rethinking the Board

The seven-person nominating committee of the board for the midsize Fortune 500 utility company is deciding how to think about future director nominees. The committee is concerned about whether it should further professionalize the board, adding directors who bring more experience to the managerial table. Committee discussion moves across a wide spectrum. How should you evaluate directors? one member wonders. Should directors own more stock? asks another (one current director, a grandson of the founder, holds nearly a half-million shares, but another director has less than 1,000). Should a consumer representative be brought onto the board? queries a third. Some also worry whether new professional directors may overplay their hands. Several who sit on other boards warn that outside directors who are themselves CEOs occasionally slip from supporting management into managing management.

No one asks whether a politically connected director should serve on the board. This is a given in light of tight government regulation of the utility. There is "an unalterable link between quality service, responsive regulation, and financial success," the CEO explains to his shareholders, and this dictates "an aggressive pursuit of regulatory decisions." To support that pursuit, the eleven-member board has already added an executive of another regulated company who previously served as legislative president of the state senate. The board has also brought on a lawyer who had earlier served as state attorney general.

The nominating committee's discussion turns to shareholders and how their voice might be better represented on the board. The company's unblemished record—fifteen years of steady annual increases in earnings and dividends—has instilled an investor calm that would be the envy of many companies. Still, the company's chief executive warns that he devotes far more time now to personal contact with the firm's institutional holders. At the top of his shareholder list are two of the nation's leading indexers, but in the next tier are the activist pensions, including CREF (it manages an indexed account that holds 1 percent of every company in the S&P 500), Calpers, and the New York State Common Retirement Fund. Fidelity and other investment companies known to prod companies are high on his list as well. Though he has felt little institutional prodding to date, the chief executive believes in preventive measures.

The directors are themselves well aware of the activist tide, and the nonexecutive board chairman has already met with representatives of the California and New York pension funds. The institutional-investor base is not yet angry or strong enough, however, to force a fresh review of the board's relations with its electorate. While the ninety-odd institutional investors hold 45 percent of the company's shares, family descendants and insiders still control 40 percent.

The debate turns to the possibility of bringing an institutional investor onto the board, a concept that draws no salutes. One director cites a technical problem: how can an institutional investor serve as a director and not face continuous conflicts of interest? The problem of special pleading by an activist investor seems even more insurmountable to others. "There is a difference," warns the former attorney general, "between a director who understands a cause and one who has a cause." Though the board represents all of the companies' shareholders, the directors are not yet ready to welcome any institutional holders into the room.

The Disconnected Director

In an era when shareholders preferred exit over voice and management exercised firm control, directors had little reason to bring the institutions in from the cold. The impersonal, market-driven relations between shareholders and companies required no mediating work by the directors. The professional, strategy-driven executive ranks required little outside guidance. On those infrequent occasions when the company was up for sale or its leadership was up for appointment, directors came to the fore. Otherwise, busy people that they were, they remained disconnected, formally present on behalf of shareholders but little engaged with their concerns.

Formal theory and public regulation insist, however, that directors cannot be disengaged. To be publicly traded in the United States a company must present its director nominees for periodic election to the board by the stockholders. Because of state court rulings, the elect must remember who put them in office, as a decision in a 1919 case known as *Dodge v. Ford Motor Co.* makes clear: "A business corporation is organized and carried on primarily for the profit of the stockholders," the court ruled. "The powers of the directors are to be employed for that end. The discretion of directors is to be exercised in the choice of means to attain that end, and does not extend to a change in the end itself."[1]

Though directors are told by general counsels and state courts that they must make shareholder value their first priority, in practice their attention has not always been quite so focused. Out of touch with shareholders and under the thumb of managers, directors more often looked down the formal organizational chart than up to the owners, taking their cues from inside executives instead of outside investors. A decision by the board of Paramount Communications in 1993 offers an instructive example.

The Paramount board had agreed to an attractive takeover offer by Viacom Inc. A Viacom competitor, QVC, believed it had offered Paramount a superior acquisition package, however, and it filed legal challenge in the Chancery Court of Delaware, where Paramount is incorporated, to prevent the Viacom acquisition. Memos and depositions presented as part of the court proceedings reveal that Paramount's chief executive, Martin S. Davis, withheld important data on the

acquirer from the directors. He also discouraged directors from considering alternative buyers. Delaware Court Vice Chancellor Jack B.
Jacobs found that the "board did not even ask QVC . . . to produce evidence of its financing." The court concluded that "meeting with QVC
was the last thing management wanted to do, and by skillful advocacy,
management persuaded the board that no exploration was required."
When several directors questioned the takeover plan, Davis and his
general counsel berated them for challenging management authority.

The Delaware court found a dereliction of the board's responsibility, for the "duty of the directors obligated them to have more information." The court reaffirmed, once again, the singular obligations of
directors to protect and defend shareholder interests: "From the standpoint of an equity investor," concluded the vice chancellor, "few events
in the life of a corporation are as significant as a change in corporate
control." Once such an event is in front the directors, they have no
choice but to engage it head on. Directors "exercise a power to choose
what premium the shareholders will receive in a change-of-control
transaction," and therefore "those directors, as fiduciaries, must be
deemed to have assumed the duty that accompanies the power." That
duty, Vice Chancellor Jacobs concluded, "is to do for the shareholders
what the shareholders would otherwise wish to do for themselves."

The Delaware Supreme Court later upheld the lower court ruling,
forcing Paramount to reopen the acquisition process for competitive
bidding. The state supreme court ruled that "the Paramount directors
violated their fiduciary duties." Investor advocates and corporate attorneys hailed the ruling as "an important victory for shareholder rights."
Viacom ultimately prevailed over QVC in a subsequent round of bidding—but with Paramount directors forced to exercise greater vigi-
lance on behalf of their shareholders, Viacom was forced to pay more
to Paramount stockholders. Viacom raised its original offer of $69 per
share to $107 for half the Paramount stock and securities for the
remainder of the stock, effectively upping the value of its bid from
$8 billion to $10 billion. In other words, the board's initial acquiescence
to management's badgering would have shortchanged its investors by
some $2 billion. The court instructed directors that they carry an invio-
lable obligation to perform an engaged role on behalf of their shareholders—in this case a role that was worth $2 billion to the owners.[2]

Though courts regularly reaffirm the singular obligation of company boards to their shareholders, directors in the past were rarely
called to fulfill it. More typically, directors learned instead to play the
roles of business advisers, sounding boards, and personal friends of
senior management. Board meetings faced full agendas and often tack-
led thorny problems, but rarely was there an open division between the

directors and executives on matters of shareholder rights. Only in one out of five companies, according to a 1992 survey of 546 corporate secretaries, was there an instance during the past five years in which the board rejected a major management proposal.[3]

The board's detachment from the world it represented seemed evident to many of those who traveled in directors' circles. The unflattering appraisal of one former chief executive may seem too harsh to even the most jaded: "I've been president and worked with seven boards, and I would say that the directors did not know what they were talking about and, worse, didn't care" about shareholder concerns. "Directors are really not knowledgeable about the business they are in." He illustrates his assessment with an account of one director who traveled from Europe by Concorde for the board meeting, dozed through much of it, and then reboarded the Concorde for Europe. Though perhaps overstated, the appraisal was widely shared, at least for many boards, until the mid-1990s. It seemed that board meetings were putting some directors to sleep.

Adding to the somnolence was a deliberate silencing of the board by management. Though directors unambiguously represented shareholders, management saw no contradiction in opposing any communication between the board and its constituents. The chief executive of Richards Oil offered an appraisal that many echoed. He was asked whether his outside directors had ever been involved in the company's proxy fights or otherwise had investor contact. "No, they don't," he replied. "Our view is that management is in the best position to know what to do. The board should know that management has a plan, and then let management do the talking for the company."

This means a director who talked to investors would be challenged to explain such actions. The chief executive of WWK Products, himself an outside director for several other companies, suggested a scenario for what would follow such unauthorized contact: "The next board meeting you went to, everybody would look at you like you had leprosy." The first question when you entered the room: "Who do you think you are that you're out speaking for all of us?" Managers at Richards Oil took the premise one step further. Directors "have authority to act while they're sitting in the boardroom," said the board's assistant secretary, but "they don't represent the company in any other context."

The business convention was clear. If directors were approached, they were expected to turn to the company executive office for guidance before making any response, as if they were suspects who must have legal counsel before responding to questions from the police. The guidance management offered was the instruction to leave investor contact to management. Buckingham Bank's chief executive could recall no instance in which institutional investors had ever had direct contact with his directors. "The quickest way to screw up anything," he said, "is to have multiple spokesmen on the same issue." The vice chairman could see little value in any direct dialogue: "Directors, despite all their wonderful desires and best efforts, don't understand things as well as management."

The disconnection was part and parcel of the old rules of managerial capitalism. The directors' disengagement was due neither to shortcomings nor to failings of their own. If professional managers needed little guidance from their owners, they required equally little from their board. Directors had scant need to know the mind of the investor for they would rarely be called upon to represent it. No wonder the board evolved a relatively modest role in the life of the firm. It simply could not have been otherwise.

The Reengaged Director

With the altered balance of power between companies and their owners, directors, of necessity, have come to think about their shareholders far more than in the past. When facing proxy challenges, when encountering angry shareholders, when confronting hostile buyouts, they have focused more attention on investor matters, and their appreciation for the mind of investor has become more enriched. This path has not been without detours, but directors are coming to acquire a far more active role under investor capitalism than they could ever have conceived under managerial capitalism.

Institutional investors have forced much of this change. Going over management's head, taking their grievances directly to the board, remains unorthodox but no longer unknown. Here, the investor agenda is not to extract company information from the directors, but to impress investor views upon the directors. It often works, and its cumulative impact over a decade has finally achieved what a half-century of securities regulations and court orders had failed to do.

The power of an investor's hand-carried message to the board can be seen in one director's experience. Buckingham Bank's vice chairman serves as an outside director and executive-committee member for a firm whose investors include a large and very disgruntled owner. Without warning, the banker receives a call from the unhappy investor. In keeping with convention he rebuffs any real exchange—"I'm not authorized to do any talking to you"—until he consults company executives. Because the institution holds such a large position, and because it keeps "rattling [the company's] cages," the chief executive agrees to authorize a meeting between his directors and the angry investor. In the presence of the company's general counsel and a special counsel retained by the board, and with an aura of legal formality and personal tension, the board members personally receive the investor's complaint. "They wanted to be certain that we heard their problem," observes the vice chairman, "and that we would agree to do something—whether it was in their favor or not in their favor—because they thought management was not doing enough." To make certain the message is fully appreciated, the investor threatens to unseat several board members at the next annual meeting unless the board takes action.

The investor's approach to the directors comes as a shot across the bow. But in firing such a loud and unusual shot, the institution attracts attention. The bank vice chairman, on his own initiative and through his own banking sources, checks on the reputation of the angry investor. He learns that the investor's portfolio managers are compensated on a highly contingent basis, and he infers that this explains much of its behavior. "They have no patience whatsoever," he concluded, and "it's a clear, absolute element of greed."

Though the diagnosis helps the directors understand the institution's aggressive behavior, the impatience of a large shareholder, whatever the motivation, still constitutes a large problem. The vice chairman urges the company to follow a two-pronged response. One, management should respond to the concerns raised. Two, management should call the investor's bluff, challenging it to try to unseat the incumbent directors. If management's first response fails to mollify the investor, the board is ready to respond to a proxy contest with a countercharge of investor "greed." The institution steps no further into this conflict, but it has won management's attention by going over its head.

Under duress from shareholders, some directors turn proselytizers. Believing that they understand investor interests better than do the investors themselves—which may often be the case—outside directors seek to educate their misguided stockholders. Jarred into paying attention to shareholders' concerns, directors sometimes lead their constituents to better understand their own interests.

The chief executive of National Metal Products, who also serves as an outside director for another large manufacturer, joins one such campaign. The manufacturer has received an unwanted tender offer and vigorously resists the bid, adopting a staggered board and a poison pill. The takeover group counters with a campaign to replace one-third of the company's directors up for reelection. Directors receive several dozen letters from angry investors as they resist the acquisition. One exclaims, in the director's paraphrase, "Stop trying to entrench yourself and being intransigent. . . . Take the offer!"

Since institutions hold some three-fifths of the threatened company's shares, they also hold the company's fate in their hands. Company management travels the country to appeal for support, and directors join the campaign to educate their shareholders. The outside director from National Metal Products views it as constructive dialogue: "I think you can do well with them if you spend some time talking with them" to "help them in their understanding." The tactics of resistance and education force the suitor to offer a far higher price to attract the institutions' blocks—and one so high that the company can no longer say no. In persuading their investors to remain patient, company executives—with the active assistance of their reengaged directors—obtain 20 percent more per share for their investors than the latter had initially seemed ready to accept.

Preparing the Board

Knowing that outside directors are increasingly held accountable by shareholders, and recognizing that responsibility depends on knowledgeability, managements are providing far more information to their directors. To the diverse repertoire of executive work has been added the task of educating the board.

Many managements now include analysts' reports, earnings estimates, and stock recommendations in directors' briefing materials. Chief financial officers and directors of investor relations update directors on shareholder matters during board meetings. Chief executive officers report private conversations with leading investors to select directors. The goal is to ensure that directors appreciate their shareholders' appetites and moods. WWK Products has adopted most such steps, and its chief financial officer explains why: "To give them a reflection of what the owners feel about the business."

The breadth of the educational agenda is evident in a 1993 survey of large companies. More than three-quarters regularly furnished their directors with information on the company's shareholder base, stock price, and trading volume. Nine-tenths told the board what the analysts are saying about the company. Three-quarters included copies of analysts' reports.[4]

Efforts by a large consumer-products company (not among the focus firms) exemplify the agenda's breadth. Its newly appointed chief executive has persuaded the board to create a shareholder-friendly approach to governance, including the avoidance of antitakeover devices and the adoption of stockholding requirements for directors and executives. But he discovers that his board knows "almost nothing" about the company's relations with its investors, recalls its manager of investor affairs. The CEO is shocked by their "naïveté," and he now presses an array of information on board members about the investor world they represent. Management thus frequently reports on the firm's shareholder mix; the fraction of stock held by institutions; the percentage actively traded; the top analysts following the company (along with their rankings in *Institutional Investor* magazine); how the analysts view the company (accompanied by copies of their latest reports on the firm); where portfolio managers acquire information about the company (they monitor news services, buy analysts' research, and talk with executives); and how often management has met with the institutions. The manager of investor affairs even devotes some time to elementary market principles, explaining how the relative supply of and demand for the company's stock affects its price, and how future expectations for the company more than past performance drive its price as well.

Another manufacturing firm (again, not among the focus companies) has devised a comparable directors' program and adds quarterly updates on ownership turnover. Management devotes special attention to churning among the firm's largest institutional investors: who has recently joined or left their ranks and why each has bought or sold substantial blocks of stock. It also summarizes what it has learned from its regular biweekly contact with nine sell-side analysts who actively track the firm, and its less regular contact with major buy-side representatives.

Campaigns to educate directors on shareholder concerns often necessitate a broader educational agenda. To comprehend investor anxieties and reactions requires that directors acquire greater appreciation for the company's own products and risks. Buckingham Bank, for instance, has instituted a program to educate its board on the potential downside of international lending and leveraged products. The vagaries of emerging markets, currency fluctuations, financial derivatives and other volatile and arcane devices require, in management's mind, a better-informed board. All these variables can exacerbate volatility in bank income, a topic of great importance to shareholders in the wake of the derivative-related bankruptcies of Orange County, California, and Baring Securities in the U.K.

Several years earlier, Buckingham Bank had announced a $2 billion loss as a provision against its third-world debt. "These are very risky businesses we're in," the general counsel frets, "and if you show up with a big loss," you need "a board that fully understands the issues. You just can't come in and say, we're taking a $2 billion debt provision today." Directors had to be ready to digest the news and to stand by management in the wake of investor criticism. "Huge volatility is part of the business that never existed before," he observed, "and it's important that the directors realize that—that they be brought along and buy into it." Buckingham Bank's education program is intended to help protect its directors from themselves. "We think a lot about" making the directors "understand our extremely complicated business and focus on the issues that are important," explains the bank's general counsel.

While investors value information on governance and succession issues, they are usually hungrier for detailed information on operating and performance issues. Despite management's educational campaigns, outside directors still remain out of their depth on many operational issues. When investors, executives, and directors mingle, directors often find themselves the wallflowers. One company hosts an annual retreat, with seminars and sports for its board, management, and major analysts. In search of insights into company operations, the analysts gravitate toward the executives; meanwhile, due to lack of attention, the directors gravitate toward the golf course in search of activity.

Reconstituting the Demography

Both company managements and institutional investors recognize that their governing boards often reflect past history more than current reality. The challenge is to overcome tradition and build a board that reflects and serves the new power relations between companies and their owners.

Many company executives know that investors want a modernized board, one that facilitates rather than impedes relations. They concede that the disengaged board is an anachronism, the quaint product of a bygone era. The chief executive of WWK Products, if he were to ask his largest stockholders about his board, knows that "they'd say the same thing about our company as they do about every company: they want a strong, independent board." The appraisal by Buckingham Bank's general counsel also echoes a common feeling. "We have to some extent had," he said, a "classic board that never" really met. Now "we want to move away from that toward a more involved" board. The goal is an "engaged" and "enlightened" governing body.

The vision may be clear, but the strategy for achieving it has been far less so since little is known about what works. Classic pitfalls of interpretation await the unwary. When IBM performed as one of the great corporate success stories, when Thomas Peters and Robert

Waterman placed it on a 1982 list of America's "best-run companies" after their search for "excellence," few IBM practices were questioned. When IBM fell from grace in the early 1990s, few IBM practices went unquestioned.[5]

Similarly, when firms deliver shareholder value, few governance policies are questioned; when share prices drop, all policies become fair game. The general counsel of National Metal Products summarizes his own experience this way: "If the stock is performing very well," institutional investors "find that those companies have perfect corporate governance." By contrast, if their stock is "not behaving well, and they're not doing well on their investment side," he said, they "find that corporate governance at [those companies] is totally inadequate." Institutional investors often corroborate the assessment. The chief executive of Calpers notes that many observers believe that his pension fund is "all fired up" about the high levels of executive compensation. But he observes that his fire is really conditional: "The only time we become concerned about executive compensation is when it heads north, and economic performance heads south." If side-by-side comparison of "perfect" and "totally inadequate" governance systems reveals little real difference, management could find few unambiguous lessons on how to reengage their board.[6]

With few proven models to draw upon, companies are inventing their future, and they have pursued one or both of the two avenues for change: replace the people or transform the organization. The first is considered here, the second in this chapter's last section on redesigning the board.

In retooling the people side of the board to be more effective as a bridge between owners and companies, managements have worked to mitigate the negatives and to accent the positives. Reducing the negatives means fewer directors with blind loyalty to management; stressing the positives means more directors looking out for the interests of shareholders. Companies have found that the first objective is less daunting than the second.

Many firms have sought to bring on directors less loyal to incumbent management, an awkward but necessary first step. A starting criterion for such independence is simply whether the directors are neither current nor former executives. A more stringent criterion is whether the nonexecutive directors consult for the company or represent customers, suppliers, bankers, or law firms, or are otherwise engaged in commerce with the company. Many institutions prefer the more restrictive standard. CREF, for instance, defines independence as "no present or former employment by the company or any significant financial or personal tie to the company or its management which could interfere with the director's loyalty to shareholders." So too does the New York Stock Exchange, which defines a director's independence to preclude material advisory, consulting, or legal relationship with the company either as an individual or as a representative of an organization with such a relationship.

By the first, less stringent criterion of whether the director is a current or former executive of the firm, companies have modestly expanded their board's independence. In one twenty-year tracking of board membership among a cross-section of large firms, during the early 1970s the typical board included eight nonexecutive directors on a board of thirteen; during the 1980s, the average board had nine nonexecutive directors out of thirteen. By the first half of the 1990s, nine of twelve members, on average, were nonexecutives.[7]

Pressed by shareholders, most company managements have embraced the majority-outsider principle, though they vary in its implementation. At Stewart Drugs, for instance, insiders had long dominated the board. More than two-thirds of the board's seats during the mid-1980s were still held by current or former executives and members of the founding family. But the company has moved to embrace the dominant model for board design. "It's healthy for the company to have outside views," the general counsel offered by way of explanation. He had never received any direct suggestions from institutions to adopt the outsider convention. Some smaller shareholders, however, pressed for more outsiders. For a decade the company had used an oversize proxy card with an invitation that shareholders use it as a suggestion box, and many suggested a more independent board. Their suggestions registered. By 1994, the company had reduced the fraction of insiders to less than half (table 7.1).

Table 7.1 Number of Inside and Outside Directors Serving on the Board of Stewart Drugs, 1984–94

Year	Directors		Total
	Nonindependent*	Independent	
1984	10	4	14
1986	9	4	13
1988	9	5	14
1990	8	6	14
1992	7	5	12
1994	6	7	13

*Nonindependent includes current or former executives or members of the founding family.

Source: Company proxy statements.

National Metal Products moved in the same direction, though large shareholders were more responsible for the change in its board. In continuing contact with institutions, the company's general counsel "heard more and more that we ought to keep a major balance of outside directors." The rationale was that such balance created a more acceptable appearance. "It gave the institutions a higher degree of confidence," he said, "that we weren't just running the company for the benefit of management." More outsiders on their board symbolized a management attitude, a tip of the hat in the right direction.

Still, residual pockets of resistance can easily be found. Though reluctant to buck the trend publicly, some executives privately complain that fewer insiders is a sure formula for a poorly informed board. Outsiders might bring independence to the boardroom, but insiders bring true understanding of the company and industry. The general counsel of Chase Chemical Products expressed the critique privately held by some. "The enormous drive toward outside directors means that you've got a ton of people on the board who are not nearly as conversant with the business as if you had a substantial number of inside directors. It is exactly the opposite of what I would do if I were looking for good corporate governance." Chemical technology, product liability, and other issues of the business can "take a career for an insider to learn," in the view of the general counsel. Outsiders are often unfamiliar with even basic industry concepts. "It results in a board which doesn't understand the business nearly as well as if it had a group of inside people."

The future nonetheless points toward more independence from management. Set against trends in other demographic characteristics, the angle of ascent on this issue appears modest. Conference Board comparison of the age of cross-sections of board members in 1972 and 1989 provides a baseline: the average age stood at fifty-eight in 1972 and fifty-nine in 1989. The number of boards with at least one non-U.S. member displayed a slight uptick, rising from 12 percent to 17 percent. The number of boards with at least one African-American showed a greater incline, from 6 percent to 21 percent. And the number of boards with at least one woman displayed the sharpest growth of all, from 8 percent to 41 percent. Drawing on an annualized database for 1973–93, an executive search firm reports the same: the percentage of company boards with one or more minority members rose over this twenty-year period from 9 percent to 39 percent; those with women increased from 11 percent to 67 percent (figure 7.1).[8]

While these upward trends draw on a momentum predating institutional power and activism, by the mid-1990s they are reinforced by the latter as well. Among CREF's new policy guidelines instituted in

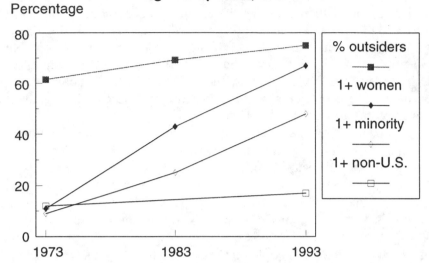

Figure 7.1 Composition of Boards of Directors of Large Companies, 1973-93

Percentage

Note: Figures for non-U.S. directors are for 1972 and 1989.
Source: Korn/Ferry International, 1993, 1994; Bacon, 1990.

1993 is a call for board heterogeneity: "The board should be composed of qualified individuals who reflect diversity of experience, gender, race and age." The Investor Responsibility Research Center's annual survey of institutional investors in 1993 found that two-fifths avowed that the absence of women or minorities on a board could affect their voting decisions. Church groups have pressed for diversity through proxy resolutions for years, but CREF and a number of public pension funds joined such efforts during the 1990s, and even a few private investors, such as U.S. Trust Co. of Boston, report voting against undiversified boards at behest of their clients.[9]

Even before the advent of investor power, managements had been chipping away at nonindependent directors as defined by the second, more stringent criterion that they have no commercial relationship with the firm. Relatively few such directors remained by the late 1980s. A 1989 survey of 589 large firms found more than half saying they no longer retained even a single outside director whose own organization had a special relationship with the company. One-quarter of the boards were still graced with a representative from an outside law firm retained by the company, but less than one-tenth included an executive from a major supplier, customer, or bank of the company. A 1992 survey of 546 companies found three-fifths claiming no directors representing any commercial relationships. Detailed analysis of the 1993 proxy statements for companies in the S&P 500 stock index, however, reveals less change, with more than half the companies still having at least one director representing an outside commercial relationship. Nonetheless, while the "ties that blind" are still in evidence, they have largely receded into the past.[10]

Consistent with investor and management expectations, the new demography should move boards to adopt policies more independent of management. Other things being equal, research studies report that boards with more independent directors are more likely to resist green-mail payments (the purchase of a block of shares at above market price from a large stockholder threatening to take control or unseat management). They are less likely to be sued by shareholders for breach of fiduciary obligations. They are more likely to take active part in the company's strategic decision making. Like any organizational record, however, the tally in this case is mixed. Boards with more independent directors are neither more nor less likely to resist adoption of a poison pill or to preside over firms that resist tender offers. They are more likely to adopt golden parachutes for top management. And under some conditions, independent boards are more likely to dismiss chief executives of poorly performing companies, while under other conditions they are less likely to do so. Whatever the research record, the demography of directors is being reconstituted to create more space between the board and its executives.[11]

The Investor Director

While managements have moved to place more independent directors on their boards, this itself facilitates only half the agenda. It reduces loyalty to management, but does not necessarily inspire loyalty to investors. The latter might have been achieved through another kind of demographic revolution, the direct placement of institutional holders on the board. When groups feel unrepresented among those who shape their fortunes, few better solutions exist than to invite their representatives into the inner circle. When long-term institutional investors feel unrepresented among corporate directors who control their wealth, perhaps one of their representatives should be offered a seat on the board.

Theory might thus point to the elevation of the investor director. On this demographic front, however, the board's composition is unlikely to change at all, despite a certain logic to the contrary. Institutional investors are not soon to be welcomed into the boardroom.

Precedent for the institutional-investor director might be found in the occasional large shareholder who already has such a position. Five representatives of Seagram Company Ltd., holder of 24 percent of DuPont's stock, served by agreement on DuPont's board until Seagram disposed of its stock in 1995 to make way for its acquisition of the entertainment company MCA from Japan's Matsushita. Warren Buffet, chief executive of Berkshire Hathaway, the holder of 18 percent of Capital Cities/ABC stock, served by agreement on its board until the latter was acquired in 1995 by the Walt Disney Company. Chrysler named John B. Neff, long-time manager of the Windsor Fund, to its board in 1996 just after his retirement from the fund. Two members of the Ford family, which controls 40 percent of Ford Motor's voting stock, serve as Ford directors. Surveys of corporations during the early 1990s, drawn largely from the Fortune 1,000 rosters, reveal that one company in four included at least one major shareholder representative who was not also an officer of the company.[12]

These major stockholders, however, are not seen as representing institutional investors at large. Institutional investors view it that way because they had no hand in selecting such directors. Executives, for their part, view all directors as representing all shareholders. When Buckingham Bank's vice chairman is asked whether he would welcome an institutional investor on the bank's board, even the question seems to make little sense. His response: "If we're doing our job right, all of us are representing [institutional investors] anyway."

When an occasional institutional investor without a dominant stake in the company finds his or her way onto a corporate board, company managements usually view that person as representing no special constituency at all. Columbia Foods, for instance, has placed the chief executive of a major investment company on its board. It is not because his firm is a major investor in the corporation, which it is not. The firm holds less than 10,000 shares, placing it near the bottom of some 400 institutional investors with stock in the company. His presence draws no special attention from the other investors. Nor does senior management see him as bringing special powers or a presence distinct from that of any other directors. It views him as one among equals, formally representing all shareholders like all directors, informally a source of useful counsel like any outside director.

Similarly, the board of Hutchins Motors includes the executive director of one of the nation's largest institutional investors. He is treated much the same way. When proxy proposals from institutions come before the board, he quietly excuses himself from the room. When questions of investor responses to company actions are raised, he is *not* asked to give or represent the investor's point of view.

The situation is analogous to that of the labor leader who is asked to join a corporate board, which happens on occasion. Douglas Fraser, president of the United Autoworkers (UAW), had been invited onto the board of Chrysler Corporation as part of a rescue plan in 1979–80 that included federal guarantees to avert bankruptcy. Chief Executive Lee Iacocca allowed that the action was constituency related: "Some people would say, 'No, you can never have a labor guy.' So then why can we have bankers and a top supplier? What the hell's the difference if the guy involved is a purveyor of labor? He's pretty key to making the joint run." Still, other companies did not like the precedent: "The only guys who are mad at me," said Iacocca, "are the other chief executives." Despite Iacocca's comments, Chrysler executives backed off from any hint of constituency representation, steadfastly maintaining that Fraser serves in the same generic capacity as any other director, not as a representative of organized labor. When Fraser stepped down as UAW president in 1984, his successor, Owen Bieber, sought nomination to the open directorship, but Chrysler contended that there was no "labor" seat on the board. As a matter of realpolitik, the company finally seated Bieber but reiterated that he would represent all stockholders, not employees. With similar acts of labeling, companies declare that the few institutional investors who do serve on company boards have no special calling from or obligation to their institutional brethren.[13]

Some company executives find money managers, in principle, to be appealing prospects for their board. Many are exceptionally knowledgeable about the particular industry, far more so than some of the sitting directors. And many bring a critical intelligence sorely lacking in some boardrooms. Yet even here management finds their personal and professional qualifications more appealing than their ownership stakes.

Buckingham Bank's vice chairman says he would consider inviting an institutional investor onto his board, for instance, not as an ambassador from the investor world but only because the person represented the best thinking available. The vice chairman singled out the portfolio manager for one of the bank's largest investors, whom he had come to know through investor-relations work, as particularly appealing. "The way he approaches issues," said the banker, "the way his mind works, he goes well beyond doing institutional investing. He's just got a very bright mind, so someone like him might not be a bad choice to go on the board." The investor's command over a portfolio is coincidental: "I wouldn't pick him because he's an institutional investor. I'd pick him because of his mind and the fact that I know something about him." The added value would come from his critical intelligence. "We want someone [who is] going to challenge us," said the vice chairman, and "he would always ask a difficult question."

The preeminent investor Warren Buffet would also be an appealing choice for the Buckingham Bank board, but again for the insight rather than the occupation. "Guys like that," offers the vice chairman, "are two, three, four steps ahead of everybody else. When you're discussing a problem, they're going to ask you the off-the-wall question that everybody else is going to say two minutes later, 'Why didn't I think of that?'" The hypothetical advantages have not been translated into practical actions, however, and no institutional investor has yet been invited onto Buckingham's board.

Whatever the perceived special advantages of an exceptional institutional investor, disadvantages are seen by managements as outweighing them. Executives worry that investors on a board cannot dissociate themselves from their external fiduciary obligations. "If you actually picked some guy who was a representative of a major institutional holder and he comes to the board meetings," the general counsel of Chase Chemical Products warns, "he ipso facto becomes privy to information which you would not be willing to reveal to the outside." The conflict appears irresolvable: "Don't you compromise this guy's ability to be a fund manager?" Similarly, WWK Products' chief executive draws the line against investor directors for fear of special pleading. "I wouldn't want Ross Perot, I wouldn't want Dale Hanson," he said, "because they have their own agendas." WWK Product's chief financial officer sees it the same way: "Both [the CEO] and I like Dale. The more time we spend with him, the more we like him, and probably the board would feel the same way if they knew him. On the other hand, he does have [an] agenda"—and that is more than enough to kill his board candidacy.

Even large shareholders not known for their activist agendas are not considered appealing candidates. Among management's objections: they might demand divisional divestitures, dividend increases, stock buybacks, or other cash disgorging that would tie the hands of management or otherwise undermine its strategy. When the chief executive of Industrial Products Corporation was asked by Zacker, the purveyor of the soft bear hug, if Zacker might find a place on the board, the response was therefore predictable. The phrasing from the demanding Zacker was low-key. "I don't suppose you would want to have me on your board?" The CEO snapped back: "That's a correct assumption."

The conundrum of preferring more investor input to board decisions but perceiving institutional investor service on boards as unworkable has led to a hybrid proposal to form what is known as a shareholder "advisory" committee. In theory an *advisory* body would seemingly solve both problems, articulating investor concerns without giving investors formal authority, and the concept attracted some attention during the early 1990s. Calpers sponsored a proxy proposal at Avon Products in 1990 to create such a committee, and the proposal drew 45 percent of the vote. Zacker formed his own "shareholder enhancement committee" to "advise" Industrial Products Corporation as part of his bear-hug strategy, and management met informally with the committee (though more as a defensive tactic than as a concession of legitimacy).

The concept of the shareholder advisory committee, however, reached an early (and not particularly high) watermark. Surveys of institutional investors during the early 1990s reveal tepid support for the concept: less than one-fifth would generally vote for a shareholder advisory committee. Only 8 percent of the 1992 Exxon shareholder vote backed a proposal by the shareholder activist Robert A. G. Monks to create a committee of shareholder representatives. And the concept itself became tarnished in the minds of many managers. Calpers and other early proponents had urged such committees for companies they designated as poorly managed. For a company then to accept the formation of such a body was to concede its premise (putting itself in a position akin to that of the U.S. Senator who called a press conference to deny an obscure magazine's claim that he was the least intelligent member of the Senate). Once proponents "put a stigma on it," observed the general counsel of National Metal Products, "it was predictable that it was going to be opposed. It was not going to be something that any company would embrace." In the end, the concept remained just that.[14]

While bringing investors in from the cold might in theory ensure that directors have shareholder concerns much on their minds, management resistance has in practice proven prohibitive. When asked in 1991 whether institutional investors would be welcome on their board, only one-tenth of the CEOs of 322 large companies said yes. When asked in 1993 whether they had drawn on nominations by institutional investors, less than one-tenth of 348 large companies affirmed they had. Adding investor directors to the board, a plausible demographic transformation to make the board more shareholder friendly, is not in the cards.[15]

Redesigning the Board

Corporate planners know that you can change the people, you can change the organization, or you can change both. The most powerful effects usually follow the combined course, and management views of governance have run in the much the same direction. Companies are altering both the demographic composition of the boardroom and its architecture.

Consider the advice from two long-time board members, one a

former CEO. They compared what they deemed to be five of the best corporate boards in 1994, including those of Dayton-Hudson Corporation and Avon Products, with five of the worst boards, including those of W. R. Grace and Apple Computer. "The composition of the board alone does not make it a good one or a bad one," they conclude from their study. Rather, "a board's success or failure depends on how the group of individuals, with proper leadership, organizes itself to govern the corporation."[16]

Many executives recognize that their board, a body that had served their company well during a long era of shareholder passivity, is not well endowed with the leadership and organization to govern the company in a period of investor power. The strategy-structure dictum applies here as well as anywhere: board structure should follow company strategy. In the same sense that organizational restructuring should follow strategic redirection, board redesign should follow governance redefinition. The era of managerial preeminence had led to a board design that had served it well; the era of shared influence calls for a new design if it too is to be well served.[17]

The object of the new design: decision making should be more continuous, company directors should be more vigilant, and shareholder value should be more central. Whatever organizational schemes give the board more of the above should be applied.

In one area, directors' terms of office, the board's organization has moved in a contrarian direction. During the 1970s, most company directors came up for reelection every year. While incumbency for as little as a single year would seem to be a sure prescription for inexperience, corporate directors were actually far more secure in office than members of Congress. Single-year director terms, however, did present a would-be raider with an opportunity to replace the entire board at the company's annual meeting. By the late 1980s, as a result, a majority of large firms had converted to three-year staggered terms for board members, and during the early 1990s extended terms continued to spread (table 2.1 and figure 7.2). The result has been to make them less, not more, accountable to shareholders.

Otherwise, however, companies are moving their boards in the opposite direction, refashioning them to be more independent of management and more responsive to investors. Many companies have given their boards stronger operating hands in the form of specialized committees for financial audit, director nomination, and executive compensation. The directors' audit committee received early impetus from the New York Stock Exchange, which ruled in 1978 that all listed companies must have such committees. At the same time, investor capitalism has given impetus to all three, and most firms now operate them all.[18]

**Figure 7.2 Length of Terms for
Company Directors, 1972 and 1989**

Percentage of companies

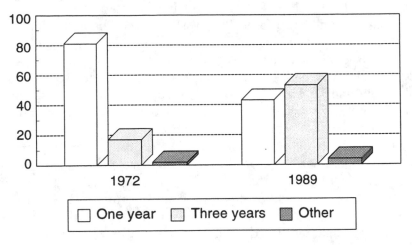

Source: Bacon, 1990.

Some companies are also taking the remaking of the board's architecture a step further, adding a specialized board committee on governance itself. During the 1990s, Campbell Soup has transformed its nominating committee into a governance committee; Gerber Products has
formed a "corporate governance review committee"; and Westinghouse
has established a nominating and governance committee. IBM created
a "directors and corporate governance committee" in 1993 to process
nominations, oversee compensation, respond to investor proposals, and
meet large holders. General Motors formed a committee of outside
directors in 1994 and instituted a "lead director"—a director selected
by the outside directors to provide independent leadership in reviewing
the performance of the chief executive.[19]

Other proposals that might arguably enhance the board's status
have gained far less momentum. These include term limits for directors,
an independent staff for the board, and separation of the chairman and
chief executive roles.

In revising its governance policies in 1994, General Motors rejected
term limits, finding that "they hold the disadvantage of losing the contribution of directors who have been able to develop, over a period of
time, increasing insight into the Company and its operations." The
board continues its practice of being serviced by management staff

rather than its own. And although after the 1992 ouster of the chairman and CEO, it had divided this top position into two, the board nonetheless ruled against the separation concept as a matter of standing principle: "the Board does not have a policy, one way or the other, on whether or not the role of Chief Executive and Chairman should be separate." In 1995, with confidence in its CEO restored, the board reunited the two positions.[20]

What is good for General Motors is evidently good for most companies: virtually none has adopted fixed term limits; almost none has added full-time board staff (though half contract with independent compensation consultants and a few retain outside counsel); and three-fourths continue to combine the chair and CEO roles in one person.[21]

One other area of board redesign, however, has drawn widespread support. It could hardly be otherwise without violating the culture of performance and accountability that has become so dominant under investor capitalism. Traditionally, corporate directors have received a fixed fee for their services. It varied only to the extent the directors chose to participate in board affairs. In addition to a flat annual payment for service, most companies had dispensed their directors' fees according to how often the directors attended board meetings and the number of board committees on which they served. In 1992, a survey of 824 large companies found that about three-fifths of the typical directors' compensation came from a fixed retainer, and most of the balance derived from meeting fees and committee assignments. Some made virtually the entire fee contingent upon attendance. WWK Products, for example, had traditionally handed a check to directors at the end of every meeting for simply being there.[22]

Since neither institutional shareholders nor senior managers expect to see the bulk of their income in fixed form, companies have pressed boards to move in the same direction. The number of companies providing some director compensation in the form of stock has risen sharply during the early 1990s, from under 40 percent in 1989 to almost 80 percent in 1995 (figure 7.3). A few firms, such as Scott Paper Company until it was acquired in 1995, moved to compensate outside directors solely through company stock.[23]

Research on large companies reveals that directors' contingent compensation is indeed associated with investors' improved income. One study, for instance, compares two sets of nine companies during the early 1990s. One set comprises firms such as IBM and Sears that have been targeted by at least three shareholder groups; the other comprises companies such as Merck and Wal-Mart that lead *Fortune*'s "most admired" company lists. Directors in the two groups were found to receive about the same total compensation (annual medians of $43,000

**Figure 7.3 Percentage of Large Firms Offering
Stock Compensation to Directors, 1989-95**

Percentage

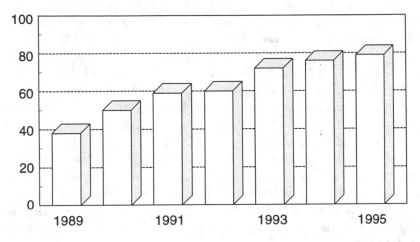

Source: Towers Perrin.

and $38,000, respectively), but they held radically different levels of stock in the firm: the average stock ownership among directors of the first group stood at $43,000, but for the second group it stood at $311,000. Company performance for stockholders also differed radically: the median return to investors for the targeted companies declined by 5 percent in 1991, while for the admired companies it rose by 60 percent.[24]

Some executives are not enamored with the concept of contingent compensation for directors, fearing it misdirects their oversight function. Applying the same compensation schemes used to reward managers, they worried, could inadvertently make directors behave too much like managers. "I think they should buy stock the way other people do," cautions the chief executive of WWK Products, "but the business of how the company performs is theirs to judge, not theirs to do." Several pension funds have pressed the company to offer restricted stock to the directors—grants of stock contingent upon the company's achievement of certain financial goals—but management has resisted and resented the demand. We "felt in this company that restricted stock was for special accomplishments for management, not to give to the board," concluded the CEO. "If the board wanted to buy stock, they could."

A company's board of directors remains the instrument for share-holder sovereignty. To assert otherwise is to challenge official portrayal, legal claim, and corporate charter. In reality, of course, the board had often evolved into a lesser instrument, largely disconnected from its shareholder base. The remoteness has come as a logical product of the managerial era, an expected corollary of executive strength and investor weakness. With investors and executives in accord on trans-forming their boards to reduce that disengagement, companies have now altered both the composition and the organization of their boards.

The evolution of the governing board of Columbia Foods is emblematic. As characterized by company executives, the board has moved away from an "authoritarian" arrangement in which directors formally ratified management decisions but did little else. The company has imposed limits on directors' terms and shifted director compensa-tion from cash to stock. It has also cut the number of meetings from twelve to six per year on the premise that this would infuse meeting agenda with more weight and less ritual. But above all, the company has transformed relations between directors and executives from formal oversight to informal consultation. "The board is a resource," offered the chief executive, "and if you think your board is anything other than a resource, you are making a mistake." In this mode, management reporting to its board has become less stiff and more substantive. The board now, said the CEO, is "much more of a peer."

Among a group of 327 chief executives surveyed in 1992, four-fifths expected that pressure from institutional investors would lead their boards to cast a more critical eye on their own performance.[25] If boards become too intrusive, however, if they slip from strategic oversight into micromanagement, investor influence could lose the buffers still required if management is to make effective decisions. "Director activism," in the words of one critic, "is like spelling the word 'banana.' It is important to know when to stop."[26]

8

§

Transforming Company Leadership

IN RESPONSE TO INVESTOR PRESSURES, senior managers are transforming their companies. In so doing they are also transforming their worlds. As they pull up the ladders that have taken them to the top, they are dropping down new ladders requiring different climbing skills. Career success under the new rules of investor capitalism depends increasingly upon an executive's ability to focus on shareholder value—and deliver it.

For those who have mastered the new leadership demands and have reached the corporate apex, staying there also requires skills less familiar to their predecessors. The old era of managerial capitalism had allowed executives to pursue priorities apart from those of the shareholders. The era of investor capitalism is less tolerant of such forays. Managerial capitalism permitted executives to ignore their shareholders; investor capitalism does not. Where managerial capitalism encouraged executives to disengage their directors from shareholders, investor capitalism will not.

Investor power and the restructuring it has wrought have redefined executive performance. Companies place more compensation at risk and make it more contingent on the expansion of investor wealth.

Senior managers face higher risk of personal loss or dismissal if they fall short. They are expected to produce more with less, and they demand the same of the middle ranks.

Top managers under the reign of managerial capitalism had enjoyed the privilege of no longer having to "manage up." They were at the top. Having paid their dues during the many years on the way up, they could savor the moment of finally arriving. They no longer had, or needed, a boss. Some of their contemporaries had earlier left promising careers to found their own ventures, each realizing a long-suppressed desire to be his or her own boss. Those who reached the executive suite achieved much the same thing. Having climbed so high that no rungs on the ladder yet remained, they had also become the undisputed masters of their own universe.

Investor capitalism, however, adds another ladder to the terrain. Vigilant investors are now also perched high above the landscape. The chief executive and his or her immediate associates are, as a result, less their own undisputed masters. Executive stature remains preeminent, executive compensation princely. Unlike their predecessors, however, company executives no longer enjoy the perquisite of going to work in a boss-free environment.

Moreover, the hierarchies of power and career are no longer quite so coterminous. Traditionally, each upward step on the corporate ladder brings the rising manager more power. With exceptional talent, much diligence, and a little luck, aspiring managers can one day expect a shot at the topmost posts of corporate authority. Now, however, those who succeed in reaching the executive suite face still another power level—and one that remains beyond their reach. Having overcome all previous barriers on their upward ascent, senior managers now confront their own glass ceiling, one through which they can peer but not pass.

Much of the core of company leadership is little different from what Gordon Donaldson and Jay Lorsch found in their 1983 study of *Decision Making at the Top,* or from what Rosabeth Moss Kanter revealed in her 1977 analysis of *Men and Women of the Corporation,* or from what Henry Mintzberg discovered in his 1975 ethnography of the "the manager's job." Chester Barnard's *The Functions of the Executive* (1938) and James March and Herbert Simon's *Organizations* (1958) remain enduring classics because they capture much of what senior managers in large organizations have always done, and probably always will do.

Still, the nature of work around many of these core activities has acquired fresh definition. Outstanding performance is more fully rewarded, lackluster achievements more harshly penalized. Bolstering share price and raising dividends can make an executive wealthy.

Unlike in the past, however, falling short today can quickly eclipse a career. The rewards for managing the status quo have declined, while the rewards for leaders who bring about change have risen.

This chapter begins with a look at the easy executive security that once prevailed and the insecurity that now prevails as tenure depends increasingly on performance. Focus turns to the new criteria in executive promotion that emphasize neither loyalty nor longevity. Finally, in this new corporate environment, executive pay becomes both more variable and more contingent upon enhancing shareholder wealth.

Executive Security

To appreciate the altered world in which company executives now manage, it is useful to consider an idealized image of big business before the deluge. Take the moment of its employment zenith in 1979. The Fortune 500 had created employment for more than 16 million workers. The economies of scale had served large firms well, giving them a privileged place in a world where manufacturing clout, marketing reach, and vertical integration were still the formula for strong earnings.

The nation's 500 great industrials had more than doubled their employment rolls in just twenty-five years. The growth engine showed no sign of slowing, corporate concentration no evidence of slackening. A 1976 article speculated on what the editors of *Fortune* magazine would do when, in the year 1998, they could find no more than 479 companies to constitute their famous 500 list. Mergers, acquisitions, and the economies of scale had eliminated or decimated all but the nation's greatest corporations. Would the editors allow the cover of the annual "Fortune 500" issue the literary license of preserving a national trademark whose numbers no longer added up?[1]

If a classic organizational form then existed, it can be characterized as a functionally defined hierarchy, with managers arrayed in tall lines of authority presiding over narrow spans of control. The central tendency was a seven-by-seven: seven layers of managers, each responsible for seven subordinates. No firm precisely fit any model, but many of the largest tended toward this one.

Though the company had been a creature of the market, it had also learned how to tame the market. It would, for instance, create steadier growth by drawing a host of unrelated products under one tent. Such diversification allowed the momentary peaks of prosperity for some products to make up for the valleys of others. With the uncertainty of the marketplace controlled, or at least buffered through sectorial diversity, company employment systems could achieve a stability unknown outside the civil service. As things turned out, of course, assured employment in American firms rarely reached the legendary standards of the Japanese lifetime-employment model. Few American executives would echo Akio Morita, Sony's chief executive, on the *first* principle of business ethics: "Management has the moral responsibility to nurture its employees." Nonetheless, for the approximately 25 million employees who found themselves inside the walls of the Fortune 500s, it was a comfortable career of respectable income, solid benefits, and job security.[2]

Reaching the apex of the corporate pyramid had been a career goal, a crowning achievement. With a hold on office secure—and along with it a secure financial future and a secure recognition of one's achievements—a successful executive could expect to pass the baton with proper ceremony and personal dignity. Other than the company's formal retirement age, little could be expected to interfere with the self-election of a retirement date. The executive suite had seemed a perch from which one would eventually depart at a moment of one's own timing and with a reputation of one's own making.[3]

Executive Insecurity

While this ideal type seemed immortal during the postwar era, its life span proved surprisingly brief. Companies that had given rise to William Whyte's "organization man" and David Riesman's "other-directed" manager would also give rise during the 1980s to the corporate raider Carl Icahn and the buyout specialist Henry Kravis—and during the 1990s to the activist investor Dale Hanson and the money manager Jeffrey Vinik. The ensuing dismissals of the chief executives of IBM, General Motors, and Eastman Kodak signaled that executive security could no longer be taken for granted. The executive suite had become a hot seat from which, on short notice, one might be ignominiously ejected.

The likelihood of ejection still remains modest. About one in ten of the CEOs of the nation's 1,000 largest companies annually steps down, and most departures are voluntary retirements. But one analysis, drawing on a host of public sources to identify the forced retirements during the 1988–93 period, finds that about one in five of the departures can be considered involuntary (figure 8.1). Most chief executives have reached the helm after two decades with the same company, and most remain at the helm for nearly a decade (table 8.1).

Yet the world confronted by today's CEOs is substantially less stable than that faced by their predecessors. This is confirmed in a study of

Figure 8.1 Turnover Among Chief Executives of 1,000 Large Companies, 1988-92

Percentage of 1,000 company CEOs

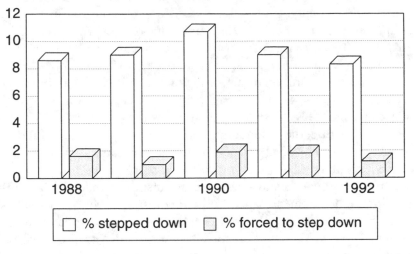

☐ % stepped down   ☐ % forced to step down

Source: Ward, 1995, Business Week.

Table 8.1 CEO Age, Years in Office, and Salary and Bonuses for Largest 1,000 Companies, 1986-92

	Average years as CEO	Average years with company	Average age	Average salary and bonuses
1986	9	23	56	$651,000
1987	9	24	56	685,000
1988	9	23	56	787,000
1989	8	23	56	841,000
1990	8	22	56	868,000
1991	8	21	56	878,000
1992	9	21	56	984,000

Source: Business Week, various issues.

114 industrial firms from 1960 to 1990 that assesses the likelihood of a chief executive's departure five years after taking office. Comparing those brought into the CEO's office in 1980 with those hired two decades earlier, the 1980s' executives are more than twice as likely to find themselves stepping down from office prematurely—five years after appointment rather than the usual eight or nine. And for CEOs hired in 1985, the most recent year for which data are available, the rate of turnover in 1990 is the highest in three decades (figure 8.2).

The American tradition of deflecting blame onto others, of embracing responsibility for what goes right and avoiding responsibility for what goes wrong, is less feasible under the new regime. In *Moral Mazes*, Robert Jackall discerns a tendency, pervasive a decade ago, for the managers of large chemical firms to point their fingers of blame in any direction except their own. Evidence for a more general application comes from a study of senior-management dismissal following a company's downslide in performance. Drawing on sixty-seven semiconductor manufacturers from 1968 to 1989, the analysis compares firms whose chief executives were powerfully ensconced with those whose CEOs had a more precarious hold on power. Ensconced chief executives are defined as those whose boards are less independent and whose stockholders are less institutional. The study finds that performance

Figure 8.2 CEO Turnover During Fifth Year in Office Among Large Manufacturers, by Year of CEO Appointment, 1960-85

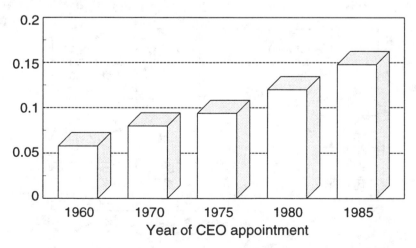

Likelihood of turnover

Year of CEO appointment

Source: Ocasio, 1994.

downturn at a firm with a powerful chief executive led to the dismissal of the CEO's top managers. Downturn at a firm with a more powerful board and investors, by contrast, led to the CEO's dismissal instead.[4]

Executive Promotion

Reaching the firm's apex requires a complex blend of career achievements, leadership qualities, and personal loyalties. It also depends much upon the most vexing company problems. If regulatory issues are paramount, executives who understand how Washington or state capitals work have an edge. If manufacturing challenges are critical, those executives with production experience push ahead. If financial restructuring or market share have been key, executives with financial backgrounds or marketing skills gain the upper hand.[5]

Investor power has now emerged as one of the era's critical contingencies. Working to assuage shareholder unrest has come to be as important to the future of the firm as fixing failed strategy, securing external financing, or reengineering business processes. Those who do it best become more valued by the organization; those who cannot become less so. To those managers who work well with investors go the kudos of success with a key constituency. To those who do not goes the taint of falling short.[6]

Company emphasis on effective executive work with investors varies from firm to firm. Within those companies most challenged by shareholder pressure, successful experience in managing shareholders is a highly valued asset for the aspiring executive. Within those companies whose strong performance has kept investors at bay, experience in working with stockholders carries less weight. Yet for both sets of companies, a demonstrated ability to produce shareholder value—or at least divisional contributions to the corporate whole—constitutes far more of a career asset under the rules of investor capitalism than under those of managerial capitalism.

The importance of these qualities is evident in National Metal Products. Its chief operating officer, who had come up on the financial side of the firm, has worked extensively with inside managers and outside investors over many years. He has had ample opportunity to witness not only what the institutions have to say to the company, but also how his own executives responded. "Over the years," says the COO, "you observe their ability to project themselves in rating agency meetings and in meeting with institutional investors." For those aspiring managers who might one day serve as chief financial officer, treasurer, or comptroller, conduct with shareholders has come to carry cachet at appraisal time.

The simultaneous exposure to outside investors and top executives has become particularly important for rising middle managers in National Metal Products, beleaguered as it has been by a hostile shareholder environment. Assistant treasurers and assistant comptrollers often join the company's meetings with its large holders. Sometimes they sit in for their bosses, while in other instances they are invited to take over when the questions become arcane. Either way, their bosses make sure they participate as part of their career development. Top executives attending the meetings—typically the CEO, COO, and divisional heads—field questions from investors at the outset. But they soon begin redirecting queries to subordinates ("Bob is better equipped to handle that one than anybody"). Sometimes the subordinates are too long-winded for their bosses' taste, furnishing details that allow them to shine but go well beyond what investors want. Afterward, they receive constructive coaching. "We try to get them to sharpen the message," offers the chief operating officer, "to leave an impression with a few sentences instead of pages."

Regardless of the value of the meetings to either shareholders or the company, they prove a forum for management development, a good training venue for high-potential prospects. Senior managers, observes National Metal Products' chief operating officer, make it "apparent to their next layer down that this was something that they probably ought to develop some skills with." Executives rarely articulate the need explicitly. Nobody says "you've got to get your ass in gear and be able to handle these meetings," offers the COO. But like so many organizational challenges that are personally experienced, the quick mastery of investor relations is self-evidently important.

Senior managers learn which subordinates work effectively in such meetings and request return appearances by those who, in the words of the chief operating officer, "seem to have the ability to convey ideas with an air of sincerity, understandableness and simplicity." The investor meetings also provide a convenient if unacknowledged forum for management assessment. "It's a pretty good way to observe" how middle managers "react in terms of salesmanship, integrity, and ability under hard questioning," concludes the chief operating officer. The company's struggle to ward off Frank Zacker's bear hug contains a silver lining. "We've had a lot of opportunity—because of all these meetings during the past four or five years—to measure people and how they perform" with investors.

Effective handling of company relations with major shareholders is a managerial asset even in companies where the investor environment has not proven terribly troublesome. Columbia Food Products has been more trouble free than most. The company nonetheless seeks to bring investors into direct contact with many senior managers. This is partly to facilitate owners' familiarity with the managers, and partly to facilitate managers' familiarity with the owners. In the chief executive's assessment, the personal contact provides "good training" for those moving toward top management. It builds experience in how to make an effective presentation to the stock analysts and money managers. And it offers insight into the minds of those with whom a rising manager will increasingly have to reckon. "Security analysts are by nature worried you're going to fall off a cliff," observed the CEO, and "I want our guys to hear about those huge chasms."

Some companies invest explicitly in the investor education of senior managers they are grooming for ever more senior assignments. Such initiatives often include increased exposure to leading shareholders and company analysts. Watching the ways of Wall Street helps. So also does experience in translating company results into language investors can understand and investor concerns into language managers can appreciate. This is evident at MFL Network, where the chief executive is grooming a division manager as a potential chief operating officer. Though the executive is not on the board, the CEO has arranged for the executive to consult with one of the outside directors who happens to hold a large block of stock. The CEO has also introduced the executive to other major shareholders. The executive confesses that he still has much to learn about the investment world, and he and the company are working hard to fill the gap.

WWK Products offers another case in point. Its two executive vice presidents are both considered viable candidates to succeed the chief executive. The company brings both into all of its quarterly meetings with sell-side analysts and into its frequent meetings with money managers. The chief executive explicitly fosters their involvement "because that's part of the training program, if you will, for the next generation." As meetings with investors close, the CEO will often tell them that "far more important than some of the things you're talking about here numerically are your meetings with" the two executives identified as "potential successors." The chief executive is disappointed by the tepid response to his advice by some investors, but most analysts embrace the proffered contact with both executives (nurturing a personal relationship with each promises good access to high office no matter who wins the succession contest). The two executives' effectiveness in these contacts is the subject of regular review by the CEO and his board.

Executive Riches

Reaching the apex brings less security than in the past, but in keeping with the risk-reward formula, it can also bring more fortune. The executive perch is less steady, but if one performs well, the rewards for being there are richer.

Compensation for chief executives has grown steadily during the late 1980s and 1990s, outpacing economic inflation, employee raises, and GNP growth. This can be seen in a tracking of the cash compensation of the chief executives of large corporations from 1984 to 1994. During that period, the percentage annual increase in CEO compensation, including both salary and bonuses, exceeded that of the consumer price index in all years except one. CEO compensation has also grown faster than that of white-collar (exempt) employees throughout the decade except for two years (1985 and 1991). The consumer price index in 1994 rose by 3 percent, white-collar salaries by 4 percent, and chief executive compensation by 12 percent (figure 8.3).

The CEO's compensation has also grown faster than that of immediate subordinates. The average CEO compensation and the average compensation of the seven top officers of a panel of forty-five large industrial firms has been annually tracked from 1982 to 1995. During this fourteen-year period, the top seven executives' average annual compensation (including benefits, perquisites, bonuses, and stock

Figure 8.3 Annual Changes in CEO Cash Compensation, Exempt Employees Compensation, Corporate Profits, and Consumer Price Index, 1984-94

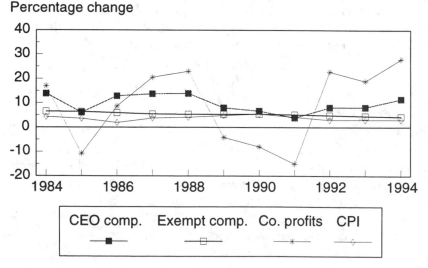

Source: William M. Mercer, Inc.

options) has risen from $455,000 to $1,459,000, a 321 percent increase. Across the same stretch, the average compensation of the chief executive officers climbed from $1,007,000 to $4,334,000 a year, a 431 percent expansion (figure 8.4).

Despite criticism by the media, labor, and Congress of the high levels of executive compensation, institutional investors express little concern over the level of pay. In an era of wage stagnation, million-dollar compensation packages are often a lightning rod for attacks on corporate power, callous management, and job decline. In an era of investor capitalism, however, seven-figure incomes bother few investors. Successful portfolio managers and stock analysts themselves often draw pay packages that match the best of the company executives. When the high compensation of the chief executive of WWK Products attracted media criticism, one of the company's million-share owners privately offered reassurance to the CEO: "I don't want someone telling me how much money I should make, and I don't expect someone to tell you how much money you should make." The manager of investor affairs for WWK Products had concluded that the amount is simply not the issue: "Serious investors expect people to be well compensated if they get good results."

What investors do despise is high compensation levels displaying little relationship to company performance. Million-dollar pay packages contingent on little except coming to work are a sure red flag. And,

Figure 8.4 Total Compensation of CEO and Average Total Compensation of Top Seven Executives, 1982-95

$ (thousands)

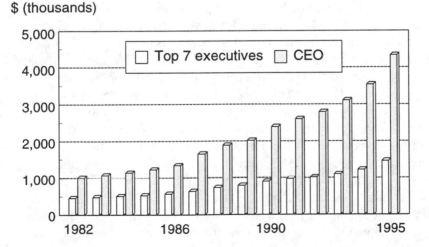

Note: Data for forty-five large industrial companies.
Source: Hewitt Associates annual surveys.

for investors, the enduring measure of company performance is their return—that combination of company dividends and stock appreciation that is the reason they part with their money in the first place. A common investor question for executives: "How is the company providing incentives to management to account for the well-being of the shareholders?"

Making Compensation Contingent

From their continuing dialogue, executives have learned to appreciate that investors oppose fixed compensation, favor variable compensation, and are indifferent to amount—so long as it varies with shareholder value. Managers of many companies have, as a result, placed more income at risk, put more managers on contingent compensation, and linked more of the contingency to expanding shareholder wealth.

The major holders of stock in Harrington Stores often ask the chief financial officer about the firm's compensation formulas. He explains that the upper management tier can earn another 50 percent or more on top of their base salary after a good year, and zero over base after a bad one. Moreover, the baseline for good and bad is not the company's budget or last year's performance, but the performance of major competitors in the same markets. Investors applaud the contingency but still question the baseline. Are you "doing this to make sure that executives don't go to the competition," one asks, "or to make sure executives perform better than the competition?" Another asks whether the baseline should be return to shareholders rather than measuring up to the competition. The CFO knows he has to do more fine-tuning if he is to meet investor standards: "The shareholder has a reasonable question there."

WWK Products has revamped its compensation to give it the contingent twist required. The company has expanded the number of senior managers with a large fraction of pay at risk, and for the top 500 it revised what the risk consisted of. The company has moved away from an earnings-per-share criterion for their bonuses and restricted stock awards. It has recast management bonuses around return-on-equity yardsticks, and it has introduced stock options that cannot be exercised until their price has risen at least 40 percent above that on the day of issue. These changes, explains the chief executive, are intended to make "the key decision makers act like owners," a change the company learned is music to the investment community's ears. The firm's liaison with investors has found that "the more our management thinks like and appreciates owners' points of view, the more positive feeling I'll get from our owners and potential owners." A large shareholder of

WWK Products confirms the liaison's view: "As long as I feel that we have an opportunity to make a lot of money in the stock, I don't object to the chairman earning a lot of money too."

Columbia Foods has frozen most executives' base salaries since 1990, placing all additional compensation on the variable side. To test the waters prior to doing so, the company's chief executive and chief counsel met several times with the chief executive and chief counsel of one of the largest public pension funds. The value of going to the latter, said the general counsel, is that they are "activist and yet at the same time we have found them to be very reasonable." The fund managers seemed to like what they heard, the company managers liked what they said, and the company plunged ahead. The company calculates the new bonus as a product of individual and corporate performance for the year, with the latter measured on growth in earnings per share and return on equity relative to other large companies. For maximum bonus payoff, the firm must rank among the top 10 percent of the S&P 500. It offered the top eighty managers the choice of staying with the old scheme or going onto the new plan. Despite its stiff performance standards, nine out of ten opted for the new regimen.

Columbia Foods' stock-option plan carries great risk for the managers, but it also promises great benefit if the company prospers. With a large portion of their income now leveraged around stock performance, executives face daily reminders of how they and the company are faring. As they leave the executive parking garage, a video monitor displays the company's closing share price on the New York Stock Exchange, tangible reminder of how their work had been judged that day by the owners, and, not coincidentally, how much richer—or poorer—it had made them personally. During the early years after the plan's introduction, the report card had been favorable as company returns and share price both soared. Investors "love" the options, observes the chief executive, "and we like [them] even better." The compensation scheme "puts us on the side of the angels," he concludes, "while we're all getting rich doing what they like us to do."

Buckingham Bank, in similar fashion, has sharply increased the contingent proportion of its officers' compensation and linked it to share-price appreciation. The board's compensation committee, observes the bank's vice chairman, "had decided that they want to be absolutely certain that our interests are the same as the shareholder interests."

Expanding variability is more generally evident in the compensation of top executives of forty-five large companies tracked from 1982 to 1995. The total income of the seven senior-most managers is divided into a fixed portion, comprising salary and benefits, and two variable portions: short term in the form of annual bonuses, and long term in the form of stock options and other stock-based incentive schemes. In 1982, about a third—37 percent—of top management's total compensation fell in the variable portion. By 1995, over three-fifths—61 percent—has become variable. Virtually all of the drop in the fixed fraction has been filled by long-term incentive pay, which rises from 17 percent to 40 percent of the compensation pie (figure 8.5).

The trend line has been even steeper for the chief executives. In 1982, two-fifths (41 percent) of the CEO's total compensation came from variable sources. By 1995, over two-thirds—70 percent—does so. Again, the long-term component drives the change. Multiyear incentive compensation in 1982 constituted 17 percent of the CEO's income package. By 1995, the multiyear fraction stands at 47 percent, larger than any other source of income (figure 8.6).

Another way to view the pay changes is to ask how a CEO might have sized up the major components of his or her compensation plan. In 1982, long-term incentives for the seven top executives of the forty-five industrial firms on average equaled 27 percent of base salary. By 1995, they equal 150 percent. For the CEO, the ratio of long-term to base pay rose from 29 percent to 154 percent. A comparable growth in variability is evident during the early 1990s for compensation of the chief executives of a larger and more diverse set of firms. In 1990, the average contingent income of the CEOs of 350 firms drawn from

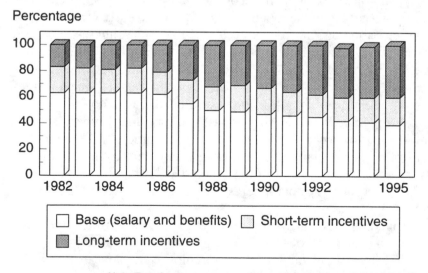

Figure 8.5 Percentage of Senior Management Compensation That Is Fixed or Variable, 1982-95

Note: Data for top seven executives at forty-five large industrial companies.
Source: Hewitt Associates annual surveys.

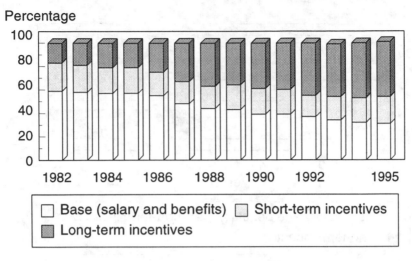

Figure 8.6 Percentage of Chief Executive Officer Compensation That Is Fixed or Variable, 1982-95

Percentage

Legend:
- ☐ Base (salary and benefits)
- ☐ Short-term incentives
- ▨ Long-term incentives

Note: Data for forty-five large industrial companies.
Source: Hewitt Associates annual surveys.

among the 1,000 largest constituted 61 percent of their total compensation. Two years later it had risen to 69 percent (figure 8.7).

Performance Contingency and Shareholder Wealth

As companies have increased the contingency of their senior managers' compensation, the marching orders from the investment community have been to tighten the linkage with shareholder wealth. Large shareholders look askance at companies that are "rewarding A while hoping for B."[7]

Executive compensation is shareholder sensitive to the extent that it includes stock-based incentives, cash awards driven by changes in shareholder return, and long-term nonstock compensation agreements contingent upon movements in investor wealth. A compact way to summarize the relationship is to examine the shareholder pay-performance sensitivity for corporate chief executives. As developed by researcher Kevin Murphy, this criterion measures how much a CEO's compensation increases in the wake of having increased investors' wealth. If the chief executive builds shareholder value by $1,000, pay-performance sensitivity gauges the number of dollars the CEO adds to his or her own

Figure 8.7 Percentage of Chief Executive Compensation That Is Fixed or Variable, 1990-1992

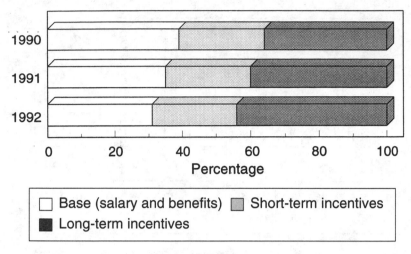

Note: Based on 350 companies among the 1,000 largest.
Source: Towers Perrin, 1992, 1993.

personal wealth at the same time. The greater the pay sensitivity, the greater the presumed CEO sensitivity to investor concerns.

Utility companies registered the lowest industry average on the pay-performance sensitivity scale in 1992, with 113 firms displaying a median $0.61. In the communication industry, 27 companies did little better, with a median value of $1.41. At the other end of the spectrum, 14 companies in health care displayed an average sensitivity score of $46.23, and 14 firms in entertainment and electronic media reached an industry-high average of $50.90. The typical utilities chief executive was $0.60 richer for having made investors $1,000 wealthier. The typical entertainment CEO was $51—or 85 times—richer.[8]

Time-trend analysis reveals, as expected, that CEO pay performance has become more sensitive to shareholder value. Analysis of the 250 largest companies in 1988 reveals a median sensitivity of $2.59 for adding $1,000 to shareholders' wealth. The median figure for the 1,000 largest firms in 1991 rose to $5.44. It 1992 it reached $7.48 (figure 8.8).[9]

Analysis of other trend data yields much the same picture. Of a set of large manufacturing firms surveyed by the Conference Board in 1982, four-fifths utilized stock-option plans to compensate their executives. By 1992, that fraction remained little changed for manufacturers, but the decade proved a watershed for companies in financial services and even utilities. Two-fifths of large financial-service companies surveyed in 1982 employed such plans, but by 1992 three-quarters did so.

**Figure 8.8 Shareholder Pay-Performance Sensitivity
for Compensation of Chief Executives of Large Firms**

$ change in CEO wealth with $1,000 change in shareholder wealth

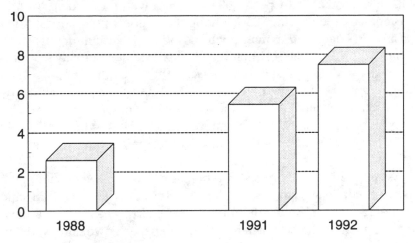

Source: United Shareholders Assoc., 1993; Jensen and Murphy, 1990.

In 1982, one-fifth of large utilities operated stock-option incentive plans for executives, but a decade later half did so.[10]

The fuel in CEO stock options can be illustrated with the terms of appointment for the new chief executive of Eastman Kodak who took office in December 1993, following the ouster of his predecessor by disgruntled directors and investors. The Kodak board recruited George Fisher from the chief executiveship of Motorola Inc., and in making the appointment it granted him 742,090 shares at $59.97. The new CEO could purchase the shares in 20 percent cumulative annual increments beginning in November 1994. Fisher also received 20,000 shares as a restricted stock grant that cannot be sold until he has been employed by Kodak for five years, a kind of "golden handcuff." If Kodak's share price has fallen below $59.97 when the option-exercise time arrives, the options are worth nothing. To the extent that the stock price rises above this waterline, however, Fisher stands to gain handsomely. Depending on price expectations, compensation consultants value the option package at $13 million to $17 million. The restricted stock grant was already worth $1.3 million at the time of issue, and it too grows as a function of the stock's price. As further incentive, Fisher purchased 107,400 Kodak shares outright just before taking office, tying up an additional $6.79 million of his own wealth in the company's fate and his performance.[11]

If Eastman Kodak's shareholders do well, Fisher thus stands to do well. Or, restated to reflect the preferred causal order, if Fisher does well professionally, both he and investors will also do well; if he does not, neither will. By contrast, the pay of Kodak's preceding CEO, Kay Whitmore, had been one of the least investor-wealth-contingent packages in the industry. In 1992, the pay-performance sensitivity estimate for Kodak stood at $0.61 per $1,000, on a par with the median for utility companies and ranking 925th among the nation's 1,000 largest firms. Whitmore's salary and annual bonus stood at $1.46 million; his stock options were valued at $0.4 million. In 1992, as the company's performance wavered, Kodak shareholders saw their wealth shrink by $1.89 billion, about 12 percent of total value. Whitmore's own company-related wealth declined by $1.2 million. Had his pay-performance sensitivity stood near the 1,000-company average ($7.48), Whitmore would instead have suffered a more than ten times greater personal loss of $14.1 million.[12]

As companies have pressed contingent compensation deeper in the ranks, the challenge has been to ensure that it is leveraged around shareholder wealth. Below the top officer level this has required measures that include the performance of the manager's own unit as well as that of the firm as a whole. Many firms now reward senior managers on the basis of their own performance, divisional success, and company results. One-third of their year-end bonuses and stock grants might thus depend on how they fare, one-third on how their division comes in, and one-third on how the company delivers to the shareholder. Xerox Corporation's prolonged remaking of its architecture has taken such a scheme a step further. To stimulate its restructuring agenda, Xerox has transformed the conventional additive formula into a multiplicative calculus. A manager's performance depends now on a product of all three factors. If the manager falls short in any one of the three areas, the variable portion is zeroed out.[13]

A New Career Rung

For those who reached the higher circles of corporate management by the 1980s and 1990s, shareholder power and investor relations had been of little company concern during their early career years. Their M.B.A. programs contained little training in valuation techniques or organizational designs for optimizing shareholder value. Their early years with the company furnished scant foundation for thinking about the nature of the investor universe or how to manage its main attractions. Many managers had begun their careers in marketing, engineering, or manufacturing. They knew that ascent into general management would require mastery of all these areas and more. But few had anticipated that reaching the highest stage would also require mastery of share-holder management.

Even those now primarily responsible for managing their company's investor affairs typically began their corporate careers with little inkling of the skills they would one day require. The absence of such background experience among those in the company foreground can be illustrated with reference to the careers of two individuals who carry primary responsibility for managing their firm's relations with major investors. One serves as vice president for investor affairs at Shaw Communications, the other carries a similar title at Western Chemical Company. One had joined the company as a marketing specialist, the other as a chemical engineer. Neither's early career anticipates the roles both now play.

The marketing specialist had joined Shaw Communications as a manager after ten years with a publishing and information services company, where he held a variety of positions, ranging from running a business operation to strategic planning at headquarters. On joining the telecommunications firm, he worked initially on the marketing side, but later, despite the fact that he had no formal background or experience in investor relations, the company asked him to run the investor affairs department. By company policy, the appointment is rotated, with line managers serving two to three years and then returning to line responsibilities. Like so many of his counterparts at other companies, the vice president would never have anticipated that he would one day be managing the company's network of investor contacts.

The chemical engineer had joined Western Chemical during the late 1950s, fresh out of an Ivy League bachelor's program in engineering. Over the next two decades he held diverse positions as he circum-navigated his way to the senior ranks. He began as a technical supervisor for a class of chemical products but soon gained promotion to general product manager. From there he moved into district and national sales positions for successively larger groups of products, and later into their marketing. By the early 1980s he had been elevated to vice president and general manager of a product division, and he later moved on to head two other divisions, the last with annual sales of $2 billion. At one point he also joined the strategic planning office, with special responsibility for a redesign of the company around the concept of profit sharing. With more than twenty years' experience in chemical engineering and management, he was asked by the chief executive in the early 1990s to take charge of the company's investor relations.

Though the engineer assumed Western Chemical's investor-affairs appointment with no background in the area, he had another, invaluable asset. He had worked for years with those now in senior management and he retained a line-manager's credibility with them. This has proved important both inside and outside the firm. On the inside, it facilitates his insistence that he be kept informed of all developments within the company's operating divisions. He tells division heads that he cannot afford to be wrong in communicating with investors, but also that he cannot afford to reveal what should not be known. Given his veteran status, line managers entrust their information to him, confident that he will use it to company advantage without divulging the proprietary side. Outside the firm, analysts acquire their information from him, confident that his years of line experience help extract the data they need.

A False Summit

During the era of managerial dominance, reaching the summit of the corporate pyramid had provided an unimpeded view. For the newly ascendant executive, the landscape sloped downward as far as the eye could see. No other summits blocked the commanding vista. The successful manager could savor the view in all directions, knowing that all lay below.

As the managerial era closed, however, the landscape acquired other imposing features. As if a geological eon had been compressed into moments, other pyramids appeared almost overnight. Their foundations resided not on the production of value, but on the possession of wealth. Their summits rose so swiftly and so high that few executives had anticipated during their own long climb to the top that they might find a disappointing view once there. But the corporate top is now dominated by still higher—and unattainable—summits. In the mountaineer's parlance, today's executives have mounted a "false summit." Moreover, they can see no way across to the truer peaks. To reach those heights would have required a long career ascent of an entirely different slope.

Even on their own now-diminished peaks, some managers have felt the perch far more perilous, and reaching the summit far more arduous. For all of those in and around the corporate apex, however, personal rewards have come to depend less upon merely being there and more upon actually achieving results. Company performance and personal accountability have become more important, service length and lofty title less so. "Companies need to recognize that part of the job of running a public company is to manage the ownership base," offers one observer, "and that part of the job is just as important as managing operations."[14]

9

§

The Expanding Universe

SENIOR MANAGERS PRESIDING over America's largest companies during the 1990s confront the same kinds of problems that challenged their predecessors. Rethinking strategic directions, repositioning company products, and retooling production designs are among the tasks upon which they—and their successors—are sure to dwell. Unlike senior managers a generation earlier, however, executives now face the added challenge of an aroused, informed, and demanding investment community.

Managing a publicly traded company in this new environment requires skills and strategies that their predecessors had little reason to master. But for today's executive, working effectively with investors has emerged as an important skill for advancement and achievement. Effective executive work means building enduring relations with large investors and building improved internal structures to support such relations. Ineffective work in either area can lead to languishing stock price, sub-par performance, and a restless board.

As in the emergence of any institutional order, new conventions have come to prevail. Consistent executive reference to "shareholder value" is de rigueur. So, too, is a willingness to share detailed company information with investors and to build personal relations with the company's largest shareholders. The chief executive of WWK, the

diversified-products company, signals the widely shared, albeit grudg-
ing, acceptance of the new rules. "Realistically," he concedes, institutional shareholding in the company "is going to grow. I mean there's no
way you can stop it. The big funds are growing, the mutual funds are
growing." He can read the handwriting on the wall and knows where his
company is headed. As shareholding "becomes more and more institutional, we're going to have to be organized so that we're accessible and
talking to the major owners."

The emergence of concentrated owner power has created the new
order. Long-disenfranchised shareholders—or, more precisely, institutional investors—are doing what community organizers urge dispos-
sessed communities to do anywhere. By identifying the points of political leverage, learning the process of pressure politics, and mastering
the art of mobilizing others, communities with little influence over their
own fate can acquire far more. Large investors have followed the pre-
scribed path. That course is far easier for them than for most, for
investors have leveraged a base of wealth dwarfing what other disen-
franchised groups could ever hope to deploy. A rallying cry for mobilizing the powerless to protest rallies during the tumultuous 1960s was
that all power is in the streets. A parallel slogan for the era of the 1990s
reads: All power is on the Street.[1]

This final chapter considers where investor power is continuing to
consolidate and how it is likely to further reshape the operation and
organization of business. The chapter identifies three areas notable for
their continuing evolution: the growth of mutual funds, the underfunding of pension funds, and the internationalization of investments.

The chapter also considers how the rise of investor power is changing the organization of the American business community. The focus is
on two aspects of that change: the emergence of boundaries between
owners and managers, and the dissolution of boundaries between organizations and markets. Investor capitalism is not only altering the
power balance between shareholders and companies; it is also creating
a new schism within the business community and, at the same time,
diminishing the divide between market and organization.

Investment Company Growth

During the 1950s, most company shares resided firmly in the hands of
individuals. The era of the "orphans and the widows" was in reality
dominated by millions of individuals (relatively few orphans or widows
among them) who picked companies and collected dividends. In 1950,
91 percent of all corporate equity holdings in the United States were

held by households. Forty-five years later, less than half is still so held. Ultimate ownership is of course not very different. Most of the money placed in mutual funds, insurance investments, pension funds, and bank trusts is managed either directly or indirectly on behalf of individuals. But the rise of the intermediary institutions has transformed the relationship between the ultimate owners and their companies. For individual beneficiaries, it has become even more arm's length. But for those picking stocks and collecting dividends for beneficiaries, the relationship is far closer.[2]

Among the five-member family of institutional investors—pension funds, insurance companies, bank trust departments, nonprofit organizations, and investment companies—the last one is of particular interest. Investment companies are directly responsible for the management of more assets than any other set of investors, and they are accumulating additional assets faster than any of them.

Strictly speaking, investment companies do not preside over the largest slice of the institutional pie: pension funds held $4.1 trillion in 1992, while investment companies controlled a mere $1.3 trillion. Still, the largest single players are to be found among the investment companies. In mid-1995, Fidelity Research and Management, the largest of the large, oversaw an investment portfolio exceeding $390 billion—a hundredfold increase from its $3.9 billion in 1972. On a typical day, it trades $1 billion in stock in some 1,000 companies.[3]

Moreover, investment companies amplify their power by managing other institutions' money as well as individual retirement plans. One-third of the total assets managed by the nation's mutual funds have come from retirement plans. Such plans account for more than two-fifths of Fidelity's and Vanguard's mutual-fund assets, and two-thirds of the new dollars going into them. Pension funds themselves retained *direct* investment control in 1993 over only 12 percent of all institutional assets. Money and mutual-fund managers, by contrast, oversaw 51 percent, making them the largest single group of active investors.[4]

Investment companies are also the fastest-growing members of the institutional-investor family. Since 1975, the compound annual growth rate of investment companies exceeds that of all other family members. The growth rate from 1975 to 1980 for all institutions averaged 13 percent, while for investment companies it averaged 21 percent. From 1980 to 1985, the respective rates were 15 percent and 30 percent; from 1985 to 1990, 11 percent and 17 percent.[5]

The growth in investment company assets can be seen at the four largest equity funds. Between 1980 and 1995, the assets of the Investment Company of America grew from $1.7 billion to $21.2 billion, a factor of 12. The Vanguard/Windsor Fund multiplied by a factor of 14,

Washington Mutual Investors by 51. The Fidelity Magellan Fund—the largest of all mutual funds—expanded by a factor of 788 (figure 9.1). A single Magellan money manager, Jeffrey N. Vinik—like his earlier counterparts Morris Smith and the legendary fund-builder Peter Lynch—presides over an enormous asset pool. By early 1996, Vinik was actively managing more than $50 billion in Magellan, and on an average business day he receives another $30 million to add to his rolling snowball.[6]

Magellan's growth rate, performance record, and huge size overshadow those of most other mutual funds, lending it a public visibility equaled by none. But the mutual-fund field as a whole has displayed rampant growth during this period. In 1977, the number of equity funds totaled 274. In 1994, that number had increased sevenfold to 1,944. The number of all mutual funds—equity, bond and income, and money-market funds included—stood at 98 in 1950. At the start of the 1990s they totaled 3,105; by 1994, they reached 5,357. Assets under management display similar acceleration. Equity fund holding stood at $41 billion in 1980, but at $867 billion by 1994. All mutual fund assets stood at $241 billion in 1980, but at $2.162 trillion in 1994 (figures 9.2 and 9.3).

The number of mutual-fund shareholders has grown in parallel fashion. In 1980, some 6 million shareholder accounts existed for equity funds, and 12 million for all mutual funds. By 1994, these numbers had reached 59 million and 115 million, respectively (figure 9.4). Looked at

Figure 9.1 Net Assets of the Four Largest U.S. Equity Funds, 1980-1995

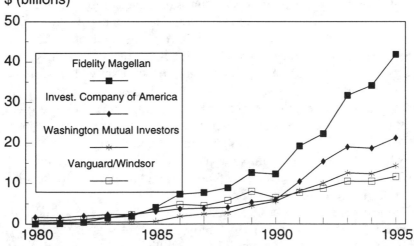

Source: Morningstar, Inc.

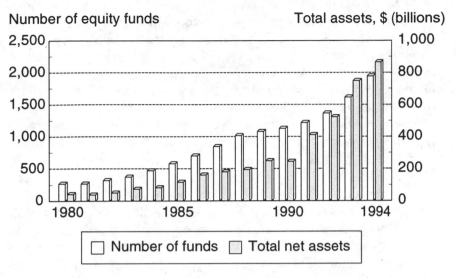

**Figure 9.2 Number and Total Assets of U.S.
Equity Funds, 1980-94**

Source: Investment Company Institute, 1995.

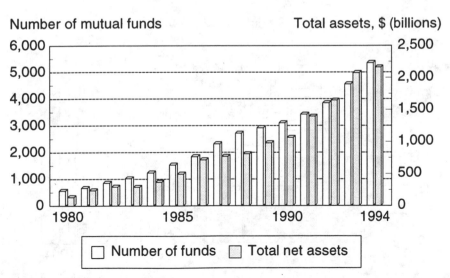

**Figure 9.3. Number and Total Assets of U.S.
Mutual Funds, 1980-94**

Source: Investment Company Institute, 1995.

differently, in 1980 one in twenty of all U.S. households had placed money in mutual funds; by 1994, one in three.[7]

The rise of mutual-fund investing has generated an ancillary industry that is devoted to informing people about the performance of funds, just as stock analysts have long been devoted to informing people about the performance of companies. Consumer services such as Morningstar and Lipper Analytical provide detailed comparative assessments. In mid-1995, Morningstar, for instance, tracked 6,512 funds, reporting current and historical data on the funds' returns, risk, turnover, composition, management, and, for those seeking a summary judgment, an overall rating system. Like hotels, funds receive up to five stars: Fidelity Magellan ranks with Ritz-Carlton.

Individual wealth has become no less important, but individual owners have receded into the shadows while mutual-fund managers have pushed into the limelight. Fewer individuals choose stocks; more equity managers do so. Picking for many households is now once-removed, a matter of selecting funds instead of stocks. In this act of relinquishing their right to pick stocks, individual owners have inadvertently created the opportunity for professional money managers to achieve what individuals could never hope—or in many cases had never intended—to achieve: a voice in company management. Though the individual mutual-fund shareholders cannot say where, how, or

Figure 9.4 Number of Shareholder Accounts in Equity Funds and All Mutual Funds, 1980-94

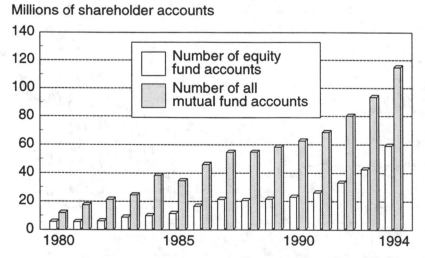

Millions of shareholder accounts

Source: Investment Company Institute, 1995.

even whether the money managers should intervene with company management, they have endowed them with the clout to do so.

Peter Drucker's early forecast of "pension fund socialism" has not come to pass in America, but something akin to mutual-fund capitalism has achieved much the same level of concentrated firepower. Should mutual funds and investment companies further consolidate their management of corporate equities during the years ahead—as they will if the course of recent history continues—mutual-fund power will also further increase. If the proverbial 800-pound gorillas exist in the world of capitalist enterprise today, they are roaming the halls of the great money-management firms.

Pension Underfunding

Pension funds have long constituted major players themselves. These funds remain the single largest component of institutional investing, and they continue to gain ground faster than any of the others except investment companies. In 1970, pensions presided over 31 percent of all institutional assets; by 1992, their share had risen to 50 percent. The number of private pension plans and participants has risen as well. In 1975, 45 million participants had enrolled in 311,000 plans with $259 billion assets. By 1990, 77 million participants were enrolled in 712,000 plans with $1,674 billion assets.[8]

Public and private pensions, of course, could not be more different in their posture toward investor activism. Public funds define the interventionist end of the spectrum, private funds the isolationist. Public pension funds have led investor unrest, while private pensions have stood for investor complacency. Despite the schism, however, many in both camps share an acute desire to improve company performance. All institutional investors seek better returns, but some public and private funds, by virtue of their underfunding, are more desperate for stronger returns than others.

Private pensions in several sectors—primarily automobiles, steel, airlines, and tires—encountered worsening conditions during the early 1990s as their parents struggled in bitterly competitive environments. By 1992, Bethlehem Steel's pension fund reported a shortfall of $1.9 billion, or 60 percent of its obligation; Uniroyal Goodrich Tire fell short by $450 million, or 47 percent; TWA by $426 million, 42 percent; and General Motors by $17.2 billion, 30 percent. The Federal Pension Benefit Guaranty Corporation tracks private funds' financial conditions (it insures a large fraction of their retirement benefits), and its picture is of substantial underfunded liabilities. Time trends in the figures for the fifty worst offenders reveal a deteriorating situation during the late 1980s and early 1990s. An aggregate underfunding in 1988 of $13.5 billion had mushroomed to $32.3 billion in 1993. However, companies sharply reduced their pension underfunding in 1994, with the aggregate underfunding dropping to $10.8 billion (figure 9.5).[9]

The worsening condition of a limited set of private pensions during the early 1990s, however, ran contrary to a more general improvement in the state of private pensions since the early 1980s. In 1981, more than half—55 percent—of private plans reported underfunding. By 1992, only one in six—15 percent—still did so (figure 9.6). While the condition of some funds has worsened markedly, the general health of private pensions in the mid-1990s is improved over that in the previous decade.[10]

The public pension sector displays similar divergence, with some funds lagging and others as flush as ever. On average, however, public funds face more underfunding than their private counterparts. In 1991, 16 percent of the private plans were underfunded. By contrast, 67 percent of the public plans reported underfunding, including 29 percent whose assets stood at less than three-quarters of their liabilities. One analysis reported that state and local pension contributions in 1989 were running 10 percent to 15 percent below what would have been required for full funding. Some of the problem may be attributed to less successful public pension investment strategies: from 1984 to 1990, pub-

Figure 9.5. Underfunding of Fifty Largest Underfunded Private Pension Plans, 1988-94

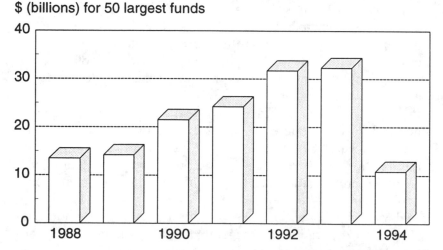

Note: Underfunding not federally guaranteed is not included.
Source: U.S. Pension Benefit Guaranty Corporation, 1995 and earlier years.

Figure 9.6 Ratio of Assets to Liabilities Among Surveyed Private Pension Plans with 1,000+ Participants, 1981-92

Percentage of companies with ratio

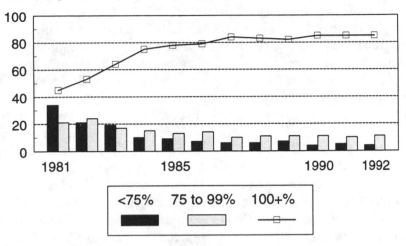

Source: Salisbury and Jones, 1994.

lic funds produced an average yield of 11 percent while securities investments in general yielded 14 percent and bonds 16 percent.[11]

Here too, however, the general picture during the early 1990s is not one of worsening underfunding. Drawing on direct surveys of several hundred state and local pensions, analysis reveals that in 1991 39 percent were underfunded (defined as those whose ratio of assets to obligations fell below 90 percent), compared with 35 percent in 1992 and 38 percent in 1993. Looked at differently, the average ratio of assets to obligations for all public funds in 1991 stood at 85 percent, in 1992 at 85 percent, and in 1993 at 90 percent. Another analysis of the 205 largest state and local funds—responsible for 91 percent of total state and local assets—from 1988 to 1992 offers corroborating evidence. It found that 33 public pension plans had been chronically underfunded. The other 172 funds, by contrast, are generally well funded and their condition has grown even stronger. Overall, the mean underfunding ratio for the 205 plans improved slightly over the five-year period from 83 percent to 86 percent.[12]

Some of the public pension underfunding is driven by regional downturns, and some of the private pension underfunding by sectorial declines. States and localities with the highest rates of unemployment are most likely to underfund their public pensions. Companies in declining sectors are most prone to underfund their private pensions.[13]

Managers of underfunded plans are under intense pressure from their parents to increase returns. The alternatives for state and local governments are to raise taxes or cut other services, neither of which is among elected officials' favorite actions. In 1994, Washington, D.C.'s pension plans for city teachers, police, firefighters, and judges held just one-third of what they should have, a nearly $5 billion shortfall. Under pressure from a city budget awash in red, the mayor sought to delay another regularly scheduled pension contribution of $230 million. The effort failed but the political and financial dilemmas persisted. "Do you pay the current cops," wonders a financial adviser to the city, "or the retired cops, or do you tax people so high they'll move out of town?"[14]

For company managements, the choices are to divert resources from dividends or cut other expenses, neither of which is an appealing option. To reduce its underfunding, General Motors developed a program in 1994 to contribute $4 billion in cash and $6 billion in stock over the following two years to the retirement program for its 600,000 current and retired wage workers. This would come on top of a regularly scheduled company contribution of $8 billion. At a time when GM was under intense market pressure to develop new products and to remake itself into a more competitive organization, the planned diversion of $12 billion carried a high price.[15]

A small set of public and private pensions thus faces short-term and, in some instances, chronic shortfalls. It is among such funds that the clamor for performance may be especially vocal, especially when stirred by alarmist media accounts. In response to reports in 1994 of continuing corporate pension shortfalls, for instance, *Fortune* cautioned: "Don't panic about your pension—yet." In reaction to 1994 reports of public pension shortfalls, the *Wall Street Journal* warned that "public pension plans are so underfunded that trouble is likely." A 1994 cartoon depicts an elderly man at home watching television; a newscaster asks, "It's 11 P.M. Do you know where your pension fund is?"[16]

Longer-term trend lines, however, do not suggest that pension underfunding is likely to be greater during the late 1990s than it was in earlier years. In the aggregate, neither public nor private pension underfunding is growing. Despite occasional alarm to the contrary, pension underfunding is unlikely to constitute a major additional source of investor pressure during the years ahead.

Internationalization of Investments

American investors have generally avoided international investments—until the 1990s. Their counterparts in the U.K. and Japan have sailed a similar course. One analysis of 1989 holdings reveals that American investors kept 94 percent of their financial assets at home. British investors were slightly more international, placing only 82 percent of their assets in the U.K. market. But Japanese investors were even more domestic, placing 98 percent in Japanese securities.[17] Few non-U.S. firms heard any of the American investors' drumbeat for steady returns, improved communication, or company restructuring. During the 1990s, however, U.S. investors have overcome their global shyness.

Dreyfus, for instance, formed its International Equity Fund in June 1993. By May 1994 it had drawn $175 million from some 12,000 investors. Paul Nix, manager of the Dreyfus fund, placed two-thirds of his newfound assets in foreign stocks, ranging from Sony and Canon to Banque Nationale de Paris, British Gas, Teléfonos de Mexico, and China Light and Power. "If you're a U.S. investor concerned with limiting volatility and seeking higher long-term returns," Dreyfus says, "there are good reasons for adding a foreign component to your portfolio." The fund does for individual investors what they cannot not do for themselves. "Fund managers can research the world's many markets, diversify the portfolios across several countries and deal with the complexities of currency fluctuations," argues Dreyfus, "activities that are beyond the scope of most individual investors."[18]

The net purchase of non-U.S. stocks soared in 1991 and 1993. With less than $4 billion net non-U.S. purchases through most of the 1980s, net non-U.S. purchases in 1989 hit $13 billion. In 1991 they reached $32 billion, and in 1993 they totaled $63 billion (figure 9.7). The outflow stems in part from the opening of new opportunities abroad. The privatization of enterprise through much of Southeast Asia (for example, Malaysia), Latin America (for example, Argentina), and Eastern Europe (for example, Hungary) has placed large numbers of new shares on the international market. Rapid growth in many emerging economies, such as Chile, China, Hong Kong, Singapore, and Thailand, has stimulated foreign opportunities as well. Capitalization of the Hong Kong equity market in 1988 stood at $74 billion but five years later reached $385 billion; the Singapore market rose from $24 billion to $133 billion during the same period.[19]

Individual investors have also acquired greater confidence in their abilities to pick equity funds that invest abroad and to give over their savings to them. During the latter half of the 1980s, international equity funds (with at least 75 percent of their holdings abroad) and global equity funds (with at least some of their holdings outside the United States) attracted net new investments of less than $3 billion per year (figure 9.8). During the first third of the 1990s, by contrast, individuals

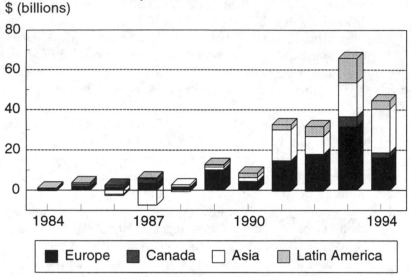

Figure 9.7 Net Purchases of Foreign Stocks by U.S. Investors, 1984-94

Source: Securities Industry Association, 1995.

poured new money into such funds. In 1993 alone, global funds drew over $12.2 billion, international funds more than $26.2 billion. Prior to the 1990s, one-fifth or less on average of new net investments in equity funds was allocated to international and global funds. By 1993, nearly 30 percent of new equity investments were going into international and global funds; during the first half of 1994, nearly 40 percent. With the precipitous devaluation of the Mexican peso at the end of 1994 and the reactive anxieties in other emerging markets, many United States investors temporarily retreated, but domestic confidence and international opportunity are now too established to permit enduring reversal.

Seen from the vantage point of emerging economies, equity investments have displaced bilateral financing as the largest single source of external financing. In 1981, equity investments accounted for 9 percent of all net new external financing. Private creditors provided 9 percent. Commercial banks furnished 59 percent, and national governments and international agencies such as the World Bank provided 24 percent. By 1993, these leadership roles were reversed. Equity investments accounted for 39 percent and private creditors 36 percent. Commercial bank financing dropped to 13 percent and public financing to 13 percent. Banks and governments were no longer the leading source of new, external financing for emerging economies—they had been displaced by pension funds, mutual funds, and investment companies. The execu-

Figure 9.8 Net Annual New Investment in International and Global Equity Funds, 1984-94

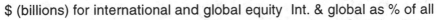

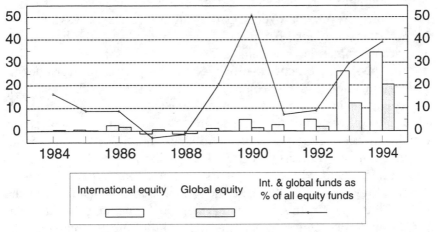

$ (billions) for international and global equity   Int. & global as % of all

Note: International funds invest 75+% outside U.S., global funds invest some; 1994 figure is 2X first of 1994 only. Source: Investment Co. Institute, 1994.

tors of world development had merged with the overseers of American equity. "The mutual funds have taken over the financing role of big banks and quasigovernmental institutions," as the coauthors of an assessment explained, and they "are trying to do what they have already been doing in the U.S.: pressure management . . . to adopt policies that will maximize returns."[20]

U.S. investors are also reaching into foreign companies without ever leaving U.S. shores through purchase of foreign stocks listed on the New York Stock Exchange, where 216 resided at the end of 1994. In 1991, under 5 percent of its trading stock volume was in foreign shares, but by 1994 the volume was over 9 percent. By 1995, trading in the exchange's non-U.S. stocks was growing three times faster—40 percent versus 13 percent—than trading in its domestic stocks.[21]

As American money managers study their international prospects, they see a welter of securities laws, reporting requirements, and board structures. Governance systems and investor-corporate relations display as much variation from country to country as almost any feature of business organization. The multidivisional structure has spread far and wide among large corporations, regardless of national setting. So too have key technologies of production. This is not the case, however, for such elementary features of governance as the composition of company boards. The boards of virtually all large, publicly traded U.S. firms include a solid majority of outsiders. The boards of virtually all large, publicly traded Japanese firms include almost no outsiders. German and Dutch governance is built around a two-tier governance structure; British and Swiss governance is designed around a single-tier, management-dominated structure. Some systems give formal voice to labor, others none: German law requires that labor representatives serve on the board, while French law places labor observers on the board, and American law mandates nothing.[22]

The days of divergent governance systems presiding over convergent organizational forms are numbered. As U.S. investors insert their moneys into other national economies, they are certain to insert themselves into other companies' management as well. Investor objections to uneven reporting requirements and shareholders rights from country to country will certainly be close behind. The U.S. Financial Accounting Standard Board is working with counterpart groups in Canada, Mexico, and Chile to harmonize accounting standards in the wake of the 1994 North American Free Trade Agreement. The International Accounting Standards Committee and the International Organization of Securities Commissions are working together to develop common accounting standards by the end of the 1990s for companies that are listed cross-nationally or are seeking to raise capital outside their home country.[23]

The U.S. government has contributed its own impetus. The Department of Labor, in its regulatory oversight of private pensions, added a provision in 1994 that pension managers must treat foreign holdings in the same active fashion in which they were already required to view domestic securities. Pension managers are now required to examine foreign proxies and cast informed votes with the same diligence as in the United States. Other governments are also inviting U.S. investors into their stock markets through liberalization of their trading rules. During the early 1990s, for instance, Taiwan, like many rapidly emerging economies, opened its stock markets to foreign securities firms and foreign direct investment. Japan opened its $200 billion in public pension funds to outside management by foreign firms.[24]

American investors are already testing the waters. For non-U.S. companies listed in the United States, investors are pressing for more information. For non-U.S. companies that are not performing as expected, shareholders are even occasionally pushing for new management. Calpers, which announced a two-year program in 1994 to expand its international holdings from 13 percent to 20 percent of its assets, could build on an already established global activism: it had openly opposed a proposed limitation of shareholder voting rights in 1992 by the French food company BSN. In late 1994 a group of investors led by

Chicago-based Harris Associates forced the chairman Maurice Saatchi to resign from the British-based advertising firm that he had founded but allowed to founder. Investors unhappy with the strategy of France's Cie. de Suez in 1995 helped force its chairman, Gerald Worms, to resign, and, in that action helped concentrate executive attention on *"Le corporate governance."* Domestic shareholders have aggressively challenged other French companies including Alcatel-Alsthom SA, Société Nationale Elf Aquitaine, and even Renault SA, their actions emboldened by American investors, especially pension funds, who have discovered the Paris Bourse.[25]

Some lag can be expected as American investors master the legal systems, reporting regimens, and capital markets outside the United States. But in time, company governance and investor relations seem likely to move toward a dominant design evolved in the American market or, more likely, some amalgam of local tradition and international model. In other words, the new rules of investor capitalism, in some modified form, are likely to extend worldwide. The process will be prolonged, with many fits and starts, judging by the domestic U.S. experience. But it is also likely to be inexorable, judging by the accumulating assets and powers of the institutional holders and their 1990s penchant for international investments.[26]

A House Divided

The institutions of American capitalism have been superb at absorbing rising groups, at transforming the nouveaux riches into an established class. Outliers appear here and there, isolated executives whose world rarely touches other executives. And of course senior managers take keenly divergent positions on matters of public policy and partisan politics. But the business community is inclusive, caring little about executive background and much about current achievement. The newly arrived, whether they are software entrepreneurs, telecommunications executives, or microchip manufacturers, are quickly drawn into the networks that define what community is all about.

The common networks stem from what researchers sometimes call "structural equivalence." While executives of sun-belt and rust-belt industries, of oil and auto companies, of insurance and defense firms evolve diverse views on specific policies, they also confront problems generic to corporate management anywhere. In facing and solving those problems, they develop a bond that is the warp and woof of mutuality.[27]

Company executives also come to know each other more personally through shared service on corporate boards and business associations. They join in fund-raising for the United Way, deserving hospitals, and other favored charities. They serve together on advisory bodies, mayor's commissions, and campaign committees. They see each other in the Business Roundtable, Committee for Economic Development, and California's exclusive retreat, the Bohemian Grove. They frequent the same clubs, sometimes the same schools, occasionally the same islands. Corporate circles in the United States never acquired the singular culture, common vision, and sharp boundaries that delineate top management in some nations. But they have achieved a sense of familiarity, a sense of acquaintanceship. The feeling of kindred spirit has not given them the consciousness of shared class or kind that has long characterized banking in Britain, manufacturing in France, and *keiretsu* in Japan. But it has imparted a sense of shared experience and mutual understanding of the problems they all face.[28]

Institutional investors, however, confront a distinct set of problems. Meeting payrolls gives way to maximizing investments. Money management replaces people management. Innovation means new portfolios, not fresh products. Though nominally part of the same world, investors and executives stand on the opposite sides of a divide. With less commonality, less mutuality, and less reciprocity, the world of American capitalism has been fractured, its house divided by the rise of investor capitalism.

The long-time manager of the Vanguard/Windsor fund until 1995, John B. Neff, exemplified one side of the divide. With assets of more than $10 billion, the Windsor fund invested heavily in a small number of companies: sixty-seven at the start of 1994. Its stakes were large: $699 million in Citicorp, $558 million in Aluminum Company of America (Alcoa), and $510 million in Bankers Trust. John Reed of Citicorp, Paul O'Neill of Alcoa, and Charles Sanford Jr. of Bankers Trust naturally took considerable interest in John Neff, and he in them. After all, he had tied up 6.2 percent of his 380,000 shareholders' hard-earned money in a bank under John Reed's leadership, 5 percent in a manufacturer under Paul O'Neill, and 4.5 percent in the bank led by Charles Sanford. But while Reed, O'Neill, and Sanford frequent the well-traveled inner circles of the national business community, they were unlikely to encounter Neff in any of them. Nor will they find the chief executive of Calpers or others who preside over the mushrooming assets of public pensions and investment companies.

Vanguard's John Neff moved in worlds far removed. A journalist characterized Neff in 1989 as one of America's great financial figures but one virtually invisible to the nation's higher circles. "He is little known outside the investment community because he is modest, gray, and unspectacular. . . . He doesn't get into the newspapers, least of all the gossip columns. Main Line society has never heard of him." Yet he had emerged as one of the nation's moving powers: "He is one of the most eminent financial figures in the country," noted the observer. In the past, dominant financial figures would have found their way into the nation's higher circles, where business, government, and celebrities enjoy access and familiarity. The new financial eminences, by contrast, display little interest in such inner byways. Nor do charter members of the corporate inner circle display much interest in bringing the new princes in from the cold.[29]

Some institutional investors have never been out in the cold. Those presiding over the nation's insurance companies, bank trust departments, and private pensions have always been very much a part of the nation's higher circles. Citicorp and Bankers Trust are counted among the nation's premier institutional investors. In a 1994 ranking of the 300 largest money managers, Bankers Trust stood third ($187 billion under management) and Citicorp twenty-second ($74 billion under management).[30] Alcoa executives preside over a pension fund with more than $3.7 billion in assets. For those toiling in these vineyards, the inner circle is tangible and familiar. John Reed serves as outside director on the boards of United Technologies and Philip Morris; Charles Sanford on the boards of Mobil Oil and General Re Corporation; Paul O'Neill on the board of GM. All participate in a range of professional, nonprofit and charitable activities. O'Neill's résumé is typical: he serves as a trustee, director, or member of the American Enterprise Institute, Business Council, Business Roundtable, California State University Foundation, Conference Board, Gerald R. Ford Foundation, Hudson Institute, Institute for International Economics, Harvard University's John F. Kennedy School of Government, Manpower Demonstration Research Corporation, and RAND Corporation.[31]

Yet for those presiding over the nation's public pension funds and investment companies, the two largest pillars of the fivefold institutional family, the higher reaches of the traditional business community remain remote. Their networks lead instead into a host of professional circuits, such as the New York Society of Security Analysts and the Association for Investment Management and Research. Few find their way into the traditional watering holes of the inner circle. For them, such byways are socially distant and professionally irrelevant. The worlds of the Business Roundtable and Bohemian Grove—and the clubbiness they engender—are to be avoided. Intimacy clouds judgment, familiarity obscures analysis. Succumbing to either is a surefire way to lose clients and shortchange beneficiaries. Social distance, not proximity, is the badge of professionalism.

A House United

With a structural and social divide between money managers and company managers, between holders of money and makers of money, between new princes and old chieftains, investor capitalism has generated a new fault line. Yet as relationships between investors and executives acquire more texture, as investor capitalism fosters new traditions, this fissure may go the way of previous divides.

A common career foundation in the halls of higher education is already facilitating that social closure, as money managers and corporate managers emerge from the same collegiate watering holes. Many have earned their M.B.A.s and undergraduate degrees from the same university programs. In that shared experience is a foundation for shared understandings.

Calpers appointed Sheryl Pressler as its chief investment officer in 1994, succeeding DeWitt Bowman, who had served in that position for five years. She had earned an M.B.A. from Washington University; he had a bachelor's degree from the University of Wisconsin. J. Gary Burkhead, chief executive of Fidelity Management & Research Company, holds a bachelor's degree in economics from Columbia University and an M.B.A. from Harvard University. Their academic profiles are not very different from those at the top of the corporate side, where college and business degrees are the norm.[32]

More generally, the M.B.A. has become a credential of choice for movement into top management at both large firms and large investors. Though many older members of both professions prospered with no formal training beyond college, by the 1990s a graduate degree in business has become de rigueur for those embarking on either professional course. Though later dividing, the careers of those traveling the two worlds of American business often share two years in the same classrooms, two years of common grounding in the fundamentals of marketing, accounting, operations, and, of course, finance and management.

The academic commingling of those whose paths are soon to separate is evident in the alumni of three institutions whose classes graduating with M.B.A.s are among the largest in the nation: the Wharton School of the University of Pennsylvania, graduating 714 in 1994; the Graduate School of Business Administration of Harvard University, granting degrees to 813; and the Graduate School of Business of Stanford University, graduating 356. Among graduates of the Wharton School, one-third of the class of 1994 entered management consulting and one-third investments. Of Stanford's 1994 graduates, one-third entered management consulting and one-fifth investments. Of Harvard's class of 1994, one-quarter entered management consulting and one-quarter chose investments (figures 9.9, 9.10, and 9.11).[33]

Assuming that the early 1990s levels persist through the decade, as the trend lines suggest they should, one-fifth to one-third of those leaving these three institutions with M.B.A.s can be expected to enter money management. Most of the remainder can be expected to enter company management, a majority through management consulting. With two years of shared training in finance and management, each of the two sides will have a lingering appreciation for the concerns and challenges of the other. With two years of shared acculturation and a lifetime of enduring contacts, the two sides will also have a personal appreciation for one another.

Organizations and Markets

The conception of the "market for corporate control" gained currency during the late 1980s as companies, investors, and buyout groups came to view firms as entities that could be bought, sold, dismembered, and reconstituted. A market of owners competed for dominance, and corporations that could not have imagined any change found themselves whipsawed by competing acquirers and hungry investors.

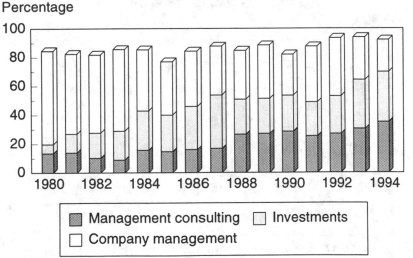

Figure 9.9 Percentage of Wharton M.B.A. Graduates Entering Management Consulting, Investments, and Company Management, 1980-94

Source: Wharton School, University of Pennsylvania.

**Figure 9.10 Percentage of Stanford M.B.A. Graduates
Entering Management Consulting, Investments,
and Company Management, 1985-94**

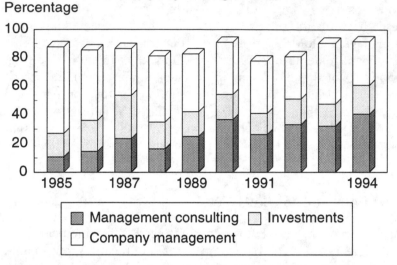

Source: Stanford University Graduate School of Business.

**Figure 9.11 Percentage of Harvard M.B.A.
Graduates Entering Management Consulting
and Investments, 1984-94**

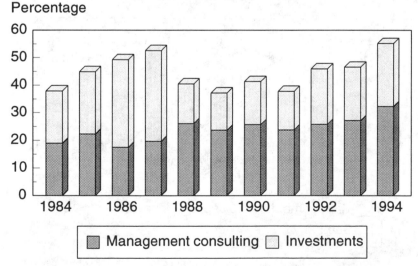

Source: Harvard Business School.

Markets for control have persisted into the 1990s as strategic acquisitions have surged in industries from banking and pharmaceuticals to entertainment and telecommunications, and institutional investors have catalyzed much of the action. Buyout funds raised $2 billion in 1990, $7 billion in 1993, and $10 billion in 1994—with public pensions providing the single largest share—29 percent—of the funds.[34]

Markets of exchange have also persisted, as institutional investors continue to trade large blocks of stock with vigor. Institutional investors in 1993 on average turned over 42 percent of their holdings. Public pension funds were the least active, with a rate of only 13 percent, and banks were close behind, with a rate of 24 percent, followed by private pension funds at 33 percent. But mutual funds turned over 48 percent, insurance companies 54 percent, and investment companies 57 percent. Seen from the standpoint of listed shares, annual turnover on the New York Stock Exchange during the 1990s has hovered around 50 percent (figure 9.12).[35]

Still, the emerging dialogue between investors and companies has added a set of enduring personal relations on top of momentary market relations. Their world is becoming not more hierarchic, but more networklike.[36] Investors come to know a company not simply through the market exchange of its shares and carefully reading its quarterly reports. They also come to know by meeting its management.

Figure 9.12 Annual Percentage of Turnover Among Stocks Traded on the New York Stock Exchange, 1980-94

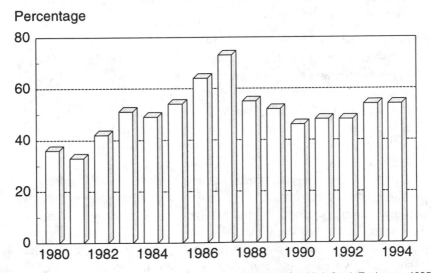

Source: New York Stock Exchange, 1995a.

If the ownership world outside the firm has become less marketlike, the organizational world within the firm has become more so. Executives' pay and promotion depend more upon performance, and, as under commercial contracts, their failure to deliver can lead to quick termination. Strategic business units acquire more autonomy, buying and selling products and services inside the firms as much as on the outside. Managers keep résumés at hand in a world where loyalty to company signifies naïveté rather than career strategy. To the enduring obligations of the traditional organization are added the fleeting relations of the virtual organization.

The imagery is one of market in and organization out. The demarcation between markets and organizations is still plain for all to see, but both sides have acquired qualities of the other.

The New Rules

Like so many areas of corporate change, the initial foundations of investor capitalism were pioneered by a few early movers. Activist investors and responsive companies tested the waters, invented solutions, and gradually built the emergent order. They initially acted haltingly, improvising and inventing, but over time they discarded what did not work well and improved what did. The rules refined over a decade of experimentation have now come to be the dominant design.

As a result, a new order has taken hold. Eight normative principles are sometimes honored more in the breach than in the observance, but they nonetheless describe and prescribe much of the evolving thrust of investor-company relations:

1. *Press for performance.* If company managers continue to underperform—or if investment managers continue to misdirect—press for strategic change, company restructuring, or, as a final resort, the replacement of management.
2. *Revitalize the governance system.* Intended to serve as the bridge between owners and managers, the governance system should be revised to recognize and support the new relations between owners and managers.
3. *Construct networks rather than markets or hierarchies.* Transcending market relations, contact between investment managers and company managers should be personalized, enduring, and a matter of equals.
4. *Disseminate information.* Information on performance and policies should flow freely between companies and institutions, giving each

party better data with which to understand and respond to the other.

5. *Enhance mutual influence.* Mutual influence between the two parties should also be openly exercised, allowing each the opportunity to reshape the visions and strategies of the other.

6. *Institutionalize the relations.* The information flow and the exercise of influence should be routinely and professionally managed, averting hostile struggles over corporate control.

7. *Contest the electoral process.* Companies and investors should actively test their visions and policies through the annual proxy process.

8. *Redefine the organization.* Company strategy and organization should be redesigned to be more responsive to shareholder concerns. Investor strategy and organization should be changed to make them more responsive to company concerns.

The state of investor relations among Japanese companies in 1994 illustrates how far American investor relations had come since 1984. A newly formed Japan Investor Relations Association surveyed some 750 Japanese companies in 1994 and found that only one-third had even formed an office for managing investor relations. Three-quarters of the executives believed the main mission of such an office was to "promote understanding of the corporation," and only one in ten saw it as contributing to shareholder value. The notion of sending information out and bringing little in is a product of a yawning shareholder/executive gap long since narrowed in the United States. "Most top [Japanese] executives tend not to think of IR as necessary," observes the association's director, "because they ignore shareholders."[37]

An Expanding Universe

Under the new rules, the institutions have created a voice in company management inconceivable at the zenith of managerial capitalism. Whether the future is one of further expansion, a new equilibrium, or a reversal of this trend remains to be seen. It depends considerably upon how well money managers and corporate managers work together in constructing their new world.

As restructuring continues its uneven but seemingly unrelenting course, corporate executives may take it in one of two directions. If company management resists change and is only finally forced to confront its competitive decline at the eleventh hour, draconian downsizing measures may be the only remaining option. In that case, the costs to employees and the company can be high as workplace insecurity and short-term pressures override long-term commitment and development of the company's workforce. The long-term costs to investors can also be high, as late actions often avert decline but do little to restore growth.

On the other hand, if company leaders build a culture stressing change and are ready for organizational innovation before the eleventh hour, creative work redesigns are a feasible alternative. If they do so, the benefits to employees, companies, and investors can be significant. For employees who remain, fewer should find themselves in plateaued, mind-numbing, or narrowly defined jobs. More should have the opportunity to experience diversity and personal renewal in their work. Fewer companies should be locked into rigid human-resource practices or product strategies. More should have the capacity to learn from experience and to revitalize their organizational form. As for corporate owners, fewer should be locked into badly performing investments from which they cannot easily exit. More should have the opportunity to find suitable buyers if they exit or to see their investment grow if they stay.

Millions of Americans have stood in the shadows during the construction of investor capitalism. To date they have been interested but largely passive participants. Most households are enrolled in pension plans, and for them, aggressive pension strategies can make the difference between a modest and a comfortable retirement. Most households carry insurance, and for them, effective investment strategies by their insurers can make for affordable coverage and generous benefits. Most households benefit from programs of private hospitals and universities, and for them wise endowment management yields better services. Many Americans households own mutual funds, and for them good money management now makes for more income later.

Most Americans thus stand behind the policies pursued by institutional investors to alter the rules in recent years. Yet so far few have concerned themselves directly with investment models, poison pills, or executive successions. They have left that to the professionals. Households have been largely concerned instead with the results—whether their pensions are solid, insurance rates are reasonable, college tuition affordable, and mutual-fund accounts are building the assets required for all of the above. Investor capitalism is thus ultimately driven by millions of households. The design of its rules, however, has been left to others.

In 1933, Lewis Gilbert, as a shareholder in Consolidated Gas Company (later absorbed into Consolidated Edison), sought to speak at an annual meeting. A company officer abruptly adjourned the meeting before Gilbert could make himself heard. For the next forty years, until his death in 1993, he and his brother attended hundreds of meetings, pressing resolution after resolution to make management more responsive. Widely regarded as eccentric gadflies, for three decades they had been voices in the wilderness.[38]

Such lone voices are no longer lonely. Finding strength in numbers, conscious of their asset power, and experienced in the art of influence, institutional investors have joined the fray on behalf of the millions of individuals they represent. Yet in that mobilization lie the seeds of another revolution. The millions of ultimate owners, like Lewis Gilbert a half-century earlier, may come to question the policies of the new powers that be. Then the questions may expand from whether the professional money managers are achieving maximum private return to whether they are fostering maximum public good. Their demands for downsizing and single-minded focus on shareholder benefits—whatever the costs—may come to constitute a new target of ownership challenge.

In the meantime, institutional investors continue their march toward better rates of return, and in so moving, they are also remaking the economy. Through dogged persistence, their campaign is succeeding. As the U.S. economy finds new momentum during the mid-1990s, in part because of the rebuilt engines inside its largest companies, institutions can enjoy some of the credit. In comparing mid-1990s trends in the U.S., German, and Japanese economies that seemingly moved the United States to the top in productivity and growth, the *New York Times* discerned a source. "Even the focus by investors . . . on last quarter's bottom line may turn out to be less of a handicap than some argue," concluded the writer. "Impatient institutional investors blew the whistle when profits shrank," forcing company turnarounds that are finally paying national dividends.[39]

One school of astrophysics argues that the physical universe is expanding; others suggest it is in stasis or they even forecast eventual collapse. But for the universe of investor capitalism, the present era is surely one of growth. Institutional investors and the millions who stand behind them are the catalysts underlying an expansionary agenda that is changing the face of American business.

Notes

Introduction

1. Associated Press, 1995; Wyatt, 1995.
2. Wyatt, 1995; McGough and Jereski, 1995; Lipin, 1995.
3. Kansas, 1995; Shapiro, 1995; ITT Corporation, 1995; Keller, 1995.
4. Shapiro and Landro, 1995; Fabrikant, 1995.

Chapter 1. The New Rules of Investor Capitalism

1. Unless otherwise noted, quoted material is derived from personal interviews and observation of company managers.
2. These figures do not include dividend payments (Eichenwald, 1992).
3. Quoted in Stevenson, 1991.
4. White and Ingrassia, 1992; White, 1992; Ingrassia and Lublin, 1992.
5. Treece, 1992.
6. Chandler, 1962, pp. 128–130; Rock, 1993.
7. Lohr and Bennet, 1994.
8. Drucker, 1976.
9. Descriptions of institutional investing can be found in Black, 1990, 1992a, 1992b, 1992c; Brancato and Gaughan, 1988, 1990; Lowenstein, 1991; Tobin, 1991; O'Barr and Conley, 1992; and Sametz, 1991; Brancato and Crum, 1993, 1994.
10. Publicly traded companies are ranked for this figure by their market value each year, defined as the share price in March multiplied by the lat-

est available number of outstanding shares. Institutional holdings are the shares held by pension funds, investment companies, insurance companies, banks, and colleges, as compiled by Vickers Stock Research Corporation. The data are reported in annual editions of *Business Week*.

11. The acquisition and buyout data are drawn from Merrill Lynch, 1993; and the data on shareholder resolutions, limited to those on corporate governance, are drawn from Sander, 1991, and more recent information releases by the Investor Responsibility Research Center. Information on the annual likelihood of a Fortune 500 company receiving a tender offer is derived from Davis and Stout, 1992. Illustrative materials on the support of institutional investors for buyout funds can be found in accounts of the nation's largest buyout practitioner, Kohlberg Kravis Roberts; see, for instance, Bartlett, 1991, pp. 119–134, and Anders, 1992, pp. 42–59.

12. The figures for the number of companies with poison pills are based on a study by Davis, 1991, of the Fortune 500 largest manufacturers; the figures for state antitakeover statutes are from the Investor Responsibility Research Center, 1992. An assessment of the contents and legal status of a leading aspect of the state statutes, their reference to company obligations to constituencies other than shareholders, can be found in Orts, 1992. The collective mobilization of business around issues of corporate control is chronicled by Davis and Thompson, 1994.

13. Blume and Zeldes, 1993.

14. Brancato and Crum, 1994; the Standard and Poor's (S&P) 500 is a list of 500 of the largest publicly traded companies as ranked by market capitalization. The companies are traded on the New York Stock Exchange, American Stock Exchange, and through NASDAQ. The index is market weighted so that a company's effect on the index depends on the size of its market value. A committee meets monthly or more often as needed to determine whether to change the index's membership. When companies in the index are acquired or enter bankruptcy, they are removed and prescreened companies are then added. The latter list is compiled according to guidelines that focus on capitalization, representativeness, and trading liquidity. The value of the S&P 500 is continually recalculated on days when the component stocks are traded. At the time of an addition of a company to the index, the new addition's stock tends to increase in value as indexers acquire it for their portfolios (Standard and Poor's Corporation, 1992; pp. 3–23; Siegel, 1994, pp. 51–52; Pettit, 1994).

15. College Retirement Equities Fund, 1990; *Fortune*, 1993, p. 59; Grant, 1992, p. D2.

16. Brancato and Crum, 1994, p. 9; Morningstar, 1994. Annual turnover rate is usually determined by dividing a fund's total stock sales or purchases during the year, whichever is less, by the average value of the stock over the year.

17. Brancato and Crum, 1994, p. 35.

18. For a developed teaching case of responding to a troubled company from the standpoint of an institutional investor, see Light and Sailer, 1992.

19. Investment Company Institute, 1995, p. 85; Silverman et al., 1995, pp. 141, 149.

Chapter 2. When Investors Challenge Company Performance

1. Readers of the *New York Times* would find no mention of Calpers during the late 1980s, but by the 1990s Calpers frequently appeared in its pages. A 1991 article appearing on the front page of the *New York Times* Business Section illustrates the tenor of the Calpers coverage. "Battling for Shareholder Rights: Giant Pension Fund Stirs Board Rooms," read the headline, accompanied by a photograph of Calpers' top officer with the caption, "Dale M. Hanson, the chief executive of the California Public Employees Retirement System, is a leader in the growing effort to make corporations more accountable to shareholders" (Stevenson, 1991). "Captain California . . . self-appointed scourge of corporate America," offered *Financial World* (Barrett, 1991).
2. Holusha, 1993a; Rigdon and Naik, 1993.
3. Cowan, 1993; Rigdon, 1993a. The other investor expressing cautious support was the Regents of the University of California, owner of 4.7 million Kodak shares.
4. Calpers' chief executive was known to his staff as "Madonna" since "he creates a stir wherever he goes" (Anders, 1993, p. A9).
5. As described in materials from the Willard Hotel, 1993.
6. Takeover tactics are described in Weston, Chung, and Hoag, 1990.
7. Stewart, 1991; Yago, 1991.
8. The following sections draw on interviews that three colleagues and I conducted with forty-eight investors (Useem, Bowman, Irvine, and Myatt, 1993). The distribution of activism among the forty-eight are as follows, where the activism levels are based on distinctions described in the text:

	Public pensions	Investment companies	Private pensions
Active	6	1	1
Moderate	5	8	3
Inactive	7	9	8

9. Investor Responsibility Research Center, *Voting by Institutional Investors on Corporate Governance Issues*, various years.
10. Concepts for viewing investor activism as a political movement are developed in Zald and Berger, 1978, and Davis and Thompson, 1994; and calls to arms can be found in Pound, 1992, 1993, and Pozen, 1994.
11. *Corporate Governance Bulletin*, March/April, 1993, pp. 25–35, Washington, D.C.: Investor Responsibility Research Center. The distinctive views of public and private pension funds regarding governance issues and the value of activism are documented in O'Barr and Conley, 1992, pp. 184–201.

12. Romano, 1993; Zorn, 1994; Roe, 1993a.
13. Zorn, 1994.
14. Much of the research is summarized in Gordon Group, 1993; see also Strickland, Wiles, and Zenner, 1996.
15. Davey, 1988. The U.S. Department of Labor warned in 1988 that the Employee Retirement Income Security Act (ERISA) of 1974 should be interpreted as "prohibiting a fiduciary from subordinating the interests of participants and beneficiaries in their retirement income to unrelated objectives."
16. Davey, 1988, 1991.
17. Landro and Jensen, 1995; Jensen, 1995.
18. Morningstar, 1994.
19. This section draws on Useem, Bowman, Irvine, and Myatt, 1993.
20. United Shareholders Association, 1990, 1991, 1992, 1993.
21. Grundfest, 1993, pp. 915–917; O'Hara, 1995; Duff, Dorfman, and Lublin, 1995; Lublin, 1995.
22. Schwartz, 1992; Passell, 1992.
23. Investor Responsibility Research Center, *Corporate Governance and Shareholder Rights*, 1987 and 1991 editions.
24. TIAA-CREF, 1993.
25. United Shareholders Association, *Shareholder 1,000*, various editions.

Chapter 3. Cultural Resistance to Shareholder Insistence

1. Associated Press, 1992; Dickson, 1992.
2. Nelson's *1993 Survey of Investment Research*, 1993.
3. Moore, 1993.
4. Hill, 1992; Kotter, 1985; Pfeffer, 1991.
5. The power and role of managerial ideologies are developed in Bendix, 1963, Fligstein, 1990, and Jackall, 1988.
6. Andrew C. Sigler, the CEO of Champion International, was responding to the takeover and buyout pressures on companies in 1986.
7. Ingrassia, 1994; Lavin and Yoshihashi, 1994; Levin, 1992; Stertz and Yoshihashi, 1992a, 1992b.
8. Ingrassia, 1994; Lavin and Yoshihashi, 1994; Levin, 1992; Stertz and Yoshihashi, 1992a, 1992b.
9. Ingrassia, 1994; Lavin and Yoshihashi, 1994; Levin, 1992; Stertz and Yoshihashi, 1992a, 1992b.
10. Templin and Lipin, 1995; Bennet, 1995a; Abelson, 1995; Bennet, 1995b; Lipin, Templin, and Yoshihashi, 1995.
11. Lipin, Templin, and Yoshihashi, 1995.
12. Stern and Hays, 1995; Stern and Lipin, 1995; Meredith, 1996.
13. *Business Week*, 1987; National Investor Relations Institute, 1989, 1994.
14. Shiller, 1991; Employee Benefit Research Institute, 1993, p. 20.
15. Gerlach, 1992.
16. *New York Times*, April 21, 1994, pp. D5–6; *New York Times*, April 19, 1995, p. D2; *Wall Street Journal*, April 20, 1995, p. A3.

17. *New York Times*, April 21, 1994, pp. D5–6; *Wall Street Journal*, April 20, 1995, p. B2; *New York Times*, April 25, 1995, p. D8.
18. Rifkin, 1994; Bulkeley, 1994; McWilliams, 1994.
19. Puffer and Weintrop, 1991.
20. Hewitt Associates, 1994.
21. Hewitt Associates, 1994; Rock and Berger, 1991.
22. Jarrell, Brickley, and Netter, 1988; Jarrell, Lehn, and Marr, 1985; Graves, 1988; Baysinger, Kosnik, and Turk, 1991; Hansen and Hill, 1991; Jones, Lehn and Mulherin, 1991; also see Shiller, 1991, and Easterbrook and Fischel, 1991, pp. 201–202.
23. Dechow and Sloan, 1991.
24. Porter, 1992; Gerlach, 1992; Jacobs, 1991; National Academy of Engineering, 1992; Dertouzos, Lester and Solow, 1989, pp. 53–66.
25. Duttweiler, 1991.
26. Chakravarthy and Lorange, 1991, p. 15; Gardner, 1990, p. xi; Burns, 1978; Kotter, 1988, p. 121.
27. The former president and chief executive officer offered his observations during a presentation at the University of Pennsylvania's Wharton School, September 10, 1993.
28. The investor's privately expressed observations were offered during a presentation at the University of Pennsylvania's Wharton School, September 10, 1993.
29. The importance of diverse professional experience for fast-tracking managers is developed by Kanter, 1977, pp. 133–134, and for joint-venture managers is developed by Nadler, Gerstein, Shaw, 1992, pp. 81–109. See also Yoshino and Rangan, 1995.
30. Gould, 1993.
31. The primary sources for the information are Standard and Poor's *Register of Directors, Executives, and Corporations,* several *Who's Who* volumes, and direct contact with investor offices. The percentages in table 3.1 are based on only those for whom data were available. For the first row, the base numbers are 21, 11, 22 and 8; for the second row, the numbers are 19, 6, 13 and 7; for the third row, the base numbers are 22, 18, 40, and 10. All individuals were assumed to appear in the Standard and Poor's *Register* if they served as directors for any major companies.
32. Wohlstetter, 1993; *Wall Street Journal*, April 21, 1993, p. R10.
33. Committee of Publicly Owned Companies, 1993; Chief Executives' Council, 1993.
34. Fligstein, 1990.
35. Shapiro, 1995; Moore, 1993.
36. National Investor Relations Institute, 1989; Mahoney, 1992a.
37. Hanson, 1993.
38. Anders, 1993; Bartlett, 1991; Hagstrom, 1994.
39. Gilson and Kraakman, 1993; Gordon Group, 1993.
40. Gilson and Kraakman, 1993; Gordon Group, 1993; Jensen, 1989.
41. Zorn, 1994; Dulebohn, 1994; Hsin, 1995.
42. National Association of Investors Corporation, 1994.

43. National Association of Investors Corporation, 1994.
44. Reich, 1993.
45. Nancy Kassenbaum sponsored the bill.
46. Andrews, 1994.
47. Noer, 1993, pp. 66, 80.
48. Kadanoff, 1992.
49. *In the Line of Fire,* Columbia Tristar, 1993.

Chapter 4. Vanquishing Opponents

1. Easterbrook and Fischel, 1991.
2. An illustrative account can be found in the publicized dismissal of a senior manager of General Electric Company. When the manager was appointed a divisional vice president of the company in 1990, one of 125 officers for a firm with one-third of a million employees, the chief executive glowingly wrote that "this is a hard-earned, well-deserved promotion." Continuing conflict over divisional priorities and decision-making style, however, led to the manager's abrupt dismissal two years later (Carley and Naj, 1993).
3. Post et al., 1983; Handler and Mulkern, 1982; Vogel, 1989; Himmelstein, 1990; Clawson et al., 1992.
4. Lev, 1991, p. 5; Rosenbaum, 1994, p. 1; quoted in Mahoney, 1990, p. 3; Mahoney, 1994b.
5. Mahoney, 1991, 1993a; Marcus and Wallace, 1991; Rosenbaum, 1994.
6. Brickley et al., 1988.
7. Conte and Svejnar, 1990.
8. Mahoney, 1993b; McDonald's Corporation, 1992, p. 1.
9. National Association of Investors Corporation, various documents; *Better Investing,* November, 1993; Gottschalk, 1994. Another organization, the American Association of Individual Investors, provides information and educational resources to its some 150,000 members for making stock and mutual-fund investments (American Association of Individual Investors, 1993).
10. The number of state and local public-pension funds with South African prohibitions is from the author's reanalysis of a 1993 survey of public systems by the Government Finance Officers Association (Zorn, 1994).
11. Mahoney, 1992b; further background on institutional "targeting" can be found in Mahoney, 1994a, and other sources cited therein.
12. *Investor Relations Newsletter*, February, 1994, pp. 1–3; *Investor Relations Update*, September, 1993, pp. 13–14; Capital Analytics, 1993; *Directorship*, June, 1995, p. 14.
13. *Investor Relations Newsletter,* February, 1994, pp. 1–3; *Investor Relations Update,* September, 1993, pp. 13–14; Capital Analytics, 1993.
14. From a national survey of publicly traded companies in 1989 and 1994 conducted by the National Investor Relations Institute (NIRI), the pro-

fessional association of those who manage investor relations for publicly traded companies.

15. The analysis is reported in Useem and Gager, 1996.
16. Rao and Sivakumar, 1995.
17. Nussbaum and Dobrzynski, 1987.
18. Rigdon and Naik, 1993, p. 3; Rigdon, 1993a, 1993b, p. 1; Rigdon and Smith, 1993.
19. Randall, 1993, p. 1; Holusha, 1993b, p. 49; Rigdon and Lublin, 1993.
20. Friedman and Singh, 1989; Puffer and Weintrop, 1991. Related studies of executive dismissal can be found in Reingenaum, 1985, Lubatkin et al., 1989, Worrell, Davidson and Glascock, 1993, and Ocasio, 1994.
21. Teitelman, 1992; Lipin, 1993; Fromson, 1993; Myatt, 1995.
22. Holusha, 1993b; Norton, 1993.
23. Boeker, 1992; Fredrickson, Hambrick, and Baumrin, 1988; Myatt, 1995; Furtado and Karan, 1990; Denis and Serrano, 1995. For analogous effects on CEO compensation, see the analysis by Westphal and Zajac, 1995. See also Denis, Denis, and Sarin, 1995.
24. Boeker, 1992.
25. Ocasio, 1994.
26. Boeker, 1992, for instance, finds that weakly performing companies with dispersed ownership are significantly more likely to fire the chief executive than weakly performing companies with concentrated ownership. Bethel and Liebeskind, 1993, find that ownership concentration increases the likelihood of a range of changes in company organization.
27. Korn/Ferry Organizational Consulting, 1993a, 1993b.
28. Cannella and Hambrick, 1993; Walsh and Ellwood, 1991; also see Walsh and Kosnik, 1993.
29. Berg, 1990; Pereira and Trachtenberg, 1990.
30. Myatt, 1995; see also Cannella and Lubatkin, 1993, and Datta and Guthrie, 1994.
31. Denis and Denis, 1995.
32. Bacon, 1990, 1993.
33. Smith and Roberts, 1993; Roberts and Smith, 1993a, 1993b; Burrough and Helyar, 1990; Bacon, 1993; Fromson, 1993; Lipin and Torres, 1993.
34. Useem and Subramanian, 1994; Directors Publications, 1992.
35. Bacon, 1990; Moore, 1988; Perot, 1988; Levin, 1989.
36. Bacon, 1990; Sailer, 1992.
37. McGurn, 1993; McGurn and Zeugner, 1992; Zeugner, 1992; Grundfest, 1993, p. 937.
38. Wade, O'Reilly, and Chandratat, 1990; Davis, 1993.

Chapter 5. Restructuring the Corporation

1. Day, 1994; Cole, Bacdayan, and White, 1993; Byrne, 1993.
2. A survey of seventy-five industry analysts during the early 1990s sug-

gested that having a feel for company cultures is indeed seen as an invaluable analytic aid by many. The analysts were asked to evaluate whether the culture of twelve companies that were performing well, and which they knew well, contributed to their success, and whether the culture of ten poorly performing companies contributed to the opposite in their cases. Nine out of ten analysts stated that the companies' cultures had indeed affected the firms' performance, both for better and for worse (Lohr, 1994; Nadler et al., 1992; Fleeson, 1994).

3. Kotter and Heskett, 1992, pp. 35–36.
4. Holusha, 1993d; Hays and Naik, 1993; Howard, 1992.
5. Freudenheim, 1993; Keller, 1994; Ramirez, 1994.
6. Worrell, Davidson, and Sharma, 1991.
7. Holusha, 1993b.
8. Bowman and Kogut, 1995.
9. Hammer and Champy, 1993; Womack, Jones and Roos, 1990.
10. Korn/Ferry Organizational Consulting, 1993a, 1993b.
11. Directors Publications, 1992.
12. Markides, 1992, 1995; Bethel and Liebeskind, 1993; Hoskisson and Hitt, 1994.
13. *Institutional Investor*, 1993a; 1994b.
14. Dorfman, 1993, 1995.
15. Hwang, 1995; Collins, 1995.
16. Shapiro, 1994.
17. Levin, 1993.
18. College Retirement Equities Fund, 1993.
19. United Shareholders Association, various years; and Bacon, 1993.
20. Ryngaert, 1988; Malatesta and Walkling, 1988; Bhagat and Brickley, 1984; Rosenstein and Wyatt, 1990.
21. Johnson and Linden, 1992; Useem, 1993b; Wyatt Company, 1993; American Management Association, 1995, and earlier years.
22. Wyatt Company, 1993; Davis and Stout, 1992; Davis et al., 1994; Lawler et al., 1992.
23. *Fortune* magazine, various annual issues reporting the Fortune 500 and Fortune Service 500.
24. Macy and Izumi, 1993; Hall, Rosenthal, and Wade, 1993; Berger and Sikora, 1994; Nadler et al., 1992; MacDuffie and Krafcik, 1992; Conte and Svejnar, 1990; Scott Morton, 1991.
25. Batt, 1996.
26. Kilborn, 1993; see also Newman, 1989.
27. Reich, 1993; Ehrlichman, 1993; Horwitz, 1993; Lublin, 1993; Berger, 1993; Uchitelle, 1993a, 1993b; Uchitelle and Kleinfeld, 1996; Sloan, 1996.
28. Randall, 1993.

Chapter 6. Managing the Shareholder

1. Kochan, Katz, and McKersie, 1986.
2. The building process for strategic alliances is described in Yoshino and Rangan, 1995, and Lewis, 1990.

3. The figures on the automaker holdings are reported in Roe, 1993.
4. The percentage figures for the top ten companies are based on data presented in Brancato, 1991; the figures for fifty-eight companies among the top one hundred were drawn from a database prepared for the present analysis.
5. Janger, 1989. The decentralization of authority within organizations and a corresponding expansion in spans of control are developed in Lawler, 1993.
6. National Investor Relations Institute, 1989, 1994; Mahoney, 1992a.
7. Katzenbach and Smith, 1993.
8. Brancato and Crum, 1994, p. 9; Brancato and Crum, 1993, p. 7.
9. Brancato and Crum, 1994, p. 9; Brancato and Crum, 1993, p. 7.
10. *Institutional Investor*, 1993b.
11. Greenwich Associates, various years; Eccles and Mavrinac, 1995.
12. The many communication channels are described in Mahoney, 1991, 1993a, and Marcus and Wallace, 1991.
13. Booth, 1995; Digital Media, 1995.
14. Waroff, 1994; Smith, 1995.
15. Marcus and Goodman, 1991, offer an analysis of stock price reactions to management reactions to accidents and disasters involving their companies.
16. Useem et al., 1993.
17. Brancato and Crum, 1994, pp. 34–38.
18. O'Brien and Lipin, 1995; Gilpin, 1995; Hansell, 1995.
19. Byrd, Johnson, and Johnson, 1993.
20. Granovetter, 1973.
21. Gerlach, 1992.
22. Lowenstein, 1996; Dobrzynski, 1993.
23. See, for instance, Gerlach, 1992, p. 123, and Gerlach and Lincoln, 1992; Harrison, 1994, pp. 150–162; Gilson and Roe, 1993.

Chapter 7. Engaging the Company Director

1. Easterbrook and Fischel, 1991; quoted in Bainbridge, 1993.
2. Smith and Roberts, 1993; Roberts and Smith, 1993b; Fabrikant, 1993; Supreme Court of Delaware, 1994; Pound, 1993b; Jarrell, 1993; *Paramount Communications Inc. v. QVC Network Inc.*
3. Bacon, 1993, p. 26.
4. *Investor Relations Update,* 1993.
5. Peters and Waterman, 1982.
6. Dale Hanson, quoted in *Chief Executive,* 1994, p. 44.
7. Korn/Ferry International, 1994.
8. Bacon, 1990; Korn/Ferry International, 1994; also see Heidrick & Struggles, 1990, 1993a, 1993b.
9. TIAA-CREF, 1993, p, 3; Zeugner, 1993.
10. TIAA-CREF, 1993, p. 2; Bacon, 1990, pp. 9–10; Bacon, 1993, p. 10; Himelstein, 1994, p. 114.

11. Singh and Harianto, 1989; Kosnik, 1987; Judge and Zeithaml, 1992; Cochran et al., 1985; Mallette and Fowler, 1992; Kesner and Johnson, 1990; Weisbach, 1988; Ocasio, 1994; Ocasio and Kim, 1994.
12. Korn/Ferry International, 1993.
13. Reich and Donahue, 1985, p. 278; Jeffreys, 1986; Moritz and Seaman, 1981.
14. Rock, 1991, pp. 490–506; Light, 1992.
15. Korn/Ferry International, 1992, 1994.
16. Lear and Yavitz, 1994, p. 39.
17. Chandler, 1962; Nadler and Tushman, 1988.
18. Korn/Ferry International, 1993; United Shareholders Association, 1993; Bacon, 1993.
19. Investor Responsibility Research Center, 1993; Simison, 1994; General Motors, 1994.
20. General Motors, 1994.
21. Discussions of these and other proposals for changes in the organization of the corporate board can be found in *Chief Executive,* 1994, *Directors and Boards,* 1994, National Association of Corporate Directors, 1994, and New Foundations Working Group, 1994; *Bacon,* 1990, 1993; Directors Publications, 1992.
22. Worell, 1993.
23. Collins, 1994.
24. Stobaugh, 1993.
25. Korn/Ferry International, 1993, p. 5.
26. Cole, 1994.

Chapter 8. Transforming Company Leadership

1. Tobias, 1976.
2. Morita, 1988; Janger, 1989; *Fortune* magazine, various annual issues reporting the Fortune 500 and Fortune Service 500.
3. Sonnenfeld, 1988.
4. Jackall, 1988; Boeker, 1992.
5. Fligstein, 1990; Ocasio and Kim, 1994.
6. Berenbeim, 1995.
7. Kerr, 1975.
8. United Shareholders Association, *Executive Compensation 1,000,* 1993.
9. United Shareholders Association, *Executive Compensation 1,000,* 1993; Jensen and Murphy, 1990.
10. Buenaventura and Peck, 1993.
11. Bounds, 1993.
12. United Shareholders Association, *Executive Compensation 1,000,* 1993.
13. Howard, 1992.
14. *Investor Relations Update,* January, 1993, p. 10.

Chapter 9. The Expanding Universe

1. Alinsky, 1972; Piven and Cloward, 1977.
2. New York Stock Exchange, 1994, p. 89.
3. Lappen, 1995; Smith, 1994.
4. Brancato and Crum, 1993, 1994; Danner, 1994; Schultz, 1995.
5. Brancato and Crum, 1993, p. 15.
6. Morningstar, 1994; Train, 1989.
7. Investment Company Institute, 1993.
8. Brancato and Crum, 1993, pp. 20–21; Mitchell and Hsin, 1994; Silverman et al., 1995, p. 141.
9. The United States reports data for the fifty largest underfunded single-employer plans (the top fifty are responsible for 72 percent of all underfunding in 1992), and it details only those fractions of the total underfunded liabilities that are insured by the federal government (83 percent of all corporate underfunding in 1992).
10. Salisbury and Jones (1994) report data compiled by the Wyatt Company, which conducts annual surveys of private pension plans with at least 1,000 active participants. The number of plans surveyed varied from 575 in 1981 (the lowest number) to 919 in 1984 (the highest number); in 1992, 762 plans were surveyed.
11. Mitchell and Hsin, 1994, p. 3.
12. Zorn, 1994; Dulebohn, 1994.
13. Mitchell and Smith, 1994; U.S. Pension Benefit Guaranty Corporation, press releases from various years.
14. Scism, 1994b, p. 1.
15. Bennet, 1994; Simison and Karr, 1994.
16. Hylton, 1994; Scism, 1994b.
17. French and Poterba, 1991.
18. Morningstar, 1994; Dreyfus advertisement, *Wall Street Journal*, August 2, 1994, p. C3; Dreyfus International Equity Fund, "Questions and Answers," 1994.
19. Securities Industry Association, 1995; World Bank, 1993; United Nations, 1993.
20. Institute of International Finance, 1994; Gilpin, 1994; Scism, 1994a; Torres and Vogel, 1994, p. 1.
21. New York Stock Exchange, 1995a, 1995b.
22. Kogut, 1993; Demb and Neubauer, 1992; Heidrick & Struggles, 1993b; Charkham, 1994.
23. Berton, 1995.
24. McGurn, 1994; Clemente and Mariano, 1993, 1994; Steiner, 1994.
25. Cossette, 1994; 1995; Berenbeim, 1994; Carpenter, 1995; Kamm, 1995; Studer, 1995.
26. Torres and Vogel, 1994; Investor Responsibility Research Center, 1994.
27. Burt, 1980, 1983; Baltzell, 1962, 1964; Christopher, 1989; Useem, 1984; Mizruchi and Schwartz, 1987; Mintz and Schwartz, 1985.

28. Useem, 1984.
29. Train, 1989, p. 138; also see Eaton, 1994.
30. *Institutional Investor*, 1994a.
31. Company records.
32. Information supplied by the respective organizations; Useem and Karabel, 1986.
33. Company management at Wharton is defined to include marketing, finance, general management, and commercial lending; investments are defined as comprising investment management and research, investment sales and trading, venture capital, corporate finance and public finance. Company management for Stanford graduates includes line management, finance, marketing, production and operations, and sales; investments are defined in the mid-1980s as investment banking, and in the early 1990s as investment management, and research and financial analysts. Investment management at Harvard is defined as investment management, banking, and brokerage. The placement data are provided by the three programs' placement office, and time trends should be interpreted cautiously since the definitions of some placement categories have evolved over time, and because the information is self-reported by those who voluntarily responded. The numbers of respondents also varies. In 1993, 554 out of Harvard's graduating class of 797 reported their job placement, and 675 of Wharton's 830 graduates so reported. In 1994, 263 of Stanford's graduating class of 356 reported their placements. The data for Wharton and Stanford are for positions classified by function rather than industry, while the data for Harvard are for positions grouped by industry rather than function.
34. *Wall Street Journal*, 1994; Steinmetz, 1994b.
35. Brancato and Crum, 1994, pp. 8–21.
36. Williamson, 1975.
37. *Investor Relations Newsletter*, April, 1994; Dattel, 1994.
38. Gilbert, 1956; Sloane, 1993.
39. Nasar, 1994.

A Note on Sources

THE ASSEMBLED ACCOUNTS and interpretations are built from an integrated use of several sources. Some of the information was already available in the public domain, but much of it could only be acquired through direct contact with company executives and institutional investors.

What proved critical here was brokerage by the Institutional Investor Project of Columbia University's Center for Law and Economic Studies. Large corporations, institutional investors, several trade unions, and the New York Stock Exchange sponsor the Institutional Investor Project, and it has assembled a prominent advisory board to guide its work. To enter a set of targeted firms, three advisory-board members approached an executive at each of the firms with whom he was personally acquainted. "I am writing about an issue that I believe is of significance to [your company] and many other large firms," the letters opened: "the evolving relationship between publicly traded companies and their major institutional investors." Elaborating on the importance of the issue and noting the dearth of information about it, the letter requested the company's participation. More specifically, on my behalf it asked for an interview with the executive and time with the firm's other senior managers.

This personalized request brought the desired response in virtually all cases. The cooperating executive identified the other executives with whom I needed to meet. In the interviews, I found them open to a wide-ranging exploration of the issues and willing to arrange for me to see still other managers and company documents. I completed the interviews in 1991–95 with an array of chief executive officers, chief operating officers, chief financial officers, general counsels, pension fund managers, directors of investor relations, and heads of divisions and operating units.

I selected the firms to represent a broad array of product sectors, ranging from automobiles and apparel to broadcasting, computers, insurance, and telecommunications. Their market capitalization ranged from $1 billion to $20 billion, annual revenues from $2 billion to nearly $100 billion, and employment from 5,000 to almost 400,000. The fraction of the company's shares held by institutions varied from 40 percent to 85 percent. For reasons of anonymity, specific values for these company measures cannot be reported for individual companies, but their ranges for 1990 can be:

Company	Market capitalization ($ billions)	Annual revenue* ($ billions)	Number of employees (1,000s)	% shares held by institutions
1	15-20	15-20	40-50	75-80
2	5-10	5-10	20-30	70-75
3	5-10	2-5	5-10	65-70
4	30-35	10-15	20-30	50-55
5	1-5	10-15	150-175	80-85
6	5-10	10-15	100-125	70-75
7	10-15	90-100	375-400	55-60
8	5-10	5-10	100-125	60-65
9	5-10	2-5	30-40	60-65
10	5-10	10-15	60-70	65-70
11	5-10	20-25	100-125	60-65
12	1-5	2-5	5-10	75-80
13	1-5	5-10	20-30	65-70
14	5-10	5-10	40-50	65-70
15	1-10	80-90	10-20	65-70
16	15-20	40-45	30-40	60-65
17	5-10	2-5	10-20	55-60
18	5-10	15-20	50-60	55-60
19	20-25	40-50	125-150	40-45
20	1-5	20-30	10-20	60-65

*Assets rather than revenues for the two commercial banks.

During this project I was also able to enter several additional corporations for interviews with senior managers. When information is reported from these companies, they are simply referenced by their main product area (for example, a consumer-products company, a utility firm).

In addition, I interviewed senior managers of another set of seven corporations in 1989–91. Although these companies were participating in a separate project with the author on corporate restructuring, many of the interviews focused on issues related to investor capitalism. Five of the seven companies are among the top one hundred firms in market value (the sixth is among the top 200, and the seventh is in the top 300). The general product areas of the seven companies are chemicals, electrical products, financial services, machinery, pharmaceuticals, retail services, and transportation (Useem, 1993).

I also codirected a project that included interviews in 1992 with fifty-eight senior officers for large institutional investors. These fund managers were drawn from among the forty largest public and private pension funds, the forty largest money managers (bank trusts, investment firms, and insurance companies), and the twenty largest foundations (Useem, Bowman, Irvine, and Myatt, 1993).

A host of other sources provided information upon which the book's accounts and interpretations are built. They included related studies conducted by both university researchers and industry analysts; company statistical data provided through SEC filings; a company survey sponsored by the National Investor Relations Institute; personal participation in meetings and conferences attended by corporate managers and institutional investors; observation of meetings between company managers and investor analysts; and use of several archival sources with information on company ownership, proxy filings, and governing policies.

References

Abelson, Alan. 1995. "Joy Ride?" *Barron's*, April 17, 3.

Alinsky, Saul. 1972. *Rules for Radicals*. New York: Vintage.

Alter, Catherine, and Jerald Hage. 1993. *Organizations Working Together*. Newbury Park, Calif.: Sage.

American Association of Individual Investors. 1993. "About AAII." Chicago: American Association of Individual Investors.

American Management Association. 1995. *1995 AMA Survey on Downsizing and Assistance to Displaced Workers*. New York: American Management Association.

Anders, George. 1992. *Merchants of Debt: KKR and the Mortgaging of American Business*. New York: Basic Books.

———. 1993. "While Head of Calpers Lectures Other Firms, His Own Board Frets." *Wall Street Journal*, January 29, A1, A9.

Andrews, Edmund L. 1994. "A.T.&T. Will Cut 15,000 Jobs to Reduce Costs." *New York Times*, February 11, D1, D14.

Appelbaum, Eileen, and Rose Batt. 1994. *The New American Workplace: Transforming Work Systems in the United States*. Ithaca, N.Y.: ILR Press.

Associated Press. 1992. "Shifts Hinted by ITT Chief." *New York Times*, March 6, D3.

———. 1995. "Investor Takes Big Stake in Chase Bank." *New York Times*, April 6, D1, D6.

Bacon, Jeremy. 1990. *Membership and Organization of Corporate Boards*. New York: Conference Board.

————. 1993. *Corporate Boards and Corporate Governance*. New York: Conference Board.

Bainbridge, Stephen M. 1993. "In Defense of the Shareholder Wealth Maximization Norm," *Washington and Lee Law Review* 50 (Fall): 1423–1447.

Baltzell, E. Digby. 1962. *An American Business Aristocracy*. New York: Collier Books.

————. 1964. *The Protestant Establishment: Aristocracy and Caste in America*. New York: Random House.

Barnard, Chester Irving. 1938. *The Functions of the Executive*. Cambridge, Mass.: Harvard University Press.

Barrett, Amy. 1991. "Captain California." *Financial World* (October 1): 20–22.

Bartlett, Sarah. 1991. *The Money Machine: How KKR Manufactured Power & Profits*. New York: Warner Books.

Batt, Rosemary. 1996. From Bureaucracy to Enterprise? The Changing Jobs and Careers of Managers in Telecommunications Services. In *Broken Ladders: Managerial Careers in the New Economy*, edited by Paul Osterman. New York: Oxford University Press (forthcoming).

Baysinger, Barry, Rita D. Kosnik, and Thomas A. Turk. 1991. "Effects of Board and Ownership Structure on Corporate R&D Strategy." *Academy of Management Journal* 34: 205–214.

Bendix, Reinhard. 1963. *Work and Authority in Industry: Ideologies of Management in the Course of Industrialization*. New York: Harper and Row.

Bennet, James. 1994. "$10 Billion for G.M. Pensions." *New York Times*, May 12, D1, D7.

————. 1995a. "Investor Plans Offer for Chrysler in a $22.8 Billion Takeover Deal." *New York Times*, April 13, A1.

————, 1995b. "Chrysler Shares Tumble 5.5% as Kerkorian's Chances Fade." *New York Times*, April 27, D1.

Berenbeim, Ronald E. 1994. *Company Relations with Institutional Investors*. New York: Conference Board.

————. 1995. *Corporate Boards: CEO Selection, Evaluation and Succession*. New York: Conference Board.

Berg, Eric N. 1990. "Ames Stores Files for Bankruptcy." *New York Times*, April 27, C1, C17.

Berger, Joseph. 1993. "The Pain of Layoffs for Ex-Senior I.B.M. Workers." *New York Times*, December 22, B1, B5.

Berger, Lance A., and Martin J. Sikora, eds. 1994. *The Change Management Handbook*. New York: Irwin Professional Publishing.

Berton, Lee. 1995. "All Accountants Soon May Speak the Same Language." *Wall Street Journal*, August 29, A15.

Bethel, Jennifer E., and Julia Liebeskind. 1993. "The Effects of Ownership Structure on Corporate Restructuring." *Strategic Management Journal* 14: 15–31.

Bhagat, Sanjai, and James A. Brickley. 1984. "Cumulative Voting: The Value of Minority Shareholder Voting Rights." *Journal of Law and Economics* 27: 339–365.

Black, Bernard S. 1990. "The Legal and Historical Contingency of Shareholder Passivity." *Michigan Law Review* 89: 520–608.

———. 1992a. "Agents Watching Agents: The Promise of Institutional Investor Voice." *UCLA Law Review* 39: 812–893.

———. 1992b. "The Value of Institutional Investor Monitoring: The Empirical Evidence." *UCLA Law Review* 39: 896–939.

———. 1992c. "Institutional Investors and Corporate Governance: The Case for Institutional Voice." *Journal of Applied Corporate Finance* (Fall): 19–32.

Blair, Margaret M. 1995. *Ownership and Control: Rethinking Corporate Governance for the Twenty-First Century.* Washington, D.C.: Brookings Institution.

Blume, Marshall E., and Stephen P. Zeldes. 1993. "The Structure of Stockownership in the U.S." Philadelphia, Pa.: Finance Department, the Wharton School, University of Pennsylvania.

Boeker, Warren. 1992. "Power and Managerial Dismissal: Scapegoating at the Top." *Administrative Science Quarterly* 37: 400–421.

Booth, Richard A. 1995. "Selective Disclosure in Cyberspace." *Off-Line* (May–June): 1–3.

Bounds, Wendy. 1993. "Kodak Gives Fisher Options to Purchase 750,000 of Its Shares." *Wall Street Journal,* December 20, B2.

Bowman, Edward H., and Bruce Kogut, eds. 1995. *Redesigning the Firm.* New York: Oxford University Press.

Brancato, Carolyn. 1991. *Institutional Investor Concentration of Economic Power: A Study of Institutional Holdings and Voting Authority in U.S. Publicly Held Corporations.* New York: Columbia University Institutional Investor Project.

Brancato, Carolyn Kay, and Kevin J. Crum. 1993. "Financial Assets and Equity Holdings," *The Brancato Report on Institutional Investment,* Vol. 1 (December). Washington: Victoria Group and Riverside Economic Research.

———. 1994. "Equity Turnover & Investment Strategies," *The Brancato Report on Institutional Investment,* Vol. 1 (April). Washington: Victoria Group and Riverside Economic Research.

Brancato, Carolyn Kay, and Patrick A. Gaughan. 1988. *The Growth of Institutional Investors in U.S. Capital Markets.* New York: Columbia University Institutional Investor Project.

———. 1990. *The Growth of Institutional Investors, Updated Data: 1981–1988.* New York: Columbia University Institutional Investor Project.

Brickley, James A., Ronald C. Lease, and Clifford W. Smith, Jr. 1988. "Ownership Structure and Voting on Antitakeover Amendments." *Journal of Financial Economics* 20: 267–291.

Brockner, Joel, Steven Grover, Thomas F. Reed, and Rocki Lee DeWitt. 1992. "Layoffs, Job Insecurity, and Survivors' Work Effort: Evidence of an Inverted-U Relationship." *Academy of Management Journal* 35: 413–425.

Brockner, Joel, Steven Grover, Michael N. O'Malley, Thomas F. Reed, and Mary Ann Glynn. 1993. "Threat of Future Layoffs: Self-Esteem, and Survivors' Reactions: Evidence from the Laboratory and the Field." *Strategic Management Journal* 14: 153–166.

Buenaventura, Maria Ruth M., and Charles Peck. 1993. *Stock Options: Motivating Through Ownership.* New York: Conference Board.

Bulkeley, William M. 1994. "Digital Equipment Promises Overhaul After Reporting Wider 3rd-Period Loss." *Wall Street Journal,* April 18, A3, A7.

Burns, James MacGregor. 1978. *Leadership.* New York: Harper and Row.

Burrough, Bryan, and John Helyar. 1990. *Barbarians at the Gate: The Fall of RJR Nabisco.* New York: Harper and Row.

Burt, Ronald S. 1980. Models of Network Structure. In *Annual Review of Sociology,* edited by Alex Inkeles and Neil J. Smelser. Palo Alto, Calif.: Annual Reviews.

———. 1983. *Corporate Profits and Cooptation.* New York: Academic Press.

Business Week. 1987. "Business Week/Harris Executive Poll." *Business Week,* October 23, 28.

Byrd, John F., Marilyn F. Johnson, and Mark S. Johnson. 1993. "Investor Relations and the Cost of Capital." Ann Arbor, Mich.: University of Michigan, School of Business Administration.

Byrne, John A. 1986. "Business Fads: What's In—What's Out: Executives Latch on to Any Idea That Looks Like a Quick Fix," *Business Week,* January 20, 52–61.

———. 1993. "The Virtual Corporation." *Business Week,* February 8, 99–102.

Cannella, Albert A., Jr., and Donald C. Hambrick. 1993. "Effects of Executive Departures on the Performance of Acquired Firms." *Strategic Management Journal* 14: 137–152.

Cannella, Albert A., Jr., and Michael Lubatkin. 1993. "Succession as a Sociopolitical Process: Internal Impediments to Outsider Selection." *Academy of Management Journal* 36: 763–793.

Capital Analytics. 1993. *The Hidden Market: A Survey of Corporate Attitudes toward Marketing to Shareholders.* New York: Capital Analytics.

Cappelli, Peter, and Michael Useem. 1996. "The Forces Driving the Restructuring of Employment." In *Change at Work,* edited by Peter Cappelli. New York: Oxford University Press (forthcoming).

Carley, William M., and Amal Kumar Naj. 1993. "Firing of Executive Gives Rare Glimpse of Intrigue Inside GE." *Wall Street Journal,* November 23, A1, A7.

Carpenter, Richard. 1995. "Pushing the Boundaries." *Investor Relations* (Summer): 22–26.

Cates, David C. 1994. "Making Shareholder Value More than Just a Slogan." *American Banker,* May 17, 19, 22.

Chakravarthy, Balaji S., and Peter Lorange. 1991. *Managing the Strategy Process: A Framework for a Multibusiness Firm.* Englewood Cliffs, N.J.: Prentice-Hall.

Chandler, Alfred A., Jr. 1962. *Strategy and Structure.* Cambridge, Mass.: MIT Press.

Charkham, Jonathan. 1994. *Keeping Good Company: A Study of Corporate Governance in Five Countries.* New York: Oxford University Press.

Chief Executive. 1994. "The New Governance Paradigm." *Chief Executive* (April): 40–54.

Chief Executives' Council. 1993. "Getting the Best from Your Board." *Directors and Boards* (Spring): 62–64.

Chisholm, Donald. 1989. *Coordination without Hierarchy: Informal Structures in Multiorganizational Systems.* Berkeley: University of California Press, 1989.

Christopher, Robert C. 1989. *Crashing the Gates: The De-Wasping of America's Power Elite.* New York: Simon and Schuster.

Clawson, Dan, Alan Neustadtl, and Denise Scott. 1992. *Money Talks: Corporate PACs and Political Influence.* New York: Basic Books.

Clemente, Lilia C., and Roberto S. Mariano, eds. 1993. *Asian Capital Markets: Dynamics of Growth and World Linkages.* New York: Asian Securities Industry Institute.

———. 1994. *Asian Capital Markets: Strategic Investing in Asia.* New York: Asian Securities Industry Institute.

Cochran, Philip L., Robert A. Wood, and Thomas B. Jones. 1985. "The Composition of Boards of Directors and Incidence of Golden Parachutes." *Academy of Management Journal* 28: 664–671.

Cole, Robert E., Paul Bacdayan, and B. Joseph White. 1993. "Quality, Participation, and Competitiveness." *California Management Review* (Spring): 68–81.

Cole, Thomas A. 1994. "Drawing the Line in Corporate Boards." *New York Times,* January 16, F11.

College Retirement Equities Fund. 1990. Letter of November 8, 1990, to U.S. Securities and Exchange Commission. New York: College Retirement Equities Fund.

———. 1992. *Semi-Annual Report* (June 30). New York: College Retirement Equities Fund.

———. 1993. *Policy Statement on Corporate Governance.* New York: College Retirement Equities Fund.

Collins, Glenn. 1994. "Scott Paper to Pay Directors in Stock." *New York Times,* August 31, D3.

———. 1995. "RJR Nabisco Shuffles Leaders to Help Lift Tobacco Unit." *New York Times,* June 30, D3.

Committee of Publicly Owned Companies. 1993. "COPOC v. Calpers," Letter of February, 1993. Washington, D.C.: Committee of Publicly Owned Companies.

Conte, Michael A., and Jan Svejnar. 1990. The Performance Effects of Employee Ownership Plans. In *Paying for Productivity: A Look at the Evidence,* edited by Alan S. Blinder. Washington, D.C.: The Brookings Institution.

Cossette, Jeff. 1994. "Exporting Proxy Power." *Investor Relations,* June, 35–39.

———. 1995. "Fund Management Profile: Calpers." *Investor Relations* (October): 82–86.

Cowan, Alison Leigh. 1993. "Kodak's Chief Wins Support from Calpers," *New York Times,* April 6, D4.

Danner, Christina R. 1994. *Corporate Pension Funds: Construction and Management.* New York: Conference Board.

Datta, Deepak K., and James P. Guthrie. 1994. "Executive Succession: Organizational Antecedents of CEO Characteristics." *Strategic Management Journal* 15: 569–577.

Dattel, Eugene R. 1994. *The Sun That Never Rose.* Chicago: Probus Publishing.

Davey, Patrick J. 1988. *Managing Pension Funds in a Volatile Environment.* New York: Conference Board.

———. 1991. *Voting Corporate Pension Fund Proxies.* New York: Conference Board.

Davis, Gerald F. 1991. "Agents without Principles? The Spread of the Poison Pill Through the Intercorporate Network." *Administrative Science Quarterly* 36: 583–613.

———. 1993. "Who Gets Ahead in the Market for Corporate Directors: The Political Economy of Multiple Board Memberships." *Academy of Management Best Paper Proceedings 1993,* Dorothy Moore, ed. Ada, Ohio: Academy of Management.

Davis, Gerald F., Kristina A. Diekmann, and Catherine H. Tinsley. 1994. "The Decline and Fall of the Conglomerate Firm in the 1980s: Deinstitutionalization of an Organizational Form." *American Sociological Review* 59: 547–570.

Davis, Gerald F., and Walter W. Powell. 1992. "Organization-Environment Relations." *Handbook of Industrial and Organizational Psychology,* 2d ed., Marvin Dunnette, ed. Palo Alto: Consulting Psychologists Press.

Davis, Gerald F., and Suzanne K. Stout. 1992. "Organization Theory and the Market for Corporate Control: A Dynamic Analysis of the Characteristics of Large Takeover Targets, 1980–90." *Administrative Science Quarterly* 37: 605–633.

Davis, Gerald F., and Tracy A. Thompson. 1994. "A Social Movement Perspective on Corporate Control." *Administrative Science Quarterly* 39: 141–173.

Day, George S. 1994. "Continuous Learning About Markets." *California Management Review* 36 (Summer): 9–31.

Dechow, Patricia M., and Richard G. Sloan. 1991. "Executive Incentives and the Horizon Problem." *Journal of Accounting and Economics* 14: 51–89.

Demb, Ada, and F.-Friedrich Neubauer. 1992. *The Corporate Board.* New York: Oxford University Press.

Denis, David J., and Diane K. Denis. 1995. "Performance Changes Following Top Management Dismissals." *Journal of Finance* (September).

Denis, David J., Diane K. Denis, and Atulya Sarin. 1995. "Ownership Structure and Top Management Turnover." Blacksburg, Va.: Virginia Polytechnic Institute and State University.

Denis, David J., and Jan M. Serrano. 1996. "Active Investors and Management Turnover Following Unsuccessful Control Contests." *Journal of Financial Economics* (forthcoming).

Dertouzos, Michael, Richard K. Lester, and Robert M. Solow. 1989. *Made in America: Regaining the Competitive Edge.* Cambridge, Mass.: MIT Press.

Dickson, Martin. 1992. "ITT Unlikely to Spin Off Hartford." *Financial Times,* March 6, 20.

Digital Media. 1995. "Virtual Investor Relations." *Digital Media* (Spring): 42–44.

Directors and Boards. 1994. Special Issue on "Revitalizing Your Board." (Spring.)

Directors Publications. 1992. *Fortune 1000 Directors Survey.* Westport, Conn.: Directors Publications.

Dobrzynski, Judith H. 1993. "Relationship Investing." *Business Week,* March 15, 68–75.

Doeringer, Peter B., Kathleen Christensen, Patricia M. Flynn, Douglas T. Hall, Harry C. Katz, Jeffrey H. Keefe, Christopher J. Ruhm, Andrew M. Sum, and Michael Useem. 1991. *Turbulence in the American Workplace.* New York: Oxford University Press.

Donaldson, Gordon. 1994. *Corporate Restructuring: Managing the Change Process from Within.* Boston: Harvard Business School Press.

Donaldson, Gordon, and Jay W. Lorsch. 1983. *Decision Making at the Top: The Shaping of Strategic Direction.* New York: Basic Books.

Dorfman, John R. 1993. "300 Take Honors as Best Stock Pickers and Profit Prophets." *Wall Street Journal,* September 15, R1–13.

———. 1995. "Ranking the Analysts: A Tougher Year for the All-Stars." *Wall Street Journal,* June 20, R1–12.

Drucker, Peter F. 1976. *The Unseen Revolution: How Pension Fund Socialism Came to America.* New York: Harper and Row.

Duff, Christina, John R. Dorfman, and Joann S. Lublin. 1995. "Kmart's Embattled CEO Resigns Post Under Pressure from Key Shareholders." *Wall Street Journal,* March 22, A3, A10.

Dulebohn, James. 1994. "A Longitudinal and Comparative Analysis of the Funded Status of State and Local Public Pension Plans." Urbana, Ill.: University of Illinois, Institute of Labor and Industrial Relations.

Duttweiler, E., ed. *Factbook 1991.* New York: New York Stock Exchange.

Easterbrook, Frank H., and Daniel R. Fischel. 1991. *The Economic Structure of Corporate Law.* Cambridge, Mass.: Harvard University Press, 1991.

Eaton, Leslie. 1994. "The Kids Managing America's Money." *New York Times,* May 22, Section 3, 1, 6.

Eccles, Robert G., and Dwight B. Crane. 1988. *Doing Deals: Investment Banks at Work.* Boston: Harvard Business School Press.

Eccles, Robert G., and Sarah C. Mavrinac. 1995. "Improving the Corporate Disclosure Process." *Sloan Management Review* (Summer): 11–25.

Eckstein, Rick, and Kevin Delaney. 1993. "Institutional Investment Patterns in Troubled Corporations." *American Journal of Economics and Sociology* 52.

Ehrlichman, John. 1993. "Who Will Hire Me Now?" *Parade,* August 29, 4–6.

Eichenwald, Kurt. 1992. "A Sorry Record for G.M. Stock." *New York Times,* October 27, D1.

Employee Benefit Research Institute. 1993. "Pension Fund Portfolio Turnover and Performance Evaluation," *EBRI Issues Brief* (November).

Fabrikant, Geraldine. 1993. "QVC Network Wins Court Round in Its Bid to Take Over Paramount." *New York Times,* November 25, 1993, A1, D6.

————. 1995. "The Motives for a Mating Game: Is Time Warner Breaking Its Mold or Acting in Self-Defense?" *New York Times*, August 31, D1, D4.

Fisher, Lawrence M. 1994. "AST Stock Drops 18% on Report." *New York Times*, March 3, D3.

Fleeson, Lucinda. 1994. "At Reinvented Firms, Perks Are Out of Style." *Philadelphia Inquirer*, April 17, A1, A15.

Fligstein, Neil. 1985. "The Spread of the Multidivisional Form." *American Sociological Review* 50: 377–391.

————. 1990. *The Transformation of Corporate Control*. Cambridge, Mass.: Harvard University Press.

————. 1991. "The Structural Transformation of American Industry: An Institutional Account of the Causes of Diversification in the Largest Firms, (1919–1979)," in *The New Institutionalism in Organizational Analysis*, Walter W. Powell and Paul J. DiMaggio, eds. Chicago: University of Chicago Press.

Fortune. 1993. "What Activist Investors Want." *Fortune*, March 8, 59–63.

Fredrickson, James W., Donald C. Hambrick, and Sara Baumrin. 1988. "A Model of CEO Dismissal." *Academy of Management Review* 13: 255–270.

French, Kenneth, and James M. Poterba. 1991. "Investor Diversification and International Equity Market." *American Economic Review* 81: 222–226.

Freudenheim, Milt. 1993. "Merck Cuts 2,100 Jobs and Takes Huge Charge," *New York Times*, July 21, D3.

Friedman, Stewart D., and Harbir Singh. 1989. "CEO Succession and Stockholder Reaction: The Influence of Organizational Context and Event Content." *Academy of Management Journal* 32: 718–744.

Fromson, Brett D. 1993. "American Express: Anatomy of a Coup." *Washington Post*, February 11, A1ff.

Furtado, Eugene P. H., and Vijan Karan. 1990. "Causes, Consequences, and Shareholder Wealth Effects of Manpower Turnover: A Review of Empirical Evidence. *Financial Management*, Summer: 60–75.

Gabarro, John J., and John P. Kotter. 1980. "Managing Your Boss," *Harvard Business Review* 58 (January–February): pp. 92–100.

Galaskiewicz, Joseph. 1985. *Social Organization of an Urban Grants Economy: A Study of Business Philanthropy and Nonprofit Organizations*. New York: Academic Press.

Gardner, John W. 1990. *On Leadership*. New York: Free Press.

General Motors Corporation. 1994. "GM Board Guidelines on Significant Corporate Governance Issues." Detroit: General Motors Corporation.

Gerlach, Michael L. 1992. *Alliance Capitalism: The Social Organization of Japanese Business*. Berkeley, Calif.: University of California Press.

Gerlach, Michael L., and James R. Lincoln. 1992. "The Organization of Business Networks in the U.S. and Japan." In *Networks and Organization Theory*, edited by Robert Eccles and Nitin Nohria. Boston: Harvard Business School Press.

Gilbert, Lewis. 1956. *Dividends and Democracy*. Larchmont, New York: American Research Council.

Gilpin, Kenneth N. 1994. "New Third World Fear: Investors Could Walk Away." *New York Times*, April 24, F4.

————. 1995. "Involuntary Retirement for Grace's Chairman." *New York Times,* March 18, D1, D19.

Gilson, Ronald J., and Reinier Kraakman. 1993. "Investment Companies as Guardian Shareholders: The Place of the MSIC in the Corporate Governance Debate." *Stanford Law Review* 45: 985–1010.

Gilson, Ronald J., and Mark J. Roe. 1993. "Understanding the Japanese Keiretsu: Overlaps Between Corporate Governance and Industrial Organization." New York: Columbia University School of Law.

Gordon Group. 1993. *Active Investing in the U.S. Equity Market: Past Performance and Future Prospects.* Newton, Mass.: Gordon Group, Inc.

Gordon, Jeffrey N. 1994. "Institutions as Relational Investors: A New Look at Cumulative Voting." *Columbia Law Review* 94: 124–192.

Gould, Carole. 1993. "Thousands of Funds Competed, but Only Three Finished on Top." *New York Times,* April 3, D35.

Gottschalk, Earl C., Jr. 1994. "Market Experts Identify Seven Traps That Could Be Hazardous to a Portfolio." *Wall Street Journal,* March 3, C1.

Granovetter, Mark. 1973. "The Strength of Weak Ties." *American Journal of Sociology* 78: 1360–1380.

Grant, Linda. 1992. "GM Shuffle May Be Watershed in Reining in CEOs." *Los Angeles Times,* April 13, D1–2.

Graves, Samuel B. 1988. "Institutional Ownership and Corporate R&D in the Computer Industry." *Academy of Management Journal* 31: 417–428.

Greenwich Associates, various years. *Institutional Equity Services, Report to Participants.* Greenwich, Conn.: Greenwich Associates.

Grundfest, Joseph A. 1993. "Just Vote No: A Minimalist Strategy for Dealing with Barbarians Inside the Gates." *Stanford Law Review* 45: 857–937.

Hagstrom, Robert G., Jr. 1994. *The Warren Buffet Way: Investment Strategies of the World's Greatest Investor.* New York: Wiley.

Hall, Gene, Jim Rosenthal, and Judy Wade. 1993. "How to Make Reengineering *Really* Work." *Harvard Business Review* (November–December): 191–131.

Hammer, Michael, and James Champy. 1993. *Reengineering the Corporation: A Manifesto for Business Revolution.* New York: Harper Business.

Handler, Edward, and John R. Mulkern. 1982. *Business in Politics.* Lexington, Mass.: Lexington Books.

Hansell, Saul. 1995. "Chase and Chemical Agree to Merge in $10 Billion Deal Creating Largest U.S. Bank." *New York Times,* August 29, A1, D6.

Hanson, Dale M. 1993. "The Bureaucrats Strike Back." *Harvard Business Review* (January–February): 78.

Hansen, Gary S., and Charles W. L. Hill. 1991. "Are Institutional Investors Myopic? A Time-Series Study of Four Technology-Driven Industries." *Strategic Management Journal* 12: 1–16.

Harrison, Bennett. 1994. *Lean and Mean: The Changing Landscape of Corporate Power in the Age of Flexibility.* New York: Basic Books.

Hays, Laurie. 1994. "Gerstner Is Struggling as He Tries to Change Ingrained IBM Culture." *Wall Street Journal,* May 13, A1, A8.

Hays, Laurie, and Gautam Naik. 1993. "Xerox to Cut 10,000 Jobs, Shut Facilities." *Wall Street Journal,* December 9, A2, A4.

Heidrick & Struggles. 1990. *The Changing Board*. Chicago: Heidrick & Struggles.
————. 1993a. *Women and Minorities on Corporate Boards*. Chicago: Heidrick & Struggles.
————. 1993b. *The Global Outside Director*. Chicago: Heidrick & Struggles.
Hewitt Associates. 1994. Personal communication of data. Lincolnshire, Ill.: Hewitt Associates.
Hill, Charles W. L., and Scott A. Snell. 1989. "Effects of Ownership Structure and Control on Corporate Productivity." *Academy of Management Journal* 32: 25–46.
Hill, Linda. 1992. *Becoming a Manager*. Boston: Harvard Business School Press.
Himelstein, Linda. 1994. "Boardrooms: The Ties That Bind?" *Business Week*, May 2, 112–114.
Himmelstein, Jerome L. 1990. *To the Right: The Transformation of American Conservatism*. Berkeley, Calif.: University of California Press.
Hirschman, Albert. 1970. *Exit, Voice and Loyalty: Responses to Decline in Firms, Organizations and States*. Cambridge, Mass.: Harvard University Press.
Holusha, John. 1993a. "Kodak Stock Drops After Officer Quits." *New York Times*, April 29, D1, D5.
————. 1993b. "Eastman Kodak Chief Is Ousted by Directors." *New York Times*, August 7, 37, 49.
————. 1993c. "At Kodak, Lower Expectations Begin with Stock." *New York Times*, December 16, D1, D6.
————. 1993d. "A Profitable Xerox Plans to Cut Staff by 10,000." *New York Times*, December 9, D1, D5.
Horwitz, Tony. 1993. "Jobless Male Managers Proliferate in Suburbs, Causing Subtle Malaise." *Wall Street Journal*, September 20, A1, A6.
Hoskisson, Robert E., and Michael A. Hitt. 1994. *Downscoping: How to Tame the Diversified Firm*. New York: Oxford University Press.
Howard, Robert. 1992. "The CEO as Organizational Architect." *Harvard Business Review* (September–October): 107–119.
Hsin, Ping Lung. 1995. "Are Public Sector Pension Plans Administratively Efficient?" Presented at the Pension Research Council Symposium, University of Pennsylvania.
Hwang, Suein L. 1995. "RJR, in Shake-Up, Appoints Greeniaus to Run Troubled U.S. Cigarette Line." *Wall Street Journal*, June 30, B8.
Hylton, Richard D. 1994. "Don't Panic About Your Pension—Yet." *Fortune*, April 18, 121–123.
Ingrassia, Paul. 1994. "Memo to Board: Management Isn't Always Wrong." *Wall Street Journal*, November 23, A14.
Ingrassia, Paul, and Joann S. Lublin. 1992. "Who's on First at the No. 1 Auto Maker." *Wall Street Journal*, April 8, B1.
Institute of International Finance. 1994. Personal communication of data. Washington, D.C.: Institute of International Finance.
Institutional Investor. 1993a. "The 1993 All-America Research Team." *Institutional Investor* (October): 53–149.

————. 1993b. "Pitching the Firm." *Institutional Investor* (February): 165.

————. 1994a. "America's Top 300 Money Managers." *Institutional Investor* (July): 113–156.

———— 1994b. "The 1994 All-American Research Team." *Institutional Investor* (October): 76–171.

Investment Company Institute. 1993. *1993 Mutual Fund Fact Book*. Washington, D.C.: Investment Company Institute.

————. 1994. *1994 Mutual Fund Fact Book*. Washington, D.C.: Investment Company Institute.

————. 1995. *1995 Mutual Fund Fact Book*. Washington, D.C.: Investment Company Institute.

Investor Relations Newsletter. 1994. "IR Practice in Japan Lags," *Investor Relations Newsletter*. Chicago: Remy Publishing Company, April, 4.

Investor Relations Update. 1993. "The NIRI Forum." *Investor Relations Update*, September, 18.

Investor Responsibility Research Center. 1992. *State Takeover Laws*. Washington, D.C.: Investor Responsibility Research Center.

————. Various years. *Voting by Institutional Investors on Corporate Governance Issues*. Washington, D.C.: Investor Responsibility Research Center.

————. 1993. "Boards Form Governance Committees." *Corporate Governance Bulletin* (July–August): 16.

————. 1994. "Regulations Extended to Foreign Proxies." *Corporate Governance Bulletin* (July–August): 3.

ITT Corporation. 1995. *Preliminary Proxy Materials*. New York: ITT Corporation.

Jackall, Robert. 1988. *Moral Mazes: The World of Corporate Managers*. New York: Oxford University Press.

Jacobs, Michael T. 1991. *The Causes and Cures of Our Short-Term Myopia*. Boston: Harvard Business School Press.

————. 1993. *Break the Wall Street Rule: Outperform the Stock Market by Investing as an Owner*. Reading, Mass.: Addison-Wesley.

Janger, Allen. 1989. *Measuring Managerial Layers and Spans*. New York: Conference Board.

Jarrell, Gregg A. 1993. "A Victory for Shareholders." *Wall Street Journal*, December 1, A20.

Jarrell, Gregg A., James A. Brickley, and Jeffrey M. Netter. 1988. "The Market for Corporate Control: The Empirical Evidence Since 1980." *Journal of Economic Perspectives* 2: 49–68.

Jarrell, Gregg A., Ken Lehn, and Wayne Marr. 1985. "Institutional Ownership, Tender Offers, and Long-Term Investments." Washington, D.C.: Securities and Exchange Commission, Office of Economic Analysis.

Jeffreys, Steve. 1986. *Management and Managed: Fifty Years of Crisis at Chrysler.* New York: Cambridge University Press.

Jensen, Elizabeth. 1995. "CBS's Tisch Is Faulted by Insiders, Affiliates for Network's Struggle." *Wall Street Journal*, May 22, A1, A6.

Jensen, Michael C. 1989. "Eclipse of the Public Corporation." *Harvard Business Review* 67 (September–October): 61–74.

Jensen, Michael C., and Kevin J. Murphy. 1990. "CEO Incentives—It's Not How Much You Pay, but How" (May–June): 138–153.

Johnson, Arlene S., and Fabian Linden. 1992. *Availability of a Quality Workforce*. New York: Conference Board.

Jones, Jonathan, Kenneth Lehn, and J. Harold Mulherin. 1991. Institutional Ownership of Stock Equity: Effects on Stock Market Liquidity and Corporate Long-Term Investments, in *Institutional Investing: The Challenges and Responsibilities of the 21st Century*, edited by Arnold W. Sametz. Homewood, Ill.: Business One Irwin.

Judge, William Q., Jr., and Carl P. Zeithaml. 1992. "Institutional and Strategic Choice Perspectives on Board Involvement in the Strategic Decision Process." *Academy of Management Journal* 35: 766–794.

Kadanoff, Leo P. 1992. "Hard Times." *Physics Today* 45 (October): 9, 11.

Kamm, Thomas. "Another Head Rolls in French Revolution: Suez Chief Latest Victim of Shareholder Activism." *Wall Street Journal*, July 10, A10.

Kansas, Dave. 1995. "ITT Holders Vote Thursday on Breakup Plan, But Any Delay in Deal May Cost Investors Big." *Wall Street Journal*, September 19, C3.

Kanter, Rosabeth Moss. 1977. *Men and Women of the Corporation*. New York: Basic Books.

Katzenbach, Jon R., and Douglas K. Smith. 1993. *The Wisdom of Teams: Creating the High-Performance Organization*. Boston: Harvard Business School Press.

Keller, John J. 1994. "GTE to Trim 13% of Workers, Post Big Charge." *Wall Street Journal*, January 14, A3.

———. 1995. "Defying Merger Trend, AT&T Plans to Split into Three Companies." *Wall Street Journal*, September 21, A1, A16.

Kerr, Steven. 1975. "On the Folly of Rewarding A While Hoping for B." *Academy of Management Journal* 18: 769–683.

Kesner, Idalene F., and Roy B. Johnson. 1990. "An Investigation of the Relationship between Board Composition and Stockholder Suits." *Strategic Management Journal* 11: 327–336.

Kilborn, Peter T. 1993. "The Workplace, After the Deluge." *New York Times,* September 5, Business Section, 3–4.

Knowlton, Winthrop and Millstein, Ira M. 1988. "Can the Board of Directors Help the American Corporation Earn the Immortality It Holds So Dear?" In *The U.S. Business Corporation: An Institution in Transition,* edited by John R. Meyer and James M. Gustafson. Cambridge, Mass: Ballinger Publishing Company.

Kochan, Thomas A., Harry C. Katz, and Robert B. McKersie. 1986. *The Transformation of American Industrial Relations*. New York: Basic Books.

Kogut, Bruce, ed. 1993. *Country Competitiveness: Technology and the Organizing of Work*. New York: Oxford University Press.

Kogut, Bruce, and David Parkinson. 1993. The Diffusion of American Organizing Principles to Europe. In *Country Competitiveness: Technology and the Organizing of Work,* edited by Bruce Kogut. New York: Oxford University Press.

Korn/Ferry International. 1992. *Board of Directors: Nineteenth Annual Study, 1992.* New York: Korn/Ferry International.

―――. 1993. *Board of Directors: Twentieth Annual Study, 1993.* New York: Korn/Ferry International.

―――. 1994. *Board of Directors: Twenty-First Annual Study, 1994.* New York: Korn/Ferry International.

Korn/Ferry Organizational Consulting. 1993a. *Reinventing Corporate Governance: Directors Prepare for the 21st Century.* Boston: Korn/Ferry Organizational Consulting.

―――. 1993b. *Affirming Corporate Governance: Fortune CEOs Endorse Tradition.* Boston: Korn/Ferry Organizational Consulting.

Kosnik, Rita D. 1987. "Greenmail: A Study of Board Performance in Corporate Governance." *Administrative Science Quarterly* 32: 163–185.

Kotter, John P. 1985. *Power and Influence: Beyond Formal Authority.* New York: Free Press.

―――. 1988. *The Leadership Factor.* New York: Free Press.

Kotter, John P., and James L. Heskett. 1992. *Corporate Culture and Performance.* New York: Free Press.

Landro, Laura, and Elizabeth Jensen. 1995. "A CBS Holder, Capital Group, Declines to Vote for Management-Backed Board." *Wall Street Journal,* May 25, B2.

Lappen, Alyssa A. 1995. "Fidelity Grapples with Gigantism." *Institutional Investor* (September): 78–90.

Lavin, Douglas, and Pauline Yoshihashi. 1994. "Kerkorian Plans to Raise Stake in Chrysler Corp." *Wall Street Journal,* November 15, A3.

Lawler, Edward E., III. 1993. *The Ultimate Advantage: Creating the High-Involvement Organization.* San Francisco: Jossey-Bass.

Lawler, Edward E., III, Susan Mohrman, and Gerald Ledford. 1992. *Employee Involvement and Total Quality Management: Practices and Results in Fortune 500 Companies.* San Francisco: Jossey-Bass.

Lear, Robert W., and Boris Yavitz. 1994. "America's Best and Worst Boards." *Chief Executive* (April): 32–39.

Lev, Baruch. 1991. *Identifying the Preferences of Institutional Investors and Implementing a Strategy for Change.* Washington, D.C.: National Investor Relations Institute.

Levin, Doron. 1989. *Irreconcilable Differences: Ross Perot versus General Motors.* Boston: Little Brown.

―――. 1992. "Truce for Chrysler and Kerkorian." *New York Times,* August 14, D2.

―――. 1993. "The Cousins Who Would Be King." *New York Times,* January 10, Section 3, 1, 6.

Lewis, Jordan D. 1990. *Partnerships for Profit: Structuring and Managing Strategic Alliances.* New York: Free Press.

Light, Sharon Pamepinto. 1992. *Voting by Institutional Investors on Corporate Governance Issues, 1992.* Washington, D.C.: Investor Responsibility Research Center.

Light, Jay O., and James E. Sailer. 1992. "Cleveland-Cliffs, Inc." Boston: Harvard Business School.

Lipin, Steven. 1993. "Golub Solidifies Hold at American Express, Begins to Change Firm." *Wall Street Journal*, June 30, A1, A6.

———. 1995. "Chemical and Chase Set $10 Billion Merger, Forming Biggest Bank." *Wall Street Journal*, August 28, A1, A6.

Lipin, Steven, and Craig Torres. 1993. "American Express Lineup Strikes Out with Investors." *Wall Street Journal*, January 27, C1, C2.

Lipin, Steven, Neal Templin, and Pauline Yoshihashi. 1995. "Chrysler Moves to Bolster the Backing of Big Investors After Kerkorian Duel." *Wall Street Journal*, April 27, A3.

Lohr, Steve. 1994. "I.B.M. May Quit Hilltop Headquarters." *New York Times*, January 13, 1, D3.

Lohr, Steve, and James Bennet. 1994. "Lessons of Rebound from G.M. and I.B.M." *New York Times*, October 24, D1, D4.

Lorsch, Jay W. 1989. *Pawns or Potentates: The Reality of America's Corporate Boards*. Boston: Harvard Business School Press.

Lowenstein, Louis. 1991. *Sense and Nonsense in Corporate Finance*. Reading, Mass.: Addison-Wesley.

———, ed. 1996. *Relational Investing*. New York: Oxford University Press (forthcoming).

Lubatkin, Michael H., Kae H. Chung, Ronald C. Rogers, and James E. Owens. 1989. "Stockholder Reactions to CEO Changes in Large Corporations." *Academy of Management Journal* 32: 47–68.

Lublin, Joann. 1993. "Survivors of Layoffs Battle Angst, Anger, Hurting Productivity." *Wall Street Journal*, December 6, A1, A16.

———. 1995. "Pension Funds Take Aim Again at Weak Stocks." *Wall Street Journal*, October 2, A4.

MacDuffie, John Paul, and John Krafcik. 1992. Integrating Technology and Human Resources for High Performance Manufacturing: Evidence from the International Auto Industry. In *Transforming Organizations*, edited by Thomas Kochan and Michael Useem. New York: Oxford University Press.

Macy, Barry A., and Hiroaki Izumi. 1993. Organizational Change, Design, and Work Innovation: A Meta-Analysis of 131 North American Field Studies— 1961–1991. In *Research in Organizational Change and Development*, edited by Richard W. Woodman and William A. Pasmore. Greenwich, Conn.: JAI Press.

Mahoney, William F. 1990. "Recession Can Provide Extraordinary Opportunity for Investor Relations Practice." *Investor Relations Update* (November): 1–7.

———. 1991. *Investor Relations: The Professional's Guide to Financial Marketing and Communications*. New York: Simon and Schuster.

———. 1992a. "NIRI Survey: IR Practice Evolving with Absence of Dramatic Change," *Investor Relations Update* (June): 12–14.

———. 1992b. "Market Intelligence Grows as Basis of Investor Relations Strategies and Programs." *Investor Relations Update* (September): 1–15.

———. 1993a. *The Active Shareholder*. New York: Wiley.

———. 1993b. "McDonald's Platform with Investors: Recruit, Service and Communicate." *Investor Relations Update* (March): 1, 4–7.

————. 1994a. "Institutional Targeting Services Continue to Grow." *Investor Relations Update* (May): 16–17.

————. 1994b. "Successful Companies: Pattern Used to Change Mix, Increase Stock Price." *Investor Relations Update* (December): 14–16.

Malatesta, Paul H., and Ralph A. Walkling. 1988. "Poison Pill Securities: Stockholder Wealth, Profitability, and Ownership Structure." *Journal of Financial Economics* 20: 347–376.

Mallette, Paul, and Karen L. Fowler. 1992. "Effects of Board Composition and Stock Ownership on the Adoption of 'Poison Pills,'" *Academy of Management Journal* 35: 1010–1035.

March, James G., and Herbert A. Simon. 1957. *Organizations.* New York: Wiley.

Marcus, Alfred A., and Robert S. Goodman. 1991. "Victims and Shareholders: The Dilemmas of Presenting Corporate Policy During a Crisis." *Academy of Management Journal* 34: 281–305.

Marcus, Bruce W., and Sherwood Lee Wallace. 1991. *Competing in the New Capital Markets: Investor Relations Strategies for the 1990s.* New York: Harper Business.

Markides, Constantinos C. 1992. "Consequences of Corporate Refocusing: Ex Ante Evidence." *Academy of Management Journal* 35: 398–412.

————. 1995. "Diversification, Restructuring, and Economic Performance." *Strategic Management Journal* 16: 101–118.

Marks, Mitchell. 1993. "Restructuring and Downsizing." In *Building a Competitive Workforce: Investing in Human Capital for Corporate Success*, edited by Philip H. Mirvis. New York: John Wiley.

McDonald's Corporation. 1992. *Annual Report, 1991.* Oak Brook, Ill.: McDonald's Corporation.

McGough, Robert, and Laura Jereski. 1995. "How an Investor Pushed Banks Toward Merger." *Wall Street Journal*, August 29, B1, B9.

McGurn, Patrick S. 1993. "Few Votes Withheld from Directors in 1993." *Corporate Governance Bulletin* (May–June): 14–15.

————. 1994. "DOL Issues New Guidelines on Proxy Voting, Active Investing." *Corporate Governance Bulletin* (July–August): 1–7.

McGurn, Patrick, and Leita K. Zeugner. 1992. "'Just Vote No' Effort Faces New Challenges." *Corporate Governance Bulletin*, (May–June): 15–18.

McKinsey & Company. 1993. *Manufacturing Productivity.* Washington, D.C.: McKinsey Global Institute.

McTaggart, James M., Peter W. Kontes, and Michael C. Mankins. 1994. *The Value Imperative: Managing for Superior Shareholder Returns.* New York: Free Press.

McWilliams, Gary. 1994. "How DEC's 'Minicompanies' Led to Major Losses." *Business Week*, February 7, 32.

Meredith, Robyn. 1996. "In Deal to End Takeover Effort, Chrysler Selling Non-Auto Lines." *New York Times*, February 9, A1, D6.

Merrill Lynch Business Brokerage and Valuation. 1993. *Mergerstat Review, 1992.* Schaumburg, Ill.: Merrill Lynch Business Brokerage and Valuation.

Millstein, Ira M. 1995. "The Professional Board." *The Business Lawyer* (November).

Mintz, Beth, and Michael Schwartz. 1985. *The Power Structure of American Business*. Chicago: University of Chicago Press.

Mintzberg, Henry. 1975. "The Manager's Job: Folklore and Fact." *Harvard Business Review* (July–August): 49–61.

Mitchell, Olivia S., and Ping Lung Hsin. 1994. "Public Pension Governance and Performance." Cambridge, Mass.: National Bureau of Economic Research.

Mitchell, Olivia S., and Robert S. Smith. 1994. "Public Sector Pension Funding." *Review of Economics and Statistics*. (May): 278–290.

Mizruchi, Mark S. 1992. *The Structure of Corporate Political Action*. Cambridge, Mass.: Harvard University Press.

Mizruchi, Mark S., and Joseph Galaskiewicz. 1993. "Networks of Interorganizational Relations." *Sociological Methods & Research* 22: 46–70.

Mizruchi, Mark S., and Michael Schwartz, eds. 1987. *Intercorporate Relations: The Structural Analysis of Business*. New York: Cambridge University Press.

Monks, Robert A. G., and Nell Minow. 1991. *Power and Accountability*. New York: Harper Business.

———. 1995. *Corporate Governance*. Cambridge, Mass.: Blackwell Publishers.

Moore, Margaret D. 1993. "Evaluating Results and Establishing Accountability for Investor Relations," presentation to the National Investor Relations Institute, Philadelphia Chapter, December 7, 1993.

Moore, Thomas. 1988. "Make or Break Time for General Motors." *Fortune*, February 15, 33–42.

Morita, Akio. 1988. *Speaking Out*. Tokyo: CBS/Sony Group Inc.

Moritz, Michael, and Barrett Seaman. 1981. *Going for Broke: The Chrysler Story*. New York: Doubleday.

Morningstar, Inc. 1994. "Mutual Funds on Disc." Chicago: Morningstar, Inc.

Myatt, Jennifer. 1995. "Why CEOs Lose Their Jobs: The Role of Alignment and Discipline Mechanisms in CEO Forced Exit." Philadelphia, Pa.: University of Pennsylvania, Wharton School, Ph.D. dissertation.

Nadler, David A., Marc S. Gerstein, Robert B. Shaw, and Associates. 1992. *Organizational Architecture: Designs for Changing Organizations*. San Francisco: Jossey-Bass.

Nadler, David A., and Michael L. Tushman. 1988. *Strategic Organization Design*. Glenview, Ill.: Scott, Foresman.

Nasar, Sylvia. 1994. "The American Economy, Back on Top." *New York Times*, February 27, F1, F6.

National Academy of Engineering, Committee on Time Horizons and Technology Investments. 1992. *Time Horizons and Technology Investments*. Washington, D.C.: National Academy of Engineering.

National Association of Corporate Directors, Blue Ribbon Commission. 1994. *Performance Evaluation of Chief Executive Officers, Boards, and Directors*. Washington, D.C.: National Association of Corporate Directors.

National Association of Investors Corporation. 1994. *A White Paper for the Individual Investor*. Royal Oak, Mich.: National Association of Investors Corporation.

National Investor Relations Institute. 1989. *Emerging Trends in Investor Relations*. Washington, D.C.: National Investor Relations Institute.

————. 1993. *An Analysis of Survey Responses from NIRI Members Pertaining to the Annual Report.* Washington, D.C.: National Investor Relations Institute.

————. 1994. *Investor Relations Trends and Compensation Survey.* Washington, D.C.: National Investor Relations Institute.

New Foundations Working Group. 1994. "Improving Communications Between Corporations and Shareholders." Cambridge, Mass.: New Foundations Working Group.

Newman, Katherine S. 1989. *Falling from Grace: The Experience of Downward Mobility in the American Middle Class.* New York: Random House.

New York Stock Exchange. 1994. *Factbook for the Year 1993.* New York: New York Stock Exchange.

————. 1995a. *Factbook for the Year 1994.* New York: New York Stock Exchange.

————. 1995b. "New Chairman's Views of NYSE's Future." *The Exchange* (July): 1–2.

Noer, David M. 1993. *Healing the Wounds: Overcoming the Trauma of Layoffs and Revitalizing Downsized Organizations.* San Francisco: Jossey-Bass.

Nohria, Nitin, and Robert G. Eccles, eds. 1992. *Networks and Organizations: Structure, Form, and Action.* Boston: Harvard Business School Press.

Norton, Erle. 1993. "Westinghouse Names Jordan to Top Posts." *Wall Street Journal,* July 1, A3–4.

Nussbaum, Bruce, and Judith H. Dobrzynski. 1987. "The Battle for Corporate Control." *Business Week* (May 18): 102–109.

O'Barr, William M., and John M. Conley. 1992. *Fortune and Folly: The Wealth and Power of Institutional Investing.* Homewood, Ill.: Business One Irwin.

O'Brien, Timothy L., and Steven Lipin. 1995. "Bank of Boston's Ira Stepanian Resigns After Failed Quests for a Merger Partner." *Wall Street Journal,* July 28, A3.

Ocasio, William. 1994. "Political Dynamics and the Circulation of Power: CEO Succession in U.S. Industrial Corporations, 1960–1990," *Administrative Science Quarterly* 39: 285–312.

Ocasio, William, and Hyosun Kim. 1994. "The Rise and Fall in Subunit Power and the Decline of the Financial Conception of Control in Large U.S. Manufacturing Firms, 1981–1992." Cambridge, Mass.: Sloan School, MIT.

O'Hara, Peg. 1995. "Three Big Funds Announce Targets, Settlements." *Corporate Governance Bulletin* (January–March): 10–12.

Orts, Eric W. 1992. "Beyond Shareholders: Interpreting Corporate Constituency Statutes." *George Washington Law Review* 61 (November): 14–135.

Paramount Communications Inc. v. QVC Network Inc., 637 A.2d 34 (Del. 1994).

Passell, Peter. 1992. "Those Big Executive Salaries May Mask a Bigger Problem." *New York Times,* April 20, D1, D5.

Pereira, Joseph, and Jeffrey A. Trachtenberg. 1990. "Ames Seeks Protection Under Chapter 11 After Retailer's Talks with Lenders Stall." *Wall Street Journal,* April 27, A3, A5.

Perot, Ross. 1988. "How I Would Turn Around GM." *Fortune,* February 15, 44–48.

Peters, Thomas J., and Robert H. Waterman Jr. 1982. *In Search of Excellence: Lessons from America's Best-Run Companies*. New York: Harper and Row.

Pettit, Dave. 1994. "Buying Spree for Microsoft to Heat Up as Stock Prepares to Join S&P 500 Index." *Wall Street Journal*, June 3, A7B.

Piacentini, Joseph S., and Jill D. Foley. 1992. *EBRI Databook on Employee Benefits*. Washington, D.C.: Employee Benefit Research Institute.

Piven, Frances Fox, and Richard A. Cloward. 1977. *Poor People's Movements: Why They Succeed, How They Fail*. New York: Pantheon.

Pfeffer, Jeffrey. 1991. *Managing with Power*. Cambridge, Mass.: Harvard Business School Press.

Pope, Kyle. 1994. "Dell's Earnings for 4th Quarter Exceed Forecast." *Wall Street Journal*, March 4, B7.

Porter, Michael. 1985. *Competitive Advantage*. New York: Free Press.

———. 1987. "From Competitive Advantage to Corporate Strategy." *Harvard Business Review* 65 (May–June): 43–59.

———. 1992. *Capital Choices: Changing the Way America Invests in Industry*. Washington, D.C.: Council on Competitiveness.

Post, James S., Edwin A. Murray, Jr., Robert D. Dickie, and John F. Mahon. 1983. "Managing Public Affairs: The Public Affairs Function." *California Management Review* 26: 135–150.

Pound, John. 1992. "Beyond Takeovers: Politics Comes to Corporate Control." *Harvard Business Review* 70 (March–April): 83–93.

———. 1993a. "Creating Relationships Between Institutional Investors and Corporations: A Proposal to Restore the Balance in the American Corporate Governance Process." New York: Conference on Relational Investing, May, 1993, sponsored by the Columbia University Institutional Investor Project.

———. 1993b. "Where Shareholder Activism Is Paramount." *Wall Street Journal*, December 7, A16.

Powell, Walter W. 1990. Neither Market Nor Hierarchy: Network Forms of Organization, in *Research in Organizational Behavior*, 12, edited by Barry M. Staw and L. L. Cummings. Greenwich, Conn.: JAI Press.

Pozen, Robert C. 1994. "Institutional Investors: The Reluctant Activists." *Harvard Business Review* (January–February): 140–149.

Puffer, Sheila M., and Joseph B. Weintrop. 1991. "Corporate Performance and CEO Turnover: A Comparison of Performance Indicators." *Administrative Science Quarterly* 36: 1–19.

Ramirez, Anthony. 1994. "GTE Says It Will Cut 17,000 Jobs." *New York Times*, January 14, D1, D2.

Randall, Eric D. 1993. "Kodak Chief's Exit Good for Stock, Bad for Staff." *USA Today*, August 9, 2B.

Rao, Hayagreeva, and Kumar Sivakumar. 1995. "The Spread of Investor Relations: An Institutional Analysis." Atlanta: Emory Business School.

Reich, Robert B. 1993. "Companies Are Cutting Their Hearts Out." *New York Times Magazine*, December 19, 54–55.

Reich, Robert B., and John Donahue. 1985. *New Deals: The Chrysler Revival and the American System*. New York: Time Books.

Reilly, Anne H., Jeane M. Brett, and Linda K. Stroh. 1993. "The Impact of Corporate Turbulence on Managers' Attitudes." *Strategic Management Journal* 14: 167–179.

Reinganum, Marc R. 1985. "The Effect of Executive Succession on Stockholder Wealth." *Administrative Science Quarterly* 30: 46–60.

Reisman, David. 1950. *The Lonely Crowd: A Study of the Changing American Character.* New Haven, Conn.: Yale University Press.

Rifkin, Glenn. 1994. "A Deepening of Digital's Losses." *New York Times*, April 16, 35, 41.

Rigdon, Joan E. 1993a. "Kodak's Chief Gains Support from 2 Holders, Whitmore Assures Calpers He Will Make Changes to Boost Productivity," *Wall Street Journal*, April 6, A4.

———. 1993b. "The New Finance Chief at Kodak Has a Style Quite Unlike His Boss's." *Wall Street Journal*, April 28, A1, A13.

Rigdon, Joan E., and Joann S. Lublin. 1993. "Kodak Seeks Outsider to Be Chairman, CEO." *Wall Street Journal*, August 9, A3, A14.

Rigdon, Joan E., and Gautam Naik. 1993. "Kodak's Financial Officer Quits in Rift with Chief." *Wall Street Journal*, April 29, A3, A6.

Rigdon, Joan E., and Randall Smith. 1993. "Kodak's Chairman Reassures Investors, Promises to Sell a 'Major Asset.'" *Wall Street Journal*, April 30, A4.

Roberts, Johnnie L., and Randall Smith. 1993a. "Paramount Is Told by Court to Consider Offer by QVC." *Wall Street Journal*, December 10, A3–A4.

———. 1993b. "Who Gets the Blame for Paramount Gaffes? Big Cast of Characters." *Wall Street Journal,* December 13, A1, A6.

Rock, Edward B. 1991. "The Logic and (Uncertain) Significance of Institutional Shareholder Activism." *Georgetown Law Review* 79: 445–506.

———. 1993. "Controlling the Dark Side of Relational Investing." Philadelphia, Pa.: University of Pennsylvania Law School.

Rock, Milton L., and Lance A. Berger, eds. 1991. *The Compensation Handbook,* 3d ed. New York: McGraw-Hill.

Roe, Mark J. 1993. "Some Differences in Corporate Structure in Germany, Japan, and the United States," *Yale Law Journal* (June): 1927–2003.

———. 1993a. "The Modern Corporation and Private Pensions." *UCLA Law Review* 41: 75–116.

———. 1994. *Strong Managers, Weak Owners: The Political Roots of American Corporate Finance.* Princeton, N.J.: Princeton University Press.

Romano, Roberta. 1993. "Public Pension Fund Activism in Corporate Governance Reconsidered." *Columbia Law Review* 93: 795–853.

Rosenbaum, Michael A. 1994. *Selling Your Story to Wall Street.* Chicago: Probus Publishing Company.

Rosenstein, Stuart, and Jeffrey G. Wyatt. 1990. "Outside Directors, Board Independence, and Shareholder Wealth." *Journal of Financial Economics* 26: 175–191.

Ryngaert, Michael. 1988. "The Effect of Poison Pill Securities on Shareholder Wealth." *Journal of Financial Economics* 20: 377–418.

Sailer, James E. 1991. "California PERS" (Case). Boston: Harvard Business School.

———. 1992. "Cleveland-Cliffs Inc." (Case). Boston: Harvard Business School.

Salisbury, Dallas L., and Nora Super Jones, eds. 1994. *Pension Funding & Taxation: Implications for Tomorrow*. Washington, D.C.: Employee Benefit Research Institute.

Sametz, Arnold W., ed. 1991. *Institutional Investing: The Challenges and Responsibilities of the 21st Century*. Homewood, Ill.: Business One Irwin.

Sander, William F. 1991. *Shareholding Voting Almanac*. Washington, D.C.: Investor Responsibility Research Center.

Santoli, Michael. 1994. "The Hunt Is on for Research Analysts." *Wall Street Journal, May 27, B4F.*

Schrader, Stephan. 1992. "Informal Information Trading Between Firms." In *Transforming Organizations*, edited by Thomas Kochan and Michael Useem. New York: Oxford University Press.

Schultz, Ellen E. 1995. "Tidal Wave of Retirement Cash Anchors Mutual Funds." *Wall Street Journal*, September 27, C1, 25.

Schwartz, Jerry. 1992. "Coke's Chairman Defends $86 Million Pay and Bonus." *New York Times*, April 16, D1, D11.

Scism, Leslie. 1994a. "Pension Funds Venture Abroad in Search of Big Returns." *Wall Street Journal*, January 19, C1, C12.

———. 1994b. "Public Pension Plans Are So Underfunded That Trouble Is Likely." *Wall Street Journal*, April 16, pp. A1, A4.

Scott Morton, Michael S., ed. 1991. *The Corporation of the 1990s: Information Technology and Organizational Transformation*. New York: Oxford University Press.

Securities Industry Association. 1994. *1994 Securities Industry Fact Book*. New York: Securities Industry Association.

———. 1995. *1995 Securities Industry Fact Book*. New York: Securities Industry Association.

Shapiro, Eben. 1994. "Philip Morris's New Management Faces Pressure for Split-Up from Big Holders." *Wall Street Journal*, June 21, A3.

———. 1995. "ITT Holders Vote Thursday on Breakup Plan, but Any Delay in Deal May Cost Investors Big." *Wall Street Journal*, September 19, C3.

Shapiro, Eben, and Laura Landro. 1995. "Frustrated Investors Ratchet Up Pressure on Time Warner Chief." *Wall Street Journal*, A1, A5.

Shiller, Robert J. 1991. The Significance of the Growth of Institutional Investing, in *Institutional Investor Fact Book 1991*, edited by Jean E. Tobin. New York: New York Stock Exchange.

Siegel, Jeremy J. 1994. *Stocks for the Long Run*. New York: Irwin Professional Publishing.

Silverman, Celia, et al. 1995. *EBRI Databook on Employee Benefits*. Washington, D.C.: Employee Benefit Research Institute.

Simison, Robert L. 1994. "GM Board Adopts Formal Guidelines on Stronger Control over Management." *Wall Street Journal*, March 29, A4.

Simison, Robert L., and Albert R. Karr. 1994. "GM Is Backed on Plan to Cut Pension Liability." *Wall Street Journal,* May 12, A3.

Singh, Harbir, and Farid Harianto. 1989. "Management-Board Relationships, Takeover Risk, and the Adoption of Golden Parachutes." *Academy of Management Journal* 32: 7–24.

Sloan, Allan. 1996. "Corporate Killers: Wall Street Loves Layoffs. But the Public is Scared. Is There a Better Way?" *Newsweek*, February 26, Cover, 44–48.

Sloane, Leonard. 1993. "Lewis Gilbert, 86, Advocate of Shareholder Rights." *New York Times*, December 8, B8.

Smith, Geoffrey. 1994. "Inside Fidelity: How the Fund Giant's Stock-Picking Machine Works." *Business Week*, October 10, 88–96.

Smith, Randall. 1995. "Conference Calls to Big Investors Often Leave Little Guys Hung Up." *Wall Street Journal*, June 21, C1, C20.

Smith, Randall, and Johnnie L. Roberts. 1993. "Court Blocks Acquisition of Paramount by Viacom." *Wall Street Journal*, November 26, A3.

Smoot, George, and Keay Davidson. 1993. *Wrinkles in Time*. New York: Morrow.

Sonnenfeld, Jeffrey A. 1988. *The Hero's Farewell: What Happens When CEOs Retire*. New York: Oxford University Press.

Standard and Poor's Corporation. 1992. *1992 S&P 500 Directory*. New York: Standard and Poor's Corporation.

Steiner, Robert. 1994. "Japanese May Permit Foreign Firms to Help Manage Public Pension Fund." *Wall Street Journal*, December 23, A6.

Steinmetz, Greg. 1994a. "Aetna Mulls Another Revamping Amid Sluggish Profits." *Wall Street Journal*, January 14, B4.

———. 1994b. "LBO Funds Lure Investors, But Returns Worry Some." *Wall Street Journal*, June 29, C1.

Stern, Gabriella, and Laurie Hays. 1995. "Chrysler Doubles Buyback of Its Shares to $2 Billion." *Wall Street Journal*, September 8, A3.

Stern, Gabriella, and Steven Lipin. 1995. "Why Kirk Kerkorian Has a (Slim) Chance to Win Over Chrysler." *Wall Street Journal*, September 15, A1, A5.

Stertz, Bradley A., and Pauline Yoshihashi. 1992a. "Kerkorian Urges Chrysler to Give Role to Iacocca." *Wall Street Journal*, August 10, A3.

———. 1992b. "Kerkorian Ends Threat to Join Chrysler Board." *Wall Street Journal*, August 14, A4.

Stevenson, Richard W. 1991. "Battling for Shareholder Rights." *New York Times*, January 31, D1.

Stewart, James B. 1991. *Den of Thieves*. New York: Simon and Schuster.

Stewart, Thomas A. 1993. "The King Is Dead," *Fortune*, January 11, 34–48.

Stobaugh, Robert. 1993. "Director Compensation: A Lever to Improve Corporate Governance." *Director's Monthly* 17 (August): 1–4.

Strickland, Deon, Kenneth W. Wiles, and Marc Zenner. 1996. "A Requiem for the USA: Is Small Shareholder Monitoring Effective?" *Journal of Financial Economics* 40: 319–338.

Studer, Margaret. 1995. "Shareholders Must Work to Maximize Investments in European Companies." *Wall Street Journal*, August 21, A5E.

Supreme Court of Delaware. 1994. *Paramount Communications Inc. v. QVC Network Inc.* February 4.

Teitelman, Robert. 1992. "Image vs. Reality at American Express." *Institutional Investor* (February): 36–46.

Templin, Neal, and Steven Lipin. 1995. "Many Analysts Agree with Kerkorian That Chrysler Cash Hoard Is Too Big." *Wall Street Journal*, April 17, B3.

TIAA-CREF. 1993. "TIAA-CREF Policy Statement on Corporate Governance." New York: TIAA-CREF.

Tobias, Andrew. 1976. "The Merging of the 'Fortune 500.'" *New York Magazine* (December 20): 23–25, 49, 67.

Tobin, Jean E., ed. 1991. *Institutional Investor Fact Book 1991*. New York: New York Stock Exchange.

Torres, Craig, and Thomas T. Vogel, Jr. 1994. "Some Mutual Funds Wield Growing Clout in Developing Nations." *Wall Street Journal*, June 14, A1, A6.

Towers Perrin. 1992. *Perspectives on Management Pay*, July. New York: Towers Perrin.

———. 1993. *Perspectives on Management Pay*, August. New York: Towers Perrin.

———. 1994. Personal communication of data. New York: Towers Perrin.

———. 1995. Personal communication of data. New York: Towers Perrin.

Train, John. 1989. *The New Money Masters*. New York: HarperCollins.

Treece, James B. 1992. "The Board Revolt: Business as Usual Won't Cut It Anymore at a Humbled GM." *Business Week*, April 20, 30–36.

Uchitelle, Louis. 1993a. "Strong Companies Are Joining Trend to Eliminate Jobs." *New York Times*, July 26, A1, D3.

———. 1993b. "More Are Forced into Ranks of Self-Employed at Low Pay." *New York Times*, November 15, A1, B8.

Uchitelle, Louis, and N. R. Kleinfield. 1996. "On the Battlefield of Business, Millions of Casualties." *New York Times*, March 3, 1, 26, 28–29.

United Nations. 1993. *World Investment Report: Transnational Corporations and Integrated International Production*. New York: United Nations.

———. 1994. *World Investment Report: Transnational Corporations, Employment, and the Workplace*. New York: United Nations.

United Shareholders Association. Various years. *Shareholder 1,000*. Washington, D.C.: United Shareholders Association.

———. Various years. *Executive Compensation 1,000*. Washington, D.C.: United Shareholders Association.

U.S. Pension Benefit Guaranty Corporation. 1995. "Pension Underfunding Drops Among Largest Plans." Washington, D.C.: U.S. Pension Benefit Guaranty Corporation (and various earlier press releases).

Useem, Michael. 1984. *The Inner Circle: Large Corporations and the Rise of Business Political Activity in the U.S. and U.K.* New York: Oxford University Press.

———. 1993a. *Executive Defense: Shareholder Power and Corporate Reorganization*. Cambridge, Mass.: Harvard University Press.

———. 1993b. "Management Commitment and Company Policies on Education and Training," *Human Resource Management Journal* 32: 411–434.

Useem, Michael, Edward Bowman, Craig Irvine, and Jennifer Myatt. 1993. "U.S. Investors Look at Corporate Governance in the 1990s," *European Management Journal* 11 (June): 175–189.

Useem, Michael, and Constance Gager. 1996. "Employee Shareholders or Institutional Investors? When Corporate Managers Replace their Shareholders." Philadelphia: University of Pennsylvania Press.

Useem, Michael, and Jerome Karabel. 1986. "Pathways to Top Corporate Management," *American Sociological Review* 51: 184–200.

Useem, Michael, and Saskia Subramanian. 1994. "Leveraged Buyouts and Corporate Political Action." *Social Science Quarterly* 75: 475–493.

Vogel, David, 1989. *Fluctuating Fortunes: The Political Power of Business in America*. New York: Basic Books.

von Hippel, Eric. 1987. "Cooperation Between Rivals: Information Know-How Trading." *Research Policy* 16: 291–302.

Wade, James, Charles A. O'Reilly, III, and Ike Chandratat. 1990. "Golden Parachutes: CEOs and the Exercise of Social Influence." *Administrative Science Quarterly* 35: 587–603.

Wall Street Journal. 1994. "Big Is Back in Style as Corporate America Deals, Buys and Merges." *Wall Street Journal*, August 4, A1, A6.

Walsh, James P., and John W. Ellwood. 1991. "Mergers, Acquisitions, and the Pruning of Managerial Deadwood." *Strategic Management Journal* 12: 201–217.

Walsh, James P., and Rita D. Kosnik. 1993. "Corporate Raiders and their Disciplinary Role in the Market for Corporate Control." *Academy of Management Journal* 36: 671–700.

Ward, Andrew. 1995. "The Harder They Fall? What Happens When CEOs Are Fired." Philadelphia, Pa.: University of Pennsylvania, Wharton School, Ph.D. dissertation.

Ward, Andrew, Jeffrey A. Sonnenfeld, and John R. Kimberly. 1995. "In Search of a Kingdom: Determinants of Subsequent Career Outcomes for Chief Executives Who Are Fired." *Human Resource Management* 34: 117–139.

Waroff, Deborah. 1994. "The Well-Connected IR Officer: IR Officers Have Whole New Ways to Communicate with Investors, Mostly for the Better." *Institutional Investor* (May): 134–139.

Wasserman, Stanley, and Joseph Galaskiewicz, eds. 1994. *Advances in Social Network Analysis*. Thousand Oaks, Calif.: Sage Publications.

Weisbach, Michael S. 1988. "Outside Directors and CEO Turnover," *Journal of Financial Economics* 20: 431–460.

Westphal, James D., and Edward J. Zajac. 1995. "Who Shall Govern? CEO/Board Power, Demographic Similarity, and New Director Selection." *Administrative Science Quarterly* 40: 60–83.

Weston, J. Fred, Kwang S. Chung, and Susan E. Hoag. 1990. *Mergers, Restructuring, and Corporate Control*. Englewood Cliffs, N.J.: Prentice-Hall.

White, Joseph B. 1992. "Corporate Lawyer Is General in Battle for Separation of Powers at Top of GM." *Wall Street Journal*, October 29, B1.

White, Joseph B., and Paul Ingrassia. 1992. "Behind Revolt at GM, Lawyer Ira Millstein Helped Call the Shots." *Wall Street Journal*, April 13, A1, A13.

Whyte, William H. 1956. *The Organization Man*. New York: Simon and Schuster.

Williamson, Oliver. 1975. *Markets and Hierarchies*. New York: Free Press.

Wohlstetter, Charles. 1993. "Pension Fund Socialism: Can Bureaucrats Run the Blue Chips?" *Harvard Business Review* (January–February): 78.

Womack, James P., Daniel T. Jones, and Daniel Roos. 1990. *The Machine That Changed the World*. New York: Rawson Associates (Macmillan).

World Bank. 1993. *Argentina's Privatization Program: Experience, Issues and Lessons.* Washington, D.C.: World Bank.

Worrell, Dan L., Wallace N. Davidson III, and John L. Glascock. 1993. "Stockholder Reactions to Departures and Appointments of Key Executives Attributable to Firings." *Academy of Management Journal* 36: 387–401.

Worrell, Dan L., Wallace N. Davidson III, and Varinder M. Sharma. 1991. "Layoff Announcements and Stockholder Wealth." *Academy of Management Journal* 34: 662–678.

Worrell, Kay. 1993. *Corporate Directors' Compensation, 1993 edition.* New York: Conference Board.

Wyatt, Edward. 1995. "Mutual-Fund Winners Had Put Their Money in the Banks." *New York Times*, August 29, D1, D7.

Wyatt Company. 1993. *Best Practices in Corporate Restructuring.* New York: Wyatt Company.

Yago, Glenn. 1991. *Junk Bonds: How High Yield Securities Restructured Corporate America.* New York: Oxford University Press.

Yoshino, Michael Y., and U. Srinivasa Rangan. 1995. *Strategic Alliances: An Entrepreneurial Approach to Globalization.* Boston: Harvard Business School Press.

Zald, Mayer N., and Michael A. Berger. 1978. "Social Movements in Organizations: Coup d'Etat, Insurgency, and Mass Movements," *American Journal of Sociology* 83: 823–861.

Zeugner, Leita K. 1992. "Funds Experiment with Withholding Votes." *Corporate Governance Bulletin* (May–June): 12–13.

———. 1993. "Institutions Campaign for Greater Board Diversity." *Corporate Governance Bulletin*, (November–December): 8–12.

Zorn, Paul. 1994. "Survey of State and Local Government Employee Retirement Systems." Washington, D.C.: Government Finance Officers Association.

Acknowledgments

I WOULD LIKE TO THANK the many company executives and investment managers who have shared their time and experience during my extended discussions with them. Their insightful and candid appraisals of the world that they are jointly constructing have been the critical foundation of the account related here.

Special gratitude is extended to the Institutional Investor Project of the Center for Law and Economic Studies of Columbia University. The Institutional Investor Project, sponsored by a number of companies, investors, unions, and the New York Stock Exchange, has generously provided financial support, conceptual guidance, and company access. Thanks go to the Board of Advisors for its backing, to Louis Lowenstein for his early guidance, and to Ira M. Millstein, H. Bruce Atwater Jr., Carolyn Kay Brancato, James R. Gillen, and James P. Melican for their opening of a number of company doors. Helpful assistance has also been rendered by those who have worked with the Institutional Investor Project, including Bernard Black, Jonathan P. Charkham, Kathleen Chojnicki, James Cochrane, Kevin Crum, Jeffrey Gordon, Reginald H. Jones, Richard H. Koppes, Jay W. Lorsch, and Mark J. Roe. Invaluable research assistance has been provided by Constance T. Gager, Mori H. Insinger, and Saskia Subramanian.

Price Waterhouse and the Reginald H. Jones Center for Management Policy, Strategy and Organization of the Wharton School, University of Pennsylvania, provided financial assistance for one aspect of the project, and special thanks here are extended to Edward H. Bowman, Raymond Bromark, Craig Irvine, Jennifer Myatt, and Rosemary Schlank.

A number of colleagues and associates at the University of Pennsylvania have provided helpful discussion or assistance, including Michael T. Baltes, James Beirne, Janice R. Bellace, Peter Cappelli, Marshall L. Fisher, Thomas P. Gerrity, Joseph W. Harder, Chris Hardwick, Richard J. Herring, Robert J. House, Karen Jehn, Howard S. Kaufold, Stephen J. Kobrin, Bruce Kogut, David F. Larcker, Thomas Malnight, Marshall Meyer, Olivia S. Mitchell, Robert Mittelstaedt, S. Philip Morgan, Edith C. Needleman, Tina Nemetz, Eric Orts, Samuel H. Preston, Edward Rock, Michael Seitchik, Jeffrey A. Sheehan, Harbir Singh, Jitendra Singh, Rosemary A. Stevens, James A. Sumner, Andrew Ward, Ross A. Webber, and Jerry Wind.

I would also like to extend my appreciation for the guidance or assistance of the following individuals: William T. Allen and Jack B. Jacobs, Chancery Court of Delaware; Michael Atkin, Institute of International Finance; James Auerbach, National Planning Association; Dan Clawson, University of Massachusetts–Amherst; Jean Crumrine, Investment Company Institute; Gerald F. Davis, Andrej Rus, and Harrison C. White, Columbia University; Amitai Etzioni, George Washington University; Neil D. Fligstein, University of California, Berkeley; Peter C. Garrett, *Directorship*; Barbara Gertz, Morningstar, Inc.; Melvyn Goetz and George J. Kirk, Westinghouse Electric Corporation; Robert Hagstrom, Lloyd, Leith & Sawin; Carolyn Harper, Edward Jarvis, and Paula Todd, Towers Perrin; Carl Kaysen, Thomas Kochan, Paul Osterman, and Maureen Scully, the Massachusetts Institute of Technology; Mary Lowengard; William F. Mahoney and Louis M. Thompson Jr., National Investor Relations Institute; Patrick S. McGurn and Peg O'Hara, Investor Responsibility Research Center; Elizabeth H. Gorman, David Kang, Peter Marsden, Kevin J. Murphy, Sally Petersen, and Aage Sorensen, Harvard University; Michael Powers, Hewitt Associates; Jeffrey Pfeffer, Stanford University; Anita Orellana and Rafael Rodriguez, Seminarium; Stephanie Rosenfelt, Korn/Ferry International; Paul Starr, Princeton University; Kelly J. Trottier, Stanford University; and Paul Zorn, Government Finance Officers Association.

A number of organizations provided valuable information, including the Association for Investment Management Research; *Business Week*; California Public Employees' Retirement System; Conference Board; *Corporate Governance Advisor*; *Directors & Boards*; Director Publications; *Fortune*; Georgeson & Co.; Government Finance Officers Association; Harvard Graduate School of Business Administration (Office of Career Development); Heidrick & Struggles, Inc.; Hewitt Associates; Institute of International Finance; Investment Company Institute; *Investor Relations Newsletter*; *Investor Relations Update*; *Institutional Investor*; Investor Responsibility Resource Center; Korn/Ferry International; Korn/Ferry Organizational Consulting; Morningstar, Inc.; National Association of Corporate Directors; National Investor Relations Institute; National Planning Association; New York Stock Exchange; Riverside Economic Research; Securities Industry Association; Stanford Graduate School of Business (MBA Career Management Center); Spencer Stuart Executive Search Consultants; Towers Perrin; United Shareholders Association; Victoria Group; Wharton School of the University of Pennsylvania (Graduate

Division Career Development and Placement); William M. Mercer, Inc.; and Wyatt Company.

The early editorial advice of Martin Kessler has been invaluable, as has the later editorial guidance of Linda Carbone, Peter Cowen, Paul Golob, and Kermit Hummel.

Index